"A HYENA IN

This was but one of the ~~many~~ ~~invec~~tions hurled at Mary Wollstonecraft during her lifetime. Her writings, which eloquently and unanswerably challenged the relegation of women to a level of intellect and occupation far below men and demanded an end to all social injustice, occasioned many of these attacks. But even more infuriating to contemporary defenders of the status quo was her private life, involving a notorious love affair, an illegitimate baby, and a persistent refusal to bow to social convention.

It took nearly two centuries for Mary Wollstonecraft to receive her due as one of history's great champions of human liberation. And now some of her finest writings are available to us in—

A MARY WOLLSTONECRAFT READER

BARBARA H. SOLOMON, chairperson of the Department of English at Iona College, is the editor of four other Mentor anthologies: AIN'T WE GOT FUN; THE AWAKENING AND SELECTED STORIES OF KATE CHOPIN; THE SHORT FICTION OF SARAH ORNE JEWETT AND MARY WILKINS FREEMAN; and THE EXPERIENCE OF THE AMERICAN WOMEN.

PAULA S. BERGGREN, Associate Professor at Baruch College of the City University of New York, has taught at Yale and is the author of numerous scholarly articles on women in literature.

MENTOR Anthologies You'll Want to Read

(0451)

A
Mary Wollstonecraft Reader

Edited, with an Introduction and Notes,

BY

Barbara H. Solomon
and
Paula S. Berggren

A MENTOR BOOK
NEW AMERICAN LIBRARY
TIMES MIRROR
New York and Scarborough, Ontario

MENTOR TRADEMARK REG. U.S. PAT. OFF. AND FOREIGN COUNTRIES
REGISTERED TRADEMARK—MARCA REGISTRADA
HECHO EN CHICAGO, U.S.A.

SIGNET, SIGNET CLASSICS, MENTOR, PLUME, MERIDIAN AND NAL BOOKS
are published *in the United States* by The New American Library, Inc.,
1633 Broadway, New York, New York 10019,
in Canada by The New American Library of Canada Limited,
81 Mack Avenue, Scarborough, Ontario M1L 1M8

First Printing, April, 1983

1 2 3 4 5 6 7 8 9

PRINTED IN THE UNITED STATES OF AMERICA

Stars, I have seen them fall
　But when they drop and die
No star is lost at all
　From all the star-sown sky.

　　　　　—A. E. Housman

Acknowledgments

The editors wish to express their gratitude for the Faculty Enrichment Grant awarded by Iona College to Barbara Solomon for the spring 1982 semester. At the college, a great deal of assistance was supplied by Eileen Liebeskind and Doris Viacava of Ryan Library; by Mary A. Bruno, Mariann Bisignano, Hyacinth Fyffe, and Nancy Girardi, of the Secretarial Services Center; and by Patricia D. Francis and Anne F. Tetro, student assistants.

Contents

Introduction

LATE IN 1778, ignoring the objections of her parents, a young woman named Mary Wollstonecraft agreed to become the paid companion of a wealthy widow, Mrs. Dawson, and set out for Bath, one of the most fashionable resorts of the period. As Wollstonecraft well knew, there were very few respectable jobs open to a female of the middle class, and she was destined to experience most of these within the next few years: companion, seamstress, teacher, and governess.

Although she understood that her job required her to obey Mrs. Dawson unquestioningly, nineteen-year-old Mary was no doubt greatly relieved to leave her family's household, headed by a tyrannical, drunken, and sometimes brutal father, a broken-spirited yet harsh mother, two remaining brothers (the eldest was already living away from home), and two sisters—Eliza and Everina—whose temperaments were never truly congenial to her own.

Edward and Elizabeth Dickson Wollstonecraft, her parents, had begun their married life in 1757 with every expectation of a pleasant and prosperous future, but they were sorely and continually disappointed. Edward, whose father had amassed considerable wealth, left London and purchased his first farm at Epping while Mary was a young child. Each successive move of the Wollstonecraft family signaled another of Edward's failures to adapt to the farm life he seemed determined to pursue. By the time Mary was eighteen, the family had moved some six times, and the substantial fortune inherited from Edward's father had been lost.

Mary's closest tie was not with any member of her family, but with a girlhood friend, Fanny Blood. The two faced very similar circumstances: as oldest daughters in impoverished households, both had cared for younger brothers and sisters, sympathized with their ill-used mothers, and detested their drunken, undependable fathers. Both were superior in intellect and spirit to the other members of their respective households, and Mary quickly imbued her side of the friendship with passionate idealism, finding inspiration in Fanny's superior accomplishments and gentle character.

If at the time she left home Mary Wollstonecraft had been the heroine of a work of romantic fiction, she would have been destined for a joyful reward as a result of her decision to accompany Mrs. Dawson to Bath. She might have displayed such patience, virtue, and good cheer that even so demanding and quarrelsome an employer as she served would have been moved to become her benefactress, to provide some extra money, or to take an interest in the girl's future. But that did not happen because the worldly widow was preoccupied with her own nieces and because the real Mary Wollstonecraft was too decisive a character to be always pliant and agreeable, too independent in her opinions and values to be easy in fashionable social circles, and in fact had a temperament marked by moodiness and a strong critical faculty.

A second, more pleasant alternative would have been to attract a strong and discriminating man determined to choose an intelligent, lively wife and indifferent to the young woman's social status, lack of great beauty, or fortune. But, alas, Mary did not meet a hero such as Jane Austen's Mr. Darcy or Charlotte Brontë's Mr. Rochester. Instead she met Joshua Waterhouse, a handsome but thoroughly egotistical and dissipated young man who was incongruously studying for the ministry. Apparently, he flirted with Wollstonecraft, inspired hopes of love, and received a number of love letters (which have not survived) from her. In light of his character and later misfortune (he eventually became an Anglican clergyman, the rector of Stukeley, but was also a miser and was killed by a thief), Mary was clearly better off without him, but her unhappy introduction to courtship set a bitter pattern that recurred throughout her life. She would respond with strong feelings to men whose interest in her was only superficial.

Moreover, no matter what fiction might promise its heroines, Wollstonecraft's firsthand experience of patriarchal oppression caused her to view marriage as a questionable source of security. With neither a benefactress nor a lover to lean on, she would be needed shortly to help support members of both her own family and Fanny Blood's. Although she managed to perform her work as a paid companion satisfactorily, and left Mrs. Dawson's employ only because she was summoned home in 1781 to nurse her dying mother, Mary chose not to return to Bath after Mrs. Wollstonecraft's death the following year. Instead she moved into the Blood household at Walham Green, which Fanny and Mrs. Blood contrived to support by sewing, since Mr. Blood seemed incapable of providing for them. For the next year and a half Mary shared their labor, often sewing from daylight to after dusk in an attempt to eke out a bare living.

Their hardships were intensified by Fanny's poor health—she had contracted tuberculosis—and unresolved marital status—she had long been engaged to a young man named Hugh Skeys, who seemed reluctant to go through with their marriage, probably fearful of linking his future to that of the impecunious Bloods. Initially, Mary resented Skeys, believing him conceited and lacking generosity because he postponed his wedding while he attempted to improve his financial situation. Fanny, powerless to control events, awaited Skeys's decision, hoping to follow him to Lisbon, where he had taken a job.

Unexpectedly, Mary was called away from the Bloods in the winter of 1783 by Meredith Bishop, her sister Eliza's husband. Eliza had given birth to a daughter a few months earlier and was suffering a severe breakdown. When Mary Wollstonecraft arrived at the Bishops' house in Bermondsey to nurse her sister, she found her fluctuating between irrational and lucid moments and soon became convinced that Eliza's condition was related to her growing aversion to her husband. Wollstonecraft concluded that Eliza could not recover in his household. But Bishop's marital rights were formidable: according to English law, a married woman had no legal identity because she had become one with her husband. She and her children were virtually the property of her husband, and only under extraordinary circumstances was it possible for a woman to resist her husband, no matter how brutal or dissolute he might be.

Through a series of dramatic ploys—switching carriages to elude detection and cowering in rented rooms—the sisters fled Bishop's household, leaving behind the five-month-old infant who was being cared for by a nurse. Wollstonecraft's actions in masterminding their flight were the first outward signs of the extent to which she would prove capable of acting without family support, following her own convictions, and withstanding the opprobrium of society.

When the danger of a confrontation with Bishop had passed,

Wollstonecraft faced the all-too-familiar problem of earning a living, intensified by her sense of responsibility for both her sisters, Everina and Eliza, as well as for Fanny. Within a month Mary had determined that they would open a school and support themselves. The first site she chose, Islington, yielded few pupils; so she moved to a large house at Newington Green, a village northeast of London.

The choice of location was propitious, not merely because a greater number of pupils were attracted to the school, but because Newington Green had attracted many distinguished writers and philosophers—among them a gentle and kindly scholar who became Mary's friend, the renowned Dissenting minister, Dr. Richard Price. The Dissenters, so called because they dissented from the Anglican Communion, were excluded from military service and the privilege of university education. As a result, they formed their own school system of Dissenting Academies, many of which were housed in Newington Green. Opposed to orthodox positions of the Established Church, the Dissenters took a generally liberal attitude in religious and political matters and extolled reason as the basis of their optimistic view of human potential. Significantly, they had a greater respect for women than Wollstonecraft had previously encountered.

Among the other congenial inhabitants of the Green were two widows of schoolmasters who had been interested in educational reform, Mrs. Burgh and Mrs. Cockburn. Dr. Price's visitors included men of established reputation, like Joseph Priestly, the great chemist who was also a Dissenting clergyman, and young intellectuals who had yet to make their names. One of the latter was John Hewlett, a fledgling writer who would later become a minister, publish *Sermons on Different Subjects*, and most importantly, *The Holy Bible with Apocrypha and Notes*. Wollstonecraft could not consciously have chosen a more supportive atmosphere for the period of informal higher education that she now began.

During her childhood, she had attended various village day schools rather than a boarding school, partly as a result of her father's rejection of the idea of female education. Her first important exposure to the life of the mind probably took place in 1774, when the Wollstonecrafts moved to Hoxton. There the independent fifteen-year-old Mary had been welcomed almost as a foster child by a childless couple, the Clares. The Reverend Mr. Clare, an invalid who loved literature, lent Mary books and directed her reading. It

seems likely that under his friendly instruction she first
made the acquaintance of those poets to whom she alludes
so frequently in her own writings in later years: Shakespeare, Milton, and, from her own century, Alexander Pope,
James Thomson (author of *The Seasons*), and Edward Young
(author of *Night Thoughts*). It was in the warmth of the
Clare household that she had met their other protegée, her
dear friend Fanny Blood.

In 1785, just as the school at Newington Green had established itself, Mary abruptly left for Portugal, rushing to be
with Fanny—who had been married to Skeys for a little less
than a year and, now in the final months of pregnancy, was
mortally ill. Mary's deepest emotional bond was still to Fanny,
and to Fanny she went, arriving in Lisbon after a stormy
passage to find her friend four hours short of prematurely
delivering her child and only a few days short of death. The
baby lived but a while longer. Morbid and depressed, Mary
returned to Newington Green in February, 1786, only to
encounter more bad news, for Eliza and Everina had not
been able to stem a tide of student defections and debts that
had built up during Mary's absence of a few months. They
closed the school in the spring.

Wollstonecraft had reached a crucial point in her life. If
the school at Newington Green had proved a failure, her
friendships there did not. Mrs. Burgh lent Mary the money
for her fare to Lisbon. John Hewlett gave her the where-
withal for another kind of departure: he did not lend her
money, but he urged her to follow his example and write a
book. He introduced her to his publisher, Joseph Johnson of
London, who gave Mary a ten-pound advance to write a
book on the education of girls. Books offering such advice
had become a popular commodity, and Mary, who up to this
point had done no writing for publication, had always filled
her letters to friends and family with general observations.
Far from being intimidated by the prospect of putting her
thoughts into print, she seems to have adopted a somewhat
cavalier attitude towards the project, completing the manuscript within weeks. (Typically, despite the many debts that
encumbered her personally, Mary used the money she earned
by it to send Fanny's parents to Ireland, where they joined
their son, George, to whom Mary had long acted as a solicitous older sister; to him, she was "the Princess.") She then
turned her attentions to repaying her own creditors and
embarked on the last of her genteel, ladylike employments:

she became a governess and, like the Bloods, headed off to Ireland.

Mary's acquaintance, the Reverend John Prior, a schoolmaster at Eton, referred her to Lord and Lady Kingsborough, a wealthy Irish couple who needed a governess for their daughters. While preparing for her journey to their castle in Ireland, Mary visited the Priors at Eton, where she had an opportunity to observe an educational establishment of an order quite different from the schools of Newington Green. She saw enough of Eton, the prestigious, traditional training ground of many young English aristocrats, to form an intense dislike of its methods.

Wollstonecraft made a new circle of friends in Ireland. Aboard ship she met a young clergyman who was to become a favorite of hers, Henry Gabell; and her new employers introduced her to several people of talent and distinction, including a poet and member of Parliament, George Ogle, and his family. On the surface, the Kingsboroughs should have been ideal to work for. Robert King, Viscount Kingsborough, was a remarkable Anglo-Irish landowner in that he actually lived in Ireland and tried to improve his holdings. Eventually to become the Earl of Kingston, he was married young to a cousin, Caroline Fitzgerald, in order to unite their estates. The Kingsboroughs farmed her property, Mitchelstown, developed a model town, built a great library, and even allowed the governess to mingle with their friends. But Mary still remained a kind of servant in their opulent household. Whatever she might have admired in Mitchelstown had she observed it from afar, actually living at Mitchelstown Castle and having to cope with Lady Kingsborough, who directly oversaw the new governess's work, proved more frustrating than rewarding.

Lady Kingsborough, a spoiled, pretty woman whose preference for her dogs over her children appalled Mary, became jealous of the governess whom her girls preferred to their mother—particularly Margaret, the oldest, who was fourteen and suffering from a fever when Mary arrived. Always a skilled nurse, Mary found her first responsibility with her new charge was to nurture her body before her mind. The bond that developed between the two in the sickroom was to last long after Wollstonecraft left the Kingsboroughs.

At best a governess's position is ambiguous: she may succeed too well with her job, as was clearly the case at Mitchelstown; even worse, if she joins the family socially, she may shine more brightly than the lady of the house and this may have been the crux of Mary's dismissal. George Ogle or Lord Kingsborough himself may have been too attentive to Mary for Caroline's composure. Whatever the circumstances, Wollstonecraft never again permitted herself to serve in another woman's household.

The year in Ireland was not wasted, although Mary's health suffered greatly there. Always prey to nervous complaints, she seems to have been especially beset by them at this point in her life. On the positive side, she was paid a good salary and, while educating her charges, continued to educate herself. She wrote to Everina from Dublin of reading Rousseau's *Emile*, and of visits to a series of operatic, symphonic, and theatrical performances. Throughout her life, she seemed capable of enriching her mind no matter what the state of her nerves. Indeed, the tension of her situation generated enough creative energy for Wollstonecraft to make her first attempt at a novel. *Mary, a Fiction* presents an unflattering portrait of a woman not unlike Caroline King as a minor character, and its heroine, "Mary," loves a man she cannot marry, named Henry. Of the book, she wrote to Henry Gabell, who was about to be married (and who had not told Wollstonecraft when they first met that he was already engaged), "I have drawn from Nature."

Although its literary merits may be disputed, *Mary* confirmed Wollstonecraft's vocation: from the moment she left the Kingsboroughs, she was a writer. Boldly, after she had been fired, she chose to go to London to see Joseph Johnson, who had published her first book, rather than to Newington Green. (She hardly would have chosen to return to her unsympathetic father, now living in Wales after his remarriage.) Even as the Dissenters had sustained her with a ready-made philosophy and employment in 1784, in 1787 Johnson gave her the scope to secure a mode of living all her own. In a gesture of rare generosity to a delinquent governess, he offered the twenty-eight-year-old Mary Wollstonecraft her own home and a job. After brief visits to her sisters, separately employed as schoolmistresses still, Mary returned to London to settle in a house Johnson had found for her and took up the sort of career a man might pursue. Her employer, Johnson, had published the works of Mary's Dissenting friends and many other celebrated figures. He would become Wordsworth's first publisher and gave the strongest encouragement to the poet William Cowper, but was probably most

important as the center of a literary and intellectual circle
of far-reaching radical significance. Thomas Paine, for example, dined regularly at Johnson's table at No. 72 St.
Paul's Churchyard, as did Wollstonecraft, who met the great
liberal activists of late eighteenth-century England over
dinner. She was not the only woman in Johnson's set, but
she was virtually unique in earning her keep as a writer.
Shortly after Wollstonecraft moved in, Johnson began to
assign book reviews to her for a newly founded periodical,
The Analytical Review, to which Mary was to contribute
hundreds of short pieces over the next decade. Johnson's
household was her university: she seized the opportunity of
conversing with the brightest members of her generation.
She learned French and German well enough to translate
for Johnson's printing house important works of philosophy,
including Christian Salzmann's *Elements of Morality*. She
wrote another book on the education of children, *Original
Stories from Real Life*. In 1788, two of her original books
and her translation of the French minister Jacques Necker's
Of the Importance of Religious Opinions went to press.

Early in 1788 she rejected Johnson's assignment of an
Italian manuscript to translate. Eager and industrious, she
was never servile, as the accents of her note of refusal to
him indicate. She could not make out the handwriting of the
foreign author and saw no prospect of completing this assignment: "I cannot bear to do any thing I cannot do well."
Her dedication is revealed in another note to Johnson, written perhaps a year or two later, when she asks for a German
grammar: "While I live, I am persuaded, I must exert my
understanding to procure an independence, and render myself useful. To make the task easier, I ought to store my
mind with knowledge." In 1789, using a pseudonym, she
edited an anthology called *The Female Reader* (a copy of
which has only recently come to light) to encourage other
women to educate themselves. She included excerpts from
Shakespeare, the Bible, William Cowper, and (among other
experts on the education of daughters) Mary Wollstonecraft.
Strong religious sentiments were urged, since the *Reader*
was primarily to be used as a textbook in schools such as
she had run in Newington Green. Mary herself, it is worth
noting, was an Anglican and still subscribed to orthodox
doctrines. But her scholarly and political researches were
drawing her away from the pieties of her youth, making her
more self-sufficient than ever.

Without systematic academic training, working under the constant pressure of paying the debts of family and friends, neglecting her own appearance and diet, in her little house on George Street, Mary Wollstonecraft assiduously listened, read, and studied. In an age of intellectual and revolutionary ferment, she was preparing herself to make a remarkable contribution to the great political debate of her time. This ferment culminated in the French Revolution. The aging Dr. Price, Mary's old friend and mentor from Newington Green, asserted that the freedoms to which the French overthrow of the Bourbons was leading were akin to those that had been opened up in England by the parliamentary removal of James II in 1688 for his absolute monarchist tendencies. James was replaced by William and Mary, who agreed to the notion of a limited monarchy, thus shifting ultimate political power from King to Parliament and marking the inevitable growth of English democracy. In a sermon on the fourth of November, 1789, delivered to the Society for Commemorating the Glorious Revolution of 1688, Price implied that as a result of the National Assembly's actions in Paris, the French were perhaps even freer than the English, for were not the Dissenters, despite the relaxation of strictures against them granted in 1688, still deprived of their basic civil rights in 1789? This speech alarmed conservatives, who had been dismayed by the approbation with which the French Revolution was being hailed in Great Britain. It led one of the century's greatest articulators of conservative principles, Edmund Burke, to write a work that was to shift the tide of public opinion in England. Spurred by Price's sermon, as his subtitle indicates, Burke wrote his *Reflections on the Revolution in France and On the Proceedings in Certain Societies in London Relative to that Event*, which was published on the first of November, 1790. Burke argued that the rights praised by Dr. Price and annually endorsed by the Society were, contrary to what the Society's name implied, the product not of revolution—which is an evil—but of centuries of English tradition which the Glorious (and bloodless) Revolution of 1688 had only confirmed.

Before the end of November, an anonymous pamphlet rebutting Burke's attack on Price was published by Joseph Johnson. So popular did it prove that a second, revised edition was put out less than a month later. This second edition of *A Vindication of the Rights of Men* bore its author's name—Mary Wollstonecraft. Wollstonecraft's earlier

books were respectably confined to feminine, domestic concerns; her private revolution was crystallized in this ambitious public work. With this publication she makes her own
claim to a level of humanity beyond the boundary lines
habitually drawn according to gender, boldly taking on one
of the Great Men of her age, demonstrating the qualities
that transformed her into the person she wanted to be instead of the woman her society expected her to become. She
reveals a fierce devotion to her beliefs, asserting the rectitude of her old friend, Dr. Price (whom Burke accused of
profaning his religious privilege), and explicitly making the
cause of freedom her subject for the first, but not the last
time. Freedom had been the implicit motif of every daring
act she had thus far attempted. When she had written Everina
of her intention to stay in London and work for Johnson, she
had tried to explain herself: "You know I am not born to
tread in the beaten track." More untrodden paths lay ahead.

The French experiment which so exhilarated Mary Wollstonecraft's circle was soon revealed to have a flaw that,
among her friends, only she perceived: the rights being
debated in Paris were not those of all human beings, but
applied only to men. In the fall of 1791, Talleyrand presented to the Constituent Assembly of France a plan for free
public education—for males. Urged on again by Johnson,
Wollstonecraft feverishly wrote a successor to her previous
pamphlet. Respectfully dedicated to Talleyrand (unlike
Burke's, his error was presumed to be open to reasonable
correction), A Vindication of the Rights of Woman by its
very title acknowledged the folly of a woman's protesting to
safeguard the rights of men when they so palpably belong
only to men. In her analysis of the ways in which the
subservience of women had been perpetuated across centuries and continents, Wollstonecraft brought together all the
themes that her various writings had individually stressed:
the way we educate our daughters ultimately determines
whether they can ever be free and full human beings. No
one was better equipped to understand this from personal
experience than Mary Wollstonecraft. By temperament, by
circumstances, and by profession, she was able to codify
what countless women of distinction had demonstrated in
their own lives but never abstracted into theory. Her Vindication proclaimed that unless women are taught to think,
not merely to imitate models of behavior, they will never
enjoy the rights that men had begun to demand as their

natural inheritance. Wollstonecraft set out to prove that women and men share the same nature, but that in women, "the mind is left to rust." To defend Dr. Price, Mary took on Edmund Burke; to defend her sex, she took on the world, sparing neither women nor men in her condemnation of "a false system of education." The confidence of this self-educated woman is staggering even today, when her arguments seem so sensible that it is almost impossible to understand how they outraged her contemporaries.

This book made Mary a literary celebrity. Diligently, she worked on, writing her reviews and, increasingly, guiding others. She became a friend of Mary Hays, another writer of the "new genus" (a term Wollstonecraft had coined in her letter of self-explanation to Everina), who had begun corresponding with her after the publication of *A Vindication of the Rights of Woman.* Hays sent Wollstonecraft some of her own work for comment, and in her reply, Wollstonecraft revealed that even an accomplished and celebrated female professional must cope with the condescension of her male associates. Apparently Mary Hays had written a self-deprecatory preface which Mary Wollstonecraft criticized: "If the writer has not sufficient strength of mind to overcome the common difficulties which lie in his way, nature seems to command him, with a very audible voice, to leave the task of instructing others to those who can. This kind of vain humility has ever disgusted me." Conversely, she warned that Hays's conclusion ". . . is so full of vanity, your male friends will still treat you like a woman. . . . An author, especially a woman, should be cautious lest she too hastily swallows the crude praises which partial friends and polite acquaintances bestow thoughtlessly when the supplicating eye looks for them. In short, it requires great resolution to try rather to be useful than to please."

For candor, this advice shared by one woman with another in the same profession cannot be excelled today. Such shrewdness enabled Wollstonecraft to maintain a position of equality among talented and well-educated men, and this sense of camaraderie and absence of rivalry seems to have informed all her literary dealings. Unfortunately, all too often in her romantic life, Mary was to become another woman's rival in a futile attempt to win or retain a man's love. Tragically, she never learned to discipline her emotions as she trained her intellect. She used her mind lest it rust; but perhaps she abused her heart.

Among the more exotic participants in the Johnson set were the great visionary poet and artist William Blake, who contributed the remarkable engravings which illustrate the second edition of *Original Stories* (published in 1791), and his admirer, the Swiss artist who anglicized his name to Henry Fuseli when he settled in London. In 1787, when Mary began her association with Johnson, Fuseli was forty-six and about to marry a young artist's model, Sophia Rawlins. Fuseli, who knew eight languages, was ordained as a Protestant minister in Zurich but made his living as a translator and painter. A talented, early Romantic, he fascinated Mary, and she—so different from Sophia, whom he did soon marry—intrigued him. They developed an intense intellectual relationship. For Mary, however, the intellectual exchange led to a desire for greater intimacy.

When Parisian politics began to heat up, many English sympathizers crossed the Channel. Johnson, the Fuselis, and Mary Wollstonecraft set off on such a venture and got as far as Dover in mid-1792 before deciding to return to London. The frustration of being so close to Fuseli apparently drove Wollstonecraft to ask Sophia Fuseli if they might share her husband in London as a threesome. Not surprisingly, the outraged Mrs. Fuseli cured the naive, thirty-three-year-old Mary of her illusions. Fuseli remained aloof, seemingly content with his wife's response, and Mary felt crushed and humiliated. Others of her friends reached Paris, despite the increasingly alarming reports of revolutionary fervor out of control, but to Wollstonecraft, mere physical violence must have seemed less threatening than the internal emotional riot she could not subdue. She ended the year which had begun with the publication of *A Vindication of the Rights of Woman* by fleeing to London in self-disgust. In December of 1792, she sailed for Paris alone.

Her lodgings had been arranged by the daughter of the French-born schoolmistress at Putney for whom Eliza and Everina had taught. She provided Wollstonecraft with room and board in her Paris home (although she and her husband, like many prudent Parisians, chose to absent themselves from the center of turmoil). Although Mary had traveled alone, she was not alone for long. She had an extraordinary gift for building interesting friendships wherever she went. Left on her own, Mary improved her spoken French and entered the salons of Anglo-American expatriates. Tom Paine was also in revolutionary Paris, as were others whom she knew from the dining room in St. Paul's Churchyard: Thomas Christie, co-founder with Johnson of *The Analytical Review*, and Ruth and Joel Barlow, Americans who became her close friends. In Paris Mary met for the first time a number of unconventional women, including the English poet, Helen Maria Williams; and French political activists and writers, notably Madame de Genlis (a commentator on women's education whose work Mary already knew) and Manon Roland (who went to the guillotine during the Reign of Terror). Unlike her London friends, some of these daring seekers after Revolution openly lived with lovers outside of marriage, favored divorce, and saw no shame in illegitimacy. In such a world, Mary met the American adventurer Gilbert Imlay, who became her lover within weeks of their introduction.

By mid-February, 1793, with France and England officially at war, Paris had become a dangerous place for British citizens. In June Mary moved to a little house at Neuilly, near a tollgate (*la barrière*) northwest of Paris. There she was intermittently joined by Imlay, and there she became pregnant with a child who would be called Fanny (for Fanny Blood) and nicknamed "the barrier girl" (for the romantic circumstances of her conception). Mary moved back to Paris once she knew of her pregnancy and was registered as Imlay's wife with the American Embassy in September, but this measure, taken for her political protection, belied the case. Mary and Imlay were never married, although she sometimes signed herself "Mary Imlay."

Fanny Imlay was born on May 14, 1794, in Le Havre, where Wollstonecraft had gone to stay with Imlay. But by August, 1794, not much more than a year after their affair had begun, Imlay had tired of the intensity of Mary's devotion. He was forty years old, had loved many women (most recently Mary's English friend, Helen Maria Williams), and finally cared more for business (with Joel Barlow, he was importing soap and other necessities into war-torn Paris) and far-fetched political schemes (he and Barlow were involved in a stillborn plot to capture the Lousiana Territory, then under Spanish rule, for France) than for the serene domesticity which Mary craved.

Her letters to Imlay, published soon after her death, expose a hysterical and despairing side of Wollstonecraft—a woman deprived of affection from her earliest days and who had shouldered the financial burdens of her family and cared for others, but whom no one had ever loved with a self-denial to equal hers. What attracted her to Imlay? Her emotional distress after Mrs. Fuseli's indignant dismissal, the heightened excitement of wartime living, and the libertine customs she encountered in France obviously made Wollstonecraft more vulnerable to love than she had ever been before. In all her failed and confused relationships with men over the years—with Joshua Waterhouse, Henry Gabell, Henry Fuseli—it appears that Mary sought reassurance as much as she desired erotic experience. When she met Imlay, however, her letters attest to a sexual arousal that deserves to be called an awakening. But if the dashing American overwhelmed her senses, her response overwhelmed him, driving him away when she most wanted to hold him.

During her pregnancy, spent mostly alone while Imlay tended to his commercial interests, Wollstonecraft wrote *An Historical and Moral View of the Origin and Progress of the French Revolution*, her longest book. Published by Johnson in 1794, it sold well enough for a second edition to be brought out the following year, in the spring of which Wollstonecraft, with little Fanny, returned to London, hoping to establish a home with Imlay. At this point, Imlay, involved with an attractive young actress, made it abundantly clear that he would never revive their liaison, and Mary attempted to kill herself. The details of this attempt are not known, but what followed was remarkable: Imlay had great difficulty completely dissociating himself from so strong a personality and he asked her to take a business trip, proposing that she travel to Scandinavia (a partner who supplied the goods Imlay and Barlow imported lived in Gothenburg, Sweden). Thus—with baby and nursemaid in tow—Wollstonecraft set off on another journey, completing whatever transactions she was supposed to undertake and composing a travel chronicle as she went. Her desperation and anguish notwithstanding, Wollstonecraft's professionalism never faltered, but she returned to London in October, 1795, depressed and once more without hope. Pulled from the Thames River where she had tried to drown herself in a second suicide attempt, she was nursed back to health by Thomas Christie's wife and published the lovely *Letters Written during a Short Residence in Sweden, Norway, and Denmark* in 1796. In the spring of that year she also wrote the last farewell (of many) to Gilbert Imlay: "It is strange that, in spite of all you do, something like conviction forces me to believe, that you are not what you appear to be. I part with you in peace."

This parting was made easier for Wollstonecraft by her renewed acquaintance with William Godwin, then at the height of his fame and influence as a philosopher and writer. Brought up to be a Dissenting minister, Godwin left the church at an early age and moved to London, where he contributed political and cultural commentaries to a liberal journal, *The New Annual Register*. He had first met Mary Wollstonecraft at Johnson's dinner table in 1791 in the company of Tom Paine, the first part of whose *Rights of Man* had just appeared. Godwin later recorded that he had been vexed at the time: he had come to talk to Paine and had instead to listen to Mary Wollstonecraft. He was much readier to listen to her five years later. In 1793 he had published *An Enquiry Concerning the Principles of Political Justice and its Influence on General Virtue and Happiness*, a major work of rational economic and social analysis inspired by the French Revolution. *Political Justice* established Godwin as one of the leading proponents of democracy of his day. When he brought out a psychological novel, *Caleb Williams*, the following year, his reputation was further enhanced. Although Godwin's radical theories included opposition to marriage, he enjoyed friendships with many cultured women and in his fortieth year, when he and Mary were reintroduced, appears to have begun actively looking for a wife. Mary Hays had the two radical authors to tea in January, 1796. Mary Wollstonecraft called on him in his rooms in the spring, and by late summer, Godwin and Wollstonecraft were lovers. If she had first been awakened to her sexuality by Imlay, she seems to have aroused a similar passion in Godwin. By the beginning of 1797, Mary was pregnant again, but she and Godwin did not immediately share a household, and when they did, shortly after their marriage, Godwin maintained a separate apartment to serve as his study. The ceremony, on March 29, 1797, took most of their friends—and perhaps themselves—by surprise.

Once again Mary simultaneously worked at producing a book and a baby. She wrote and rewrote the drafts of her second novel, *The Wrongs of Woman*, and awaited the birth of little "William." She and Godwin pursued separate social lives, often dining out and greeting visitors individually rather than as a couple. Less than three months after they were wed, Godwin upset Mary by setting off on a tour of

Staffordshire with a friend and staying longer than he had expected. Unlike Imlay, however, Godwin had truly pledged himself to her, and they lived companionably together during the final months of her pregnancy.

Mary gave careful thought to the arrangements for her delivery. Despite her lifelong complaints of digestive trouble and despite her attempts at suicide, she was in good health. She had had an easy first labor; following her own surprisingly modern sense of what was medically desirable, she had begun to exercise eight days after Fanny's birth, and she had delighted in the physical experience of motherhood as she had rejoiced in the twinges occasioned by fetal movements. She reported to Ruth Barlow that her baby girl sucked her breast "so *manfully* that her father reckons saucily on her writing the second part of the *Rights of Woman*." For her second confinement, she chose to have a female attendant, a midwife from the Westminster Lying-in Hospital. Anticipating an uneventful birth, she saw no need for a male physician; but, after an exhausting labor, the placenta did not emerge. The baby, a daughter, was safe, but a doctor had to be summoned. Working without anesthetic, or a modern knowledge of the ways in which germs are spread, the doctor had manually to remove the placenta, in bits and pieces. Mary, not untypically, developed an infection, but for a short time it appeared as though she might survive her ordeal. Concerned physicians and friends visited her bedside, but there were insufficient medical procedures to save women from the complications of childbirth in the eighteenth century. Her death, as had her life, reflected her struggle against the constraints that enslaved her sex. The infant, Mary Godwin, was born on August 30, 1797, and her mother died on September 10.

Godwin was left in grief with two little girls to raise, and he keenly felt the lack of Mary's special qualifications for such an enterprise. He purged his sorrow in a biographical tribute, *Memoirs of the Author of "A Vindication of the Rights of Woman*," published in 1798. He brought out as well her *Posthumous Works*, containing letters to Imlay. These letters, openly declaring of Mary's passion for Imlay and her seeming indifference to the illegitimacy of her first child, shocked and outraged several generations of readers. Thus for many years, Mary Wollstonecraft's name was known more for her life than for her work and was often confused with her daughter's. While Fanny Imlay grew up to commit suicide in a hotel room at the age of twenty-two, Mary

Wollstonecraft Godwin grew up to marry Percy Bysshe Shelley (after an affair with the young poet) and to write the novel *Frankenstein*, an embodiment of her parents' quests for justice and for love. She and Shelley were befriended by one of Mary Wollstonecraft's charges, Margaret King of the Irish Kingsboroughs, who had deserted her husband to live with another man in Italy. Margaret took the name "Mrs. Mason," the same name as the heroic educator of *Original Stories* (suggesting the lasting influence of her governess), and when Shelley died, she was able to help Mary Shelley and her baby son.

To conclude a sketch of Mary Wollstonecraft's life with the lives and deaths of her daughters, Fanny and Mary, obscures her lasting impact on the world. For she has thousands, perhaps millions, of daughters, the young and old women to whom she has left the legacy of her books and the poignant memory of her story. And Mary Wollstonecraft's own story was always an essential component of her work. During her thirty-eight years she continually strove to reshape her life, becoming a "new genus," an emblem of what she believed: that women's inferior status was the result of external barriers and not of natural, internal deficiencies.

When Wollstonecraft was born, the fabric of western civilization was so thoroughly permeated by misogynistic attitudes that most men and women were not even vaguely aware of the extent to which their culture denigrated women and debased their self-image. In century after century, the perception was fostered that nature had ordained a social order which rightly dictated male domination and female subordination. To the Greek philosopher Aristotle, "Females are weaker and colder in nature, and we must look upon the female character as being a sort of natural deficiency" (*De Generatione Animalium*). To the Christian theologian St. Thomas Aquinas, "It would seem that women should not have been made in the first production of things" (*Summa Theologicae*). To the Protestant revolutionary Martin Luther, "No dress or garment is less becoming to a woman than a show of intelligence."

The eighteenth-century French philosopher Jean-Jacques Rousseau began *The Social Contract* with a clarion call to freedom: "Man was born free, but is everywhere in bondage." Yet even to the liberal Rousseau, women belonged in bondage:

The man should be strong and active; the woman should be weak and passive; the one must have both the power and the will; it is enough that the other should offer little resistance.

If woman is made to please and to be in subjection to man, she ought to make herself pleasing in his eyes and not provoke him to anger; her strength is in her charms.

Women do wrong to complain of the inequality of man-made laws; this inequality is not of man's making, or at any rate it is not the result of mere prejudice, but of reason.

Little wonder, then, that Wollstonecraft, filled with respect for Rousseau and revering him as a force for human dignity, felt impelled to use her *Vindication of the Rights of Woman* as a forum to argue against his disappointing advocacy of the age-old views on the subjection of all women despite his ringing rejection of such views when applied to men. Rousseau, the man, was safely dead and in his grave; his ideas, though published thirty years earlier, lived on, irritating Wollstonecraft so that she could not rest until she had quoted and refuted the most offensive examples of his masculine complacency.

Wollstonecraft's arguments in turn live on in *A Vindication of the Rights of Woman*. Within a hundred years this ground-breaking work went through six English and four American editions and was also republished in *The Revolution*, the feminist newspaper edited by Susan B. Anthony in the 1860's. Wollstonecraft's arguments formed the basis of a feminist intellectual tradition wherever feminists gathered to encourage, educate, and support one another. Her ideas lived on in such "daughters" as Elizabeth Cady Stanton, Margaret Fuller, Sarah Grimké, Charlotte Perkins Gilman, Lucy Stone, Susan B. Anthony, Lucretia Mott, Margaret Sanger, Carrie Chapman Catt, and Emmeline Pankhurst. Her story lives on each time a woman refuses to accept a patriarchal notion of her abilities or rights and depends upon her own experience and self-knowledge in order to define herself.

The young woman who left her family behind to become Mrs. Dawson's companion was the heroine of a difficult life and not a pleasant fiction. Mary Wollstonecraft could not teach us how to go about securing a kindly and protective husband with whom to live happily ever after. Instead, she taught us that women must acquire a sound education to survive in a competitive world, that they may be offered servile and low-paying jobs because they are women, and that they may well face the responsibility for bearing and nurturing their young with little outside help. She continues to teach us that many of her problems and the tragic experiences of other women she knew or imagined were not personal but universal, the common burden of one half of the human race.

—BARBARA H. SOLOMON
Iona College
New Rochelle, New York

—PAULA S. BERGGREN
Baruch College
City University of New York

A Note on the Text

THE SPELLING AND SOME INCONSISTENT PUNCTUATION the selections in this volume have been revised to bring them into conformity with modern American usage. For example, Wollstonecraft's "fewel" becomes "fuel," "Mussulman" becomes "Moslem," and all British spellings such as "labour," "enquiry," and "theatre" have been changed to the American equivalents. Occasionally, quotation marks have been added or deleted to clarify Wollstonecraft's original intentions.

Chronology

1759   Mary Wollstonecraft, second child and first daughter of Edward John and Elizabeth Dickson Wollstonecraft, is born in late April.

1765   The death of her grandfather leaves Mary's father with a substantial fortune, which is squandered in frequent family moves and unsuccessful attempts at farming.

1774   The family relocates in Hoxton, near London.

1775   Mary meets Fanny Blood at the home of the Clares in Hoxton.

1778   Mary leaves home to join Mrs. Dawson in Bath as a paid companion.

1780   Summoned home, Mary returns to nurse her mother in her last illness.

1782   After Elizabeth's death, Mary moves in with the Blood family.

1784   In January, Mary arranges for her sister, Eliza Bishop, to escape from her husband's household. Later in the year, with Eliza and Fanny, she opens a school for girls at Newington Green.

1785   Fanny Blood and Hugh Skeys marry in Lisbon. In November, Mary journeys to Lisbon to nurse Fanny, who dies after delivering a child.

1786   Upon returning from Lisbon in the spring, Mary is forced to close the school. She writes *Thoughts on the Education of Daughters*, receiving £10 in payment from Joseph Johnson. In October, after a short wait at Eton, she sails to Ireland, where she will be governess to the daughters of the Kingsborough family at Mitchelstown Castle.

1787　She writes *Mary, A Fiction* while in Ireland. During the summer, she is dismissed by Lady Kingsborough while the family is vacationing in England at Bristol Hot Wells. By November, she settles into a house at 49 George Street, found by Johnson, who will employ her as a writer and translator.

1788　Her active publishing career begins with *Mary, a Fiction, Original Stories from Real Life*, a translation of Necker's *Of the Importance of Religious Opinions*, and articles or reviews for *The Analytical Review*.

1789　She writes the preface for and edits the anthology *The Female Reader*, attributed to "Mr. Cresswick." The French Revolution begins in July. Dr. Price delivers his sermon before the Society for Commemorating the Glorious Revolution of 1688 in November.

1790　Mary translates Christian Salzmann's *Elements of Morality* and answers Edmund Burke's *Reflections on the French Revolution* in the anonymously published *A Vindication of the Rights of Men*.

1791　The second edition of *Vindication* bears Wollstonecraft's name. She meets William Godwin at Johnson's house, but is preoccupied by a relationship with Henry Fuseli.

1792　*A Vindication of the Rights of Woman* appears in print. In December, she leaves for Paris after a breach in her relationship with the Fuselis.

1793　During the spring, she meets Gilbert Imlay in Paris and within a few months she has moved to Neuilly and become pregnant by him.

1794　Fanny Imlay, her illegitimate daughter, is born on May 14 in Le Havre. In December, *An Historical and Moral View of the Origin and Progress of the French Revolution* is published.

1795　During the spring, Mary attempts suicide in London, but shortly thereafter travels to Scandinavia with Fanny on business for Imlay. She returns to London in the fall and tries to drown herself on learning that Imlay has taken a mistress. Mrs. Thomas Christie nurses her back to health.

1796 Mary publishes *Letters Written during a Short Residence in Sweden, Norway, and Denmark* and meets Godwin again in Mary Hays's rooms. Her affair with Godwin begins during the summer and she starts to write *The Wrongs of Woman*.

1797 On March 29, she marries Godwin. Her second child, Mary Wollstonecraft Godwin, is born on August 30. On September 10, Mary Wollstonecraft dies of childbirth complications.

1798 Godwin publishes his *Memoirs* and Mary's four-volume *Posthumous Works*, including *The Wrongs of Woman: or, Maria, a Fragment* and *Letters to Imlay*.

Selected Bibliography

WORKS BY MARY WOLLSTONECRAFT

Thoughts on the Education of Daughters: With Reflections on Female Conduct, in the More Important Duties of Life. London: Joseph Johnson, 1787.

Mary, A Fiction. London: Joseph Johnson, 1788.

Original Stories from Real Life: With Conversations Calculated to Regulate the Affections and Form the Mind to Truth and Goodness. London: Joseph Johnson, 1788.

The Female Reader: Or, Miscellaneous Pieces, in Prose and Verse: Selected From the Best Writers, and Disposed Under Proper Heads: For the Improvement of Young Women. London: Joseph Johnson, 1789.

A Vindication of the Rights of Men, in a Letter to the Right Honourable Edmund Burke. London: Joseph Johnson, 1790.

A Vindication of the Rights of Woman with Strictures on Political and Moral Subjects. London: Joseph Johnson, 1792.

An Historical and Moral View of the Origin and Progress of the French Revolution; and the Effect it has Produced in Europe. London: Joseph Johnson, 1794.

Letters Written during a Short Residence in Sweden, Norway, and Denmark. London: Joseph Johnson, 1796.

Posthumous Works of the Author of a Vindication of the Rights of Woman. London: Joseph Johnson, 1798. *The Wrongs of Woman: or, Maria: A Fragment* was first published in this edition.

BIOGRAPHY AND CRITICISM

Boulton, James T. *The Language of Politics in the Age*

of Wilkes and Burke. London: Routledge and Kegan Paul, 1963.

Bouten, Jacob. *Mary Wollstonecraft and the Beginnings of Female Emancipation in France and England.* Amsterdam: H. J. Paris, 1922.

Brailsford, H. N. *Shelley, Godwin and Their Circle.* London: William and Norgate, 1913.

William and Norgate, 1913.

Cameron, Kenneth Neill, ed. *Shelley and His Circle: 1773–1822.* Cambridge, Mass.: Harvard University Press, 1961.

Detre, Jean. *A Most Extraordinary Pair: Mary Wollstonecraft and William Godwin.* New York: Doubleday, 1975.

Dowden, Edward. "Theorists of Revolution, Godwin, Mary Wollstonecraft" in *The French Revolution and English Literature.* London: K. Paul, Trench, Trubnerer, 1897.

Ferguson, Moira. "The Discovery of Mary Wollstonecraft's *The Female Reader.*" *Signs: Journal of Women in Culture and Society* 3 (1978):945–57.

Flexner, Eleanor. *Mary Wollstonecraft: A Biography.* New York: Coward, McCann and Geoghegan, 1972.

George, Margaret. *One Woman's "Situation": A Study of Mary Wollstonecraft.* Urbana: University of Illinois Press, 1970.

Godwin, William. *Memoirs of the Author of a Vindication of the Rights of Woman.* London: J. Johnson and G. G. and J. Robinson, 1798; Philadelphia (*The Memoirs of Mary Wollstonecraft Godwin*): James Carey, 1799.

Guralnick, Elissa S. "Radical Politics in Mary Wollstonecraft's *A Vindication of the Rights of Woman.*" *Studies in Burke and His Time: A Journal Devoted to British, American, and Continental Culture* 18 (1977):155–66.

———. "Rhetorical Strategy in Mary Wollstonecraft's *A Vindication of the Rights of Woman.*" *The Humanities Association Review* 30 (1979):174–85.

Kelly, Gary. "Mary Wollstonecraft as *Vir Bonus.*" *English Studies in Canada* 5 (1979):275–91.

Janes, R. M. "On the Reception of Mary Wollstonecraft's *A Vindication of the Rights of Woman.*" *Journal of the History of Ideas* 39 (1978):293–302.

Myers, Mitzi. "Mary Wollstonecraft's *Letters Written . . . in Sweden: Toward Romantic Autobiography.*" *Studies in 18th-Century Culture* 8 (1979):165–85.

———. "Unfinished Business: Wollstonecraft's *Maria.*" *The Wordsworth Circle* 11 (1980):107–14.

Nicholes, Eleanor L. "Mary Wollstonecraft." In *Romantic Rebels: Essays on Shelley and His Circle*, ed. Kenneth Neill Cameron. Cambridge, Mass.: Harvard University Press, 1973.

Nixon, Edna. *Mary Wollstonecraft: Her Life and Times*. London: J. M. Dent and Sons, 1971.

Pennell, Elizabeth R. *Mary Wollstonecraft*, London, 1885. Reprinted New York: Gordon Press, 1972.

Rauschenbusch-Clough, Emma. *A Study of Mary Wollstonecraft and the Rights of Woman*. London: Longmans, Green, 1896.

Sunstein, Emily W. *A Different Face: The Life of Mary Wollstonecraft*. New York: Harper and Row, 1975.

Theriot, Nancy M. "Mary Wollstonecraft and Margaret Fuller: A Theoretical Comparison." *International Journal of Women's Studies* 2 (1979):560–74.

Tomalin, Claire. *The Life and Death of Mary Wollstonecraft*. New York: Harcourt Brace Jovanovich, 1974.

Todd, Janet M. *Mary Wollstonecraft: A Bibliography*. New York: Garland Publishing, 1976.

Wardle, Ralph M. "Mary Wollstonecraft, Analytical Reviewer." *Publications of the Modern Language Association of America* vol. 62, December 1947, pp. 1000–1009.

———. *Mary Wollstonecraft: A Critical Biography*. 1951. Reprinted Lincoln: University of Nebraska Press, 1966.

Wardle, Ralph M., ed. *Godwin and Mary: Letters of William Godwin and Mary Wollstonecraft*. Lawrence: University of Kansas Press, 1966.

———. *Collected Letters of Mary Wollstonecraft*. Ithaca, N.Y.: Cornell University Press, 1979.

ON THE
EDUCATION
OF WOMEN

Thoughts on the Education
of Daughters

MANY OF the deeply felt convictions that were to make Mary Wollstonecraft a symbol of rebellious feminism appear throughout her first book. If read with hindsight, it becomes revealing and touching in ways that the neophyte writer probably did not suspect. Written in 1786, after she closed her school at Newington Green and before she sailed for Ireland as governess to the Kingsborough family, *Thoughts on the Education of Daughters* is a random assortment of ideas that she developed in fulfilling her tutorial role. While her topics may be confined to the narrow range of traditional female concerns in the eighteenth century (whole chapters are devoted to "The Observance of Sunday" and "Card-Playing," for instance) and her counsel is for women to seek tranquility through reason and self-discipline, her private passions and fears color her otherwise unexceptionable educational philosophy.

She begins with many sensible suggestions for "The Nursery," but her experience as a teacher seems less central to her perceptions than her own rankling sense of childhood deprivation. Her view of parents can be caustic: "Indolence, and a thoughtless disregard of everything except the present indulgence, make many mothers, who may have momentary starts of tenderness, neglect their children." With an insight that seems quite modern, this sensitive observer writing two hundred years ago urges mothers to breastfeed so they can develop a rational affection for their offspring.

She places great value on domestic skills—one of her "Desultory Thoughts" recommends "a little knowledge of physic," knowledge which Wollstonecraft prided herself on (it was always she who was called to nurse relatives and friends on their sickbeds)—but already she was arguing that the practical education to which women had been limited neglected their minds. Throughout her career she called for women to enter into the "severe exercise" of independent thought.

Thoughts on the Education of Daughters becomes most probing when it goes beyond advice and begins to question the underlying purposes of education. Here Wollstonecraft condemns the frivolity of the contemporary curriculum for females: whether her fate be to marry or not, no woman can expect a life so cushioned that she need only learn the art of dress and social graces. Even in happy marriages, there will be vacuums to fill. How much more problematical, writes the twenty-seven-year-old spinster, becomes the education of women who never marry, for whose attainments society can find no use. It is an unmistakably personal judgment.

The book's most idiosyncratic chapter, "Unfortunate Situation of Females, Fashionably Educated, and Left without a Fortune," also warns against the disappointments visited upon maidens by "male coquets." Wollstonecraft, the disciple of reason, argues that women can exercise self-control to blunt the indignities of sexual relations, before or after matrimony. This attitude of maidenly (or virginal) reserve evaporated as her contacts with the opposite sex deepened, but the crucial vision in this initial volume grew stronger with time: "In a comfortable situation, a cultivated mind is necessary to render a woman contented; and in a miserable one, it is her only consolation."

THOUGHTS
ON THE
EDUCATION
OF
DAUGHTERS:
WITH
REFLECTIONS ON FEMALE CONDUCT,
IN
THE MORE IMPORTANT DUTIES OF LIFE

THE NURSERY

As I conceive it to be the duty of every rational creature to attend to its offspring, I am sorry to observe that reason and duty together have not so powerful an influence over human conduct as instinct has in the brute creation. Indolence, and a thoughtless disregard of everything except the present indulgence, make many mothers, who may have momentary starts of tenderness, neglect their children. They follow a pleasing impulse, and never reflect that reason should cultivate and govern those instincts which are implanted in us to render the path of duty pleasant—for if they are not governed they will run wild; and strengthen the passions which are ever endeavoring to obtain dominion—I mean vanity and self-love.

The first thing to be attended to is laying the foundation of a good constitution. The mother (if there are not very weighty reasons to prevent her) ought to suckle her children. Her milk is their proper nutriment, and for some time is quite sufficient. Were a regular mode of suckling adopted,

it would be far from being a laborious task. Children who
are left to the care of ignorant nurses have their stomachs
overloaded with improper food, which turns acid, and renders them very uncomfortable. We should be particularly
careful to guard them in their infant state from bodily pain;
as their minds can then afford them no amusement to alleviate it. The first years of a child's life are frequently made
miserable through negligence or ignorance. Their complaints
are mostly in their stomach or bowels; and these complaints
generally arise from the quality and quantity of their food.

The suckling of a child also excites the warmest glow of
tenderness. Its dependent, helpless state produces an affection, which may properly be termed maternal. I have even
felt it, when I have seen a mother perform that office, and
am of opinion that maternal tenderness arises quite as much
from habit as instinct. It is possible, I am convinced, to
acquire the affection of a parent for an adopted child; it is
necessary, therefore, for a mother to perform the office of
one in order to produce in herself a rational affection for her
offspring.

Children very early contract the manners of those about
them. It is easy to distinguish the child of a well-bred person, if it is not left entirely to the nurse's care. These women
are of course ignorant, and to keep a child quiet for the moment, they humor all its little caprices. Very soon does it
begin to be perverse, and eager to be gratified in everything.
The usual mode of acting is complying with the humors
sometimes, and contradicting them at others—just according to the dictates of an uncorrected temper. This the infant
finds out earlier than can be imagined, and it gives rise to
an affection devoid of respect. Uniformity of conduct is the
only feasible method of creating both. An inflexible adherence to any rule that has been laid down makes children
comfortable, and saves the mother and nurse much trouble,
as they will not often contest if they have not once conquered. They will, I am sure, love and respect a person who
treats them properly, if someone else does not indiscreetly
indulge them. I once heard a judicious father say, "He would
treat his child as he would his horse: first convince it he was
its master, and then its friend." But yet a rigid style of
behavior is by no means to be adopted; on the contrary, I
wish to remark that it is only in the years of childhood that
the happiness of a human being depends entirely on others—
and to embitter those years by needless restraint is cruel. To

conciliate affection, affection must be shown, and little proofs of it ought always to be given—let them not appear weaknesses, and they will sink deep into the young mind, and call forth its most amiable propensities. The turbulent passions may be kept down till reason begins to dawn.

In the nursery, too, they are taught to speak; and there they not only hear nonsense, but that nonsense retailed out in such silly, affected tones as must disgust; yet these are the tones which the child first imitates, and its innocent playful manner renders them tolerable, if not pleasing; but afterwards they are not easily got the better of—nay, many women always retain the pretty prattle of the nursery, and do not forget to lisp, when they have learned to languish.

Children are taught revenge and lies in their very cradles. If they fall down, or strike their heads against any thing, to quiet them they are bid return the injury, and their little hands held out to do it. When they cry, or are troublesome, the cat or dog is chastised, or some bugbear called to take them away; which only terrifies them at first, for they soon find out that the nurse means nothing by these dreadful threatenings. Indeed so well do they discover the fallacy that I have seen little creatures who could scarcely speak play over the same tricks with their doll or the cat.

How, then, when the mind comes under discipline, can precepts of truth be enforced, when the first examples they have had would lead them to practice the contrary?

MORAL DISCIPLINE

It has been asserted, "That no being, merely human, could properly educate a child." I entirely coincide with this author; but though perfection cannot be attained, and unforeseen events will ever govern human conduct, yet still it is our duty to lay down some rule to regulate our actions by, and to adhere to it, as consistently as our infirmities will permit. . . . Parents must have subdued their own passions, which is not often the case in any considerable degree.

The marriage state is too often a state of discord; it does not always happen that both parents are rational, and the weakest have it in their power to do most mischief.

How then are the tender minds of children to be cultivated? —Mamma is only anxious that they should love her best, and perhaps takes pains to sow those seeds, which have produced such luxuriant weeds in her own mind. Or, what still more frequently occurs, the children are at first made playthings of, and when their tempers have been spoiled by indiscreet indulgence, they become troublesome, and are mostly left with servants. . . .

Children should be permitted to enter into conversation; but it requires great discernment to find out such subjects as will gradually improve them. Animals are the first objects which catch their attention; and I think little stories about them would not only amuse but instruct at the same time, and have the best effect in forming the temper and cultivating the good dispositions of the heart. . . .

Whenever a child asks a question, it should always have a reasonable answer given it. Its little passions should be engaged. They are mostly fond of stories, and proper ones would improve them even while they are amused. Instead of these, their heads are filled with improbable tales and superstitious accounts of invisible beings, which breed strange prejudices and vain fears in their minds.

. . . .

Above all, try to teach them to combine their ideas. It is of more use than can be conceived for a child to learn to compare things that are similar in some respects, and different in others. I wish them to be taught to think—thinking, indeed, is a severe exercise, and exercise of either mind or body will not at first be entered on, but with a view to pleasure. Not that I would have them make long reflections; for when they do not arise from experience, they are mostly absurd.

EXTERIOR ACCOMPLISHMENTS

Under this head may be ranked all those accomplishments which merely render the person attractive; and those half-learned ones which do not improve the mind. . . .

. . . I have known children who could repeat things in the order they learned them, that were quite at a loss when put out of the beaten track. If the understanding is not exercised, the memory will be employed to little purpose.

Girls learn something of music, drawing, and geography; but they do not know enough to engage their attention, and render it an employment of the mind. If they can play over a few tunes to their acquaintance, and have a drawing or two (half done by the master) to hang up in their rooms, they imagine themselves artists for the rest of their lives. It is not the being able to execute a trifling landscape, or anything of the kind, that is of consequence—these are at best but trifles, and the foolish, indiscriminate praises which are bestowed on them only produce vanity. But what is really of no importance, when considered in this light, becomes of the utmost when a girl has a fondness for the art, and a desire of excellence. Whatever tends to make a person in some measure independent of the senses is a prop to virtue. Amusing employments must first occupy the mind; and as an attention to moral duties leads to piety, so whoever weighs one subject will turn to others, and new ideas will rush into the mind. The faculties will be exercised, and not suffered to sleep, which will give a variety to the character.

Dancing and elegance of manners are very pleasing, if too great a stress is not laid on them. . . .

The lively thoughtlessness of youth makes every young creature agreeable for the time; but when those years are flown, and sense is not substituted in the stead of vivacity, the follies of youth are acted over, and they never consider that the things which please in their proper season disgust out of it. It is very absurd to see a woman whose brow time has marked with wrinkles aping the manners of a girl in her teens.

I do not think it foreign to the present subject to mention the trifling conversations women are mostly fond of. In general, they are prone to ridicule. As they lay the greatest stress on manners, the most respectable characters will not escape its lash, if deficient in this article. Ridicule has been, with some people, the boasted test of truth—if so, our sex ought to make wonderful improvements; but I am apt to think they often exert this talent till they lose all perception of it themselves. Affectation, and not ignorance, is the fair game for ridicule; and even affectation some good-natured persons will spare. We should never give pain without a design to amend.

DRESS

Many able pens have dwelt on the peculiar foibles of our sex. We have been equally desired to avoid the two extremes in dress, and the necessity of cleanliness has been insisted on, "As from the body's purity the mind receives a sympathetic aid."

By far too much of a girl's time is taken up in dress. This is an exterior accomplishment; but I chose to consider it by itself. The body hides the mind, and it is, in its turn, obscured by the drapery. I hate to see the frame of a picture so glaring as to catch the eye and divide the attention. Dress ought to adorn the person, and not rival it. It may be simple, elegant, and becoming, without being expensive; and ridiculous fashions disregarded, while singularity is avoided. The beauty of dress (I shall raise astonishment by saying so) is its not being conspicuous one way or the other; when it neither distorts [n]or hides the human form by unnatural protuberances. If ornaments are much studied, a consciousness of being well dressed will appear in the face—and surely this mean pride does not give much sublimity to it.

"Out of the abundance of the heart the mouth speaketh." And how much conversation does dress furnish, which surely cannot be very improving or entertaining.

It gives rise to envy, and contests for trifling superiority, which do not render a woman very respectable to the other sex.

Arts are used to obtain money; and much is squandered away, which if saved for charitable purposes might alleviate the distress of many poor families, and soften the heart of the girl who entered into such scenes of woe.

In the article of dress may be included the whole tribe of beauty washes, cosmetics, Olympian dew, oriental herbs, liquid bloom, and the paint which enlivened Ninon's face, and bid defiance to time. These numerous and essential articles are advertised in so ridiculous a style that the rapid sale of them is a very severe reflection on the understanding of those females who encourage it. The dew and herbs, I imagine, are very harmless, but I do not know whether the same may be said of the paint. White is certainly very prejudicial to the health, and never can be made to resemble nature. The red, too, takes off from the expression of the countenance, and the beautiful glow which modesty, affection, or any other emotion of the mind gives can never be seen. It is not "a mind-illumined face." "The body does not charm, because the mind is seen," but just the contrary; and if caught by it a man marries a woman thus disguised, he may chance not to be satisfied with her real person. A made-up face may strike visitors, but will certainly disgust domestic friends. And one obvious inference is drawn: truth is not expected to govern the inhabitant of so artificial a form. The false life with which rouge animates the eyes is not of the most delicate kind; nor does a woman's dressing herself in a way to attract languishing glances give us the most advantageous opinion of the purity of her mind.

I forgot to mention powder among the deceptions. It is a pity that it should be so generally worn. The most beautiful ornament of the features is disguised, and the shade it would give to the countenance entirely lost. The color of every person's hair generally suits the complexion, and is calculated to set it off. What absurdity then do they run into, who use red, blue, and yellow powder! And what a false taste does it exhibit!

The quantity of pomatum is often disgusting. We laugh at the Hottentots, and in some things adopt their customs.

Simplicity of dress, and unaffected manners, should go together. They demand respect, and will be admired by people of taste, even when love is out of the question.

. . . .

UNFORTUNATE SITUATION OF FEMALES, FASHIONABLY EDUCATED, AND LEFT WITHOUT A FORTUNE

I have hitherto only spoken of those females, who will have a provision made for them by their parents. But many who have been well, or at least fashionably educated, are left without a fortune, and if they are not entirely devoid of delicacy, they must frequently remain single.

Few are the modes of earning a subsistence, and those

very humiliating. Perhaps to be an humble companion to some rich old cousin, or what is still worse, to live with strangers who are so intolerably tyrannical that none of their own relations can bear to live with them, though they should even expect a fortune in reversion. It is impossible to enumerate the many hours of anguish such a person must spend. Above the servants, yet considered by them as a spy, and ever reminded of her inferiority when in conversation with the superiors. If she cannot condescend to mean flattery, she has not a chance of being a favorite; and should any of the visitors take notice of her, and she for a moment forget her subordinate state, she is sure to be reminded of it.

Painfully sensible of unkindness, she is alive to everything, and many sarcasms reach her which were perhaps directed another way. She is alone, shut out from equality and confidence, and the concealed anxiety impairs her constitution; for she must wear a cheerful face, or be dismissed. The being dependent on the caprice of a fellow creature, though certainly very necessary in this state of discipline, is yet a very bitter corrective, which we would fain shrink from.

A teacher at a school is only a kind of upper servant, who has more work than the menial ones.

A governess to young ladies is equally disagreeable. It is ten to one if they meet with a reasonable mother; and if she is not so, she will be continually finding fault to prove she is not ignorant, and be displeased if her pupils do not improve, but angry if the proper methods are taken to make them do so. The children treat them with disrespect, and often with insolence. In the meantime life glides away, and the spirits with it; "and when youth and genial years are flown," they have nothing to subsist on; or, perhaps, on some extraordinary occasion, some small allowance may be made for them, which is thought a great charity.

The few trades which are left are now gradually falling into the hands of the men, and certainly they are not very respectable.

It is hard for a person who has a relish for polished society to herd with the vulgar, or to condescend to mix with her former equals when she is considered in a different light. What unwelcome heartbreaking knowledge is then poured in on her! I mean a view of the selfishness and depravity of the world; for every other acquirement is a source of pleasure, though they may occasion temporary inconveniences.

How cutting is the contempt she meets with! A young mind looks round for love and friendship; but love and friendship fly from poverty: expect them not if you are poor! The mind must then sink into meanness, and accommodate itself to its new state, or dare to be unhappy. Yet I think no reflecting person would give up the experience and improvement they have gained, to have avoided the misfortunes; on the contrary, they are thankfully ranked amongst the choicest blessings of life, when we are not under their immediate pressure.

How earnestly does a mind full of sensibility look for disinterested friendship, and long to meet with good unalloyed. When fortune smiles they hug the dear delusion; but dream not that it is one. The painted cloud disappears suddenly, the scene is changed, and what an aching void is left in the heart! a void which only religion can fill up—and how few seek this internal comfort!

A woman who has beauty without sentiment is in great danger of being seduced; and if she has any, cannot guard herself from painful mortifications. It is very disagreeable to keep up a continual reserve with men she has been formerly familiar with; yet if she places confidence, it is ten to one but she is deceived. Few men seriously think of marrying an inferior; and if they have honor enough not to take advantage of the artless tenderness of a woman who loves, and thinks not of the difference of rank, they do not undeceive her until she has anticipated happiness, which, contrasted with her dependent situation, appears delightful. The disappointment is severe; and the heart receives a wound which does not easily admit of a complete cure, as the good that is missed is not valued according to its real worth: for fancy drew the picture, and grief delights to create food to feed on.

If what I have written should be read by parents who are now going on in thoughtless extravagance, and anxious only that their daughters may be *genteelly educated*, let them consider to what sorrows they expose them; for I have not overcolored the picture.

. . . .

LOVE

. . . .

. . . Though it is not easy to say how a person should act under the immediate influence of passion, yet they certainly have no excuse who are actuated only by vanity, and deceive by an equivocal behavior in order to gratify it. There are quite as many male coquets as female, and they are far more pernicious pests to society, as their sphere of action is larger, and they are less exposed to the censure of the world. A smothered sigh, downcast look, and the many other little arts which are played off may give extreme pain to a sincere, artless woman, though she cannot resent, or complain of, the injury. This kind of trifling, I think, much more inexcusable than inconstancy; and why it is so appears so obvious, I need not point it out.

. . . .

. . . Love, unsupported by esteem, must soon expire, or lead to depravity; as, on the contrary, when a worthy person is the object, it is the greatest incentive to improvement, and has the best effect on the manners and temper. We should always try to fix in our minds the rational grounds we have for loving a person, that we may be able to recollect them when we feel disgust or resentment; we should then habitually practice forbearance, and the many petty disputes which interrupt domestic peace would be avoided. A woman cannot reasonably be unhappy, if she is attached to a man of sense and goodness, though he may not be all she could wish.

I am very far from thinking love irresistible, and not to be conquered. "If weak women go astray," it is they, and not the stars, that are to be blamed. A resolute endeavor will almost always overcome difficulties. I knew a woman very early in life warmly attached to an agreeable man, yet she saw his faults; his principles were unfixed, and his prodigal turn would have obliged her to have restrained every benevolent emotion of her heart. She exerted her influence to improve him, but in vain did she for years try to do it. Convinced of the impossibility, she determined not to marry him, though she was forced to encounter poverty and its attendants.

....

Nothing can more tend to destroy peace of mind than platonic attachments. They are begun in false refinements, and frequently end in sorrow, if not in guilt. The two extremes often meet, and virtue carried to excess will sometimes lead to the opposite vice. Not that I mean to insinuate that there is no such thing as friendship between persons of different sexes; I am convinced of the contrary. I only mean to observe that if a woman's heart is disengaged, she should not give way to a pleasing delusion, and imagine she will be satisfied with the friendship of a man she admires, and prefers to the rest of the world. The heart is very treacherous, and if we do not guard its first emotions, we shall not afterwards be able to prevent its sighing for impossibilities. If there are any insuperable bars to an union in the common way, try to dismiss the dangerous tenderness, or it will undermine your comfort, and betray you into many errors. To attempt to raise ourselves above human beings is ridiculous; we cannot extirpate our passions, nor is it necessary that we should, though it may be wise sometimes not to stray too near a precipice, lest we fall over before we are aware. We cannot avoid much vexation and sorrow, if we are ever so prudent; it is then the part of wisdom to enjoy those gleams of sunshine which do not endanger our innocence, or lead to repentance. Love gilds all the prospects of life, and though it cannot always exclude apathy, it makes many cares appear trifling. . . .

MATRIMONY

Early marriages are, in my opinion, a stop to improvement. If we were born only "to draw nutrition, propagate and rot," the sooner the end of creation was answered the better; but as women are here allowed to have souls, the soul ought to be attended to. In youth a woman endeavors to please the other sex, in order, generally speaking, to get married, and this endeavor calls forth all her powers. If she has had a tolerable education, the foundation only is laid, for the mind does not soon arrive at maturity, and should not be engrossed by domestic cares before any habits are fixed. The passions also have too much influence over the judgment to suffer it to direct her in this most important affair; and many women, I am persuaded, marry a man before they are twenty, whom they would have rejected some years after. Very frequently, when the education has been neglected, the mind improves itself, if it has leisure for reflection, and experience to reflect on; but how can this happen when they are forced to act before they have had time to think, or find that they are unhappily married? Nay, should they be so fortunate as to get a good husband, they will not set a proper value on him; he will be found much inferior to the lovers described in novels, and their want of knowledge makes them frequently disgusted with the man, when the fault is in human nature.

When a woman's mind has gained some strength, she will in all probability pay more attention to her actions than a girl can be expected to do; and if she thinks seriously, she will choose for a companion a man of principle; and this perhaps young people do not sufficiently attend to, or see the necessity of doing. A woman of feeling must be very much hurt if she is obliged to keep her children out of their father's company, that their morals may not be injured by his conversation; and besides, the whole arduous task of education devolves on her, and in such a case it is not very practicable. Attention to the education of children must be irksome, when life appears to have so many charms, and its pleasures are not found fallacious. Many are but just returned from a boarding school, when they are placed at the head of a family, and how fit they are to manage it, I leave the judicious to judge. Can they improve a child's understanding, when they are scarcely out of the state of childhood themselves?

Dignity of manners, too, and proper reserve are often wanting. The constant attendant on too much familiarity is contempt. Women are often before marriage prudish, and afterwards they think they may innocently give way to fondness, and overwhelm the poor man with it. They think they have a legal right to his affections, and grow remiss in their endeavors to please. There are a thousand nameless decencies which good sense gives rise to, and artless proofs of regard which flow from the heart, and will reach it, if it is not depraved. It has ever occurred to me that it was sufficient for a woman to receive caresses, and not bestow them. She ought to distinguish between fondness and tenderness. The latter is the sweetest cordial of life, but, like all other cordials, should be reserved for particular occasions; to exhilarate the spirits, when depressed by sickness, or lost in sorrow. Sensibility will best instruct. Some delicacies can never be pointed out or described, though they sink deep into the heart, and render the hours of distress supportable.

A woman should have so proper a pride, as not easily to forget a deliberate affront, though she must not too hastily resent any little coolness. We cannot always feel alike, and all are subject to changes of temper without an adequate cause.

Reason must often be called in to fill up the vacuums of life; but too many of our sex suffer theirs to lie dormant. A little ridicule and smart turn of expression often confutes without convincing; and tricks are played off to raise tenderness, even while they are forfeiting esteem.

Women are said to be the weaker vessel, and many are the miseries which this weakness brings on them. Men have in some respects very much the advantage. If they have a tolerable understanding, it has a chance to be cultivated. They are forced to see human nature as it is, and are not left to dwell on the pictures of their own imaginations. Nothing, I am sure, calls forth the faculties so much as the being obliged to struggle with the world; and this is not a woman's province in a married state. Her sphere of action is not large, and if she is not taught to look into her own heart, how trivial are her occupations and pursuits! What little arts engross and narrow her mind! "Cunning fills up the mighty void of sense"; and cares, which do not improve the heart or understanding, take up her attention. Of course, she falls a prey to childish anger, and silly capricious humors, which render her rather insignificant than vicious.

In a comfortable situation, a cultivated mind is necessary to render a woman contented; and in a miserable one, it is her only consolation. A sensible, delicate woman, who by some strange accident, or mistake, is joined to a fool or a brute, must be wretched beyond all names of wretchedness, if her views are confined to the present scene. Of what importance, then, is intellectual improvement, when our comfort here, and happiness hereafter, depends upon it.

DESULTORY THOUGHTS

As every kind of domestic concern and family business is properly a woman's province, to enable her to discharge her duty she should study the different branches of it. Nothing is more useful in a family than a little knowledge of physic, sufficient to make the mistress of it a judicious nurse. Many a person who has had a sensible physician to attend them have been lost for want of the other; for tenderness without judgment sometimes does more harm than good.

The ignorant imagine there is something very mysterious in the practice of physic. They expect a medicine to work like a charm, and know nothing of the progress and crisis of disorders. The keeping of the patient low appears cruel, all kind of regimen is disregarded, and though the fever rages, they cannot be persuaded not to give them inflammatory food. "How (say they) can a person get well without nourishment?"

The mind, too, should be soothed at the same time; and indeed, whenever it sinks, soothing is, at first, better than reasoning. The slackened nerves are not to be braced by words. When a mind is worried by care, or oppressed by sorrow, it cannot in a moment grow tranquil, and attend to the voice of reason.

. . . .

Original Stories from
Real Life

The theoretical *Thoughts on the Education of Daughters* had been written prior to Wollstonecraft's service as a governess. *Mary, a Fiction*, a story of such an education, written in Ireland, incorporated some aspects of her life there with the Kingsborough family. Her third published book also looked at the education of women, turning a different aspect of her Irish year into another sort of fiction. *Original Stories from Real Life*, written in 1787 and published anonymously in April of the following year, explains its method in its subtitle: "with conversations, calculated to regulate the affections, and form the mind to truth and goodness." Two motherless girls have been sent by their father to profit from conversations with a female relative blessed with flawless discernment and high moral probity. The twelve-year-old Caroline (too vain of her beauty) and fourteen-year-old Mary (too quick to ridicule others) bear the names of the two younger King daughters; the name of the eldest, Mary's favorite Margaret, is not used, but she is apparently the model for Mary. While the saintly Mrs. Mason may occasionally be an idealized self-portrait, the generous and cultivated Mrs. Burgh of Newington Green appears to be Wollstonecraft's real-life prototype.

As in her two previous works, Wollstonecraft's central motivation was her strong sense of parental dereliction. She was haunted by the image of wealthy parents shunting their offspring into the arms of ignorant and uncaring servants. *Original Stories*, her only major work directed at a youthful audience, takes a more aggressively didactic tone than her other writing; nevertheless, its polemical use of fiction was for her not the exception but the rule. Through a series of moralized vignettes, Wollstonecraft demonstrates the virtues of teaching by example. The essential lesson the children learn, to respect the rights of others, is systematically illustrated. After they are brought to feel the pain that

45

even snails and birds and dogs can suffer, they are ready to
empathize with human beings from different levels of society but almost universally victims of neglect or injustice
that has left them declassed. The parallel with the writer's
own childhood is unmistakable. Wollstonecraft, the daughter of a man who had squandered a sizeable inheritance,
imagines a series of tragic falls, of once-proud families humbled, of loss of rank and prestige. In cumulative impact, the
stories provide an early sketch for the fictional case histo-
ries that ten years later would form a pattern in her *Wrongs
of Woman*.

Only a few characters in these stories have the strength
to pull themselves up from the ruins of their former selves.
We can more easily understand the tinge of smugness in
some of Mrs. Mason's remarks after she reveals the price
she has had to pay for her self-mastery. Having lost both
child and husband, she keeps herself from despairing only
through the practice of charity, which reconciles her to her
own continuing existence. "When our bowels yearn to our
fellow creatures, we feel that the love of God dwelleth in
us—and then we cannot always go on our way sorrowing."
But if Mary herself has a counterpart in these tales of virtue
brought low, it is the schoolmistress Anna, determined to be
independent: "When I am my own mistress, the crust I earn
will be sweet, and the water that moistens it will not be
mingled with tears of sorrow or indignation." The plots of
Original Stories from Real Life were, in fact, highly unorig-
inal, but the biblical phrases Wollstonecraft employed demonstrate her intense identification with their motif of fall
and redemption. The passion of her expression points the
way to the mature work that lies just ahead.

ORIGINAL STORIES,
FROM
REAL LIFE;
WITH
CONVERSATIONS,
CALCULATED TO
REGULATE THE AFFECTIONS,
AND
FORM THE MIND
TO
TRUTH AND GOODNESS

MORAL CONVERSATIONS
AND
STORIES

CHAPTER I

*The treatment of animals—The ant—The bee—Good-
ness—The lark's nest—The asses*

One fine morning in spring, some time after Mary and
Caroline were settled in their new abode, Mrs. Mason proposed a walk before breakfast, a custom she wished to teach
them, by rendering it amusing to them.

The sun had scarcely dispelled the dew which hung on
every blade of grass, and filled the half-shut flowers; every
prospect smiled, and the freshness of the air conveyed the

most pleasing sensations to Mrs. Mason's mind; but the children were regardless of the surrounding beauties, and ran eagerly after some insects to destroy them. Mrs. Mason silently observed them, without appearing to do it; and stepped suddenly out of the footpath into the long grass. Her buckle was caught in it, and striving to disentangle herself, she wet her feet; a thing the children knew she wished to avoid, as she had been lately sick. This circumstance roused their attention; and they forgot their amusement to inquire *why* she had left the path; and Mary could hardly restrain a laugh when she was informed that it was to avoid treading on some snails that were creeping across the narrow footway. Surely, said Mary, you do not think there is any harm in killing a snail, or any of those nasty creatures that crawl on the ground? I hate them, and should I scream, if any one of them was to find its way from my clothes to my neck! With great gravity, Mrs. Mason asked how she dared to kill anything, but to prevent its hurting her? Then, resuming a smiling face, she said, You have been neglected, my child; as we walk along attend to what I say, and make the best answers you can; and do you, Caroline, join in the conversation.

You have already heard that God created the world, and every inhabitant of it. He is then called the Father of all creatures; and all are made to be happy. He made those snails you despise, and caterpillars, and spiders; and when he made them, did not leave them to perish, but placed them where the food that is most proper to nourish them is easily found. They do not live long, but *their* Father, as well as yours, directs them to deposit their eggs on the plants that are fit to support the young, when they are not able to get food for themselves. And when such a great and wise Being has taken care to provide everything necessary for the meanest creature, would you dare to kill it, merely because it appears, as you think, ugly? Mary began to be attentive, and followed Mrs. Mason's example, who allowed a caterpillar and a spider to creep on her hand. You find them very harmless; but too great a quantity would destroy our vegetables and fruit: to prevent this mischief, birds are permitted to eat them, and in spring there are always more than at any other time of the year, to furnish food for the young birds. Half-convinced, Mary said, but worms are of little consequence in the world. Yet, replied Mrs. Mason, God cares for them, and gives them everything that is necessary to render their existence comfortable. You are often troublesome—I am stronger than you—yet I do not kill you.

Observe those ants; they have a little habitation in yonder hillock; they carry food to it for the winter, and live very snug in it during the cold weather. The bees, too, have comfortable towns, and lay in a store of honey to support them when the flowers die, and snow covers the ground: and this forecast is as much the gift of God, as any quality you possess.

Do you know the meaning of the word Goodness? I see you are unwilling to answer. I will tell you. It is, first, to avoid hurting anything; and then, to contrive to give as much pleasure as you can. If any insects are to be destroyed, to preserve my garden from desolation, I have it done in the quickest way. Domestic animals that I keep, I provide the best food for, and never suffer them to be tormented; and this caution arises from two motives: I wish to make them happy; and, as I love my fellow creatures still better than them, I would not allow those I have any influence over to grow habitually thoughtless and cruel, and by these means lose the greatest pleasure life affords—that of resembling God, by doing good.

A lark now began to sing, as it soared aloft. The children watched it, and listened to its melody. They wondered what it was thinking of—of its young family, they concluded: it flew over the hedge, and drawing near, they heard the young ones chirp. Very soon both the old birds took their flight together, to look for food to satisfy their craving young, who were almost fledged. An idle boy, who had borrowed a gun, fired at them—they fell: and before he could take up the wounded pair, he saw Mrs. Mason; and expecting a very severe reprimand, ran away. They drew near; one was not much hurt; but the other, the cock, had one leg broke, and both its wings shattered; and its little eyes seemed starting out of their sockets, it was in such exquisite pain. The children turned from it. Look at it, said Mrs. Mason; do you not see it suffers as much, and more than you did when you had the smallpox; then you were tenderly nursed. Take up the hen; I will bind her wing together; perhaps it will heal. As to the other, though I hate to kill it, I must put it out of pain; to leave it in its present state would be cruel; and avoiding an unpleasant sensation myself, I should allow the bird to die by inches, and call this treatment tenderness, when it would be weakness or selfishness. Saying so, she put her foot on the bird's head, turning her own another way.

They walked on; when Caroline remarked that the nestlings, deprived of their parents, would now perish; and the mother began to flutter in her hand as they drew near the hedge, but the poor creature could not fly, though she tried to do it. The girls, with one voice, begged to take the nest, and provide food in a cage; and try if the mother could not contrive to hop about to feed them. The nest and the old mother were instantly in Mary's handkerchief, and a little opening left to admit the air; and Caroline peeped into it every moment to see how they looked. I give you leave, said Mrs. Mason, to take those birds, because an accident has rendered them helpless; if that had not been the case, they should not have been confined.

They had scarcely reached the next field when they met another boy with a nest in his hand, and on a tree near him saw the mother, who, forgetting her natural timidity, followed the spoiler; and her intelligible tones of anguish reached the ears of the children, whose hearts now first felt the emotions of humanity. Caroline called him, and taking sixpence out of her little purse, offered to give it to him for the nest, if he would show her where he took it from. The boy consented, and away ran Caroline to replace it—crying all the way, how delighted the old bird will be to find her brood again. The pleasure that the parent-bird would feel was talked of till they came to a large common, and heard some young asses, at the door of an hovel, making a most dreadful noise. Mrs. Mason had ordered the old ones to be confined, lest the young should suck before the necessary quantity had been saved for the sick. After milking them, the thoughtless boy left them still in confinement, and the young in vain implored the food nature designed for them. Open the hatch, said Mrs. Mason, the mothers have still enough left to satisfy their young. It was opened, and they saw them suck.

Now we will return to breakfast; give me your hands, my little girls, you have done good this morning, you are my fellow creatures. Look, what a fine morning it is. Insects, birds, and animals are all enjoying the day. Thank God for permitting you to see it, and to imitate himself by doing good. Other creatures only think of themselves; but man is allowed to *retrace* the image of God first implanted in him; he feels disinterested love; every part of the creation affords an exercise for virtue, and a *consequent* source of pleasure.

. . . .

CHAPTER X

The danger of delay—Description of a mansion house in ruins—The history of Charles Townley

Very frequently Mrs. Mason had to wait for the children, when she wished to walk and had desired them to be ready. Mary in particular had a trick of putting everything off till the last moment, and then she did but half do it, or left it undone. This indolent way of delaying made her miss many opportunities of obliging and doing good; and whole hours were lost in irresolute idleness, which she afterwards wished had been properly employed.

This was the case one day, when she had a letter to write to her father; though it was mentioned to her early in the morning, they were obliged to let the finest part of the evening slip away while she was finishing it; and her haste made her forget what she intended to have said. Out of breath she joined them, and after they had crossed several fields, Mrs. Mason turned down a long avenue and bid them look at a large old mansion house. It was now in ruins: ivy grew over the substantial walls, which still resisted the depredations of time, and almost concealed a noble arch, on which maimed lions crouched; and vultures and eagles, who had lost their wings, seemed to rest forever there. Near it was a rookery, and the rooks lived safe in the high trees, whose trunks were all covered with ivy or moss, and a number of funguses grew about their large roots. The grass was long, and remained undisturbed, save when the wind swept across: it was of course pathless; here the mower never whet his scythe, nor did the haymakers mix their songs with the hoarse croaking of the rooks. A spacious basin was overspread with slime; water plants grew on the margin, and afforded a shelter for toads and adders. In many places lay the remains of ornaments and sun-dials; and pedestals that had crushed the figures they before supported. Making your way through the grass, you would frequently stumble over a headless statue, or the head would impede your progress. When you spoke, the voice seemed to return again, as if unable to penetrate the thick stagnated air; the sun could not dart into it his purifying rays, and the fallen leaves contributed to choke up the way, and render the air more noxious.

To this place I brought you on purpose this evening, said Mrs. Mason to the children, who clung about her, to tell you the story of the last inhabitant; but, as this part is unwholesome, we will sit on the broken stones of the drawbridge.

Charles Townley was a boy of uncommon abilities, and strong feelings, and he ever permitted those feelings to direct his conduct; I mean the present emotion governed him. He had not any strength or consistency of character; one moment he enjoyed a pleasure, and the next felt the pangs of remorse, on account of some duty he had neglected. He always indeed intended to act right in every particular *tomorrow*; but *today* he followed the prevailing whim.

He heard of a man in great distress, he determined to relieve him, and left his house in order to follow the humane impulse; but meeting an acquaintance, he was persuaded to go to the play, and *tomorrow* he thought he would do the act of charity. The next morning some company came to breakfast with him, and took him with them to view some fine pictures; in the evening he went to a concert; the day following he was tired, and lay in bed till noon; then read a dismal story, well wrought up, *wept* over it—fell asleep—and forgot to *act* humanely. An accident reminded him of his intention, he sent to the man, and found that he had too long delayed— the relief was useless.

In this thoughtless manner he spent his time and money; never applying to any profession, though formed to shine in all. His friends were offended, and allowed him to languish in a jail; as there appeared no probability of reforming or fixing him, they left him to struggle with adversity. Severely did he reproach himself—He was almost lost in despair, when a friend visited him: this friend loved the latent sparks of virtue which he imagined would some time or other light up, and animate his conduct. He paid his debts, and gave him a sum of money sufficient to enable him to prepare for a voyage to the East Indies, where Charles wished to go, to try to regain his lost fortune. Through the intercession of his kind, considerate friend, his relations were reconciled to him, and his spirits raised.

He sailed with a fair wind, and fortune favored his most

romantic wishes; in the space of fifteen years, he gained large acquisitions, and thought of visiting, nay, settling in his native country.

Though impressed by the most lively sense of gratitude, he soon dropped his friend's correspondence; yet, as he knew he had a daughter, a large portion of his wealth he determined to reserve for her, to give the most substantial proof of his gratitude. The thought pleased him, and that was sufficient to divert him some months; but accidentally he heard that his friend had been very unsuccessful in trade; and this information made him wish to hasten his return to his native country. Still a procrastinating spirit possessed him, and he delayed the arduous task of settling his affairs, previous to his departure: he wrote however to England, and transmitted a considerable sum to a correspondent, desiring that this house might be prepared for him, and the mortgage cleared.

I can scarcely enumerate the various trifling pursuits that prevented his embarking. When he arrived in England, he came here, and sent for different workmen, and actually trifled away a month, before he went to visit his friend.

But his negligence was now severely punished. He learned that he had been reduced to great distress, and thrown into the very jail, out of which he took Townley, who, hastening to it, found there only his dead body; he died the day before. On the table lay a letter, directed in an unsteady hand to Charles Townley. He seized it, it contained but a few lines; but they smote his heart. He read as follows:

"I have been reduced by unforeseen misfortunes; when I heard of your arrival, a gleam of joy cheered my heart—*I thought I knew yours*, and that my latter days might still have been made comfortable in your society, for I loved you, I expected pleasure; but I was mistaken; you are ungrateful, and death is my only friend."

He read it over and over again and cried out, Gracious God, had I arrived but one day sooner I should have seen him, and he would not have died thinking me the most ungrateful wretch that ever burdened the earth! He then knocked his clinched fist against his forehead, looked wildly round the dreary apartment, and exclaimed in a choked, though impatient tone, You sat here yesterday, thinking of my ingratitude—where are you now? Oh! that my repenting sighs could reach you! He ordered the body to be interred, and returned home a prey to grief and despondency; indulging it, he neglected to inquire about the daughter; he intended to provide amply for her, but now he could only grieve. Some time elapsed, then he sent, and the intelligence he procured aggravated his distress, and gave it an additional sting.

The poor gentle girl, had, during her father's life, been engaged to a worthy young man; but, after his death, the relations of her lover sent him to sea to prevent the match taking place. She was helpless, and had not sufficient courage to combat with poverty; to escape from it, she married an old rake she detested. He was ill-humored, and his vicious habits rendered him a most dreadful companion. She tried in vain to please him, and banish the sorrow that bent her down, and made wealth and all the pleasures it could procure tasteless. Her tender father was dead—she had lost her lover—without a friend or confidant, silent grief consumed her. I have told you friendship is only to be found amongst the virtuous; her husband was vicious.

Oh! why did she marry? said Mary.

Because she was timid; but I have not told you all; the grief that did not break her heart, disturbed her reason; and her husband confined her in a madhouse.

Charles heard of this last circumstance, he visited her. Fanny, said he, do you recollect your old friend? Fanny looked at him and reason for a moment resumed her seat, and informed her countenance to trace anguish on it—the trembling light soon disappeared—wild fancy flushed in her eyes, and animated her incessant rant. She sung, talked of her husband's ill-usage—inquired if he had lately been to sea? And addressed her father's ghost, which she imagined was behind her chair.

Charles could not bear it. If I could lose like her a sense of woe, he cried, this intolerable anguish would not tear my heart. The money he intended for her could not restore her reason; but, had he sent for her soon after her father's death, he might have saved her and comforted himself.

This last stroke was worse than the first; he retired to this abode; melancholy crept on him, he let his beard grow, and the garden run wild. One room in the house the poor lunatic inhabited; and he had a proper person to attend her, and guard her from the dangers she wished to encounter. Every day he visited her, the sight of her would almost have unhinged a sound mind—How could he bear it, when his conscience was wounded, and whispered him that he had neglected to do good, to live to any rational purpose—the sweets of friendship were denied, and he every day contemplated the saddest of all sights—the wreck of a human understanding.

He died without a will—the estate was litigated, and as the title to this part could not be proved, the house was let fall into its present state.

But the night will overtake us, we must make haste home—And, Mary, need I desire you to remember this story—And remember, my child, you must attend to trifles; do all the good you can the present day, nay hour. This circumspection may not produce dazzling actions, nor will your silent virtue be supported by human applause; but your Father, who seeth in secret, will reward you.

CHAPTER XI

Dress—A character—Remarks on Mrs. B's manner of dressing—Trifling omissions undermine affection

Mary's procrastinating temper produced many ill consequences; she would lie in bed till the last moment, and then appear without washing her face or cleaning her teeth. Mrs. Mason had often observed it, and hinted dislike; but, unwilling to burden her with precepts, she waited for a glaring example; one was soon accidentally thrown in her way, and she determined it should not pass unobserved.

A lady who was remarkable for her negligence in this respect spent a week with them; and, during that time, very frequently disconcerted the economy of the family. She was seldom fit to be seen, and if any company came by chance to dinner, she would make them wait till it was quite cold, while she huddled on some ill-chosen finery. In the same style, if a little party of pleasure was proposed, she had to dress herself, and the hurry discomposed her, and tired those, who did not like to lose time in anticipating a trifling amusement. A few hours after she had left them, Mrs. Mason inquired of Mary, what effect this week's experience had had on her mind? ... Mrs. F's negligence arises from indolence; her mind is not employed about matters of importance; and, if it was, it would not be sufficient excuse for her habitually neglecting an essential part of a woman's duty....

. . . .

Of all the women I ever met with, Mrs. B. seems the freest from vanity, and those *littlenesses* which degrade the female character. Her virtues claim respect, and the practice of them engrosses her thoughts; yet her clothes are apparently well-chosen, and you always see her in the same attire. Not like many women who are eager to set off their persons to the best advantage, when they are only going to take a walk, and are careless, nay slovenly, when forced to stay at home. Mrs. B's conduct is just the reverse of this. She tries to avoid singularity, she does not wish to disgust the generality; but it is her family, her friends, she studies to please.

In dress it is not little minute things, but the *whole* that should be attended to; never desire to excel in trifles, if you do—there is an end to virtuous emulation, the mind cannot attend to both; if the main pursuit is trivial, the character will of course be insignificant. Habitual neatness is laudable; but, if you wish to be reckoned a well, and elegant dressed girl; and feel that praises on account of it give you pleasure, you are vain; and a laudable ambition will not dwell with vanity.

CHAPTER XVI

The benefits arising from devotion—The history of the village schoolmistress—Fatal effects of inattention to expenses, in the history of Mr. G.

The next morning Mrs. Mason desired the children to get their work and in the afternoon, if the weather was fine, they should visit the village schoolmistress.

Her father . . . was the youngest son of a noble family; his education had been liberal, though his fortune was small. His relations, however, seemed determined to push him forward in life, had not disobliged them by marrying the daughter of a country clergyman, an accomplished, sensible woman.

. . . .

This amiable parent died when Anna was near eighteen, and left her to the care of her father, whose high spirit she had imbibed. The religious principles her mother had instilled, regulated her notions of honor, and elevated her character; and her heart was regulated by her understanding.

After the death of her father, her aunt treated her as if she was a mere dependent on her bounty; and expected her to be an humble companion in every sense of the word; the company took the tone from her ladyship, and numberless were the mortifications she had to bear.

CHAPTER XVII

The benefits arising from devotion—The history of the village schoolmistress concluded

Anna endured this treatment some years, and had an opportunity of acquiring a knowledge of the world and her own heart. She visited her mother's father, and would have remained with him, but she determined not to lessen the small pittance he had anxiously saved out of a scanty income for two other grandchildren. She thought continually of her situation, and found, on examining her understanding, that the fashionable circle could not at any rate have afforded her much satisfaction, or even amusement; though their neglect and contempt rendered her very uncomfortable. She had her father's spirit of independence, and determined to shake off the galling yoke, and try to earn her own subsistence. Her acquaintance expostulated with her, and represented the miseries of poverty, and the mortifications and difficulties she would have to encounter. Let it be so, she replied, it is much preferable to swelling the train of the vicious great, and despising myself for bearing their impertinence, for eating their bitter bread; better, indeed, is a dinner of herbs with contentment. My wants are few; when I am my own mistress, the crust I earn will be sweet, and the water that moistens it will not be mingled with tears of sorrow or indignation.

To shorten my story: she came to me, after she had attempted several plans, and requested my advice; she would not accept of any considerable favors, and declared the greatest would be, to put her in a way of supporting herself, without forfeiting her highly valued liberty. I knew not what to advise; but while I was debating the matter with myself, I happened to mention, that we were in want of a schoolmistress. She eagerly adopted the plan, and has persevered in these last ten years, and I find her a valuable acquisition to our society.

She was formed to shine in the most brilliant circle—yet she relinquished it, and patiently labors to improve the children consigned to her management, and tranquilize her own mind; and she succeeds in both.

. . . .

CHAPTER XIX

Charity—The history of Peggy and her family—The sailor's widow

I have often remarked to you, said Mrs. Mason, one morning, to her pupils, that we are all dependent on each other, and this dependence is wisely ordered by our Heavenly Father, to call forth virtue, to exercise the best affections of the human heart, and fix them into habits. While we impart pleasure we receive it, and feel the grandeur of our immortal soul, as it is constantly struggling to spread itself into futurity.

Perhaps the greatest pleasure I have ever received has arisen from the habitual exercise of charity in its various branches: the view of a distressed object has made me now think of conversing about one branch of it, giving alms.

You know Peggy, the young girl I wish to have most about my person; I mean, I wish it for her own sake, that I may have an opportunity of improving her mind, and cultivating a good capacity. As to attendance, I never give much trouble to any fellow creature, I choose to be independent of caprice and artificial wants; except, indeed, when I am sick, then I thankfully receive the assistance I would willingly give to others in the same situation. I believe I have not in the world a more faithful friend than Peggy; and her earnest desire to please me gratifies my benevolence, for with delight I observe the workings of a grateful heart.

I lost a darling child, said Mrs. Mason, smothering a sigh, in the depth of winter—death had before deprived me of her father, and when I lost my child, he died again—every remnant of him was gone. The wintry prospects suited the temper of my soul; I have sat looking at a wide waste of trackless snow for hours; and the heavy sullen fog, that the feeble rays of the sun could not pierce, gave me back an image of my mind: I was unhappy, and the sight of dead nature accorded with my feelings—for all was dead to me.

As the snow began to melt, I took a walk, and observed the birds hopping about with drooping wings, or mute on the leafless bough. The mountains, whose sides had lost the snow, looked black; yet still it remained on the summit, and formed a contrast to diversify the dreary prospect.

I walked thoughtfully along, when the appearance of a man, who did not beg, struck me very forcibly. His shivering limbs were scarcely sheltered from the cold by the tattered garments which covered him; and he had a sharp, famished look. I stretched out my hand with some relief in it, I would not inquire into the particulars of such obvious distress; the poor wretch caught my hand, and hastily dropped on his knees, to thank me in an ecstasy, as if he had forgot to hope, and the sudden relief overcame him. His attitude and eager thanks oppressed my weak spirits, I could not for a moment ask him any more questions, but as soon as I recollected myself, I learned from him the circumstance that had reduced him to such extreme distress, and he hinted, that I could not easily guess the good I had done; I imagine he was meditating his own destruction when I saw him, to spare himself the misery of seeing his infant perish, starved to death in every sense of the word. I will now hasten to the sequel of the account. His wife had lately had a child, she was very ill at the time, and want of proper food, and a defense against the inclemency of the weather, hurried her out of the world. The poor child, Peggy, had sucked in disease and nourishment together, and now even they were denied—the breast was cold that had afforded the impoverished stream; and the little innocent smiled, unconscious of its misery. I sent for it, added Mrs. Mason, and the father dying a few years after, it has ever been a favorite charge, and the nursing of it, in some measure, dispelled the gloom in which I had been enveloped.—Ah! my children, you know not how many "houseless heads bide the pitiless storm."

I received soon after a lesson of resignation from a poor woman who was a practical philosopher.

She had lost her husband, a sailor, and lost his wages too, as she could not prove his death; she came to me to beg some pieces of silk, to make pincushions of to sell to the boarders of a neighboring school. Her lower weeds were patched with different colored rags; but they spoke not variety of wretchedness, on the contrary, they showed a mind so content with want, and all the miseries of life, as to attend to the opinion of casual observers. This woman had lost a husband and a child, and her daily bread was precarious. I cheered the widow's heart, and my own was not quite solitary. But I am growing melancholy—I am only desirous of pointing out how very beneficial charity is—as it enables us to find comfort when all our worldly comforts are lowering: and besides, when our bowels yearn to our fellow creatures, we feel that the love of God dwelleth in us—and then we cannot always go on our way sorrowing.

. . . .

CHAPTER XXII

Journey to London

The girls were visibly improved; an air of intelligence began to animate Caroline's fine features; and benevolence gave her eyes the humid sparkle which is so beautiful and engaging. The interest we take in the fate of others, attaches them to ourselves.

Mary's judgment every day grew clearer; or, more properly speaking, she acquired experience every hour, and her lively feelings fixed the conclusions in her mind. While Mrs. Mason was rejoicing in their apparent improvement, she received a letter from their father, requesting her to allow his daughters to spend the winter in town, as he wished to procure them the best masters, an advantage the country did not afford. With reluctance she consented, determining to remain with them a short time. Preparations were quickly made for the journey.

. . . .

For some time after their arrival, everything they saw excited wonder and admiration; and not till they were a little familiarized with the new objects, did they ask reasonable questions.

. . . .

CHAPTER XXIII

Charity—Shopping—The distressed stationer—Mischievous consequences of delaying payment

As they walked in search of a shop, they both determined to purchase pocketbooks; and their friend desired them not to spend all the money they had received, as they would meet many objects of charity in the numerous streets of the metropolis. . . .

. . . In the shop they entered, they did not find the kind of pocketbook they had fixed on; and wished precipitately to leave it; but were detained by their more considerate friend. While they had been turning over the trinkets, the countenance of the woman who served them caught her eye, and she observed her eager manner of recommending the books. You have given much unnecessary trouble, said she, to the mistress of the shop, the books are better, and more expensive than you intended to purchase, but I will make up the deficiency. A beam of pleasure enlivened the woman's swollen eyes; and Mrs. Mason, in the mild accents of compassion, said, if it is not an impertinent question, will you tell me from what cause your visible distress arises? Perhaps I may have it in my power to relieve you. The woman burst into tears. Indeed, madam, you have already relieved me; the money you have laid out will enable me to procure some food for my poor little grandchildren, and send a meal to their poor father, who is now confined for debt, though a more honest man never breathed. Ah! Madam, I little thought I should come to this. Yesterday his wife died, poor soul! I really believe things going so cross broke her heart. He has been in jail these five months; I could not manage the shop, or buy what was proper to keep up the credit of it, so business has been continually falling off; yet, if he could collect in his debts, he would now be here, and we should have money in our pockets. . . .

. . . My son, before his misfortunes, was one of the most sober, industrious young men in London; but now he is not like the same man. He had nothing to do in the jail, and to drive away care he learned to drink; he said it was a comfort to forget himself, and he would add an oath—I never heard him swear till then. . . . And yet I pity my poor boy, he is shut up with such a number of profligate wretches, who laugh at religion. Every farthing I send him he spends in liquor, and used to make his wife pawn her clothes to buy him drink—she was happy to die, it was well for her not to live to see the babes she gave suck to despise her!

. . . .

Mrs. Mason gave her something to supply her present wants, and promised to call on her again before she left town.

They walked silently down two or three streets; I hope you have learned to think, my dear girls, said Mrs. Mason, and that your hearts have felt the emotions of compassion; need I make any comments on the situation of the poor woman we have just left. You perceive that those who neglect to pay their debts, do more harm than they imagine. . . .

CHAPTER XXIV

Visit to a poor family in London—Idleness the parent of vice—Prodigality and generosity incompatible—The pleasures of benevolence—True and false motives for saving

After the impression the story, and the sight of the family had made, was a little worn off; Caroline begged leave to buy one toy, and then another, till her money was exhausted. When Mrs. Mason found it was all expended, she looked round for an object in distress; a poor woman soon presented herself, and her meager countenance gave weight to her tale—a babe, as meager, hung at her breast, which seemed not to contain sufficient moisture to wet its parched lips.

On inquiry they found that she lodged in a neighboring garret. Her husband had been out of employment a long time, and was now sick; the master who formerly gave him work, had gradually lost great part of his business; his best customers were grown so fond of French goods. The consequence was the dismission of a number of hands, who could not immediately find employment elsewhere, and of course were reduced to the most extreme distress. The truth of this account a reputable shopkeeper attested; and he added, many of the unhappy creatures, who die unpitied, were first led into vice by accidental idleness.

They ascended the dark stairs scarcely able to bear the different effluvia that flew from every part of a small house, which contained in each room a family, occupied in such an anxious manner to obtain the necessaries of life, that its comforts never engaged their thoughts. The precarious meal was snatched, and the stomach did not turn, though the cloth on which it was laid was dyed in dirt. When tomorrow's bread is uncertain, who thinks of cleanliness? Thus does despair increase the misery, and consequent disease aggravate the horrors of poverty!

They followed the woman into a low garret, which was never visited by the cheerful rays of the sun; a man with a sallow complexion and long beard, sat shivering over a few cinders in the bottom of a broken grate, and two more children were on the ground, half-naked, near him, breathing the noxious air. The gaiety natural to their age, animated not their eyes, half-sunk in their sockets; and, instead of smiles, premature wrinkles had found a place in their lengthened visages. Life was nipped in the bud; shut up just as it began to unfold itself. "A frost, a killing frost," destroyed the parents' hopes: they seemed to come into the world only to crawl half-formed, to suffer, and to die.

Mrs. Mason desired the girls to relieve the family; Caroline hung down her head abashed; and wished the paltry ornaments she had bought, in the bottom of the sea. Mary, proud of the new privilege, emptied her purse; and Caroline, in a supplicating tone, entreated to be allowed to give her handkerchief to the little infant.

Mrs. Mason desired the woman to call on her the next day; they left the family cheered by their bounty.

Caroline expected the reproof that soon proceeded from the mouth of her true friend. I am glad that this accident has occurred, to prove to you that prodigality and generosity are incompatible. Economy and self-denial are necessary, to enable us to be generous, and act conformably to the rules of justice.

Mary may this night enjoy peaceful slumbers; foolishly indulged fancies will not float in her brain; she may, ere she closes her eyes, thank God for allowing her to be His instrument of mercy: will the trifles you have purchased, afford you such heartfelt delight, Caroline?

CHAPTER XXV

Mrs. Mason's farewell advice to her young friends

The day before Mrs. Mason was to leave her pupils, she took a hand of each and pressing them tenderly in her own, tears started into her eyes—I tremble for you, my dear girls, you must practice by yourselves some of the virtues I have been endeavoring to inculcate; and I shall anxiously wait for the summer, to see the progress you have made.

. . . .

Your father will allow you a certain stipend; you have already *felt* the pleasure of doing good; ever recollect that fancy must be conquered, if you wish to gratify benevolence; and practice economy to enable you to be generous. The good you intend to do, do quickly, for know a trifling duty neglected, is a great fault, and the present time only is at your command.

. . . .

Adieu! when you think of your friend, observe her precepts; and let the recollection of my affection give additional weight to the truths I have endeavored to instil.

Preface to
The Female Reader

IN HIS *Memoirs of the Author of "A Vindication of the Rights of Woman,"* written in tribute to his wife shortly after her premature death, William Godwin mentions *The Female Reader*, a book of excerpts compiled by Wollstonecraft but attributed to "Mr. Cresswick, Teacher of Elocution." That was all anyone knew of this pseudonymous work, published in 1789, until copies were recently discovered. As in the case of *Original Stories*, Wollstonecraft presumably suppressed her authorship out of modesty; besides, not affixing her own name to the work made it more seemly for her to include in the collection several of her own pieces on the teaching of young women. *The Female Reader* was among the first of what has now become a standard educational tool: the thematic anthology.

In the preface (by "O.," one of the signatures Wollstonecraft used for *The Analytical Review*), she acknowledges the example of *The Speaker*, a collection arranged by William Enfield, head of the Warrington Dissenting Academy. As its title indicates, the purpose of his book was to provide elocutionary models for his male students, whose aspirations to civic prominence, in the face of the barriers set against them for religious reasons, made facility in public speaking essential.

In her preface, Wollstonecraft accepts the prejudice that women should be unobtrusive in public, but as we know from her discussion of lisping in *Thoughts on the Education of Daughters*, she was disgusted by the speech patterns affected by many ostensibly cultivated women who adopted infantile pronunciation in an attempt to be childlike and pleasing. She therefore recommends oratorical practice simply to help correct that fault, and not as preparation for a public career. It was equally important that her method of reading aloud encouraged depth of understanding, not mere glibness. Characteristically, she attacks superficial learning by rote and the parents who promote it in order to have "a wonderful child to exhibit." By teaching young women to attend to their minds and pursue self-improvement, Wollstonecraft gives a feminist cast to the familiar Protestant emphasis on individual responsibility for the fate of one's soul, for her advice is addressed exclusively to the conscience of women. She concludes: "As we are created accountable creatures we must run the race ourselves, and by our own exertions acquire virtue."

The Preface to *The Female Reader* emphasizes the wisdom of introducing students to knowledge in an orderly sequence. In this anthology, the experienced schoolmistress and governess exhibits her methods to the world.

THE FEMALE READER: OR MISCELLANEOUS
PIECES
IN PROSE AND VERSE: SELECTED FROM THE
BEST WRITERS.
AND DISPOSED UNDER PROPER HEADS:
FOR THE IMPROVEMENT OF YOUNG WOMEN
By Mr. Cresswick, Teacher of Elocution
TO WHICH IS PREFIXED A PREFACE, CON-
TAINING SOME
HINTS ON FEMALE EDUCATION

PREFACE

It is universally allowed that many poems, tales, and allegories are scattered through our best authors, particularly calculated to affect a young heart and improve an opening understanding, which the gay and thoughtless seldom have patience to look for, or discernment to select, and many collections have been made, in order to present in one point of view the most useful passages of many volumes, where various other subjects are mixed that were once written for minds matured by experience.

. . . .

In the present volume, which is principally intended for the improvement of females, the subjects are not only arranged in separate books, but are carefully disposed in a series that tends to make them illustrate each other; linking the detached pieces seemed to give an interest to the whole, which even the slightest connection will not fail to produce.

The main object of this work is to imprint some useful lessons on the mind, and cultivate the taste at the same time—to infuse a relish for a pure and simple style, by presenting natural and touching descriptions from the Scriptures, Shakespeare, etc. Simplicity and sincerity generally go hand in hand, as both proceed from a love of truth.

In subordination to this design, passages varying in style, in verse and prose, have been chosen to enable a scholar to learn to read well: and, at a time when female accomplishments are deemed of more consequence than they ever were, the most essential demands some attention.

Females are not educated to become public speakers or players; though many young ladies are now led by fashion to exhibit their persons on a stage, sacrificing to mere vanity that diffidence and reserve which characterizes youth, and is the most graceful ornament of the sex.

But if it be allowed to be a breach of modesty for a woman to obtrude her person or talents on the public when necessity does not justify and spur her on, yet to be able to read with propriety is certainly a very desirable attainment: to facilitate this task, and exercise the voice, many dialogues have been selected; but not always the most beautiful with respect to composition, as the taste should very gradually be formed. A contrary method may teach young people what to say, but probably will prevent their ever learning to think. It would be needless to repeat here the trite remark which proves an undeniable fact—that the ignorant never read with propriety; and they must ever be accounted ignorant who are suddenly made wise by the experience of others, never brought to a test by their own feeble unexercised reason.

Some little helps to elocution are necessary even for those who never aspire at being orators; but teachers should be very careful not to make scholars practice rules they cannot understand, as monotony is less disgusting than affectation.

In the beginning only prevent their acquiring bad habits; instruct them in the common methods of observing stops and articulating each syllable; and as the mind is stored with arranged knowledge they will insensibly read well, interested by the sentiments they understand. To guard against a dull indifferent tone, they should be allowed to read amusing tales, allegories, etc. Reasoning must be tedious and irksome to those whose passions have never led them to reason; and examples of virtue will ever most forcibly illustrate precepts of morality.

In this selection many tales and fables will be found, as it seems to be following the simple order of nature, to permit young people to peruse works addressed to the imagination, which tend to awaken the affections and fix good habits more firmly in the mind than cold arguments and mere declamation.

. . . .

It has been a custom too prevalent to make children learn by rote long passages from authors, to whose very expressions they could not annex an idea, not considering how vain, and indeed cruel it is, to compel them to repeat a round of unintelligible words. Parents are often led astray by the selfish desire of having a wonderful child to exhibit; but these monsters very seldom make sensible men or women: the wheels are impaired by being set in motion before the time pointed out by nature, and both mind and body are ever after feeble. If, however, a girl be inclined to commit poems, etc., to memory, let me warn the fond mother not to persuade her to display this trifling attainment in company; for the young and thoughtless will seldom endeavor, by virtue and propriety of behavior, to deserve praise, when they can obtain it at such an easy rate. Nay, if they wished them to learn to read well, they would not require them to run over emphatical expressions with the same voice: to teach them just tones, as far as a parrot can be taught, is still worse; for it will infallibly render them affected: and though we do not see the wires we discern that they are mere puppets. Should it then be thought necessary to exercise the memory—pray choose a simple tale or fable, and many children will find them so entertaining that they will instinctively vary their tones; but let them only be repeated to a mother or governess, if you do not mean to light a spark you will not easily extinguish when it has quietly spread through the whole mass.

When a girl arrives at a more advanced age it would be still more useful to make her read a short lesson, and then transcribe it from her memory; and afterwards let her copy the original, and lead her to remark the mistakes she has made. This method would exercise the memory and form the judgment at the same time: she would learn to write correctly, and retain the precepts which in some measure she has composed herself, and a kind of emulation would be excited from which no bad consequences could possibly flow. If this employment is allowed to occupy two mornings every week, at the end of four or five years the understanding will have received great strength, and the pupil will express herself both in speaking and writing, provided she has a tolerable capacity, with a degree of propriety that will astonish those that have not adopted the same plan. She will understand English, and express her sentiments in her native tongue; instead of which our young ladies of fashion write a mixture of French and Italian, and speak the same jargon.

If my young readers, for whom this collection is principally intended, would listen to me a few moments, I would endeavor to prove to them that the most sedulous attention to the person will never improve it, whilst a cultivated mind renders the most graceful form more pleasing:—What do I say?—there is no grace without it; nor any beauty, that will charm for half an hour, which does not arise from an artless display of virtue or sense. But it is not necessary to speak to display mental charms—the eye will quickly inform us if an active soul resides within; and a blush is far more eloquent than the best turned period.

Exterior accomplishments are not to be obtained by imitation, they must result from the mind, or the deception is soon detected, and admiration gives place to contempt. If you wish to be loved by your relations and friends, prove that you can love them by governing your temper; good humor and cheerful gaiety will then enliven every feature and dimple your cheeks—but this my young friends is not the work of a day. An attention to truth gives dignity to the manners: and a dependence on Providence banishes those fears which render many girls very ridiculous, and make them appear as insignificant as they are helpless; if they do not endeavor to conquer them they will forfeit the esteem of those whose protection they most want—the good and the wise.

Another observation I must here be allowed to dwell on; supposing a young lady has received the best education, she has advanced but a few steps towards the improvement of her mind and heart—that is the business of her whole life; she must not mistake and call blossoms fruit, for the summer often proves the hopes of spring fallacious; and it must ripen the most promising to give it real value. The plenty of autumn only rewards the industrious, and industry is never irksome when it becomes habitual.

As we are created accountable creatures we must run the race ourselves, and by our own exertions acquire virtue: the utmost our friends can do is to point out the right road, and clear away some of the loose rubbish which might at first retard our progress. If, conquering indolence and a desire of present enjoyment, we push forward, not only the tranquil joy of an approving conscience will cheer us here, but we shall anticipate in some degree, while we advance to it, that happiness of which we can form no conception in our present state, except when we have some faint glimpse from the pleasures arising from benevolence, and the hope of attaining more perfect knowledge. We are indeed all children educated by a beneficent Father for his kingdom—some are nearer the awful close than others, to their advice the young should listen—for respectable is the hoary head when found in the path of virtue.

Lessons

IN *Lessons,* another fragmentary manuscript published by William Godwin in *Posthumous Works,* Wollstonecraft, a former teacher, and the mother of a three-year-old daughter, created for her child a series of primary readings that demonstrate rational principles of organization. Godwin found this inscription on the undated manuscript: "The first book of a series which I intended to have written for my unfortunate girl." Had she lived to complete this project, Wollstonecraft might well have become known as a pioneer in the field of early childhood education; even these brief selections reveal her sensitivity to a child's perspective on the world. Like a gentler Mrs. Mason, she leads Fanny to respect the rights of others by remembering her own feelings: when her puppy falls from a stool, the little girl is urged to translate her own injuries into animal terms. Wollstonecraft encourages the child to proceed with the "severe exercise" prescribed in *Thoughts on the Education of Daughters*: "You say that you do not know how to think. Yes; you do a little," and citing her young reader's ability to connect thoughts, she illumines for a mature audience the pedagogical theories that play so central a part in her work. "When a child does wrong at first, she does not know any better. But, after she has been told that she must not disturb mamma, when poor mamma is unwell, she thinks herself, that she must not wake papa when he is tired."

These few *Lessons* have a special poignancy because in place of the manufactured stereotypes of so many modern readers of the Dick and Jane variety, Wollstonecraft offers Fanny a rosy mirror of her own small world, with a baby William (the son that a pregnant Mary imagined she would soon deliver), a self-sufficient mamma who doesn't need a maid's help in dressing, and a papa who falls asleep on the sofa when he's tired. This idyllic family life, which had eluded Wollstonecraft's grasp for so many years, was to be denied her "unfortunate girl" as well. Mary had cherished Fanny Imlay, nursing her through minor miseries like weaning and teething and major dangers like chicken pox, but Mary was to succumb to a fever more treacherous than Fanny's. These lessons survive, testaments to the maternal affection and tutorial good sense of a woman who often intuitively understood human needs and behavior and trusted her insights even when they went counter to the practices of her era's "authorities."

LESSONS

LESSON I

Cat. Dog. Cow. Horse. Sheep. Pig. Bird. Fly. Man. Boy. Girl. Child.

....

LESSON V

Come to me, my little girl. Are you tired of playing? Yes. Sit down and rest yourself, while I talk to you.

Have you seen the baby? Poor little thing. O here it comes. Look at him. How helpless he is. Four years ago you were as feeble as this very little boy.

See, he cannot hold up his head. He is forced to lie on his back, if his mamma do not turn him to the right or left side, he will soon begin to cry. He cries to tell her that he is tired with lying on his back.

....

LESSON X

See how much taller you are than William. In four years you have learned to eat, to walk, to talk. Why do you smile? You can do much more, you think: you can wash your hands and face. Very well. I should never kiss a dirty face. And you can comb your head with the pretty comb you always

74

put by in your own drawer. To be sure, you do all this to be ready to take a walk with me. You would be obliged to stay at home, if you could not comb your own hair. Betty is busy getting the dinner ready, and only brushes William's hair because he cannot do it for himself.

Betty is making an apple pie. You love an apple pie; but I do not bid you make one. Your hands are not strong enough to mix the butter and flour together; and you must not try to pare the apples, because you cannot manage a great knife.

Never touch the large knives: they are very sharp, and you might cut your finger to the bone. You are a little girl, and ought to have a little knife. When you are as tall as I am, you shall have a knife as large as mine; and when you are as strong as I am, and have learned to manage it, you will not hurt yourself.

You can trundle a hoop, you say; and jump over a stick. O, I forgot!—and march like the men in the red coats, when papa plays a pretty tune on the fiddle.

LESSON XI

What, you think that you shall soon be able to dress yourself entirely? I am glad of it: I have something else to do. You may go, and look for your frock in the drawer; but I will tie it, till you are stronger. Betty will tie it, when I am busy.

I button my gown myself: I do not want a maid to assist me, when I am dressing. But you have not yet got sense enough to do it properly, and must beg somebody to help you, till you are older.

Children grow older and wiser at the same time. William is not able to take a piece of meat, because he has not got the sense which would make him think that, without teeth, meat would do him harm. He cannot tell what is good for him.

The sense of children grows with them. You know much more than William, now you walk alone, and talk; but you do not know as much as the boys and girls you see playing yonder, who are half as tall again as you; and they do not know half as much as their fathers and mothers, who are men and women grown. Papa and I were children, like you; and men and women took care of us. I carry William, because he is too weak to walk. I lift you over a stile, and over the gutter, when you cannot jump over it.

You know already that potatoes will not do you any harm: but I must pluck the fruit for you, till you are wise enough to know the ripe apples and pears. The hard ones would make you sick, and then you must take physic. You do not love physic: I do not love it any more than you. But I have more sense than you; therefore I take care not to eat unripe fruit, or anything else that would make my stomach ache, or bring out ugly red spots on my face.

When I was a child, my mamma chose the fruit for me, to prevent my making myself sick. I was just like you; I used to ask for what I saw, without knowing whether it was good or bad. Now I have lived a long time, I know what is good; I do not want anybody to tell me.

. . . .

LESSON XIII

Poor child, she cannot do much for herself. When I let her do anything for me, it is to please her: for I could do it better myself.

Oh! The poor puppy has tumbled off the stool. Run and stroke him. Put a little milk in a saucer to comfort him. You have more sense than he. You can pour the milk into the saucer without spilling it. He would cry for a day with hunger, without being able to get it. You are wiser than the dog, you must help him. The dog will love you for it, and run after you. I feed you and take care of you: you love me and follow me for it.

When the book fell down on your foot, it gave you great pain. The poor dog felt the same pain just now.

Take care not to hurt him when you play with him. And every morning leave a little milk in your basin for him. Do not forget to put the basin in a corner, lest somebody should fall over it.

When the snow covers the ground, save the crumbs of bread for the birds. In the summer they find seed enough, and do not want you to think about them.

I make broth for the poor man who is sick. A sick man is like a child, he cannot help himself.

LESSON X [SIC]

When I caught cold some time ago, I had such a pain in my head, I could scarcely hold it up. Papa opened the door very softly, because he loves me. You love me, yet you made a noise. You had not the sense to know that it made my head worse, till papa told you.

Papa had a pain in the stomach, and he would not eat the fine cherries or grapes on the table. When I brought him a cup of camomile tea, he drank it without saying a word, or making an ugly face. He knows that I love him, and that I would not give him anything to drink that has a bad taste, if it were not to do him good.

You asked me for some apples when your stomach ached; but I was not angry with you. If you had been as wise as papa, you would have said, I will not eat the apples today, I must take some camomile tea.

You say that you do not know how to think. Yes; you do a little. The other day papa was tired; he had been walking about all the morning. After dinner he fell asleep on the sofa. I did not bid you be quiet; but you thought of what papa said to you, when my head ached. This made you think that you ought not to make a noise, when papa was resting himself. So you came to me, and said to me, very softly, Pray reach me my ball, and I will go and play in the garden, till papa wakes.

You were going out; but thinking again, you came back to me on your tiptoes. Whisper—whisper. Pray mamma, call me, when papa wakes; for I shall be afraid to open the door to see, lest I should disturb him.

Away you went.—Creep—creep—and shut the door as softly as I could have done myself.

That was thinking. When a child does wrong at first, she does not know any better. But, after she has been told that she must not disturb mamma, when poor mamma is unwell, she thinks herself, that she must not wake papa when he is tired.

Another day we will see if you can think about anything else.

ON WOMEN'S
SUFFERING

Mary, A Fiction

WRITTEN IN 1787 while Wollstonecraft was a governess at the Kingsboroughs' castle in Ireland, and published the following year, *Mary, A Fiction* is her most transparent representation of the events of her own life. The heroine, like Mary Wollstonecraft, born to a couple bearing the first names Edward and Eliza, is ignored in favor of her older brother and, seeking the affection denied her at home, devotes herself to a friend called Ann, not unlike Wollstonecraft's friend Fanny. Mary helps Ann's family and at last accompanies the sickly girl to Lisbon where, despite constant attendance, she dies. Wollstonecraft's fictional counterpart, unlike her creator, becomes an heiress when her older brother dies young, and the fictional parents, especially the mother, display the aristocratic affectations that Wollstonecraft, living at Mitchelstown as she worked on this project, found so repellent in her employers, Lord and Lady Kingsborough. Two beautiful dogs share the bed of the mistress of the house, who neglects her growing daughter, lisps, and immerses herself in sentimental novels.

Wollstonecraft, who deplored frivolous reading matter, declares her independence from it in her preface: her heroine will differ from the standard romantic models, as will her plot. Its borrowing of true-life incidents notwithstanding, the originality of *Mary, A Fiction* emerges in Wollstonecraft's conscious experiment in using a narrative form without episodes to explore the mind of an intelligent woman. Like Wordsworth, Wollstonecraft deeply believes in the indelibility of childhood impressions, and her subject, like his, is the growth of her protagonist's mind. Wollstonecraft describes the domestic environment into which her heroine will be born so that all the formative influences of her existence may be open to scrutiny. Left to herself by indifferent parents, the fictional Mary learn to think. She learns as well to pray: *Mary*, in its insistence on the superiority of spiritual claims to all others, gives expression to Wollstonecraft's early religious ideas. At this point in her development, she saw moral virtue and intellectual attainments as the twin goals of one's inner life.

Mary's history departs from her author's in the circumstances of her marriage, which seem at least partly based on Caroline King's early arranged marriage, made to unify two large estates. It is her dying mother's wish that her sole surviving child, Mary, marry a boy two years her junior in order to settle a claim on the family estate. Stunned, Mary agrees to go through with the ceremony. Her adolescent husband then goes abroad to further his education with the gentleman's traditional Grand Tour; Mary furthers hers in ever deeper self-contemplation, and later, in traveling to Lisbon in order to devote herself to Ann, whose physician had prescribed a change of climate.

As Wollstonecraft wrote to Henry Gabell, a young clergyman she met on the boat that took them both to Dublin, her tale illustrates her opinion "that a genius will educate itself." The fictional Mary displays a formidable array of accomplishments: a determined philanthropist, she seeks out poor people to succor; an enthusiast of nature, she finds pleasure in long walks and landscapes; a cultivated lover of the arts, she responds passionately to painting and music. Wollstonecraft imbues the heroine who shares her name with a flattering combination of saintliness, sensitivity, and sensibility, but even for such excellence of character, she could imagine no conventional novelistic rewards. Bound by her unconsummated marriage, the heroine, Mary, falls in love with an equally improbable hero, Henry, himself doomed to a premature death. The book ends with Mary in ill health and eagerly awaiting the joys of heaven. She is disgusted by the marital life she had finally been obliged to attempt.

Wollstonecraft was never again to write any works as unguarded as *Mary*. Despite its passive strain of pious morbidity, it looks forward toward her more mature work by subjecting its focal character to the tyrannies of family and marriage that have the power to embitter even the most gifted women. *Mary*'s thematic content, then, leads directly to Wollstonecraft's later works of persuasion. In her last year, she would turn from argument to narrative once again. Although Wollstonecraft was unable to complete a true novel, in *Mary*, for all its self-indulgence, she had sketched a rough outline of the elements that the great women novelists of the nineteenth century were to perfect. Rejecting artificially plotted incident and all-conquering love as ingredients of serious fiction, she sought, prophetically, to show that the hallmark of a genuine heroine was her sense of moral responsibility.

MARY, A FICTION

ADVERTISEMENT

In delineating the Heroine of this Fiction, the Author attempts to develop a character different from those generally portrayed. . . .

. . . .

In an artless tale, without episodes, the mind of a woman who has thinking powers is displayed. The female organs have been thought too weak for this arduous employment; and experience seems to justify the assertion. Without arguing physically about *possibilities*—in a fiction, such a being may be allowed to exist; whose grandeur is derived from the operations of its own faculties, not subjugated to opinion; but drawn by the individual from the original source.

CHAPTER I

Mary, the heroine of this fiction, was the daughter of Edward, who married Eliza, a gentle, fashionable girl, with a kind of indolence in her temper, which might be termed negative good nature: her virtues, indeed, were all of that stamp. She carefully attended to the *shows* of things, and her opinions, I should have said prejudices, were such as the generality approved of. She was educated with the expectation of a large fortune, of course became a mere machine: the homage of her attendants made a great part of her puerile amusements, and she never imagined there were any relative duties for her to fulfill: notions of her own consequence, by these means, were interwoven in her mind, and the years of youth spent in acquiring a few superficial accomplishments, without having any taste for them. When she was first introduced into the polite circle, she danced with an officer, whom she faintly wished to be united to; but her father soon after recommending another in a more distinguished rank of life, she readily submitted to his will, and promised to love, honor, and obey a vicious fool, as in duty bound.

While they resided in London, they lived in the usual fashionable style, and seldom saw each other; nor were they much more sociable when they wooed rural felicity for more than half the year, in a delightful country, where Nature, with lavish hand, had scattered beauties around; for the master, with brute, unconscious gaze, passed them by unobserved, and sought amusement in country sports. He hunted in the morning, and after eating an immoderate dinner, generally fell asleep: this seasonable rest enabled him to digest the cumbrous load; he would then visit some of his pretty tenants; and when he compared their ruddy glow of health with his wife's countenance, which even rouge could not enliven, it is not necessary to say which a *gourmand* would give the preference to. Their vulgar dance of spirits were infinitely more agreeable to his fancy than her sickly, die-away languor. Her voice was but the shadow of a sound, and she had, to complete her delicacy, so relaxed her nerves, that she became a mere nothing.

Many such noughts are there in the female world! yet she had a good opinion of her own merit—truly, she said long prayers . . . she dreaded that horrid place vulgarly called *hell*, the regions below; but whether hers was a mounting spirit, I cannot pretend to determine; or what sort of a planet would have been proper for her, when she left her *material* part in this world, let metaphysicians settle; I have nothing to say to her unclothed spirit.

As she was sometimes obliged to be alone, or only with her French waiting-maid, she sent to the metropolis for all the new publications, and while she was dressing her hair, and she could turn her eyes from the glass, she ran over those most delightful substitutes for bodily dissipation, novels. I say bodily, or the animal soul, for a rational one can find no employment in polite circles. The glare of lights, the studied inelegancies of dress, and the compliments offered up at the shrine of false beauty, are all equally addressed to the senses.

She had besides another resource, two most beautiful dogs, who shared her bed, and reclined on cushions near her all the day. These she watched with the most assiduous care, and bestowed on them the warmest caresses. This fondness for animals was not that kind ... which makes a person take pleasure in providing for the subsistence and comfort of a living creature; but it proceeded from vanity, it gave her an opportunity of lisping out the prettiest French expressions of ecstatic fondness, in accents that had never been attuned by tenderness.

She was chaste, according to the vulgar acceptation of the word; that is, she did not make any actual *faux pas;* she feared the world, and was indolent; but then, to make amends for this seeming self-denial, she read all the sentimental novels, dwelt on the love scenes, and had she thought while she read, her mind would have been contaminated; as she accompanied the lovers to the lonely arbors, and would walk with them by the clear light of the moon. She wondered her husband did not stay at home. She was jealous—why did he not love her, sit by her side, squeeze her hand, and look unutterable things? Gentle reader, I will tell thee; they neither of them felt what they could not utter. I will not pretend to say that they always annexed an idea to a word; but they had none of those feelings which are not easily analyzed.

CHAPTER II

In due time she brought forth a son, a feeble babe; and the following year a daughter. After the mother's throes she felt very few sentiments of maternal tenderness: the children were given to nurses, and she played with her dogs. Want of exercise prevented the least chance of her recovering strength; and two or three milk fevers brought on a consumption, to which her constitution tended. Her children all died in their infancy, except the two first, and she began to grow fond of the son, as he was remarkably handsome. For years she divided her time between the sofa, and the card table. She thought not of death, though on the borders of the grave; nor did any of the duties of her station occur to her as necessary. Her children were left in the nursery; and when

Mary, the little blushing girl, appeared, she would send the awkward thing away. To own the truth, she was awkward enough, in a house without any playmates; for her brother had been sent to school, and she scarcely knew how to employ herself; she would ramble about the garden, admire the flowers, and play with the dogs. An old housekeeper told her stories, read to her, and, at last, taught her to read. Her mother talked of inquiring for a governess when her health would permit; and, in the interim desired her own maid to teach her French. As she had learned to read, she perused with avidity every book that came in her way. Neglected in every respect, and left to the operations of her own mind, she considered everything that came under her inspection, and learned to think. She had heard of a separate state, and that angels sometimes visited this earth. She would sit in a thick wood in the park, and talk to them; make little songs addressed to them, and sing them to tunes of her own composing; and her native wood notes wild were sweet and touching.

Her father always exclaimed against female acquirements, and was glad that his wife's indolence and ill health made her not trouble herself about them. She had besides another reason: she did not wish to have a fine tall girl brought forward into notice as her daughter; she still expected to recover, and figure away in the gay world. Her husband was very tyrannical and passionate; indeed so very easily irritated when inebriated, that Mary was continually in dread lest he should frighten her mother to death; her sickness called forth all Mary's tenderness, and exercised her compassion so continually that it became more than a match for self-love, and was the governing propensity of her heart through life. She was violent in her temper; but she saw her father's faults, and would weep when obliged to compare his temper with her own.—She did more; artless prayers rose to Heaven for pardon, when she was conscious of having erred; and her contrition was so exceedingly painful that she watched diligently the first movements of anger and impatience, to save herself this cruel remorse.

Sublime ideas filled her young mind—always connected with devotional sentiments; extemporary effusions of gratitude, and rhapsodies of praise would burst often from her, when she listened to the birds, or pursued the deer. She would gaze on the moon, and ramble through the gloomy path, observing the various shapes the clouds assumed, and

listen to the sea that was not far distant. The wandering
spirits, which she imagined inhabited every part of nature,
were her constant friends and confidants. She began to consider the Great First Cause, formed just notions of his attributes, and, in particular, dwelt on his wisdom and goodness.
Could she have loved her father or mother, had they returned her affection, she would not so soon, perhaps, have
sought out a new world.

Her sensibility prompted her to search for an object to
love; on earth it was not to be found; her mother had often
disappointed her, and the apparent partiality she showed to
her brother gave her exquisite pain—produced a kind of
habitual melancholy, led her into a fondness for reading
tales of woe, and made her almost realize the fictitious
distress.

She had not any notion of death till a little chicken expired at her feet; and her father had a dog hung in a
passion. She then concluded animals had souls, or they
would not have been subjected to the caprice of man; but
what was the soul of man or beast? In this style year after
year rolled on, her mother still vegetating.

A little girl who attended in the nursery fell sick. Mary
paid her great attention; contrary to her wish, she was sent
out of the house to her mother, a poor woman, whom necessity obliged to leave her sick child while she earned her
daily bread. The poor wretch, in a fit of delirium stabbed
herself, and Mary saw her dead body, and heard the dismal
account; and so strongly did it impress her imagination,
that every night of her life the bleeding corpse presented
itself to her when she first began to slumber. Tortured by it,
she at last made a vow, that if she was ever mistress of a
family she would herself watch over every part of it. The
impression that this accident made was indelible.

As her mother grew imperceptibly worse and worse, her
father, who did not understand such a lingering complaint,
imagined his wife was only grown still more whimsical, and
that if she could be prevailed on to exert herself, her health
would soon be reestablished. In general he treated her with
indifference; but when her illness at all interfered with his
pleasures, he expostulated in the most cruel manner, and
visibly harassed the invalid. Mary would then assiduously
try to turn his attention to something else; and when sent
out of the room, would watch at the door, until the storm
was over, for unless it was, she could not rest. Other causes

also contributed to disturb her repose: her mother's luke-warm manner of performing her religious duties, filled her with anguish; and when she observed her father's vices, the unbidden tears would flow. She was miserable when beggars were driven from the gate without being relieved; if she could do it unperceived, she would give them her own breakfast, and feel gratified, when, in consequence of it, she was pinched by hunger.

She had once, or twice, told her little secrets to her mother; they were laughed at, and she determined never to do it again. In this manner was she left to reflect on her own feelings; and so strengthened were they by being meditated on, that her character early became singular and permanent. Her understanding was strong and clear, when not clouded by her feelings; but she was too much the creature of impulse, and the slave of compassion.

CHAPTER III

Near her father's house lived a poor widow who had been brought up in affluence but reduced to great distress by the extravagance of her husband; he had destroyed his constitution while he spent his fortune; and dying, left his wife, and five small children, to live on a very scanty pittance. The eldest daughter was for some years educated by a distant relation, a clergyman. While she was with him a young gentleman, son to a man of property in the neighborhood, took particular notice of her. It is true, he never talked of love; but then they played and sung in concert; drew landscapes together, and while she worked he read to her, cultivated her taste, and stole imperceptibly her heart. Just at this juncture, when smiling, unanalyzed hope made every prospect bright, and gay expectation danced in her eyes, her benefactor died. She returned to her mother—the companion of her youth forgot her, they took no more sweet counsel together. This disappointment spread a sadness over her countenance, and made it interesting. She grew fond of solitude, and her character appeared similar to Mary's, though her natural disposition was very different.

She was several years older than Mary, yet her refinement, her taste, caught her eye, and she eagerly sought her friendship: before her return she had assisted the family, which was almost reduced to the last ebb; and now she had another motive to actuate her.

As she had often occasion to send messages to Ann, her new friend, mistakes were frequently made; Ann proposed that in future they should be written ones, to obviate this difficulty, and render their intercourse more agreeable. Young people are mostly fond of scribbling; Mary had had very little instruction; but by copying her friend's letters, whose hand she admired, she soon became a proficient; a little practice made her write with tolerable correctness, and her genius gave force to it. In conversation, and in writing, when she felt, she was pathetic, tender and persuasive; and she expressed contempt with such energy, that few could stand the flash of her eyes.

As she grew more intimate with Ann, her manners were softened, and she acquired a degree of equality in her behavior: yet still her spirits were fluctuating, and her movements rapid. She felt less pain on account of her mother's partiality to her brother, as she hoped now to experience the pleasure of being beloved; but this hope led her into new sorrows, and, as usual, paved the way for disappointment. Ann only felt gratitude; her heart was entirely engrossed by one object, and friendship could not serve as a substitute; memory officiously retraced past scenes, and unavailing wishes made time loiter.

Mary was often hurt by the involuntary indifference which these consequences produced. When her friend was all the world to her, she found she was not as necessary to her happiness; and her delicate mind could not bear to obtrude her affection, or receive love as an alms, the offspring of pity. Very frequently had she run to her with delight, and not perceiving anything of the same kind in Ann's countenance, she had shrunk back; and, falling from one extreme into the other, instead of a warm greeting that was just slipping from her tongue, her expressions seemed to be dictated by the most chilling insensibility.

She would then imagine that she looked sickly or unhappy, and then all her tenderness would return like a torrent, and bear away all reflection. In this manner was her sensibility called forth, and exercised, by her mother's illness, her friend's misfortunes, and her own unsettled mind.

CHAPTER IV

. . . .

At a little distance ... were the huts of a few poor fishermen, who supported their numerous children by their precarious labor. In these little huts she frequently rested, and denied herself every childish gratification, in order to relieve the necessities of the inhabitants. Her heart yearned for them, and would dance with joy when she had relieved their wants, or afforded them pleasure.

In these pursuits she learned the luxury of doing good; and the sweet tears of benevolence frequently moistened her eyes, and gave them a sparkle which, exclusive of that, they had not; on the contrary, they were rather fixed, and would never have been observed if her soul had not animated them. They were not at all like those brilliant ones which look like polished diamonds, and dart from every superfice, giving more light to the beholders than they receive themselves.

Her benevolence, indeed, knew no bounds; the distress of others carried her out of herself; and she rested not till she had relieved or comforted them. The warmth of her compassion often made her so diligent that many things occurred to her which might have escaped a less interested observer.

In like manner, she entered with such spirit into whatever she read, and the emotions thereby raised were so strong that it soon became a part of her mind.

. . . .

Many nights she sat up, if I may be allowed the expression, *conversing* with the Author of Nature, making verses, and singing hymns of her own composing. She considered also, and tried to discern what end her various faculties were destined to pursue; and had a glimpse of a truth, which afterwards more fully unfolded itself.

. . . .

She was now fifteen, and she wished to receive the holy sacrament; and perusing the scriptures, and discussing some points of doctrine which puzzled her, she would sit up half the night, her favorite time for employing her mind; she too plainly perceived that she saw through a glass darkly; and that the bounds set to stop our intellectual researches, is one of the trials of a probationary state.

. . . The night before the important day, when she was to take on herself her baptismal vow, she could not go to bed; the sun broke in on her meditations, and found her not exhausted by her watching.

. . . She hailed the morn, and sung with wild delight, Glory to God on high, good will towards men. She was indeed so much affected when she joined in the prayer for her eternal preservation that she could hardly conceal her violent emotions; and the recollection never failed to wake her dormant piety when earthly passions made it grow languid.

These various movements of her mind were not commented on, nor were the luxuriant shoots restrained by culture. The servants and the poor adored her.

In order to be enabled to gratify herself in the highest degree, she practiced the most rigid economy, and had such power over her appetites and whims, that without any great effort she conquered them so entirely, that when her understanding or affections had an object, she almost forgot she had a body which required nourishment.

This habit of thinking, this kind of absorption, gave strength to the passions.

We will now enter on the more active field of life.

CHAPTER V

A few months after Mary was turned of seventeen, her brother was attacked by a violent fever, and died before his father could reach the school.

She was now an heiress, and her mother began to think her of consequence, and did not call her *the child*. Proper masters were sent for; she was taught to dance, and an extraordinary master procured to perfect her in that most necessary of all accomplishments.

A part of the estate she was to inherit had been litigated, and the heir of the person who still carried on a Chancery suit, was only two years younger than our heroine. The fathers, spite of the dispute, frequently met, and, in order to settle it amicably, they one day, over a bottle, determined to quash it by a marriage, and, by uniting the two estates, to preclude all farther inquiries into the merits of their different claims.

While this important matter was settling, Mary was otherwise employed. Ann's mother's resources were failing; and the ghastly phantom, poverty, made hasty strides to catch them in his clutches. Ann had not fortitude enough to brave such accumulated misery; besides, the cankerworm was lodged in her heart, and preyed on her health. . . .

. . . .

This ill-fated love had given a bewitching softness to her manners, a delicacy so truly feminine that a man of any feeling could not behold her without wishing to chase her sorrows away. She was timid and irresolute, and rather fond of dissipation; grief only had power to make her reflect.

In everything it was not the great, but the beautiful, or the pretty, that caught her attention. And in composition, the polish of style, and harmony of numbers, interested her much more than the flights of genius, or abstracted speculations.

She often wondered at the books Mary chose, who, though she had a lively imagination, would frequently study authors whose works were addressed to the understanding. This liking taught her to arrange her thoughts, and argue with herself, even when under the influence of the most violent passions.

Ann's misfortunes and ill health were strong ties to bind Mary to her; she wished so continually to have a home to receive her in that it drove every other desire out of her mind; and, dwelling on the tender schemes which compassion and friendship dictated, she longed most ardently to put them in practice.

Fondly as she loved her friend, she did not forget her mother, whose decline was so imperceptible that they were not aware of her approaching dissolution. The physician, however, observing the most alarming symptoms; her husband was apprised of her immediate danger; and then first mentioned to her his designs with respect to his daughter.

She approved of them; Mary was sent for; she was not at home; she had rambled to visit Ann, and found her in an hysteric fit. The landlord of her little farm had sent his agent for the rent, which had long been due to him; and he threatened to seize the stock that still remained, and turn them out, if they did not very shortly discharge the arrears.

. . . .

. . . The mother added, she had many other creditors who would, in all probability, take the alarm, and snatch from them all that had been saved out of the wreck. "I could bear all," she cried, "but what will become of my children? Of this child," pointing to the fainting Ann, "whose constitution is already undermined by care and grief—where will she go?" Mary's heart ceased to beat while she asked the question—She attempted to speak, but the inarticulate sounds died away. Before she had recovered herself, her father called himself to inquire for her, and desired her instantly to accompany him home.

Engrossed by the scene of misery she had been witness to, she walked silently by his side, when he roused her out of her reverie by telling her that in all likelihood her mother had not many hours to live; and before she could return him any answer, informed her that they had both determined to marry her to Charles, his friend's son; he added, the ceremony was to be performed directly, that her mother might be witness of it, for such a desire she had expressed with childish eagerness.

Overwhelmed by this intelligence, Mary rolled her eyes about, then, with a vacant stare, fixed them on her father's face; but they were no longer a sense; they conveyed no ideas to the brain. As she drew near the house, her wonted presence of mind returned: after this suspension of thought, a thousand darted into her mind—her dying mother—her friend's miserable situation—and an extreme horror at taking—at being forced to take, such a hasty step; but she did not feel the disgust, the reluctance, which arises from a prior attachment.

She loved Ann better than anyone in the world—to snatch her from the very jaws of destruction she would have encountered a lion. To have this friend constantly with her; to make her mind easy with respect to her family, would it not be superlative bliss?

Full of these thoughts she entered her mother's chamber, but they then fled at the sight of a dying parent. She went to her, took her hand; it feebly pressed hers. "My child," said the languid mother: the words reached her heart; she had seldom heard them pronounced with accents denoting affection. "My child, I have not always treated you with kindness—God forgive me! do you?"—Mary's tears strayed in a disregarded stream; on her bosom the big drops fell, but did not relieve the fluttering tenant. "I forgive you!" said she, in a tone of astonishment.

The clergyman came in to read the service for the sick, and afterwards the marriage ceremony was performed. Mary stood like a statue of Despair, and pronounced the awful vow without thinking of it; and then ran to support her mother, who expired the same night in her arms.

Her husband set off for the continent the same day, with a tutor, to finish his studies at one of the foreign universities.

Ann was sent for to console her, not on account of the departure of her new relation, a boy she seldom took any notice of, but to reconcile her to her fate; besides, it was necessary she should have a female companion, and there was not any maiden aunt in the family, or cousin of the same class.

CHAPTER VI

Mary was allowed to pay the rent which gave her so much uneasiness, and she exerted every nerve to prevail on her father effectually to succor the family; but the utmost she could obtain was a small sum very inadequate to the purpose, to enable the poor woman to carry into execution a little scheme of industry near the metropolis.

. . . .

After the departure of her mother, Ann still continued to languish, though she had a nurse who was entirely engrossed by the desire of amusing her. Had her health been reestablished, the time would have passed in a tranquil, improving manner.

During the year of mourning they lived in retirement; music, drawing, and reading, filled up the time; and Mary's taste and judgment were both improved by contracting a habit of observation, and permitting the simple beauties of Nature to occupy her thoughts.

She had a wonderful quickness in discerning distinctions and combining ideas, that at the first glance did not appear to be similar. But these various pursuits did not banish all her cares, or carry off all her constitutional black bile. Before she enjoyed Ann's society, she imagined it would have made her completely happy: she was disappointed, and yet knew not what to complain of.

. . . .

She had not yet found the companion she looked for. Ann and she were not congenial minds, nor did she contribute to her comfort in the degree she expected. She shielded her from poverty; but this was only a negative blessing; when under the pressure it was very grievous, and still more so were the apprehensions; but when exempt from them, she was not contented.

Such is human nature, its laws were not to be inverted to gratify our heroine, and stop the progress of her understanding, happiness only flourished in paradise—we cannot taste and live.

Another year passed away with increasing apprehensions. Ann had a hectic cough, and many unfavorable prognostics: Mary then forgot everything but the fear of losing her, and even imagined that her recovery would have made her happy.

Her anxiety led her to study physic, and for some time she only read books of that cast; and this knowledge, literally speaking, ended in vanity and vexation of spirit, as it enabled her to foresee what she could not prevent.

As her mind expanded, her marriage appeared a dreadful misfortune; she was sometimes reminded of the heavy yoke, and bitter was the recollection!

In one thing there seemed to be a sympathy between them, for she wrote formal answers to his as formal letters. An extreme dislike took root in her mind; the sound of his name made her turn sick; but she forgot all, listening to Ann's cough, and supporting her languid frame. She would then catch her to her bosom with convulsive eagerness, as if to save her from sinking into an opening grave.

CHAPTER VII

It was the will of Providence that Mary should experience almost every species of sorrow. Her father was thrown from his horse ... his recovery was not expected by the physical tribe.

Terrified at seeing him so near death, and yet so ill prepared for it, his daughter sat by his bed, oppressed by the keenest anguish, which her piety increased.

. . . .

Night after night Mary watched, and this excessive fatigue impaired her own health, but had a worse effect on Ann; though she constantly went to bed, she could not rest; a number of uneasy thoughts obtruded themselves; and apprehensions about Mary, whom she loved as well as her exhausted heart could love, harassed her mind. After a sleepless, feverish night she had a violent fit of coughing, and burst a blood vessel. The physician, who was in the house, was sent for, and when he left the patient, Mary, with an authoritative voice, insisted on knowing his real opinion. Reluctantly he gave it, that her friend was in a critical state; and if she passed the approaching winter in England, he imagined she would die in the spring, a season fatal to consumptive disorders. The spring! Her husband was then expected. Gracious Heaven, could she bear all this.

In a few days her father breathed his last. The horrid sensations his death occasioned were too poignant to be durable: and Ann's danger, and her own situation, made Mary deliberate what mode of conduct she should pursue. She feared this event might hasten the return of her husband, and prevent her putting into execution a plan she had determined on. It was to accompany Ann to a more salubrious climate.

CHAPTER VIII

I mentioned before that Mary had never had any particular attachment to give rise to the disgust that daily gained ground. Her friendship for Ann occupied her heart, and resembled a passion. She had had, indeed, several transient likings; but they did not amount to love. The society of men of genius delighted her, and improved her faculties. With beings of this class she did not often meet; it is a rare genus; her first favorites were men past the meridian of life, and of a philosophic turn.

Determined on going to the South of France, or Lisbon, she wrote to the man she had promised to obey. The physicians had said change of air was necessary for her as well as her friend. . . .

. . . .

By the return of the post she received an answer; it contained some commonplace remarks on her romantic friendship, as he termed it; "But as the physicians advised change of air, he had no objection."

CHAPTER IX

There was nothing now to retard their journey; and Mary chose Lisbon rather than France, on account of its being further removed from the only person she wished not to see.

. . . .

They had only been a week at sea when they hailed the rock of Lisbon, and the next morning anchored at the castle. . . .

. . . .

In an unknown land, she considered that the Being she adored inhabited eternity, was ever present in unnumbered worlds. When she had not anyone she loved near her, she was particularly sensible of the presence of her Almighty Friend.

The arrival of the carriage put a stop to her speculations; it was to conduct them to an hotel fitted up for the reception of invalids. Unfortunately, before they could reach it there was a violent shower of rain; and as the wind was very high, it beat against the leather curtains, which they drew along the front of the vehicle to shelter themselves from it; but it availed not: some of the rain forced its way, and Ann felt the effects of it, for she caught cold, spite of Mary's precautions.

As is the custom, the rest of the invalids, or lodgers, sent to enquire after their health; and as soon as Ann left her chamber, in which her complaints seldom confined her the whole day, they came in person to pay their compliments. Three fashionable females, and two gentlemen; the one a brother of the eldest of the young ladies, and the other an invalid, who came, like themselves, for the benefit of the air. They entered into conversation immediately.

People who meet in a strange country and are all together in a house soon get acquainted, without the formalities which attend visiting in separate houses, where they are surrounded by domestic friends. Ann was particularly delighted at meeting with agreeable society; a little hectic fever generally made her low-spirited in the morning, and lively in the evening, when she wished for company. Mary, who only thought of her, determined to cultivate their acquaintance, as she knew that if her mind could be diverted, her body might gain strength.

They were all musical, and proposed having little concerts. One of the gentlemen played on the violin, and the other on the German flute. The instruments were brought in, with all the eagerness that attends putting a new scheme in execution.

Mary had not said much, for she was diffident; she seldom joined in general conversations, though her quickness of penetration enabled her soon to enter into the characters of those she conversed with, and her sensibility made her desirous of pleasing every human creature. Besides, if her mind was not occupied by any particular sorrow, or study, she caught reflected pleasure, and was glad to see others happy, though their mirth did not interest her.

This day she was continually thinking of Ann's recovery, and encouraging the cheerful hopes, which though they dissipated the spirits that had been condensed by melancholy, yet made her wish to be silent. The music, more than the conversation, disturbed her reflections; but not at first. The gentleman who played on the German flute, was a handsome, well-bred, sensible man; and his observations, if not original, were pertinent.

The other, who had not said much, began to touch the violin, and played a little Scotch ballad; he brought such a thrilling sound out of the instrument that Mary started, and looking at him with more attention than she had done before, and saw, in a face rather ugly, strong lines of genius. His manners were awkward, that kind of awkwardness which is often found in literary men: he seemed a thinker, and delivered his opinions in elegant expressions, and musical tones of voice.

When the concert was over, they all retired to their apartments. Mary always slept with Ann, as she was subject to terrifying dreams; and frequently in the night was obliged to be supported, to avoid suffocation. They chatted about their new acquaintance in their own apartment, and, with respect to the gentlemen, differed in opinion.

. . . .

CHAPTER XI

When I mentioned the three ladies, I said they were fashionable women; and it was all the praise, as a faithful historian, I could bestow on them; the only thing in which they were consistent. I forgot to mention that they were all of one family, a mother, her daughter, and niece. The daughter was sent by her physician, to avoid a northerly winter; the mother, her niece, and nephew, accompanied her.

They were people of rank; but unfortunately, though of an ancient family, the title had descended to a very remote branch—a branch they took care to be intimate with; and servilely copied the Countess's airs. Their minds were shackled with a set of notions concerning propriety, the fitness of things for the world's eye, trammels which always hamper weak people. What will the world say? was the first thing that was thought of, when they intended doing anything they had not done before. Or what would the Countess do on such an occasion? And when this question was answered, the right or wrong was discovered without the trouble of their having any idea of the matter in their own heads. This same

Countess was a fine planet, and the satellites observed a most harmonic dance around her.

. . . Without having any seeds sown in their understanding, or the affections of the heart set to work, they were brought out of their nursery, or the place they were secluded in, to prevent their faces being common; like blazing stars, to captivate Lords.

They were pretty, and hurrying from one party of plea- sure to another, occasioned the disorder which required change of air. The mother, if we except her being near twenty years older, was just the same creature; and these additional years only served to make her more tenaciously adhere to her habits of folly, and decide with stupid gravity some trivial points of ceremony, as a matter of the last importance; of which she was a competent judge, from hav- ing lived in the fashionable world so long: that world to which the ignorant look up as we do to the sun.

. . . .

One afternoon, which they had engaged to spend together, Ann was so ill that Mary was obliged to send an apology for not attending the tea table. The apology brought them on the carpet; and the mother; with a look of solemn impor- tance, turned to the sick man, whose name was Henry, and said, "Though people of the first fashion are frequently at places of this kind, intimate with they know not who, yet I do not choose that my daughter, whose family is so respect- able, should be intimate with anyone she would blush to know elsewhere. It is only on that account, for I never suffer her to be with anyone but in my company," added she, sitting more erect; and a smile of self-complacency dressed her countenance.

"I have inquired concerning these strangers, and find that the one who has the most dignity in her manners is really a woman of fortune." "Lord, mamma, how ill she dresses." Mamma went on, "She is a romantic creature, you must not copy her, miss; yet she is an heiress of the large fortune in ———shire, of which you may remember to have heard the Countess speak the night you had on the dancing dress that was so much admired; but she is married."

She then told them the whole story as she heard it from her maid, who picked it out of Mary's servant. "She is a foolish creature, and this friend that she pays as much attention to as if she was a lady of quality, is a beggar." "Well, how strange!" cried the girls.

"She is, however, a charming creature," said her nephew. Henry sighed, and strode across the room once or twice; then took up his violin, and played the air which first struck Mary; he had often heard her praise it.

. . . The well-known sounds reached Mary as she sat by her friend—she listened without knowing that she did—and shed tears almost without being conscious of it. Ann soon fell asleep, as she had taken an opiate. Mary, then brooding over her fears, began to imagine she had deceived herself—Ann was still very ill; hope had beguiled many heavy hours; yet she was displeased with herself for admitting this welcome guest. And she worked up her mind to such a degree of anxiety that she determined, once more, to seek medical aid.

No sooner did she determine, than she ran down with a discomposed look, to inquire of the ladies who she should send for. When she entered the room she could not articulate her fears—it appeared like pronouncing Ann's sentence of death; her faltering tongue dropped some broken words, and she remained silent. The ladies wondered that a person of her sense should be so little mistress of herself; and began to administer some commonplace comfort, as, that it was our duty to submit to the will of Heaven, and the like trite consolations, which Mary did not answer; but waving her hand, with an air of impatience, she exclaimed, "I cannot live without her!—I have no other friend; if I lose her, what a desert will the world be to me." "No other friend," reechoed they, "have you not a husband?"

Mary shrunk back, and was alternately pale and red. A delicate sense of propriety prevented her replying, and recalled her bewildered reason. Assuming, in consequence of her recollection, a more composed manner, she made the intended inquiry, and left the room. Henry's eyes followed her while the females very freely animadverted on her strange behavior.

CHAPTER XII

The physician was sent for; his prescription afforded Ann a little temporary relief; and they again joined the circle. Unfortunately, the weather happened to be constantly wet for more than a week, and confined them to the house. An then found the ladies not so agreeable; when they sat whole hours together, the threadbare topics were exhausted; and, but for cards or music, the long evenings would have been yawned away in listless indolence.

The bad weather had had as ill an effect on Henry as on Ann. He was frequently very thoughtful, or rather melancholy; this melancholy would of itself have attracted Mary's notice, if she had not found his conversation so infinitely superior to the rest of the group. When she conversed with him, all the faculties of her soul unfolded themselves; genius animated her expressive countenance; and the most graceful, unaffected gestures gave energy to her discourse.

They frequently discussed very important subjects, while the rest were singing or playing cards, nor were they observed for doing so, as Henry, whom they all were pleased with, in the way of gallantry showed them all more attention than her. Besides, as there was nothing alluring in her dress or manner, they never dreamt of her being preferred to them.

Henry was a man of learning; he had also studied mankind, and knew many of the intricacies of the human heart, from having felt the infirmities of his own. His taste was just, as it had a standard—Nature, which he observed with a critical eye. Mary could not help thinking that in his company her mind expanded, as he always went below the surface. She increased her stock of ideas, and her taste was improved.

He was also a pious man; his rational religious sentiments received warmth from his sensibility; and, except on very particular occasions, kept it in proper bounds; these sentiments had likewise formed his temper; he was gentle, and easily to be entreated. The ridiculous ceremonies they were every day witness to led them into what are termed grave subjects, and made him explain his opinions, which, at other times, he was neither ashamed of nor unnecessarily brought forward to notice.

CHAPTER XIII

When the weather began to clear up, Mary sometimes rode out alone, purposely to view the ruins that still remained of the earthquake; or she would ride to the banks of the Tagus, to feast her eyes with the sight of that magnificent river. At other times she would visit the churches, as she was particularly fond of seeing historical paintings.

One of these visits gave rise to the subject, and the whole party descanted on it; but as the ladies could not handle it well, they soon adverted to portraits; and talked of the attitudes and characters in which they should wish to be drawn. Mary did not fix on one—when Henry, with more apparent warmth than usual, said, "I would give the world for your picture, with the expression I have seen in your face, when you have been supporting your friend."

This delicate compliment did not gratify her vanity, but it reached her heart. She then recollected that she had once sat for her picture—for whom was it designed? For a boy! Her cheeks flushed with indignation, so strongly did she feel an emotion of contempt at having been thrown away—given in with an estate.

. . . .

CHAPTER XIV

. . . .

. . . Henry had been some time ill and low-spirited; Mary would have been attentive to anyone in that situation; but to him she was particularly so; she thought herself bound in gratitude, on account of his constant endeavors to amuse Ann, and prevent her dwelling on the dreary prospect before her, which sometimes she could not help anticipating with a kind of quiet despair.

She found some excuse for going more frequently into the room they all met in; nay, she avowed her desire to amuse him: offered to read to him, and tried to draw him into amusing conversations; and when she was full of these little schemes, she looked at him with a degree of tenderness that she was not conscious of. This divided attention was of use to her, and prevented her continually thinking of Ann, whose fluctuating disorder often gave rise to false hopes.

A trifling thing occurred now which occasioned Mary some uneasiness. Her maid, a well-looking girl, had captivated the clerk of a neighboring countinghouse. As the match was an advantageous one, Mary could not raise any objection to it, though at this juncture it was very disagreeable to her to have a stranger about her person. However, the girl consented to delay the marriage, as she had some affection for her mistress; and, besides, looked forward to Ann's death as a time of harvest.

Henry's illness was not alarming, it was rather pleasing, as it gave Mary an excuse to herself for showing him how much she was interested about him, and giving little artless proofs of affection, which the purity of her heart made her never wish to restrain.

The only visible return he made was not obvious to common observers. He would sometimes fix his eyes on her, and take them off with a sigh that was coughed away; or when he was leisurely walking into the room, and did not expect to see her, he would quicken his steps, and come up to her with eagerness to ask some trivial question. In the same style, he would try to detain her when he had nothing to say—or said nothing.

Ann did not take notice of either his or Mary's behavior, nor did she suspect that he was a favorite, on any other account than his appearing neither well nor happy. She had often seen that when a person was unfortunate, Mary's pity might easily be mistaken for love, and, indeed, it was a temporary sensation of that kind. . . .

CHAPTER XV

One morning they set out to visit the aqueduct; though the day was very fine when they left home, a very heavy shower fell before they reached it; they lengthened their ride, the clouds dispersed, and the sun came from behind them uncommonly bright.

Mary would fain have persuaded Ann not to have left the carriage; but she was in spirits, and obviated all her objections, and insisted on walking, though the ground was damp. But her strength was not equal to her spirits; she was soon obliged to return to the carriage so much fatigued that she fainted, and remained insensible a long time.

Henry would have supported her; but Mary would not permit him; her recollection was instantaneous, and she feared sitting on the damp ground might do him a material injury: she was on that account positive, though the company did not guess the cause of her being so. As to herself, she did not fear bodily pain; and, when her mind was agitated, she could endure the greatest fatigue without appearing sensible of it.

When Ann recovered, they returned slowly home; she was carried to bed, and the next morning Mary thought she observed a visible change for the worse. The physician was sent for, who pronounced her to be in the most imminent danger.

All Mary's former fears now returned like a torrent, and carried every other care away; she even added to her present anguish by upbraiding herself for her late tranquility—it haunted her in the form of a crime.

The disorder made the most rapid advances—there was no hope! Bereft of it, Mary again was tranquil; but it was a very different kind of tranquility. She stood to brave the approaching storm, conscious she only could be overwhelmed by it.

She did not think of Henry, or if her thoughts glanced towards him, it was only to find fault with herself for suffering a thought to have strayed from Ann. Ann! This dear friend was soon torn from her—she died suddenly as Mary was assisting her to walk across the room. The first string was severed from her heart ... she seemed stunned by it; unable to reflect, or even to feel her misery.

... Mary refused to see her former companions. She desired her maid to conclude her marriage, and request her intended husband to inform her when the first merchantman was to leave the port, as the packet had just sailed, and she determined not to stay in that hated place any longer than was absolutely necessary.

She then sent to request the ladies to visit her; she wished to avoid a parade of grief—her sorrows were her own, and appeared to her not to admit of increase or softening. She was right; the sight of them did not affect her, or turn the stream of her sullen sorrow; the black wave rolled along in the same course; it was equal to her where she cast her eyes; all was impenetrable gloom.

CHAPTER XVI

Soon after the ladies left her, she received a message from Henry, requesting, as she saw company, to be permitted to visit her: she consented, and he entered immediately, with an unassured pace. She ran eagerly up to him—saw the tear trembling in his eye, and his countenance softened by the tenderest compassion; the hand which pressed hers seemed that of a fellow creature. She burst into tears; and, unable to restrain them, she hid her face with both her hands: these tears relieved her (she had before had a difficulty in breathing), and she sat down by him more composed than she had appeared since Ann's death; but her conversation was incoherent.

She called herself "a poor disconsolate creature!"—"Mine is a selfish grief," she exclaimed—"Yes, Heaven is my witness, I do not wish her back now she has reached those peaceful mansions, where the weary rest. Her pure spirit is happy; but what a wretch am I!"

Henry forgot his cautious reserve. "Would you allow me to call you friend?" said he in a hesitating voice. "I feel, dear girl, the tenderest interest in whatever concerns thee." His eyes spoke the rest. They were both silent a few moments; then Henry resumed the conversation. "I have also been acquainted with grief! I mourn the loss of a woman who was not worthy of my regard. Let me give thee some account of the man who now solicits thy friendship; and who, from motives of the purest benevolence, wishes to give comfort to thy wounded heart.

"I have myself," he said, mournfully, "shaken hands with happiness, and am dead to the world; I wait patiently for my dissolution; but, for thee, Mary, there may be many bright days in store."

"Impossible," replied she, in a peevish tone, as if he had insulted her by the supposition; her feelings were so much in unison with his that she was in love with misery.

He smiled at her impatience, and went on. "My father died before I knew him, and my mother was so attached to my eldest brother that she took very little pains to fit me for the profession to which I was destined: and, may I tell thee, I left my family, and, in many different stations, rambled about the world; saw mankind in every rank of life; and, in order to be independent, exerted those talents Nature has given me: these exertions improved my understanding; and the miseries I was witness to gave a keener edge to my sensibility. My constitution is naturally weak; and, perhaps, two or three lingering disorders in my youth first gave me a habit of reflecting, and enabled me to obtain some dominion over my passions. At least," added he, stifling a sigh, "over the violent ones, though I fear, refinement and reflection only renders the tender ones more tyrannic.

"I have told you already I have been in love, and disappointed—the object is now no more; let her faults sleep with her! Yet this passion has pervaded my whole soul, and mixed itself with all my affections and pursuits. I am not peacefully indifferent; yet it is only to my violin I tell the sorrows I now confide with thee. The object I loved forfeited my esteem; yet, true to the sentiment, my fancy has too frequently delighted to form a creature that I could love, that could convey to my soul sensations which the gross part of mankind have not any conception of."

He stopped, as Mary seemed lost in thought; but as she was still in a listening attitude, continued his little narrative. "I kept up an irregular correspondence with my mother; my brother's extravagance and ingratitude had almost broken her heart, and made her feel something like a pang of remorse, on account of her behavior to me. I hastened to comfort her—and was a comfort to her.

"My declining health prevented my taking orders, as I had intended; but I with warmth entered into literary pursuits; perhaps my heart, not having an object, made me embrace the substitute with more eagerness. But do not imagine I have always been a die-away swain. No: I have frequented the cheerful haunts of men, and wit!—enchanting wit! has made many moments fly free from care. I am too fond of the elegant arts; and woman—lovely woman! thou hast charmed me, though, perhaps, it would not be easy to find one to whom my reason would allow me to be constant.

"I have now only to tell you that my mother insisted on my spending this winter in a warmer climate; and I fixed on

Lisbon, as I had before visited the Continent." He then looked Mary full in the face; and, with the most insinuating accents, asked "if he might hope for her friendship? If she would rely on him as if he was her father; and that the tenderest father could not more anxiously interest himself in the fate of a darling child, than he did in hers."

Such a crowd of thoughts all at once rushed into Mary's mind, that she in vain attempted to express the sentiments which were most predominant. Her heart longed to receive a new guest; there was a void in it: accustomed to have some one to love, she was alone, and comfortless, if not engrossed by a particular affection.

Henry saw her distress, and, not to increase it, left the room. He had exerted himself to turn her thoughts into a new channel, and had succeeded; she thought of him till she began to chide herself for defrauding the dead, and, determining to grieve for Ann, she dwelt on Henry's misfortunes and ill health; and the interest he took in her fate was a balm to her sick mind. She did not reason on the subject; but she felt he was attached to her: lost in this delirium, she never asked herself what kind of an affection she had for him, or what it tended to; nor did she know that love and friendship are very distinct; she thought with rapture that there was one person in the world who had an affection for her, and that person she admired—had a friendship for.

He had called her his dear girl; the words might have fallen from him by accident; but they did not fall to the ground. My child! His child, what an association of ideas! If I had had a father, such a father!—She could not dwell on the thoughts, the wishes which obtruded themselves. Her mind was unhinged, and passion unperceived filled her whole soul. Lost, in waking dreams, she considered and reconsidered Henry's account of himself, till she actually thought she would tell Ann—a bitter recollection then roused her out of her reverie; and aloud she begged forgiveness of her.

By these kind of conflicts the day was lengthened; and when she went to bed, the night passed away in feverish slumbers; though they did not refresh her, she was spared the labor of thinking, of restraining her imagination; it sported uncontrolled; but took its color from her waking train of thoughts. One instant she was supporting her dying mother, then Ann was breathing her last, and Henry was comforting her.

The unwelcome light visited her languid eyes; yet, I must tell the truth, she thought she should see Henry, and this hope set her spirits in motion: but they were quickly depressed by her maid, who came to tell her that she had heard of a vessel on board of which she could be accommodated, and that there was to be another female passenger on board, a vulgar one; but perhaps she would be more useful on that account—Mary did not want a companion.

As she had given orders for her passage to be engaged in the first vessel that sailed, she could not now retract; and must prepare for the lonely voyage, as the Captain intended taking advantage of the first fair wind. She had too much strength of mind to waver in her determination; but to determine wrung her very heart, opened all her old wounds, and made them bleed afresh. What was she to do? where go? Could she set a seal to a hasty vow, and tell a deliberate lie; promise to love one man, when the image of another was ever present to her—her soul revolted. "I might gain the applause of the world by such mock heroism; but should I not forfeit my own? forfeit thine, my father!"

There is a solemnity in the shortest ejaculation, which, for a while, stills the tumult of passion. Mary's mind had been thrown off its poise; her devotion had been, perhaps, more fervent for some time past; but less regular. She forgot that happiness was not to be found on earth, and built a terrestrial paradise liable to be destroyed by the first serious thought: when she reasoned she became inexpressibly sad, to render life bearable she gave way to fancy—this was madness.

In a few days she must again go to sea; the weather was very tempestuous—what of that, the tempest in her soul rendered every other trifling—it was not the contending elements, but *herself* she feared!

. . . .

CHAPTER XVIII

The ladies heard that her servant was to be married that day, and that she was to sail in the vessel which was then clearing out at the customhouse. Henry heard, but did not make any remarks; and Mary called up all her fortitude to support her, and enable her to hide from the females her internal struggles. She durst not encounter Henry's glances when she found he had been informed of her intention; and, trying to draw a veil over her wretched state of mind, she talked incessantly, she knew not what; flashes of wit burst from her, and when she began to laugh she could not stop herself.

Henry smiled at some of her sallies, and looked at her with such benignity and compassion that he recalled her scattered thoughts; and, the ladies going to dress for dinner, they were left alone; and remained silent a few moments: after the noisy conversation it appeared solemn. Henry began. "You are going, Mary, and going by yourself; your mind is not in a state to be left to its own operations—yet I cannot dissuade you; if I attempted to do it, I should ill deserve the title I wish to merit. I only think of your happiness; could I obey the strongest impulse of my heart, I should accompany thee to England; but such a step might endanger your future peace."

Mary, then, with all the frankness which marked her character, explained her situation to him, and mentioned her fatal tie with such disgust that he trembled for her. "I cannot see him; he is not the man formed for me to love!" Her delicacy did not restrain her, for her dislike to her husband had taken root in her mind long before she knew Henry. Did she not fix on Lisbon rather than France on purpose to avoid him? and if Ann had been in tolerable health she would have flown with her to some remote corner to have escaped from him.

"I intend," said Henry, "to follow you in the next packet; where shall I hear of your health?" "Oh! let me hear of thine," replied Mary. "I am well, very well; but thou art very ill—thy health is in the most precarious state." She then mentioned her intention of going to Ann's relations. "I am her representative, I have duties to fulfill for her: during my voyage I have time enough for reflection; though I think I have already determined."

"Be not too hasty, my child," interrupted Henry; "far be it from me to persuade thee to do violence to thy feelings—but consider that all thy future life may probably take its color from thy present mode of conduct. Our affections as well as our sentiments are fluctuating; you will not perhaps always either think or feel as you do at present: the object you now shun may appear in a different light." He paused. "In advising thee in this style, I have only thy good at heart, Mary."

. . . "Yet a little while am I parted from my Ann—I could not

exist without the hope of seeing her again—I could not bear
to think that time could wear away an affection that was
founded on what is not liable to perish; you might as well
attempt to persuade me that my soul is matter, and that its
feelings arose from certain modifications of it."

"Dear enthusiastic creature," whispered Henry, "how you
steal into my soul." She still continued. "The same turn of
mind which leads me to adore the Author of all Perfection—
which leads me to conclude that he only can fill my soul;
forces me to admire the faint image—the shadows of his
attributes here below; and my imagination gives still bolder
strokes to them. . . . Every cause in nature produces an
effect; and am I an exception to the general rule? Have I
desires implanted in me only to make me miserable? Will
they never be gratified? Shall I never be happy? My feelings
do not accord with the notion of solitary happiness. In a
state of bliss, it will be the society of beings we can love,
without the alloy that earthly infirmities mix with our best
affections, that will constitute great part of our happiness.

. . . .

"Riches and honors await me, and the cold moralist might
desire me to sit down and enjoy them—I cannot conquer my
feelings, and till I do, what are these baubles to me? . . .
These struggles prepare me for eternity—when I no longer
see through a glass darkly I shall not reason about, but *feel*
in what happiness consists."

Henry had not attempted to interrupt her; he saw she was
determined, and that these sentiments were not the effusion
of the moment, but well-digested ones, the result of strong
affections, a high sense of honor, and respect for the source
of all virtue and truth. He was startled, if not entirely
convinced by her arguments; indeed her voice, her gestures
were all persuasive.

Someone now entered the room; he looked an answer to
her long harangue; it was fortunate for him, or he might
have been led to say what in a cooler moment he had
determined to conceal; but were words necessary to reveal
it? He wished not to influence her conduct—vain precaution;
she knew she was beloved; and could she forget that such a
man loved her, or rest satisfied with any inferior gratification. When passion first enters the heart, it is only a return
of affection that is sought after, and every other remembrance and wish is blotted out.

CHAPTER XIX

Two days passed away without any particular conversation; Henry, trying to be indifferent, or to appear so, was more assiduous than ever. The conflict was too violent for his present state of health; the spirit was willing, but the body suffered; he lost his appetite, and looked wretchedly; his spirits were calmly low—the world seemed to fade away— what was that world to him that Mary did not inhabit; she lived not for him.

He was mistaken; his affection was her only support; without this dear prop she had sunk into the grave of her lost, long-loved friend; his attention snatched her from despair. Inscrutable are the ways of Heaven!

The third day Mary was desired to prepare herself; for if the wind continued in the same point, they should set sail the next evening. She tried to prepare her mind, and her efforts were not useless; she appeared less agitated than could have been expected, and talked of her voyage with composure. On great occasions she was generally calm and collected, her resolution would brace her unstrung nerves; but after the victory she had no triumph; she would sink into a state of moping melancholy, and feel tenfold misery when the heroic enthusiasm was over.

The morning of the day fixed on for her departure she was alone with Henry only a few moments, and an awkward kind of formality made them slip away without their having said much to each other. Henry was afraid to discover his passion, or give any other name to his regard but friendship; yet his anxious solicitude for her welfare was ever breaking out—while she as artlessly expressed again and again, her fears with respect to his declining health.

"We shall soon meet," said he, with a faint smile; Mary smiled too; she caught the sickly beam; it was still fainter by being reflected, and not knowing what she wished to do, started up and left the room. When she was alone she regretted she had left him so precipitately. "The few precious moments I have thus thrown away may never return," she thought—the reflection led to misery.

She waited for, nay, almost wished for the summons to depart. She could not avoid spending the intermediate time with the ladies and Henry; and the trivial conversations she was obliged to bear a part in harassed her more than can be well conceived.

The summons came, and the whole party attended her to the vessel. For a while the remembrance of Ann banished her regret at parting with Henry, though his pale figure pressed on her sight; it may seem a paradox, but he was more present to her when she sailed; her tears then were all his own.

"My poor Ann!" thought Mary, "along this road we came, and near this spot you called me your guardian angel—and now I leave thee here! ah! no, I do not—thy spirit is not confined to its moldering tenement! Tell me, thou soul of her I love, tell me, ah! whither art thou fled?" Ann occupied her until they reached the ship.

The anchor was weighed. Nothing can be more irksome than waiting to say farewell. As the day was serene, they accompanied her a little way, and then got into the boat; Henry was the last; he pressed her hand, it had not any life in it; she leaned over the side of the ship without looking at the boat, till it was so far distant that she could not see the countenances of those that were in it: a mist spread itself over her sight—she longed to exchange one look—tried to recollect the last—the universe contained no being but Henry! The grief of parting with him had swept all others clean away. Her eyes followed the keel of the boat, and when she could no longer perceive its traces she looked round on the wide waste of waters, thought of the precious moments which had been stolen from the waste of murdered time.

She then descended into the cabin, regardless of the surrounding beauties of nature, and throwing herself on her bed in the little hole which was called the stateroom—she wished to forget her existence. On this bed she remained two days, listening to the dashing waves, unable to close her eyes. A small taper made the darkness visible; and the third night, by its glimmering light, she wrote the following fragment.

"Poor solitary wretch that I am; here alone do I listen to the whistling winds and dashing waves;—on no human support can I rest—when not lost to hope I found pleasure in the society of those rough beings; but now they appear not like my fellow creatures; no social ties draw me to them.

How long, how dreary has this day been; yet I scarcely wish it over—for what will tomorrow bring—tomorrow, and to-morrow will only be marked with unvaried characters of wretchedness. Yet surely I am not alone!"

Her moistened eyes were lifted up to heaven; a crowd of thoughts darted into her mind, and pressing her hand against her forehead, as if to bear the intellectual weight, she tried, but tried in vain, to arrange them. "Father of Mercies, compose this troubled spirit: do I indeed wish it to be composed—to forget my Henry?" the *my*, the pen was directly drawn across in an agony.

CHAPTER XX

. . . .

The winds then became very tempestuous, the Great Deep was troubled, and all the passengers appalled. Mary then left her bed, and went on deck to survey the contending elements: the scene accorded with the present state of her soul; she thought in a few hours I may go home; the prisoner may be released. The vessel rose on a wave and descended into a yawning gulf. Not slower did her mounting soul return to earth, for—Ah! her treasure and her heart was there. The squalls rattled amongst the sails, which were quickly taken down; the wind would then die away, and the wild undirected waves rushed on every side with a tremendous roar. In a little vessel in the midst of such a storm she was not dismayed; she felt herself independent.

. . . .

CHAPTER XXII

In England then landed the forlorn wanderer. She looked round for some few moments—her affections were not attracted to any particular part of the Island. She knew none of the inhabitants of the vast city to which she was going: the mass of buildings appeared to her a huge body without an informing soul. As she passed through the streets in an

hackney coach, disgust and horror alternately filled her
mind. She met some women drunk; and the manners of
those who attacked the sailors made her shrink into herself
and exclaim, are these my fellow creatures!

Detained by a number of carts near the waterside, for she
came up the river in the vessel, not having reason to hasten
on shore, she saw vulgarity, dirt, and vice—her soul sickened; this was the first time such complicated misery obtruded itself on her sight. Forgetting her own griefs, she
gave the world a much indebted tear; mourned for a world
in ruins. She then perceived that great part of her comfort
must arise from viewing the smiling face of nature, and be
reflected from the view of innocent enjoyments: she was fond
of seeing animals play, and could not bear to see her own
species sink below them.

In a little dwelling in one of the villages near London,
lived the mother of Ann; two of her children still remained
with her; but they did not resemble Ann. To her house Mary
directed the coach, and told the unfortunate mother of her
loss. The poor woman, oppressed by it, and her many other
cares, after an inundation of tears, began to enumerate all
her past misfortunes, and present cares. The heavy tale
lasted until midnight, and the impression it made on Mary's
mind was so strong that it banished sleep till towards morning; when tired nature sought forgetfulness, and the soul
ceased to ruminate about many things.

. . . .

. . . She deliberated, and at last informed the family that she
had a reason for not living with her husband, which must
some time remain a secret—they stared—Not live with him!
How will you live then? This was a question she could not
answer; she had only about eighty pounds remaining, of the
money she took with her to Lisbon; when it was exhausted
where could she get more? I will work, she cried, do anything rather than be a slave.

CHAPTER XXIII

Unhappy, she wandered about the village, and relieved the poor; it was the only employment that eased her aching heart; she became more intimate with misery—the misery that rises from poverty and the want of education. She was in the vicinity of a great city; the vicious poor in and about it must ever grieve a benevolent contemplative mind.

One evening a man who stood weeping in a little lane, near the house she resided in, caught her eye. She accosted him; in a confused manner, he informed her that his wife was dying, and his children crying for the bread he could not earn. Mary desired to be conducted to his habitation. . . .

It was crowded with inhabitants: some were scolding, others swearing, or singing indecent songs. What a sight for Mary! Her blood ran cold; yet she had sufficient resolution to mount to the top of the house. On the floor, in one corner of a very small room, lay an emaciated figure of a woman; a window over her head scarcely admitted any light, for the broken panes were stuffed with dirty rags. Near her were five children, all young, and covered with dirt; their sallow cheeks and languid eyes exhibited none of the charms of childhood. Some were fighting, and others crying for food; their yells were mixed with their mother's groans, and the wind which rushed through the passage. Mary was petrified; but soon assuming more courage, approached the bed, and, regardless of the surrounding nastiness, knelt down by the poor wretch and breathed the most poisonous air; for the unfortunate creature was dying of a putrid fever, the consequence of dirt and want.

Their state did not require much explanation. Mary sent the husband for a poor neighbor, whom she hired to nurse the woman, and take care of the children; and then went herself to buy them some necessaries at a shop not far distant. Her knowledge of physic had enabled her to prescribe for the woman; and she left the house with a mixture of horror and satisfaction.

She visited them every day, and procured them every comfort; contrary to her expectation, the woman began to recover; cleanliness and wholesome food had a wonderful effect; and Mary saw her rising as it were from the grave.

Not aware of the danger she ran into, she did not think of it till she perceived she had caught the fever. It made such an alarming progress that she was prevailed on to send for a physician; but the disorder was so violent that for some days it baffled his skill; and Mary felt not her danger, as she was delirious. After the crisis, the symptoms were more favorable, and she slowly recovered, without regaining much strength or spirits; indeed they were intolerably low: she wanted a tender nurse.

For some time she had observed that she was not treated with the same respect as formerly; her favors were forgotten when no more were expected. This ingratitude hurt her. . . .

Two months were elapsed; she had not seen or heard from Henry. He was sick—nay, perhaps had forgotten her; all the world was dreary, and all the people ungrateful.

She sunk into apathy, and endeavoring to rouse herself out of it, she wrote in her book another fragment:

"Surely life is a dream, a frightful one! and after those rude, disjointed images are fled, will light ever break in? Shall I ever feel joy? Do all suffer like me; or am I framed so as to be particularly susceptible of misery? . . ."

. . . .

She could not write any more; she wished herself far distant from all human society; a thick gloom spread itself over her mind: but did not make her forget the very beings she wished to fly from. She sent for the poor woman she found in the garret; gave her money to clothe herself and children and buy some furniture for a little hut, in a large garden, the master of which agreed to employ her husband, who had been bred a gardener. Mary promised to visit the family, and see their new abode when she was able to go out.

CHAPTER XXIV

Mary still continued weak and low, though it was spring, and all nature began to look gay; with more than usual brightness the sun shone, and a little robin which she had cherished during the winter sung one of his best songs. The family were particularly civil this fine morning, and tried to prevail on her to walk out. Anything like kindness melted her; she consented.

Softer emotions banished her melancholy, and she directed her steps to the habitation she had rendered comfortable.

Emerging out of a dreary chamber, all nature looked cheerful; when she had last walked out, snow covered the ground, and bleak winds pierced her through and through: now the hedges were green, the blossoms adorned the trees, and the birds sung. She reached the dwelling, without being much exhausted; and while she rested there, observed the children sporting on the grass, with improved complexions. The mother with tears thanked her deliverer, and pointed out her comforts. Mary's tears flowed not only from sympathy, but a complication of feelings and recollections; the affections which bound her to her fellow creatures began again to play, and reanimated nature.

. . . .

CHAPTER XXV

A few mornings after, as Mary was sitting ruminating, harassed by perplexing thoughts, and fears, a letter was delivered to her: the servant waited for an answer. Her heart palpitated; it was from Henry; she held it some time in her hand, then tore it open; it was not a long one; and only contained an account of a relapse, which prevented his sailing in the first packet, as he had intended. Some tender inquiries were added, concerning her health and state of mind; but they were expressed in rather a formal style: it vexed her, and the more so as it stopped the current of affection, which the account of his arrival and illness had made flow to her heart—it ceased to beat for a moment—she read the passage over again; but could not tell what she was hurt by—only that it did not answer the expectations of her affection. She wrote a laconic, incoherent note in return, allowing him to call on her the next day—he had requested permission at the conclusion of his letter.

Her mind was then painfully active; she could not read or walk; she tried to fly from herself, to forget the long hours that were yet to run before tomorrow could arrive: she knew not what time he would come; certainly in the morning, she concluded; the morning then was anxiously wished for; and every wish produced a sigh that arose from expectation on the stretch, damped by fear and vain regret.

To beguile the tedious time, Henry's favorite tunes were sung; the books they read together turned over; and the short epistle read at least a hundred times. Anyone who had seen her would have supposed that she was trying to decipher Chinese characters.

After a sleepless night, she hailed the tardy day, watched the rising sun, and then listened for every footstep, and started if she heard the street door opened. At last he came, and she who had been counting the hours, and doubting whether the earth moved, would gladly have escaped the approaching interview.

With an unequal, irresolute pace, she went to meet him; but when she beheld his emaciated countenance, all the tenderness, which the formality of his letter had damped, returned, and a mournful presentiment stilled the internal conflict. She caught his hand, and looking wistfully at him, exclaimed, "Indeed, you are not well!"

"I am very far from well; but it matters not," added he with a smile of resignation. "My native air may work wonders, and besides, my mother is a tender nurse, and I shall sometimes see thee."

Mary felt for the first time in her life envy; she wished involuntarily that all the comfort he received should be from her. She inquired about the symptoms of his disorder and heard that he had been very ill; she hastily drove away the fears that former dear-bought experience suggested: and again and again did she repeat that she was sure he would soon recover. She would then look in his face, to see if he assented, and ask more questions to the same purport. She tried to avoid speaking of herself, and Henry left her, with a promise of visiting her the next day.

Her mind was now engrossed by one fear—yet she would not allow herself to think that she feared an event she could not name. . . .

. . . .

Out of this reverie she was soon woke to keener anguish by the arrival of a letter from her husband. . . .

She could not muster up sufficient resolution to break the seal: her fears were not prophetic, for the contents gave her comfort. He informed her that he intended prolonging his tour, as he was now his own master, and wished to remain some time on the Continent. . . .

. . . .

CHAPTER XXVI

. . . .

As the summer advanced, Henry grew worse; the closeness of the air in the metropolis affected his breath; and his mother insisted on his fixing on someplace in the country, where she would accompany him. He could not think of going far off, but chose a little village on the banks of the Thames, near Mary's dwelling: he then introduced her to his mother.

They frequently went down the river in a boat; Henry would take his violin, and Mary would sometimes sing, or read, to them. She pleased his mother; she enchanted him. It was an advantage to Mary that friendship first possessed her heart; it opened it to all the softer sentiments of humanity: and when this first affection was torn away, a similar one sprung up, with a still tenderer sentiment added to it.

The last evening they were on the water, the clouds grew suddenly black, and broke in violent showers, which interrupted the solemn stillness that had prevailed previous to it. The thunder roared; and the oars plying quickly, in order to reach the shore, occasioned a not unpleasing sound. Mary drew still nearer Henry; she wished to have sought with him a watery grave; to have escaped the horror of surviving him. She spoke not, but Henry saw the workings of her mind—he felt them; threw his arm round her waist—and they enjoyed the luxury of wretchedness. As they touched the shore, Mary perceived that Henry was wet; with eager anxiety she cried, What shall I do!—this day will kill thee, and I shall not die with thee!

This accident put a stop to their pleasurable excursions; it had injured him, and brought on the spitting of blood he was subject to—perhaps it was not the cold that he caught that occasioned it. In vain did Mary try to shut her eyes; her fate pursued her! Henry every day grew worse and worse.

CHAPTER XXVII

Oppressed by her foreboding fears, her sore mind was hurt by new instances of ingratitude: disgusted with the family, whose misfortunes had often disturbed her repose, and lost in anticipated sorrow, she rambled she knew not where; when turning down a shady walk, she discovered her feet had taken the path they delighted to tread. She saw Henry sitting in his garden alone; he quickly opened the garden gate, and she sat down by him.

"I did not," said he, "expect to see thee this evening, my dearest Mary; but I was thinking of thee. Heaven has endowed thee with an uncommon portion of fortitude, to support one of the most affectionate hearts in the world. This is not a time for disguise; I know I am dear to thee—and my affection for thee is twisted with every fiber of my heart. I loved thee ever since I have been acquainted with thine: thou art the being my fancy has delighted to form; but which I imagined existed only there! In a little while the shades of death will encompass me—ill-fated love perhaps added strength to my disease, and smoothed the rugged path. Try, my love, to fulfill thy destined course—try to add to thy other virtues patience. I could have wished, for thy sake, that we could have died together—or that I could live to shield thee from the assaults of an unfeeling world! Could I but offer thee an asylum in these arms—a faithful bosom, in which thou couldst repose all thy griefs—" He pressed her to it, and she returned the pressure—he felt her throbbing heart. A mournful silence ensued. When he resumed the conversation: "I wished to prepare thee for the blow—too surely do I feel that it will not be long delayed! The passion I have nursed is so pure that death cannot extinguish it—or tear away the impression thy virtues have made on my soul. I would fain comfort thee—"

"Talk not of comfort," interrupted Mary. "It will be in heaven with thee and Ann—while I shall remain on earth the veriest wretch!" She grasped his hand.

"There we shall meet, my love, my Mary, in our Father's—" His voice faltered; he could not finish the sentence; he was almost suffocated—they both wept. Their tears relieved them;

they walked slowly to the garden gate (Mary would not go into the house); they could not say farewell when they reached it—and Mary hurried down the lane; to spare Henry the pain of witnessing her emotions.

When she lost sight of the house she sat down on the ground, till it grew late, thinking of all that had passed. Full of these thoughts, she crept along, regardless of the descending rain; when lifting up her eyes to heaven, and then turning them wildly on the prospects around, without marking them, she only felt that the scene accorded with her present state of mind. It was the last glimmering of twilight, with a full moon, over which clouds continually flitted. Where am I wandering, God of Mercy! she thought; she alluded to the wanderings of her mind. In what a labyrinth am I lost! What miseries have I already encountered—and what a number lie still before me.

Her thoughts flew rapidly to something. I could be happy listening to him, soothing his cares. Would he not smile upon me—call me his own Mary? I am not his—said she with fierceness—I am a wretch! and she heaved a sigh that almost broke her heart, while the big tears rolled down her burning cheeks; but still her exercised mind, accustomed to think, began to observe its operation, though the barrier of reason was almost carried away, and all the faculties not restrained by her were running into confusion. Wherefore am I made thus? Vain are my efforts—I cannot live without loving—and love leads to madness.—Yet I will not weep; and her eyes were now fixed by despair, dry and motionless; and then quickly whirled about with a look of distraction.

She looked for hope; but found none—all was troubled waters. Nowhere could she find rest. I have already paced to and fro in the earth; it is not my abiding place—may I not too go home! Ah! no. Is this complying with my Henry's request, could a spirit thus disengaged expect to associate with his? Tears of tenderness strayed down her relaxed countenance, and her softened heart heaved more regularly. She felt the rain, and turned to her solitary home.

Fatigued by the tumultuous emotions she had endured, when she entered the house she ran to her own room, sunk on the bed, and exhausted nature soon closed her eyes; but active fancy was still awake, and a thousand fearful dreams interrupted her slumbers.

. . . .

CHAPTER XXVIII

Just as she was going to quit her room to visit Henry, his mother called on her.

"My son is worse today," said she. "I come to request you to spend not only this day, but a week or two with me. Why should I conceal anything from you? Last night my child made his mother his confidante, and, in the anguish of his heart, requested me to be thy friend—when I shall be childless. I will not attempt to describe what I felt when he talked thus to me. If I am to lose the support of my age, and be again a widow—may I call her Child whom my Henry wishes me to adopt?"

. . . .

CHAPTER XXIX

She found Henry very ill. The physician had some weeks before declared he never knew a person with a similar pulse recover. Henry was certain he could not live long; all the rest he could obtain was procured by opiates. Mary now enjoyed the melancholy pleasure of nursing him, and softened by her tenderness the pains she could not remove. Every sigh did she stifle, every tear restrain, when he could see or hear them. She would boast of her resignation—yet catch eagerly at the least ray of hope. While he slept she would support his pillow, and rest her head where she could feel his breath. She loved him better than herself—she could not pray for his recovery; she could only say, The will of Heaven be done.

While she was in this state she labored to acquire fortitude; but one tender look destroyed it all—she rather labored, indeed, to make him believe she was resigned, than really to be so.

She wished to receive the sacrament with him, as a bond of union which was to extend beyond the grave. She did so, and received comfort from it; she rose above her misery.

His end was now approaching. Mary sat on the side of the bed. His eyes appeared fixed—no longer agitated by passion, he only felt that it was a fearful thing to die. The soul retired to the citadel; but it was not now solely filled by the image of her who in silent despair watched for his last breath. Collected, a frightful calmness stilled every turbulent emotion.

The mother's grief was more audible. Henry had for some time only attended to Mary—Mary pitied the parent, whose stings of conscience increased her sorrow; she whispered him, "Thy mother weeps, disregarded by thee; oh! comfort her!—My mother, thy son blesses thee." The oppressed parent left the room. And Mary *waited* to see him die.

. . . .

He was a long time silent; the opiate produced a kind of stupor. At last, in an agony, he cried, "It is dark; I cannot see thee; raise me up. Where is Mary? Did she not say she delighted to support me? Let me die in her arms."

Her arms were opened to receive him; they trembled not. Again he was obliged to lie down, resting on her: as the agonies increased he leaned towards her: the soul seemed flying to her, as it escaped out of its prison. The breathing was interrupted; she heard distinctly the last sigh—and lifting up to Heaven her eyes, "Father, receive his spirit," she calmly cried.

. . . .

. . . She prayed wildly—and fervently—but attempting to touch the lifeless hand—her head swum—she sunk—

. . . .

CHAPTER XXX

. . . .

. . . Mary was not able . . . to fix on the mode of conduct she ought now to pursue. But at last she conquered her disgust, and wrote her *husband* an account of what had passed since she had dropped his correspondence.

He came in person to answer the letter. Mary fainted when he approached her unexpectedly. Her disgust returned with additional force, in spite of previous reasonings, whenever he appeared; yet she was prevailed on to promise to live with him, if he would permit her to pass one year traveling from place to place; he was not to accompany her.

The time too quickly elapsed, and she gave him her hand—the struggle was almost more than she could endure. She tried to appear calm; time mellowed her grief, and mitigated her torments; but when her husband would take her hand, or mention anything like love, she would instantly feel a sickness, a faintness at her heart, and wish, involuntarily, that the earth would open and swallow her.

CHAPTER XXXI

Mary visited the Continent, and sought health in different climates; but her nerves were not to be restored to their former state. She then retired to her house in the country, established manufactories, threw the estate into small farms, and continually employed herself this way to dissipate care, and banish unavailing regret. She visited the sick, supported the old, and educated the young.

These occupations engrossed her mind; but there were hours when all her former woes would return and haunt her. Whenever she did, or said, anything she thought Henry would have approved of she could not avoid thinking with anguish of the rapture his approbation ever conveyed to her heart—a heart in which there was a void that even benevolence and religion could not fill. The latter taught her to struggle for resignation; and the former rendered life supportable.

Her delicate state of health did not promise long life. In moments of solitary sadness, a gleam of joy would dart across her mind—she thought she was hastening to that world *where there is neither marrying,* nor giving in marriage.

The Wrongs of Woman:
or, Maria

THIS UNFINISHED WORK of fiction, originally published in 1798 as the first two volumes of *The Posthumous Works of Mary Wollstonecraft*, reveals both the darker side of a complex woman and the corrupt side of her eighteenth-century world. In her public persona as the vindicator of human rights, Wollstonecraft tempered her outrage at social evils by embracing a rational, optimistic philosophy. In the heroines who bear her name, by contrast, she instilled little confidence of better things to come. *The Wrongs of Woman* opens with shattering boldness in a madhouse, as a sane woman imprisoned there by an avaricious husband tries to understand why she has been torn from her infant, drugged, and cast into this "abode of horror." A more practiced novelist probably would have softened the introduction—Mary knew her work still needed refining—and the narrative proceeds, often awkwardly, jolting the reader from one scene to the next. But intensified by this very lack of transitional ease, the unifying theme recurs. At one level of society or another, many women have only one question to ask: "Why was I not born a man, or why was I born at all?"

Maria remembers her life; at every turn, from the moment of birth, betrayal waited. Her mother loved her brother and she suckled him; little Maria, fed by a wet nurse, was of no consequence. She married in hopes of giving her sisters a competency and a home, only to have her groom laugh at so generous a notion, for her money was now his and money remained the motive for all the humiliations she endured at his hands. It is not hard to see here, as in *Mary*, a fantasy version of Wollstonecraft's childhood and adolescence; the history of her sister's escape from a tyrannical husband clearly supplied her with additional source material. The more original sections of *The Wrongs of Woman* probably owe something to the influence of her philosopher-husband, William Godwin, both as an analyst of the economic roots of

political relations and as a novelist himself. The story of
Jemima, Maria's jailer and eventual companion, plumbs the
lower depths of eighteenth-century London; another victim
of parental neglect, but born to servants (for whose degraded
lives Wollstonecraft had never shown genuine empathy before), Jemima survives child abuse, prostitution, abortion,
and worse, but, managing to educate herself somewhat when
she becomes a housekeeper to a man of intelligence, she
transforms herself into a being capable of loving and trusting the purported madwoman she has been sent to guard.

Nor are the lives of Maria and Jemima, born to different
stations but exposed to many surprisingly similar evils, the
sum of the wrongs done to woman. For the novel reinforces
the two central narratives with episode after episode of
females victimized and abused. For example, the impressing
of sailors—to which Wollstonecraft the social reformer had
devoted some pages in *A Vindication of the Rights of
Men*—comes alive in the pathetic story of Peggy, married
to a seaman who is pressed away on the river and never
returns, with the result that she is reduced to demeaning
poverty. In a series of interpolated sketches, the list of
wrongs against women is relentlessly dramatized; they are
impoverished, deceived, seduced, impregnated, prostituted,
driven to crime and even murder. A man such as Maria's
uncle or Jemima's employer occasionally displays good will
and seems likely to help. But even the best men prove weak
or undependable.

For the first time in her career, Wollstonecraft showed
that women, vulnerable to their sensual desires, compound
their own difficulties. The prim advice that the author of
Thoughts on the Education of Daughters gave on the way
women ought passively to endure caresses is repudiated
here. Maria's narrative, imbedded in a letter to be read
many years in the future by the infant daughter from whom
she was cruelly separated, insists on the profundity and
virtue of female sexuality: "When novelists or moralists
praise as a virtue, a woman's coldness of constitution, and
want of passion; and make her yield to the ardor of her lover
out of sheer compassion, or to promote a frigid plan of future
comfort, I am disgusted. . . . We cannot, without depraving
our minds, endeavor to please a lover or a husband, but in
proportion as he pleases us. . . . Let us not blush for nature
without a cause!" This extraordinary admission undercuts
the masculine complacency of the judge who tries Maria's

case for divorce. The hypocrisies incorporated by the British legal system perpetuate the wrongs of woman as surely as the sordid practices of houses of prostitution. When Maria pleads her rights to divorce on the grounds that her husband "has violated every moral obligation which binds man to man," the judge finds her argument "newfangled." "What virtuous woman thought of her feelings?" he wonders. *The Wrongs of Woman,* left unfinished, is not the polished work of art towards which its author strove; it probably never would have been even if she had lived to complete it.

Godwin notes in the middle of chapter 5 that the copy incorporating Mary Wollstonecraft's final corrections breaks off there. Throughout the text, bracketed additions occasionally appear when Godwin, by collating different copies of certain passages, attempts to give the fullest possible version of what Mary had written. Some inconsistencies therefore occur in *The Wrongs of Woman* (even before the completed portion of the manuscript ends), particularly in relation to the character of Darnford, with whom she falls in love while they are both wrongly confined in a madhouse and whose prior acquaintance with Maria is alluded to in the third chapter but never explained.

Hoping to give the reader some sense of Mary's ultimate intentions for the novel, Godwin includes a final sequence of sentences and topic headings separated by Roman numerals, with a few last paragraphs that Mary had written out under the notation, "The End." From these scattered phrases, we can deduce that Maria was to be denied a resolution of her problem that would lead to a conventional happy ending. Family ties fail her: although she dutifully provides for her father, society shuns her, and her new pregnancy ends in miscarriage. The world rejects her and so do the men she has known: divorced by her husband, separated from and eventually betrayed by Darnford, she swallows laudanum and calmly waits for death. But the compassion and concern of a female saves her at the last. Jemima, ever faithful, has tracked down the young daughter of Venables and Maria, whose death was falsely given out by Maria's deceiving brother as well as her husband. Maternal strength revives her desire to live; Maria regurgitates and expels the opiate before it takes effect. Weakened but renewed, she proclaims victoriously: "The conflict is over!—I will live for my child!"

No matter how happy the last year of her life with Godwin had been, the personal fulfillment derived from their association could not erase the lessons of three-and-a-half decades of suffering endured because she had been born female. The salvation of Maria, the righting of the wrongs of woman, could be accomplished only in feminine society. Mary Wollstonecraft's final work contains her most radical and disturbing vision: women must be prepared for sexual isolation if they hope to fulfill their own destinies.

THE
WRONGS OF WOMAN:
OR,
MARIA

AUTHOR'S PREFACE

The Wrongs of Woman, like the wrongs of the oppressed part of mankind, may be deemed necessary by their oppressors: but surely there are a few who will dare to advance before the improvement of the age, and grant that my sketches are not the abortion of a distempered fancy, or the strong delineations of a wounded heart.

In writing this novel, I have rather endeavored to portray passions than manners.

In many instances I could have made the incidents more dramatic, would I have sacrificed my main object, the desire of exhibiting the misery and oppression, peculiar to women, that arise out of the partial laws and customs of society.

In the invention of the story, this view restrained my fancy; and the history ought rather to be considered, as of woman, than of an individual.

The sentiments I have embodied.

In many works of this species, the hero is allowed to be mortal, and to become wise and virtuous as well as happy, by a train of events and circumstances. The heroines, on the contrary, are to be born immaculate, and to act like goddesses of wisdom, just come forth highly finished Minervas from the head of Jove.

[Here Godwin added the following passage from a letter Wollstonecraft wrote to a critical male friend.]

For my part, I cannot suppose any situation more distressing, than for a woman of sensibility, with an improving mind, to be bound to such a man as I have described for life; obliged to renounce all the humanizing affections, and to avoid cultivating her taste, lest her perception of grace and refinement of sentiment, should sharpen to agony the pangs of disappointment. Love, in which the imagination mingles its bewitching coloring, must be fostered by delicacy. I should despise, or rather call her an ordinary woman, who could endure such a husband as I have sketched.

These appear to me (matrimonial despotism of heart and conduct) to be the peculiar Wrongs of Woman, because they degrade the mind. What are termed great misfortunes may more forcibly impress the mind of common readers; they have more of what may justly be termed *stage-effect;* but it is the delineation of finer sensations, which, in my opinion, constitutes the merit of our best novels. This is what I have in view; and to show the wrongs of different classes of women, equally oppressive, though, from the difference of education, necessarily various.

CHAPTER 1

Abodes of horror have frequently been described, and castles, filled with specters and chimeras, conjured up by the magic spell of genius to harrow the soul, and absorb the wondering mind. But, formed of such stuff as dreams are made of, what were they to the mansion of despair, in one corner of which Maria sat, endeavoring to recall her scattered thoughts!

Surprise, astonishment that bordered on distraction, seemed to have suspended her faculties, till, waking by degrees to a keen sense of anguish, a whirlwind of rage and indignation roused her torpid pulse. One recollection with frightful velocity following another, threatened to fire her brain, and make her a fit companion for the terrific inhabitants, whose groans and shrieks were no unsubstantial sounds of whistling winds, or startled birds, modulated by a romantic fancy, which amuse while they affright; but such tones of misery as carry a dreadful certainty directly to the heart. What effect must they then have produced on one, true to the touch of sympathy, and tortured by maternal apprehension!

Her infant's image was continually floating on Maria's sight, and the first smile of intelligence remembered, as none but a mother, an unhappy mother, can conceive. She heard her half-speaking half-cooing, and felt the little twinkling fingers on her burning bosom—a bosom bursting with the nutriment for which this cherished child might now be pining in vain. From a stranger she could indeed receive the maternal aliment, Maria was grieved at the thought—but who would watch her with a mother's tenderness, a mother's self-denial?

The retreating shadows of former sorrows rushed back in a gloomy train, and seemed to be pictured on the walls of her prison, magnified by the state of mind in which they were viewed—Still she mourned for her child, lamented she was a daughter, and anticipated the aggravated ills of life that her sex rendered almost inevitable, even while dreading she was no more. To think that she was blotted out of existence was agony, when the imagination had been long employed to expand her faculties; yet to suppose her turned adrift on an unknown sea, was scarcely less afflicting.

After being two days the prey of impetuous, varying emotions, Maria began to reflect more calmly on her present situation, for she had actually been rendered incapable of sober reflection by the discovery of the act of atrocity of which she was the victim. She could not have imagined that, in all the fermentation of civilized depravity, a similar plot could have entered a human mind. She had been stunned by an unexpected blow; yet life, however joyless, was not to be indolently resigned, or misery endured without exertion, and proudly termed patience. She had hitherto meditated only to point the dart of anguish, and suppressed the heart heavings of indignant nature merely by the force of contempt. Now she endeavored to brace her mind to fortitude, and to ask herself what was to be her employment in her dreary cell? Was it not to effect her escape, to fly to the succor of her child, and to baffle the selfish schemes of her tyrant—her husband?

These thoughts roused her sleeping spirit, and the self-possession returned, that seemed to have abandoned her in the infernal solitude into which she had been precipitated. The first emotions of overwhelming impatience began to subside, and resentment gave place to tenderness, and more tranquil meditation; though anger once more stopped the calm current of reflection when she attempted to move her manacled arms. But this was an outrage that could only excite momentary feelings of scorn, which evaporated in a faint smile; for Maria was far from thinking a personal insult the most difficult to endure with magnanimous indifference.

She approached the small grated window of her chamber, and for a considerable time only regarded the blue expanse; though it commanded a view of a desolate garden, and of part of a huge pile of buildings that, after having been suffered, for half a century, to fall to decay, had undergone some clumsy repairs, merely to render it habitable. The ivy had been torn off the turrets, and the stones not wanted to patch up the breaches of time, and exclude the warring elements, left in heaps in the disordered court. Maria contemplated this scene she knew not how long; or rather gazed on the walls, and pondered on her situation. To the master of this most horrid of prisons, she had, soon after her entrance, raved of injustice, in accents that would have justified his treatment, had not a malignant smile, when she appealed to his judgment, with a dreadful conviction stifled her remonstrating complaints. By force, or openly, what could be done? But surely some expedient might occur to an active mind, without any other employment, and possessed of sufficient resolution to put the risk of life into the balance with the chance of freedom.

A woman entered in the midst of these reflections, with a firm, deliberate step, strongly marked features, and large black eyes, which she fixed steadily on Maria's, as if she designed to intimidate her, saying at the same time—"You had better sit down and eat your dinner, than look at the clouds."

"I have no appetite," replied Maria, who had previously determined to speak mildly; "why then should I eat?"

"But, in spite of that, you must and shall eat something. I have had many ladies under my care, who have resolved to starve themselves; but, soon or late, they gave up their intent, as they recovered their senses."

"Do you really think me mad?" asked Maria, meeting the searching glance of her eye.

"Not just now. But what does that prove?—only that you must be the more carefully watched, for appearing at times so reasonable. You have not touched a morsel since you entered the house."—Maria sighed intelligibly.—"Could anything but madness produce such a disgust for food?"

"Yes, grief; you would not ask the question if you knew what it was." The attendant shook her head; and a ghastly smile of desperate fortitude served as a forcible reply, and made Maria pause, before she added—"Yet I will take some refreshment: I mean not to die.—No; I will preserve my senses; and convince even you, sooner than you are aware of, that my intellects have never been disturbed, though the exertion of them may have been suspended by some infernal drug."

Doubt gathered still thicker on the brow of her guard, as she attempted to convict her of mistake.

"Have patience!" exclaimed Maria, with a solemnity that inspired awe. "My God! how have I been schooled into the practice!" A suffocation of voice betrayed the agonizing emotions she was laboring to keep down; and conquering a qualm of disgust, she calmly endeavored to eat enough to prove her docility, perpetually turning to the suspicious female, whose observation she courted, while she was making the bed and adjusting the room.

"Come to me often," said Maria, with a tone of persuasion, in consequence of a vague plan that she had hastily adopted, when, after surveying this woman's form and features, she felt convinced that she had an understanding above the common standard, "and believe me mad, till you are obliged to acknowledge the contrary." The woman was no fool, that is, she was superior to her class; nor had misery quite petrified the life's-blood of humanity, to which reflections on our own misfortunes only give a more orderly course. The manner, rather than the expostulations, of Maria made a slight suspicion dart into her mind with corresponding sympathy, which various other avocations, and the habit of banishing compunction, prevented her, for the present, from examining more minutely.

But when she was told that no person, excepting the physician appointed by her family, was to be permitted to see the lady at the end of the gallery, she opened her keen eyes still wider, and uttered a—"hem!" before she inquired—"Why?" She was briefly told, in reply, that the malady was hereditary, and the fits not occurring but at very long and irregular intervals, she must be carefully watched; for the length of these lucid periods only rendered her more mischievous, when any vexation or caprice brought on the paroxysm of frenzy.

Had her master trusted her, it is probable that neither pity nor curiosity would have made her swerve from the straight line of her interest; for she had suffered too much in her intercourse with mankind, not to determine to look for support, rather to humoring their passions, than courting their approbation by the integrity of her conduct. A deadly blight had met her at the very threshold of existence; and the wretchedness of her mother seemed a heavy weight fastened on her innocent neck, to drag her down to perdition. She could not heroically determine to succor an unfortunate; but, offended at the bare supposition that she could be deceived with the same ease as a common servant, she no longer curbed her curiosity; and, though she never seriously fathomed her own intentions, she would sit, every moment she could steal from observation, listening to the tale, which Maria was eager to relate with all the persuasive eloquence of grief.

It is so cheering to see a human face, even if little of the divinity of virtue beam in it, that Maria anxiously expected the return of the attendant, as of a gleam of light to break the gloom of idleness. Indulged sorrow, she perceived, must blunt or sharpen the faculties to the two opposite extremes; producing stupidity, the moping melancholy of indolence; or the restless activity of a disturbed imagination. She sunk into one state, after being fatigued by the other; till the want of occupation became even more painful than the actual pressure or apprehension of sorrow; and the confinement that froze her into a nook of existence, with an unvaried prospect before her, the most insupportable of evils. The lamp of life seemed to be spending itself to chase the vapors of a dungeon which no art could dissipate.—And to what purpose did she rally all her energy?—Was not the world a vast prison, and women born slaves?

Though she failed immediately to rouse a lively sense of injustice in the mind of her guard, because it had been sophisticated into misanthropy, she touched her heart. Jemima (she had only a claim to a Christian name, which had not procured her any Christian privileges) could patiently hear of Maria's confinement on false pretenses; she had felt the crushing hand of power, hardened by the exercise of injustice, and ceased to wonder at the perversions of the understanding, which systematize oppression; but, when told that her child, only four months old, had been torn from her, even while she was discharging the tenderest maternal office, the woman awoke in a bosom long estranged from feminine emotions, and Jemima determined to alleviate all in her power, without hazarding the loss of her place, the sufferings of a wretched mother, apparently injured, and certainly unhappy. A sense of right seems to result from the simplest act of reason, and to preside over the faculties of the mind, like the master-sense of feeling, to rectify the rest; but (for the comparison may be carried still farther) how often is the exquisite sensibility of both weakened or destroyed by the vulgar occupations, and ignoble pleasures of life?

The preserving her situation was, indeed, an important object to Jemima, who had been hunted from hole to hole, as if she had been a beast of prey, or infected with a moral plague. The wages she received, the greater part of which she hoarded, as her only chance for independence, were much more considerable than she could reckon on obtaining anywhere else, were it possible that she, an outcast from society, could be permitted to earn a subsistence in a reputable family. Hearing Maria perpetually complain of listlessness, and the not being able to beguile grief by resuming her customary pursuits, she was easily prevailed on, by compassion, and that involuntary respect for abilities, which those who possess them can never eradicate, to bring her some books, and implements for writing. Maria's conversation had amused and interested her, and the natural consequence was a desire, scarcely observed by herself, of obtaining the esteem of a person she admired. The remembrance of better days was rendered more lively; and the sentiments then acquired appearing less romantic than they had for a long period, a spark of hope roused her mind to new activity.

How grateful was her attention to Maria! Oppressed by a dead weight of existence, or preyed on by the gnawing worm of discontent, with what eagerness did she endeavor to shorten the long days, which left no traces behind! She seemed to be sailing on the vast ocean of life, without seeing any landmark to indicate the progress of time; to find employment was then to find variety, the animating principle of nature.

CHAPTER 2

Earnestly as Maria endeavored to soothe, by reading, the anguish of her wounded mind, her thoughts would often wander from the subject she was led to discuss, and tears of maternal tenderness obscured the reasoning page. She descanted on "the ills which flesh is heir to," with bitterness, when the recollection of her babe was revived by a tale of fictitious woe, that bore any resemblance to her own; and her imagination was continually employed, to conjure up and embody the various phantoms of misery, which folly and vice had let loose on the world. The loss of her babe was the tender string; against other cruel remembrances she labored to steel her bosom; and even a ray of hope, in the midst of her gloomy reveries, would sometimes gleam on the dark horizon of futurity, while persuading herself that she ought to cease to hope, since happiness was nowhere to be found.—But of her child, debilitated by the grief with which its mother had been assailed before it saw the light, she could not think without an impatient struggle.

"I, alone, by my active tenderness, could have saved," she would exclaim, "from an early blight, this sweet blossom; and, cherishing it, I should have had something still to love."

In proportion as other expectations were torn from her, this tender one had been fondly clung to, and knit into her heart.

The books she had obtained were soon devoured by one who had no other resource to escape from sorrow, and the feverish dreams of ideal wretchedness or felicity, which equally weaken the intoxicated sensibility. Writing was then the only alternative, and she wrote some rhapsodies descriptive of the state of her mind; but the events of her past life pressing on her, she resolved circumstantially to relate them, with the sentiments that experience, and more matured reason, would naturally suggest. They might perhaps instruct her daughter, and shield her from the misery, the tyranny, her mother knew not how to avoid.

This thought gave life to her diction, her soul flowed into it, and she soon found the task of recollecting almost obliterated impressions very interesting. She lived again in the revived emotions of youth, and forgot her present in the retrospect of sorrows that had assumed an unalterable character.

Though this employment lightened the weight of time, yet, never losing sight of her main object, Maria did not allow any opportunity to slip of winning on the affections of Jemima; for she discovered in her a strength of mind that excited her esteem, clouded as it was by the misanthropy of despair.

An insulated being, from the misfortune of her birth, she despised and preyed on the society by which she had been oppressed, and loved not her fellow creatures, because she had never been beloved. No mother had ever fondled her, no father or brother had protected her from outrage; and the man who had plunged her into infamy, and deserted her when she stood in greatest need of support, deigned not to smooth with kindness the road to ruin. Thus degraded was she let loose on the world; and virtue, never nurtured by affection, assumed the stern aspect of selfish independence.

This general view of her life Maria gathered from her exclamations and dry remarks. Jemima indeed displayed a strange mixture of interest and suspicion; for she would listen to her with earnestness, and then suddenly interrupt the conversation, as if afraid of resigning, by giving way to her sympathy, her dear-bought knowledge of the world.

Maria alluded to the possibility of an escape, and mentioned a compensation, or reward; but the style in which she was repulsed made her cautious, and determine not to renew the subject, till she knew more of the character she had to work on. Jemima's countenance, and dark hints, seemed to say, "You are an extraordinary woman; but let me consider, this may only be one of your lucid intervals." Nay, the very energy of Maria's character made her suspect that the extraordinary animation she perceived might be the effect of madness. "Should her husband then substantiate his charge, and get possession of her estate, from whence would come the promised annuity, or more desired protection? Besides, might not a woman, anxious to escape, conceal some of the circumstances which made against her? Was truth to be expected from one who had been entrapped, kidnapped, in the most fraudulent manner?"

In this train Jemima continued to argue, the moment after compassion and respect seemed to make her swerve;

and she still resolved not to be wrought on to do more than soften the rigor of confinement, till she could advance on surer ground.

Maria was not permitted to walk in the garden; but sometimes, from her window, she turned her eyes from the gloomy walls, in which she pined life away, on the poor wretches who strayed along the walks, and contemplated the most terrific of ruins—that of a human soul. What is the view of the fallen column, the moldering arch, of the most exquisite workmanship, when compared with this living memento of the fragility, the instability, of reason, and the wild luxuriancy of noxious passions? Enthusiasm turned adrift, like some rich stream overflowing its banks, rushes forward with destructive velocity, inspiring a sublime concentration of thought. Thus thought Maria—These are the ravages over which humanity must ever mournfully ponder, with a degree of anguish not excited by crumbling marble, or cankering brass, unfaithful to the trust of monumental fame. It is not over the decaying productions of the mind, embodied with the happiest art, we grieve most bitterly. The view of what has been done by man produces a melancholy, yet aggrandizing, sense of what remains to be achieved by human intellect; but a mental convulsion, which, like the devastation of an earthquake, throws all the elements of thought and imagination into confusion, makes contemplation giddy, and we fearfully ask on what ground we ourselves stand.

Melancholy and imbecility marked the features of the wretches allowed to breathe at large; for the frantic, those who in a strong imagination had lost a sense of woe, were closely confined. The playful tricks and mischievous devices of their disturbed fancy that suddenly broke out could not be guarded against, when they were permitted to enjoy any portion of freedom; for, so active was their imagination, that every new object which accidentally struck their senses awoke to frenzy their restless passions, as Maria learned from the burden of their incessant ravings.

Sometimes, with a strict injunction of silence, Jemima would allow Maria, at the close of evening, to stray along the narrow avenues that separated the dungeonlike apartments, leaning on her arm. What a change of scene! Maria wished to pass the threshold of her prison, yet, when by chance she met the eye of rage glaring on her, yet unfaithful to its office, she shrunk back with more horror and affright than if she had stumbled over a mangled corpse. Her busy fancy pictured the misery of a fond heart, watching over a friend thus estranged, absent, though present—over a poor wretch lost to reason and the social joys of existence; and losing all consciousness of misery in its excess. What a task, to watch the light of reason quivering in the eye, or with agonizing expectation to catch the beam of recollection; tantalized by hope, only to feel despair more keenly, at finding a much loved face or voice, suddenly remembered, or pathetically implored, only to be immediately forgotten, or viewed with indifference or abhorrence!

The heartrending sigh of melancholy sunk into her soul; and when she retired to rest, the petrified figures she had encountered, the only human forms she was doomed to observe, haunting her dreams with tales of mysterious wrongs, made her wish to sleep to dream no more.

Day after day rolled away, and tedious as the present moment appeared, they passed in such an unvaried tenor, Maria was surprised to find that she had already been six weeks buried alive, and yet had such faint hopes of effecting her enlargement. She was, earnestly as she had sought for employment, now angry with herself for having been amused by writing her narrative; and grieved to think that she had for an instant thought of anything but contriving to escape.

Jemima had evidently pleasure in her society: still, though she often left her with a glow of kindness, she returned with the same chilling air, and, when her heart appeared for a moment to open, some suggestion of reason forcibly closed it, before she could give utterance to the confidence Maria's conversation inspired.

Discouraged by these changes, Maria relapsed into despondency, when she was cheered by the alacrity with which Jemima brought her a fresh parcel of books; assuring her that she had taken some pains to obtain them from one of the keepers, who attended a gentleman confined in the opposite corner of the gallery.

Maria took up the books with emotion. "They come," said she, "perhaps, from a wretch condemned, like me, to reason on the nature of madness, by having wrecked minds continually under his eye; and almost to wish himself—as I do—mad, to escape from the contemplation of it." Her heart throbbed with sympathetic alarm; and she turned over the leaves with awe, as if they had become sacred from passing through the hands of an unfortunate being, oppressed by a similar fate.

Dryden's *Fables*, Milton's *Paradise Lost*, with several modern productions, composed the collection. It was a mine of treasure. Some marginal notes, in Dryden's *Fables*, caught her attention: they were written with force and taste; and, in one of the modern pamphlets, there was a fragment left, containing various observations on the present state of society and government, with a comparative view of the politics of Europe and America. These remarks were written with a degree of generous warmth, when alluding to the enslaved state of the laboring majority, perfectly in unison with Maria's mode of thinking.

She read them over and over again; and fancy, treacherous fancy, began to sketch a character, congenial with her own, from these shadowy outlines.—"Was he mad?" She reperused the marginal notes, and they seemed the production of an animated, but not of a disturbed imagination. Confined to this speculation, every time she reread them, some fresh refinement of sentiment, or acuteness of thought, impressed her, which she was astonished at herself for not having before observed.

What a creative power has an affectionate heart! There are beings who cannot live without loving, as poets love; and who feel the electric spark of genius, wherever it awakens sentiment or grace. Maria had often thought, when disciplining her wayward heart, "that to charm, was to be virtuous." "They who make me wish to appear the most amiable and good in their eyes must possess in a degree," she would exclaim, "the graces and virtues they call into action."

She took up a book on the powers of the human mind; but her attention strayed from cold arguments on the nature of what she felt, while she was feeling, and she snapped the chain of the theory to read Dryden's *Guiscard and Sigismunda*.

Maria, in the course of the ensuing day, returned some of the books, with the hope of getting others—and more marginal notes. Thus shut out from human intercourse, and compelled to view nothing but the prison of vexed spirits, to meet a wretch in the same situation, was more surely to find a friend, than to imagine a countryman one, in a strange land, where the human voice conveys no information to the eager ear.

"Did you ever see the unfortunate being to whom these books belong?" asked Maria, when Jemima brought her supper. "Yes. He sometimes walks out, between five and six, before the family is stirring, in the morning, with two keepers; but even then his hands are confined."

"What! is he so unruly?" inquired Maria, with an accent of disappointment.

"No, not that I perceive," replied Jemima; "but he has an untamed look, a vehemence of eye, that excites apprehension. Were his hands free, he looks as if he could soon manage both his guards: yet he appears tranquil."

"If he be so strong, he must be young," observed Maria.

"Three or four and thirty, I suppose; but there is no judging of a person in his situation."

"Are you sure that he is mad?" interrupted Maria with eagerness. Jemima quitted the room, without replying.

"No, no, he certainly is not!" exclaimed Maria, answering herself; "the man who could write those observations was not disordered in his intellects."

She sat musing, gazing at the moon, and watching its motion as it seemed to glide under the clouds. Then, preparing for bed, she thought, "Of what use could I be to him, or he to me, if it be true that he is unjustly confined?—Could he aid me to escape, who is himself more closely watched?—Still I should like to see him." She went to bed, dreamed of her child, yet woke exactly at half after five o'clock, and starting up, only wrapped a gown around her, and ran to the window. The morning was chill, it was the latter end of September; yet she did not retire to warm herself and think in bed, till the sound of the servants, moving about the house, convinced her that the unknown would not walk in the garden that morning. She was ashamed at feeling disappointed; and began to reflect, as an excuse to herself, on the little objects which attract attention when there is nothing to divert the mind; and how difficult it was for women to avoid growing romantic, who have no active duties or pursuits.

At breakfast, Jemima inquired whether she understood French, for, unless she did, the stranger's stock of books was exhausted. Maria replied in the affirmative, but forbore to ask any more questions respecting the person to whom they belonged. And Jemima gave her a new subject for contemplation, by describing the person of a lovely maniac, just brought into an adjoining chamber. She was singing the pathetic ballad of old Rob with the most heart-melting falls and pauses. Jemima had half-opened the door, when she distinguished her voice, and Maria stood close to it, scarcely daring to respire, lest a modulation should escape her, so exquisitely sweet, so passionately wild. She began with sympathy to portray to herself another victim, when the lovely warbler flew, as it were, from the spray, and a torrent of unconnected exclamations and questions burst from her, interrupted by fits of laughter so horrid that Maria shut the door, and, turning her eyes up to heaven, exclaimed—"Gracious God!"

Several minutes elapsed before Maria could inquire respecting the rumor of the house (for this poor wretch was obviously not confined without a cause); and then Jemima could only tell her, that it was said, "she had been married, against her inclination to a rich old man, extremely jealous (no wonder, for she was a charming creature); and that, in consequence of his treatment, or something which hung on her mind, she had, during her first lying-in, lost her senses."

What a subject of meditation—even to the very confines of madness.

"Woman, fragile flower! why were you suffered to adorn a world exposed to the inroad of such stormy elements?" thought Maria, while the poor maniac's strain was still breathing on her ear, and sinking into her very soul.

Towards the evening, Jemima brought her Rousseau's *Heloïse;* and she sat reading with eyes and heart, till the return of her guard to extinguish the light. One instance of her kindness was, the permitting Maria to have one, till her own hour of retiring to rest. She had read this work long since; but now it seemed to open a new world to her—the only one worth inhabiting. Sleep was not to be wooed; yet, far from being fatigued by the restless rotation of thought, she rose and opened her window, just as the thin watery clouds of twilight made the long silent shadows visible. The air swept across her face with a voluptuous freshness that thrilled to her heart, awakening indefinable emotions; and the sound of a waving branch, or the twittering of a startled bird, alone broke the stillness of reposing nature. Absorbed by the sublime sensibility which renders the consciousness of existence felicity, Maria was happy, till an autumnal scent, wafted by the breeze of morn from the fallen leaves of the adjacent wood, made her recollect that the season had changed since her confinement; yet life afforded no variety to solace an afflicted heart. She returned dispirited to her couch, and thought of her child till the broad glare of day again invited her to the window. She looked not for the unknown, still how great was her vexation at perceiving the back of a man, certainly he, with his two attendants, as he turned into a side path which led to the house! A confused recollection of having seen somebody who resembled him, immediately occurred, to puzzle and torment her with endless conjectures. Five minutes sooner, and she should have seen his face, and been out of suspense—was ever anything so unlucky! His steady, bold step, and the whole air of his person, bursting as it were from a cloud, pleased her, and gave an outline to the imagination to sketch the individual form she wished to recognize.

Feeling the disappointment more severely than she was willing to believe, she flew to Rousseau, as her only refuge from the idea of him, who might prove a friend, could she but find a way to interest him in her fate; still the personification of St. Preux, or of an ideal lover far superior, was after this imperfect model, of which merely a glance had been caught, even to the minutiae of the coat and hat of the stranger. But if she lent St. Preux, or the demi-god of her fancy, his form, she richly repaid him by the donation of all St. Preux's sentiments and feelings, culled to gratify her own, to which he seemed to have an undoubted right, when she read on the margin of an impassioned letter, written in the well-known hand—"Rousseau alone, the true Prometheus of sentiment, possessed the fire of genius necessary to portray the passion, the truth of which goes so directly to the heart."

Maria was again true to the hour, yet had finished Rousseau, and begun to transcribe some selected passages, unable to quit either the author or the window before she had a glimpse of the countenance she daily longed to see; and, when seen, it conveyed no distinct idea to her mind where she had seen it before. He must have been a transient acquaintance; but to discover an acquaintance was fortunate, could she contrive to attract his attention and excite his sympathy.

Every glance afforded coloring for the picture she was delineating on her heart; and once, when the window was half-open, the sound of his voice reached her. Conviction flashed on her; she had certainly, in a moment of distress, heard the same accents. They were manly, and characteristic of a noble mind; nay, even sweet—or sweet they seemed to her attentive ear.

She started back, trembling, alarmed at the emotion a strange coincidence of circumstances inspired, and wondering why she thought so much of a stranger, obliged as she had been by his timely interference . . . She found however that she could think of nothing else; or, if she thought of her daughter, it was to wish that she had a father whom her mother could respect and love.

CHAPTER 3

When perusing the first parcel of books, Maria had, with her pencil, written in one of them a few exclamations, expressive of compassion and sympathy, which she scarcely remembered, till turning over the leaves of one of the volumes, lately brought to her, a slip of paper dropped out, which Jemima hastily snatched up.

"Let me see it," demanded Maria impatiently. "You surely are not afraid of trusting me with the effusions of a madman?" "I must consider," replied Jemima; and withdrew, with the paper in her hand.

In a life of such seclusion, the passions gain undue force; Maria therefore felt a great degree of resentment and vexation, which she had not time to subdue, before Jemima, returning, delivered the paper.

"Whoever you are, who partake of my fate, accept my sincere commiseration—I would have said protection; but the privilege of man is denied me.

"My own situation forces a dreadful suspicion on my mind—I may not always languish in vain for freedom—say are you—I cannot ask the question; yet I will remember you when my remembrance can be of any use. I will inquire, *why* you are so mysteriously detained—and I *will* have an answer.

"HENRY DARNFORD."

By the most pressing entreaties, Maria prevailed on Jemima to permit her to write a reply to this note. Another and another succeeded, in which explanations were not allowed relative to their present situation; but Maria, with sufficient explicitness, alluded to a former obligation; and they insensibly entered on an interchange of sentiments on the most important subjects. To write these letters was the business of the day, and to receive them the moment of sunshine. By some means, Darnford having discovered Maria's window, when she next appeared at it, he made her, behind his keepers, a profound bow of respect and recognition.

Two or three weeks glided away in this kind of intercourse, during which period Jemima, to whom Maria had given the necessary information respecting her family, had evidently gained some intelligence, which increased her desire of pleasing her charge, though she could not yet determine to liberate her. Maria took advantage of this favorable change, without too minutely inquiring into the cause; and such was her eagerness to hold human converse, and to see her former protector, still a stranger to her, that she incessantly requested her guard to gratify her more than curiosity.

Writing to Darnford, she was led from the sad objects before her, and frequently rendered insensible to the horrid noises around her, which previously had continually employed her feverish fancy. Thinking it selfish to dwell on her own sufferings, when in the midst of wretches who had not only lost all that endears life but their very selves, her imagination was occupied with melancholy earnestness to trace the mazes of misery, through which so many wretches must have passed to this gloomy receptacle of disjointed souls, to the grand source of human corruption. Often at midnight was she waked by the dismal shrieks of demoniac rage, or of excruciating despair, uttered in such wild tones of indescribable anguish as proved the total absence of reason, and roused phantoms of horror in her mind, far more terrific than all that dreaming superstition ever drew. Besides, there was frequently something so inconceivably picturesque in the varying gestures of unrestrained passion, so irresistibly comic in their sallies, or so heart-piercingly pathetic in the little airs they would sing, frequently bursting out after an awful silence, as to fascinate the attention, and amuse the fancy, while torturing the soul. It was the uproar of the passions which she was compelled to observe; and to mark the lucid beam of reason, like a light trembling in a socket, or like the flash which divides the threatening clouds of angry heaven only to display the horrors which darkness shrouded.

Jemima would labor to beguile the tedious evenings, by describing the persons and manners of the unfortunate beings, whose figures or voices awoke sympathetic sorrow in Maria's bosom; and the stories she told were the more interesting, for perpetually leaving room to conjecture something extraordinary. Still Maria, accustomed to generalize her observations, was led to conclude from all she heard, that it was a vulgar error to suppose that people of abilities were the most apt to lose the command of reason. On the contrary, from most of the instances she could investigate, she thought it resulted, that the passions only appeared strong and disproportioned, because the judgment was weak and unexercised; and that they gained strength by the decay of reason, as the shadows lengthen during the sun's decline.

Maria impatiently wished to see her fellow sufferer; but Darnford was still more earnest to obtain an interview. Accustomed to submit to every impulse of passion, and never taught, like women, to restrain the most natural, and acquire, instead of the bewitching frankness of nature, a factitious propriety of behavior, every desire became a torrent that bore down all opposition.

His traveling trunk, which contained the books lent to Maria, had been sent to him, and with a part of its contents he bribed his principal keeper, who, after receiving the most solemn promise that he would return to his apartment without attempting to explore any part of the house, conducted him, in the dusk of the evening, to Maria's room.

Jemima had apprised her charge of the visit, and she expected with trembling impatience, inspired by a vague hope that he might again prove her deliverer, to see a man who had before rescued her from oppression. He entered with an animation of countenance, formed to captivate an enthusiast; and hastily turned his eyes from her to the apartment, which he surveyed with apparent emotions of compassionate indignation. Sympathy illuminated his eye, and, taking her hand, he respectfully bowed on it, exclaiming—"This is extraordinary!—again to meet you, and in such circumstances!" Still, impressive as was the coincidence of events which brought them once more together, their full hearts did not overflow.—*

[And though, after this first visit, they were permitted frequently to repeat their interviews, they were for some time employed in] a reserved conversation, to which all the

*At this point, Godwin noted, "The copy which had received the author's last corrections breaks off in this place, and the pages which follow, to the end of Chap. IV, are printed from a copy in a less finished state."

world might have listened; excepting, when discussing some literary subject, flashes of sentiment, enforced by each relaxing feature, seemed to remind them that their minds were already acquainted.

[By degrees, Darnford entered into the particulars of his story.] In a few words, he informed her that he had been a thoughtless, extravagant young man; yet, as he described his faults, they appeared to be the generous luxuriancy of a noble mind. Nothing like meanness tarnished the luster of his youth, nor had the worm of selfishness lurked in the unfolding bud, even while he had been the dupe of others. Yet he tardily acquired the experience necessary to guard him against future imposition.

"I shall weary you," continued he, "by my egotism; and did not powerful emotions draw me to you,"—his eyes glistened as he spoke, and a trembling seemed to run through his manly frame,—"I would not waste these precious moments in talking of myself.

"My father and mother were people of fashion, married by their parents. He was fond of the turf, she of the card table. I, and two or three other children since dead, were kept at home till we became intolerable. My father and mother had a visible dislike to each other, continually displayed; the servants were of the depraved kind usually found in the houses of people of fortune. My brothers and parents all dying, I was left to the care of guardians; and sent to Eton. I never knew the sweets of domestic affection, but I felt the want of indulgence and frivolous respect at school. I will not disgust you with a recital of the vices of my youth, which can scarcely be comprehended by female delicacy. I was taught to love by a creature I am ashamed to mention; and the other women with whom I afterwards became intimate were of a class of which you can have no knowledge. I formed my acquaintance with them at the theaters; and, when vivacity danced in their eyes, I was not easily disgusted by the vulgarity which flowed from their lips. Having spent, a few years after I was of age, [the whole of] a considerable patrimony, excepting a few hundreds, I had no resource but to purchase a commission in a new-raised regiment, destined to subjugate America. The regret I felt to renounce a life of pleasure, was counterbalanced by the curiosity I had to see America, or rather to travel; [nor had any of those circumstances occurred to my youth which might have been calculated] to bind my country to my heart.

I shall not trouble you with the details of a military life. My
blood was still kept in motion; till, towards the close of the
contest, I was wounded and taken prisoner.

"Confined to my bed, or chair, by a lingering cure, my
only refuge from the preying activity of my mind was books,
which I read with great avidity, profiting by the conversation of my host, a man of sound understanding. My political
sentiments now underwent a total change, and, dazzled by
the hospitality of the Americans, I determined to take up
my abode with freedom. I, therefore, with my usual impetu-
osity, sold my commission, and traveled into the interior
parts of the country, to lay out my money to advantage.
Added to this, I did not much like the puritanical manners
of the large towns. Inequality of condition was there most
disgustingly galling. The only pleasure wealth afforded was
to make an ostentatious display of it; for the cultivation of
the fine arts, or literature, had not introduced into the first
circles that polish of manners which renders the rich so
essentially superior to the poor in Europe. Added to this, an
influx of vices had been let in by the Revolution, and the
most rigid principles of religion shaken to the center, before
the understanding could be gradually emancipated from the
prejudices which led their ancestors undauntedly to seek an
inhospitable clime and unbroken soil. The resolution that
led them, in pursuit of independence, to embark on rivers
like seas, to search for unknown shores, and to sleep under
the hovering mists of endless forests, whose baleful damps
agued their limbs, was now turned into commercial speculations, till the national character exhibited a phenomenon in
the history of the human mind—a head enthusiastically
enterprising, with cold selfishness of heart. And woman,
lovely woman!—they charm everywhere—still there is a
degree of prudery; and a want of taste and ease in the
manners of the American women, that renders them, in
spite of their roses and lilies, far inferior to our European
charmers. In the country, they have often a bewitching
simplicity of character; but, in the cities, they have all the
airs and ignorance of the ladies who give the tone to the
circles of the large trading towns in England. They are fond
of their ornaments, merely because they are good, and not
because they embellish their persons; and are more gratified
to inspire the women with jealousy of these exterior advantages than the men with love. All the frivolity which often
(excuse me, madam) renders the society of modest women so

stupid in England here seemed to throw still more leaden fetters on their charms. Not being an adept in gallantry, I found that I could only keep myself awake in their company by making downright love to them.

"But, not to intrude on your patience, I retired to the track of land which I had purchased in the country, and my time passed pleasantly enough while I cut down the trees, built my house, and planted my different crops. But winter and idleness came, and I longed for more elegant society, to hear what was passing in the world, and to do something better than vegetate with the animals that made a very considerable part of my household. Consequently, I determined to travel. Motion was a substitute for variety of objects; and, passing over immense tracks of country, I exhausted my exuberant spirits, without obtaining much experience. I everywhere saw industry the forerunner and not the consequence of luxury; but this country, everything being on an ample scale, did not afford those picturesque views which a certain degree of cultivation is necessary gradually to produce. The eye wandered without an object to fix upon over immeasureable plains, and lakes that seemed replenished by the ocean, whilst eternal forests of small clustering trees obstructed the circulation of air and embarrassed the path, without gratifying the eye of taste. No cottage smiling in the waste, no travelers hailed us, to give life to silent nature; or if perchance we saw the print of a footstep in our path, it was a dreadful warning to turn aside; and the head ached as if assailed by the scalping knife. The Indians who hovered on the skirts of the European settlements had only learned of their neighbors to plunder, and they stole their guns from them to do it with more safety.

"From the woods and back settlements, I returned to the towns, and learned to eat and drink most valiantly; but without entering into commerce (and I detested commerce) I found I could not live there; and, growing heartily weary of the land of liberty and vulgar aristocracy, seated on her bags of dollars, I resolved once more to visit Europe. I wrote to a distant relation in England, with whom I had been educated, mentioning the vessel in which I intended to sail. Arriving in London, my senses were intoxicated. I ran from street to street, from theater to theater, and the women of the town (again I must beg pardon for my habitual frankness) appeared to me like angels.

"A week was spent in this thoughtless manner, when,

returning very late to the hotel in which I had lodged ever
since my arrival, I was knocked down in a private street,
and hurried, in a state of insensibility, into a coach, which
brought me hither, and I only recovered my senses to be
treated like one who had lost them. My keepers are deaf to
my remonstrances and inquiries, yet assure me that my
confinement shall not last long. Still I cannot guess, though
I weary myself with conjectures, why I am confined, or in
what part of England this house is situated. I imagine sometimes that I hear the sea roar, and wished myself again on
the Atlantic, till I had a glimpse of you."

A few moments were only allowed to Maria to comment
on this narrative, when Darnford left her to her own thoughts,
to the "never ending, still beginning" task of weighing his
words, recollecting his tones of voice, and feeling them re-
verberate on her heart.

CHAPTER 4

Pity, and the forlorn seriousness of adversity, have both
been considered as dispositions favorable to love, while sa-
tirical writers have attributed the propensity to the relaxing
effect of idleness; what chance then had Maria of escaping,
when pity, sorrow, and solitude all conspired to soften her
mind, and nourish romantic wishes, and, from a natural
progress, romantic expectations?

Maria was six-and-twenty. But such was the native sound-
ness of her constitution that time had only given to her
countenance the character of her mind. Revolving thought
and exercised affections had banished some of the playful
graces of innocence, producing insensibly that irregularity
of features which the struggles of the understanding to trace
or govern the strong emotions of the heart are wont to
imprint on the yielding mass. Grief and care had mellowed,
without obscuring, the bright tints of youth, and the thought-
fulness which resided on her brow did not take from the
feminine softness of her features; nay, such was the sensibility which often mantled over it that she frequently appeared,
like a large proportion of her sex, only born to feel; and
activity of her well-proportioned, and even almost voluptuous figure, inspired the idea of strength of mind, rather

than of body. There was a simplicity sometimes indeed in her manner, which bordered on infantine ingenuousness, that led people of common discernment to underrate her talents, and smile at the flights of her imagination. But those who could not comprehend the delicacy of her sentiments were attached by her unfailing sympathy, so that she was very generally beloved by characters of very different descriptions; still, she was too much under the influence of an ardent imagination to adhere to common rules.

There are mistakes of conduct which at five-and-twenty prove the strength of the mind that, ten or fifteen years after, would demonstrate its weakness, its incapacity to acquire a sane judgment. The youths who are satisfied with the ordinary pleasures of life, and do not sigh after ideal phantoms of love and friendship, will never arrive at great maturity of understanding; but if these reveries are cherished, as is too frequently the case with women, when experience ought to have taught them in what human happiness consists, they become as useless as they are wretched. Besides, their pains and pleasures are so dependent on outward circumstances, on the objects of their affections, that they seldom act from the impulse of a nerved mind, able to choose its own pursuit.

Having had to struggle incessantly with the vices of mankind, Maria's imagination found repose in portraying the possible virtues the world might contain. Pygmalion formed an ivory maid, and longed for an informing soul. She, on the contrary, combined all the qualities of a hero's mind, and fate presented a statue in which she might enshrine them.

We mean not to trace the progress of this passion, or recount how often Darnford and Maria were obliged to part in the midst of an interesting conversation. Jemima ever watched on the tiptoe of fear, and frequently separated them on a false alarm, when they would have given worlds to remain a little longer together.

A magic lamp now seemed to be suspended in Maria's prison, and fairy landscapes flitted round the gloomy walls, late so blank. Rushing from the depth of despair, on the seraph wing of hope, she found herself happy. She was beloved, and every emotion was rapturous.

To Darnford she had not shown a decided affection; the fear of outrunning his, a sure proof of love, made her often assume a coldness and indifference foreign from her character; and, even when giving way to the playful emotions of a heart

just loosened from the frozen bond of grief, there was a delicacy
in her manner of expressing her sensibility, which made
him doubt whether it was the effect of love.

One evening, when Jemima left them to listen to the
sound of a distant footstep which seemed cautiously to approach, he seized Maria's hand—it was not withdrawn.
They conversed with earnestness of their situation; and,
during the conversation, he once or twice gently drew her
towards him. He felt the fragrance of her breath, and longed,
yet feared, to touch the lips from which it issued; spirits of
purity seemed to guard them, while all the enchanting graces
of love sported on her cheeks, and languished in her eyes.

Jemima entering, he reflected on his diffidence with poignant regret, and, she once more taking alarm, he ventured,
as Maria stood near his chair, to approach her lips with a
declaration of love. She drew back with solemnity, he hung
down his head abashed; but lifting his eyes timidly, they
met hers; she had determined, during that instant, and
suffered their rays to mingle. He took, with more ardor,
reassured, a half-consenting, half-reluctant kiss, reluctant
only from modesty; and there was a sacredness in her dignified manner of reclining her glowing face on his shoulder,
that powerfully impressed him. Desire was lost in more
ineffable emotions, and to protect her from insult and
sorrow—to make her happy, seemed not only the first wish
of his heart, but the most noble duty of his life. Such angelic
confidence demanded the fidelity of honor; but could he,
feeling her in every pulsation, could he ever change, could
he be a villain? The emotion with which she, for a moment,
allowed herself to be pressed to his bosom, the tear of rapturous sympathy, mingled with a soft melancholy sentiment
of recollected disappointment, said—more of truth and faith-
fulness, than the tongue could have given utterance to in
hours! They were silent—yet discoursed, how eloquently?
till, after a moment's reflection, Maria drew her chair by the
side of his, and, with a composed sweetness of voice, and
supernatural benignity of countenance, said, "I must open
my whole heart to you; you must be told who I am, why I am
here, and why, telling you I am a wife, I blush not to"—the
blush spoke the rest.

Jemima was again at her elbow, and the restraint of her
presence did not prevent an animated conversation, in which
love, sly urchin, was ever at bo-peep.

So much of heaven did they enjoy that paradise bloomed

around them; or they, by a powerful spell, had been transported into Armida's garden. Love, the grand enchanter, "lapt them in Elysium," and every sense was harmonized to joy and social ecstasy. So animated, indeed, were their accents of tenderness, in discussing what, in other circumstances, would have been commonplace subjects, that Jemima felt, with surprise, a tear of pleasure trickling down her rugged cheeks. She wiped it away, half-ashamed; and when Maria kindly inquired the cause, with all the eager solicitude of a happy being wishing to impart to all nature its overflowing felicity, Jemima owned that it was the first tear that social enjoyment had ever drawn from her. She seemed indeed to breathe more freely; the cloud of suspicion cleared away from her brow; she felt herself, for once in her life, treated like a fellow-creature.

Imagination! who can paint thy power; or reflect the evanescent tints of hope fostered by thee? A despondent gloom had long obscured Maria's horizon—now the sun broke forth, the rainbow appeared, and every prospect was fair. Horror still reigned in the darkened cells, suspicion lurked in the passages, and whispered along the walls. The yells of men possessed, sometimes, made them pause, and wonder that they felt so happy, in a tomb of living death. They even chid themselves for such apparent insensibility; still the world contained not three happier beings. And Jemima, after again patrolling the passage, was so softened by the air of confidence which breathed around her, that she voluntarily began an account of herself.

CHAPTER 5

"My father," said Jemima, "seduced my mother, a pretty girl, with whom he lived fellow-servant; and she no sooner perceived the natural, the dreaded consequence, than the terrible conviction flashed on her—that she was ruined. Honesty, and a regard for her reputation, had been the only principles inculcated by her mother; and they had been so forcibly impressed that she feared shame more than the poverty to which it would lead. Her incessant importunities to prevail upon my father to screen her from reproach by marrying her, as he had promised in the fervor of seduction, estranged him from her so completely that her very person became distasteful to him; and he began to hate as well as despise me before I was born.

"My mother, grieved to the soul by his neglect, and unkind treatment, actually resolved to famish herself; and injured her health by the attempt; though she had not sufficient resolution to adhere to her project, or renounce it entirely. Death came not at her call; yet sorrow, and the methods she adopted to conceal her condition, still doing the work of a housemaid, had such an effect on her constitution that she died in the wretched garret, where her virtuous mistress had forced her to take refuge in the very pangs of labor, though my father, after a slight reproof, was allowed to remain in his place—allowed by the mother of six children, who, scarcely permitting a footstep to be heard during her month's indulgence, felt no sympathy for the poor wretch, denied every comfort required by her situation.

"The day my mother died, the ninth after my birth, I was consigned to the care of the cheapest nurse my father could find, who suckled her own child at the same time, and lodged as many more as she could get, in two cellarlike apartments.

"Poverty, and the habit of seeing children die off her hands, had so hardened her heart that the office of a mother did not awaken the tenderness of a woman; nor were the feminine caresses which seem a part of the rearing of a child ever bestowed on me. The chicken has a wing to shelter under; but I had no bosom to nestle in, no kindred warmth to foster me. Left in dirt, to cry with cold and hunger till I was weary, and sleep without ever being prepared by exercise, or lulled by kindness to rest; could I be expected to become anything but a weak and rickety babe? Still, in spite of neglect, I continued to exist, to learn to curse existence, [her countenance grew ferocious as she spoke,] and the treatment that rendered me miserable seemed to sharpen my wits. Confined then in a damp hovel, to rock the cradle of the succeeding tribe, I looked like a little old woman, or a hag shriveling into nothing. The furrows of reflection and care contracted the youthful cheek, and gave a sort of supernatural wildness to the ever watchful eye. During this period, my father had married another fellow servant, who loved him less, and knew better how to manage his passion, than my mother. She likewise proving with child, they agreed to keep a shop: my stepmother, if, being an illegitimate offspring, I may venture thus to characterize her, having obtained a sum of a rich relation, for that purpose.

"Soon after her lying-in, she prevailed on my father to take me home, to save the expense of maintaining me, and of hiring a girl to assist her in the care of the child. I was young, it was true, but appeared a knowing little thing, and might be made handy. Accordingly I was brought to her house; but not to a home—for a home I never knew. Of this child, a daughter, she was extravagantly fond; and it was a part of my employment to assist to spoil her, by humoring all her whims, and bearing all her caprices. Feeling her own consequence, before she could speak, she had learned the art of tormenting me, and if I ever dared to resist, I received blows, laid on with no compunctious hand, or was sent to bed dinnerless, as well as supperless. I said that it was a part of my daily labor to attend this child, with the servility of a slave; still it was but a part. I was sent out in all seasons, and from place to place, to carry burdens far above my strength, without being allowed to draw near the fire, or ever being cheered by encouragement or kindness. No wonder then, treated like a creature of another species, that I began to envy, and at length to hate, the darling of the house. Yet, I perfectly remember, that it was the caresses, and kind expressions of my stepmother, which first excited my jealous discontent. Once, I cannot forget it, when she was calling in vain her wayward child to kiss her, I ran to her, saying, 'I will kiss you, ma'am!' and how did my heart, which was in my mouth, sink, what was my debasement of soul, when pushed away with—'I do not want you, pert thing!' Another day, when a new gown had excited the highest good humor, and she uttered the appropriate *dear*, addressed unexpectedly to me, I thought I could never do enough to please her; I was all alacrity, and rose proportionably in my own estimation.

"As her daughter grew up, she was pampered with cakes and fruit, while I was, literally speaking, fed with the refuse of the table, with her leavings. A liquorish tooth is, I believe, common to children, and I used to steal anything sweet, that I could catch up with a chance of concealment. When detected, she was not content to chastise me herself at the moment, but, on my father's return in the evening (he was a shopman), the principal discourse was to recount my faults, and attribute them to the wicked disposition which I had brought into the world with me, inherited from my

mother. He did not fail to leave the marks of his resentment
on my body, and then solaced himself by playing with my
sister. I could have murdered her at those moments. To save
myself from these unmerciful corrections, I resorted to falsehood, and the untruths which I sturdily maintained were
brought in judgment against me, to support my tyrant's
inhuman charge of my natural propensity to vice. Seeing me
treated with contempt, and always being fed and dressed
better, my sister conceived a contemptuous opinion of me
that proved an obstacle to all affection; and my father,
hearing continually of my faults, began to consider me as a
curse entailed on him for his sins: he was therefore easily
prevailed on to bind me apprentice to one of my stepmother's friends, who kept a slopshop in Wapping. I was represented (as it was said) in my true colors; but she, 'warranted,'
snapping her fingers, 'that she should break my spirit or
heart.'

"My mother replied, with a whine, 'that if anybody could
make me better, it was such a clever woman as herself;
though, for her own part, she had tried in vain; but good
nature was her fault.'

"I shudder with horror when I recollect the treatment I
had now to endure. Not only under the lash of my taskmis-
tress, but the drudge of the maid, apprentices, and children,
I never had a taste of human kindness to soften the rigor of
perpetual labor. I had been introduced as an object of abhorrence into the family; as a creature of whom my stepmother,
though she had been kind enough to let me live in the house
with her own child, could make nothing. I was described as
a wretch, whose nose must be kept to the grinding stone—
and it was held there with an iron grasp. It seemed indeed
the privilege of their superior nature to kick me about, like
the dog or cat. If I were attentive, I was called fawning, if
refractory, an obstinate mule, and like a mule I received
their censure on my loaded back. Often has my mistress, for
some instance of forgetfulness, thrown me from one side of
the kitchen to the other, knocked my head against the wall,
spit in my face, with various refinements on barbarity that I
forbear to enumerate, though they were all acted over again
by the servant, with additional insults, to which the appellation of *bastard* was commonly added, with taunts or sneers.
But I will not attempt to give you an adequate idea of my
situation, lest you, who probably have never been drenched
with the dregs of human misery, should think I exaggerate.

"I stole now, from absolute necessity, bread; yet whatever else was taken, which I had it not in my power to take, was ascribed to me. I was the filching cat, the ravenous dog, the dumb brute, who must bear all; for if I endeavored to exculpate myself, I was silenced, without any inquiries being made, with 'Hold your tongue, you never tell truth.' Even the very air I breathed was tainted with scorn; for I was sent to the neighboring shops with Glutton, Liar, or Thief, written on my forehead. This was, at first, the most bitter punishment; but sullen pride, or a kind of stupid desperation, made me, at length, almost regardless of the contempt, which had wrung from me so many solitary tears at the only moments when I was allowed to rest.

"Thus was I the mark of cruelty till my sixteenth year; and then I have only to point out a change of misery; for a period I never knew. Allow me first to make one observation. Now I look back, I cannot help attributing the greater part of my misery to the misfortune of having been thrown into the world without the grand support of life—a mother's affection. I had no one to love me; or to make me respected, to enable me to acquire respect. I was an egg dropped on the sand; a pauper by nature, hunted from family to family, who belonged to nobody—and nobody cared for me. I was despised from my birth, and denied the chance of obtaining a footing for myself in society. Yes; I had not even the chance of being considered as a fellow creature—yet all the people with whom I lived, brutalized as they were by the low cunning of trade, and the despicable shifts of poverty, were not without bowels, though they never yearned for me. I was, in fact, born a slave, and chained by infamy to slavery during the whole of existence, without having any companions to alleviate it by sympathy, or teach me how to rise above it by their example. But, to resume the thread of my tale—

"At sixteen, I suddenly grew tall, and something like comeliness appeared on a Sunday, when I had time to wash my face, and put on clean clothes. My master had once or twice caught hold of me in the passage; but I instinctively avoided his disgusting caresses. One day, however, when the family were at a Methodist meeting, he contrived to be alone in the house with me, and by blows—yes—blows and menaces compelled me to submit to his ferocious desire; and, to avoid my mistress's fury, I was obliged in future to comply, and skulk to my loft at his command, in spite of increasing loathing.

"The anguish which was now pent up in my bosom seemed to open a new world to me: I began to extend my thoughts beyond myself, and grieve for human misery, till I discovered, with horror—ah! what horror!—that I was with child. I know not why I felt a mixed sensation of despair and tenderness, excepting that, ever called a bastard, a bastard appeared to me an object of the greatest compassion in creation.

"I communicated this dreadful circumstance to my master, who was almost equally alarmed at the intelligence, for he feared his wife, and public censure at the meeting. After some weeks of deliberation had elapsed, I in continual fear that my altered shape would be noticed, my master gave me a medicine in a phial, which he desired me to take, telling me, without any circumlocution, for what purpose it was designed. I burst into tears, I thought it was killing myself—yet was such a self as I worth preserving? He cursed me for a fool, and left me to my own reflections. I could not resolve to take this infernal potion; but I wrapped it up in an old gown, and hid it in a corner of my box.

"Nobody yet suspected me, because they had been accustomed to view me as a creature of another species. But the threatening storm at last broke over my devoted head—never shall I forget it! One Sunday evening when I was left, as usual, to take care of the house, my master came home intoxicated, and I became the prey of his brutal appetite. His extreme intoxication made him forget his customary caution, and my mistress entered and found us in a situation that could not have been more hateful to her than me. Her husband was 'pot-valiant,' he feared her not at the moment, nor had he then much reason, for she instantly turned the whole force of her anger another way. She tore off my cap, scratched, kicked, and buffeted me, till she had exhausted her strength, declaring, as she rested her arm, 'that I had wheedled her husband from her.—But, could anything better be expected from a wretch, whom she had taken into her house out of pure charity?' What a torrent of abuse rushed out, till, almost breathless, she concluded with saying 'that I was born a strumpet; it ran in my blood, and nothing good could come to those who harbored me.'

"My situation was, of course, discovered, and she declared that I should not stay another night under the same roof with an honest family. I was therefore pushed out of doors, and my trumpery thrown after me, when it had been contemptuously examined in the passage, lest I should have stolen anything.

"Behold me then in the street, utterly destitute! Whither could I creep for shelter? To my father's roof I had no claim, when not pursued by shame—now I shrunk back as from death, from my mother's cruel reproaches, my father's execrations. I could not endure to hear him curse the day I was born, though life had been a curse to me. Of death I thought, but with a confused emotion of terror, as I stood leaning my head on a post, and starting at every footstep, lest it should be my mistress coming to tear my heart out. One of the boys of the shop passing by, heard my tale, and immediately repaired to his master, to give him a description of my situation; and he touched the right key—the scandal it would give rise to, if I were left to repeat my tale to every inquirer. This plea came home to his reason, who had been sobered by his wife's rage, the fury of which fell on him when I was out of her reach, and he sent the boy to me with half a guinea, desiring him to conduct me to a house where beggars, and other wretches, the refuse of society, nightly lodged.

"This night was spent in a state of stupefaction, or desperation. I detested mankind, and abhorred myself.

"In the morning I ventured out, to throw myself in my master's way, at his usual hour of going abroad. I approached him, he damned me for a b———, declared I had disturbed the peace of the family, and that he had sworn to his wife never to take any more notice of me. He left me; but, instantly returning, he told me that he should speak to his friend, a parish officer, to get a nurse for the brat I laid to him; and advised me, if I wished to keep out of the house of correction, not to make free with his name.

"I hurried back to my hole, and, rage giving place to despair, sought for the potion that was to procure abortion, and swallowed it, with a wish that it might destroy me, at the same time that it stopped the sensations of newborn life, which I felt with indescribable emotion. My head turned round, my heart grew sick, and in the horrors of approaching dissolution, mental anguish was swallowed up. The effect of the medicine was violent, and I was confined to my bed several days; but, youth and a strong constitution prevailing, I once more crawled out, to ask myself the cruel question, 'Whither I should go?' I had but two shillings left in my pocket, the rest had been expended, by a poor woman who slept in the same room, to pay for my lodging, and purchase the necessaries of which she partook.

"With this wretch I went into the neighboring streets to beg, and my disconsolate appearance drew a few pence from the idle, enabling me still to command a bed; till, recovering from my illness, and taught to put on my rags to the best advantage, I was accosted from different motives, and yielded to the desire of the brutes I met, with the same detestation that I had felt for my still more brutal master. I have since read in novels of the blandishments of seduction, but I had not even the pleasure of being enticed into vice.

"I shall not," interrupted Jemima, "lead your imagination into all the scenes of wretchedness and depravity which I was condemned to view; or mark the different stages of my debasing misery. Fate dragged me through the very kennels of society: I was still a slave, a bastard, a common property. Become familiar with vice, for I wish to conceal nothing from you, I picked the pockets of the drunkards who abused me; and proved by my conduct that I deserved the epithets with which they loaded me at moments when distrust ought to cease.

Detesting my nightly occupation, though valuing, if I may so use the word, my independence, which only consisted in choosing the street in which I should wander, or the roof, when I had money, in which I should hide my head, I was some time before I could prevail on myself to accept of a place in a house of ill fame, to which a girl, with whom I had accidentally conversed in the street, had recommended me. I had been hunted almost into a fever by the watchmen of the quarter of the town I frequented; one, whom I had unwittingly offended, giving the word to the whole pack. You can scarcely conceive the tyranny exercised by these wretches: considering themselves as the instruments of the very laws they violate, the pretext which steels their conscience, hardens their heart. Not content with receiving from us, outlaws of society (let other women talk of favors), a brutal gratification gratuitously as a privilege of office, they extort a tithe of prostitution, and harass with threats the poor creatures whose occupation affords not the means to silence the growl of avarice. To escape from this persecution, I once more entered into servitude.

"A life of comparative regularity restored my health; and— do not start—my manners were improved, in a situation where vice sought to render itself alluring, and taste was cultivated to fashion the person, if not to refine the mind. Besides, the common civility of speech, contrasted with the gross vulgarity to which I had been accustomed, was something like the polish of civilization. I was not shut out from all intercourse of humanity. Still I was galled by the yoke of service, and my mistress often flying into violent fits of passion, made me dread a sudden dismission, which I understood was always the case. I was therefore prevailed on, though I felt a horror of men, to accept the offer of a gentleman, rather in the decline of years, to keep his house, pleasantly situated in a little village near Hampstead.

"He was a man of great talents, and of brilliant wit; but, a worn-out votary of voluptuousness, his desires became fastidious in proportion as they grew weak, and the native tenderness of his heart was undermined by a vitiated imagination. A thoughtless career of libertinism and social enjoyment had injured his health to such a degree that, whatever pleasure his conversation afforded me (and my esteem was ensured by proofs of the generous humanity of his disposition), the being his mistress was purchasing it at a very dear rate. With such a keen perception of the delicacies of sentiment, with an imagination invigorated by the exercise of genius, how could he sink into the grossness of sensuality!

"But, to pass over a subject which I recollect with pain, I must remark to you, as an answer to your often-repeated question, 'Why my sentiments and language were superior to my station?' that I now began to read, to beguile the tediousness of solitude, and to gratify an inquisitive, active mind. I had often, in my childhood, followed a ballad singer, to hear the sequel of a dismal story, though sure of being severely punished for delaying to return with whatever I was sent to purchase. I could just spell and put a sentence together, and I listened to the various arguments, though often mingled with obscenity,—which occurred at the table where I was allowed to preside: for a literary friend or two frequently came home with my master, to dine and pass the night. Having lost the privileged respect of my sex, my presence, instead of restraining, perhaps gave the reins to their tongues; still I had the advantage of hearing discussions from which, in the common course of life, women are excluded.

"You may easily imagine that it was only by degrees that I could comprehend some of the subjects they investigated,

or acquire from their reasoning what might be termed a
moral sense. But my fondness of reading increasing, and my
master occasionally shutting himself up in this retreat, for
weeks together, to write, I had many opportunities of improvement. At first, considering money" ("I was right!" exclaimed Jemima, altering her tone of voice) "as the only
means, after my loss of reputation, of obtaining respect, or
even the toleration of humanity, I had not the least scruple
to secrete a part of the sums entrusted to me, and to screen
myself from detection by a system of falsehood. But, acquiring new principles, I began to have the ambition of returning to the respectable part of society, and was weak enough
to suppose it possible. The attention of my unassuming
instructor, who, without being ignorant of his own powers,
possessed great simplicity of manners, strengthened the il-
lusion. Having sometimes caught up hints for thought, from
my untutored remarks, he often led me to discuss the subjects he was treating, and would read to me his productions,
previous to their publication, wishing to profit by the criticism of unsophisticated feeling. The aim of his writings was
to touch the simple springs of the heart; for he despised the
would-be oracles, the self-elected philosophers, who fright
away fancy, while sifting each grain of thought to prove
that slowness of comprehension is wisdom.

"I should have distinguished this as a moment of sunshine, a happy period in my life, had not the repugnance the
disgusting libertinism of my protector inspired daily become
more painful. And, indeed, I soon did recollect it as such
with agony, when his sudden death (for he had recourse to
the most exhilarating cordials to keep up the convivial tone
of his spirits) again threw me into the desert of human
society. Had he had any time for reflection, I am certain he
would have left the little property in his power to me: but,
attacked by the fatal apoplexy in town, his heir, a man of
rigid morals, brought his wife with him to take possession of
the house and effects, before I was even informed of his
death—'to prevent,' as she took care indirectly to tell me,
'such a creature as she supposed me to be from purloining
any of them, had I been apprised of the event in time.'

"The grief I felt at the sudden shock the information gave
me, which at first had nothing selfish in it, was treated with
contempt, and I was ordered to pack up my clothes; and a
few trinkets and books, given me by the generous deceased,
were contested, while they piously hoped, with a reprobat-

ing shake of the head, 'that God would have mercy on his sinful soul!' With some difficulty, I obtained my arrears of wages; but asking—such is the spirit-grinding consequence of poverty and infamy—for a character for honesty and economy, which God knows I merited, I was told by this— why must I call her woman?—'that it would go against her conscience to recommend a kept mistress.' Tears started in my eyes, burning tears; for there are situations in which a wretch is humbled by the contempt they are conscious they do not deserve.

"I returned to the metropolis; but the solitude of a poor lodging was inconceivably dreary, after the society I had enjoyed. To be cut off from human converse, now I had been taught to relish it, was to wander a ghost among the living. Besides, I foresaw, to aggravate the severity of my fate, that my little pittance would soon melt away. I endeavored to obtain needlework; but, not having been taught early, and my hands being rendered clumsy by hard work, I did not sufficiently excel to be employed by the ready-made linen shops, when so many women, better qualified, were suing for it. The want of a character prevented my getting a place; for, irksome as servitude would have been to me, I should have made another trial, had it been feasible. Not that I disliked employment, but the inequality of condition to which I must have submitted. I had acquired a taste for literature, during the five years I had lived with a literary man, occasionally conversing with men of the first abilities of the age; and now to descend to the lowest vulgarity was a degree of wretchedness not to be imagined unfelt. I had not, it is true, tasted the charms of affection, but I had been familiar with the graces of humanity.

"One of the gentlemen, whom I had frequently dined in company with, while I was treated like a companion, met me in the street, and inquired after my health. I seized the occasion, and began to describe my situation; but he was in haste to join, at dinner, a select party of choice spirits; therefore, without waiting to hear me, he impatiently put a guinea into my hand, saying, 'It was a pity such a sensible woman should be in distress—he wished me well from his soul.'

"To another I wrote, stating my case, and requesting advice. He was an advocate for unequivocal sincerity; and had often, in my presence, descanted on the evils which arise in society from the despotism of rank and riches.

"In reply, I received a long essay on the energy of the human mind, with continual allusions to his own force of character. He added 'that the woman who could write such a letter as I had sent him, could never be in want of resources, were she to look into herself, and exert her powers; misery was the consequence of indolence, and, as to my being shut out from society, it was the lot of man to submit to certain privations."

"How often have I heard," said Jemima, interrupting her narrative, "in conversation, and read in books, that every person willing to work may find employment? It is the vague assertion, I believe, of insensible indolence, when it relates to men; but, with respect to women, I am sure of its fallacy, unless they will submit to the most menial bodily labor; and even to be employed at hard labor is out of the reach of many, whose reputation misfortune or folly has tainted.

"How writers, professing to be friends to freedom and the improvement of morals can assert that poverty is no evil, I cannot imagine."

"No more can I," interrupted Maria, "yet they even expatiate on the peculiar happiness of indigence, though in what it can consist, excepting in brutal rest, when a man can barely earn a subsistence, I cannot imagine. The mind is necessarily imprisoned in its own little tenement; and, fully occupied by keeping it in repair, has not time to rove abroad for improvement. The book of knowledge is closely clasped against those who must fulfill their daily task of severe manual labor or die; and curiosity, rarely excited by thought or information, seldom moves on the stagnate lake of ignorance."

"As far as I have been able to observe," replied Jemima, "prejudices, caught up by chance, are obstinately maintained by the poor, to the exclusion of improvement; they have not time to reason or reflect to any extent, or minds sufficiently exercised to adopt the principles of action, which form perhaps the only basis of contentment in every station."

"And independence," said Darnford, "they are necessarily strangers to, even the independence of despising their persecutors. If the poor are happy, or can be happy, *things are very well as they are*. And I cannot conceive on what principle those writers contend for a change of system, who support this opinion. The authors on the other side of the question are much more consistent, who grant the fact; yet, insisting that it is the lot of the majority to be oppressed in this life, kindly turn them over to another, to rectify the false weights and measures of this, as the only way to justify the dispensations of Providence. I have not," continued Darnford, "an opinion more firmly fixed by observation in my mind, than that, though riches may fail to produce proportionate happiness, poverty most commonly excludes it, by shutting up all the avenues to improvement."

"And as for the affections," added Maria, with a sigh, "how gross, and even tormenting do they become, unless regulated by an improving mind! The culture of the heart ever, I believe, keeps pace with that of the mind. But pray go on," addressing Jemima, "though your narrative gives rise to the most painful reflections on the present state of society."

"Not to trouble you," continued she, "with a detailed description of all the painful feelings of unavailing exertion, I have only to tell you, that at last I got recommended to wash in a few families, who did me the favor to admit me into their houses, without the most strict inquiry, to wash from one in the morning till eight at night, for eighteen or twenty-pence a day. On the happiness to be enjoyed over a washing tub I need not comment; yet you will allow me to observe that this was a wretchedness of situation peculiar to my sex. A man with half my industry, and, I may say, abilities, could have procured a decent livelihood, and discharged some of the duties which knit mankind together; whilst I, who had acquired a taste for the rational, nay, in honest pride let me assert it, the virtuous enjoyments of life, was cast aside as the filth of society. Condemned to labor, like a machine, only to earn bread, and scarcely that, I became melancholy and desperate.

"I have now to mention a circumstance which fills me with remorse, and fear it will entirely deprive me of your esteem. A tradesman became attached to me, and visited me frequently—and I at last obtained such a power over him that he offered to take me home to his house. Consider, dear madam, I was famishing: wonder not that I became a wolf! The only reason for not taking me home immediately was the having a girl in the house, with child by him—and this girl—I advised him—yes, I did! would I could forget it!—to turn out of doors: and one night he determined to follow my advice. Poor wretch! She fell upon her knees, reminded him that he had promised to marry her, that her parents were honest! What did it avail? She was turned out.

"She approached her father's door, in the skirts of London—listened at the shutters—but could not knock. A watchman had observed her go and return several times—Poor wretch! [The remorse Jemima spoke of, seemed to be stinging her to the soul, as she proceeded.]

"She left it, and, approaching a tub where horses were watered, she sat down in it, and, with desperate resolution, remained in that attitude—till resolution was no longer necessary!

"I happened that morning to be going out to wash, anticipating the moment when I should escape from such hard labor. I passed by, just as some men, going to work, drew out the stiff, cold corpse—Let me not recall the horrid moment!—I recognized her pale visage; I listened to the tale told by the spectators, and my heart did not burst. I thought of my own state, and wondered how I could be such a monster! I worked hard; and, returning home, I was attacked by a fever. I suffered both in body and mind. I determined not to live with the wretch. But he did not try me; he left the neighborhood. I once more returned to the washtub.

"Still this state, miserable as it was, admitted of aggravation. Lifting one day a heavy load, a tub fell against my shin, and gave me great pain. I did not pay much attention to the hurt, till it became a serious wound, being obliged to work as usual, or starve. But, finding myself at length unable to stand for any time, I thought of getting into an hospital. Hospitals, it should seem (for they are comfortless abodes for the sick), were expressly endowed for the reception of the friendless; yet I, who had on that plea a right to assistance, wanted the recommendation of the rich and respectable, and was several weeks languishing for admittance; fees were demanded on entering; and, what was still more unreasonable, security for burying me, that expense not coming into the letter of the charity. A guinea was the stipulated sum—I could as soon have raised a million; and I was afraid to apply to the parish for an order, lest they should have passed me, I knew not whither. The poor woman at whose house I lodged, compassionating my state, got me into the hospital; and the family where I received the hurt, sent me five shillings, three and sixpence of which I gave at my admittance—I know not for what.

"My leg grew quickly better; but I was dismissed before

my cure was completed, because I could not afford to have my linen washed to appear decently, as the virago of a nurse said, when the gentlemen (the surgeons) came. I cannot give you an adequate idea of the wretchedness of an hospital; everything is left to the care of people intent on gain. The attendants seem to have lost all feeling of compassion in the bustling discharge of their offices; death is so familiar to them that they are not anxious to ward it off. Everything appeared to be conducted for the accommodation of the medical men and their pupils, who came to make experiments on the poor, for the benefit of the rich. One of the physicians, I must not forget to mention, gave me half a crown, and ordered me some wine, when I was at the lowest ebb. I thought of making my case known to the ladylike matron, but her forbidding countenance prevented me. She condescended to look on the patients, and make general inquiries, two or three times a week; but the nurses knew the hour when the visit of ceremony would commence, and everything was as it should be.

"After my dismission, I was more at a loss than ever for a subsistence, and, not to weary you with a repetition of the same unavailing attempts, unable to stand at the washing tub, I began to consider the rich and poor as natural enemies, and became a thief from principle. I could not now cease to reason, but I hated mankind. I despised myself, yet I justified my conduct. I was taken, tried, and condemned to six months' imprisonment in a house of correction My soul recoils with horror from the remembrance of the insults I had to endure, till, branded with shame, I was turned loose in the street, penniless. I wandered from street to street, till, exhausted by hunger and fatigue, I sunk down senseless at a door, where I had vainly demanded a morsel of bread. I was sent by the inhabitant to the workhouse, to which he had surlily bid me go, saying, he 'paid enough in conscience to the poor,' when, with parched tongue, I implored his charity. If those well-meaning people who exclaim against beggars, were acquainted with the treatment the poor receive in many of these wretched asylums, they would not stifle so easily involuntary sympathy, by saying that they have all parishes to go to, or wonder that the poor dread to enter the gloomy walls. What are the common run of workhouses, but prisons, in which many respectable old people, worn out by immoderate labor, sink into the grave in sorrow, to which they are carried like dogs!"

Alarmed by some indistinct noise, Jemima rose hastily to

listen, and Maria, turning to Darnford, said, "I have indeed been shocked beyond expression when I have met a pauper's funeral. A coffin carried on the shoulders of three or four ill-looking wretches, whom the imagination might easily convert into a band of assassins, hastening to conceal the corpse, and quarreling about the prey on their way. I know it is of little consequence how we are consigned to the earth; but I am led by this brutal insensibility, to what even the animal creation appears forcibly to feel, to advert to the wretched, deserted manner in which they died."

"True," rejoined Darnford, "and, till the rich will give more than a part of their wealth, till they will give time and attention to the wants of the distressed, never let them boast of charity. Let them open their hearts, and not their purses, and employ their minds in the service, if they are really actuated by humanity; or charitable institutions will always be the prey of the lowest order of knaves."

Jemima, returning, seemed in haste to finish her tale. "The overseer farmed the poor of different parishes, and out of the bowels of poverty was wrung the money with which he purchased this dwelling, as a private receptacle for madness. He had been a keeper at a house of the same description, and conceived that he could make money much more readily in his old occupation. He is a shrewd—shall I say it?—villain. He observed something resolute in my manner, and offered to take me with him, and instruct me how to treat the disturbed minds he meant to entrust to my care. The offer of forty pounds a year, and to quit a workhouse, was not to be despised, though the condition of shutting my eyes and hardening my heart was annexed to it.

"I agreed to accompany him; and four years have I been attendant on many wretches, and"—she lowered her voice—"the witness of many enormities. In solitude my mind seemed to recover its force, and many of the sentiments which I imbibed in the only tolerable period of my life returned with their full force. Still, what should induce me to be the champion for suffering humanity? Who ever risked anything for me? Who ever acknowledged me to be a fellow creature?"

Maria took her hand, and Jemima, more overcome by kindness than she had ever been by cruelty, hastened out of the room to conceal her emotions.

Darnford soon after heard his summons, and, taking leave of him, Maria promised to gratify his curiosity, with respect to herself, the first opportunity.

CHAPTER 6

Active as love was in the heart of Maria, the story she had just heard made her thoughts take a wider range. The opening buds of hope closed, as if they had put forth too early, and the happiest day of her life was overcast by the most melancholy reflections. Thinking of Jemima's peculiar fate and her own, she was led to consider the oppressed state of women, and to lament that she had given birth to a daughter. Sleep fled from her eyelids while she dwelt on the wretchedness of unprotected infancy, till sympathy with Jemima changed to agony, when it seemed probable that her own babe might even now be in the very state she so forcibly described.

Maria thought, and thought again. Jemima's humanity had rather been benumbed than killed, by the keen frost she had to brave at her entrance into life; an appeal then to her feelings, on this tender point, surely would not be fruitless; and Maria began to anticipate the delight it would afford her to gain intelligence of her child. This project was now the only subject of reflection; and she watched impatiently for the dawn of day, with that determinate purpose which generally ensures success.

At the usual hour, Jemima brought her breakfast, and a tender note from Darnford. She ran her eye hastily over it, and her heart calmly hoarded up the rapture a fresh assurance of affection, affection such as she wished to inspire, gave her, without diverting her mind a moment from its design. While Jemima waited to take away the breakfast, Maria alluded to the reflections that had haunted her during the night to the exclusion of sleep. She spoke with energy of Jemima's unmerited sufferings, and of the fate of a number of deserted females, placed within the sweep of a whirlwind, from which it was next to impossible to escape. Perceiving the effect her conversation produced on the countenance of her guard, she grasped the arm of Jemima with that irresistible warmth which defies repulse, exclaiming—
"With your heart, and such dreadful experience, can you lend your aid to deprive my babe of a mother's tenderness, a mother's care? In the name of God, assist me to snatch her

from destruction! Let me but give her an education—let me but prepare her body and mind to encounter the ills which await her sex, and I will teach her to consider you as her second mother, and herself as the prop of your age. Yes, Jemima, look at me—observe me closely, and read my very soul; you merit a better fate"—she held out her hand with a firm gesture of assurance—"and I will procure it for you, as a testimony of my esteem, as well as of my gratitude."

Jemima had not power to resist this persuasive torrent; and, owning that the house in which she was confined was situated on the banks of the Thames, only a few miles from London, and not on the seacoast, as Darnford had supposed, she promised to invent some excuse for her absence, and go herself to trace the situation, and inquire concerning the health, of this abandoned daughter. Her manner implied an intention to do something more, but she seemed unwilling to impart her design; and Maria, glad to have obtained the main point, thought it best to leave her to the workings of her own mind; convinced that she had the power of interesting her still more in favor of herself and child by a simple recital of facts.

In the evening, Jemima informed the impatient mother that on the morrow she should hasten to town before the family hour of rising, and received all the information necessary, as a clue to her search. The "Good night!" Maria uttered was peculiarly solemn and affectionate. Glad expectation sparkled in her eye; and, for the first time since her detention, she pronounced the name of her child with pleasureable fondness; and, with all the garrulity of a nurse, described her first smile when she recognized her mother. Recollecting herself, a still kinder "Adieu!" with a "God bless you!" that seemed to include a maternal benediction, dismissed Jemima.

The dreary solitude of the ensuing day, lengthened by impatiently dwelling on the same idea, was intolerably wearisome. She listened for the sound of a particular clock, which some directions of the wind allowed her to hear distinctly. She marked the shadow gaining on the wall; and, twilight thickening into darkness, her breath seemed oppressed while she anxiously counted nine. The last sound was a stroke of despair on her heart; for she expected every moment, without seeing Jemima, to have her light extinguished by the savage female who supplied her place. She was even obliged to prepare for bed, restless as she was, not to dislodge her new attendant. She had been cautioned not to speak too freely to her; but the caution was needless, her countenance would still more emphatically have made her shrink back. Such was the ferocity of manner, conspicuous in every word and gesture of this hag, that Maria was afraid to inquire why Jemima, who had faithfully promised to see her before her door was shut for the night, came not?—and, when the key turned in the lock, to consign her to a night of suspense, she felt a degree of anguish which the circumstances scarcely justified.

Continually on the watch, the shutting of a door, or the sound of a footstep, made her start and tremble with apprehension, something like what she felt, when, at her entrance, dragged along the gallery, she began to doubt whether she were not surrounded by demons?

Fatigued by an endless rotation of thought and wild alarms, she looked like a specter when Jemima entered in the morning; especially as her eyes darted out of her head, to read in Jemima's countenance, almost as pallid, the intelligence she dared not trust her tongue to demand. Jemima put down the tea things, and appeared very busy in arranging the table. Maria took up a cup with trembling hand, then forcibly recovering her fortitude, and restraining the convulsive movement which agitated the muscles of her mouth, she said, "Spare yourself the pain of preparing me for your information, I adjure you!—My child is dead!" Jemima solemnly answered, "Yes;" with a look expressive of compassion and angry emotions. "Leave me," added Maria, making a fresh effort to govern her feelings, and hiding her face in her handkerchief, to conceal her anguish—"It is enough—I know that my babe is no more—I will hear the particulars when I am"—*calmer,* she could not utter; and Jemima, without importuning her by idle attempts to console her, left the room.

Plunged in the deepest melancholy, she would not admit Darnford's visits; and such is the force of early associations even on strong minds, that, for a while, she indulged the superstitious notion that she was justly punished by the death of her child, for having for an instant ceased to regret her loss. Two or three letters from Darnford, full of soothing, manly tenderness, only added poignancy to these accusing emotions; yet the passionate style in which he expressed what he termed the first and fondest wish of his heart, "that his affection might make her some amends for the cruelty and injustice she had endured," inspired a sentiment of gratitude to heaven; and her eyes filled with delicious tears, when, at the conclusion of his letter, wishing to supply the place of her unworthy relations, whose want of principle he execrated, he assured her, calling her his dearest girl, "that it should henceforth be the business of his life to make her happy."

He begged, in a note sent the following morning, to be permitted to see her, when his presence would be no intrusion on her grief; and so earnestly entreated to be allowed, according to promise, to beguile the tedious moments of absence, by dwelling on the events of her past life, that she sent him the memoirs which had been written for her daughter, promising Jemima the perusal as soon as he returned them.

CHAPTER 7

"Addressing these memoirs to you, my child, uncertain whether I shall ever have an opportunity of instructing you, many observations will probably flow from my heart, which only a mother—a mother schooled in misery—could make.

"The tenderness of a father who knew the world, might be great; but could it equal that of a mother—of a mother, laboring under a portion of the misery, which the constitution of society seems to have entailed on all her kind? It is, my child, my dearest daughter, only such a mother who will dare to break through all restraint to provide for your happiness—who will voluntarily brave censure herself, to ward off sorrow from your bosom. From my narrative, my dear girl, you may gather the instruction, the counsel, which is meant rather to exercise than influence your mind. Death may snatch me from you before you can weigh my advice or enter into my reasoning: I would then, with fond anxiety, lead you very early in life to form your grand principle of action, to save you from the vain regret of having, through irresolution, let the spring tide of existence pass away, unimproved, unenjoyed. Gain experience—ah! gain it—while experience is worth having, and acquire sufficient fortitude to pursue your own happiness; it includes your utility, by a direct path. What is wisdom too often but the owl of the goddess, who sits moping in a desolated heart; around me she shrieks, but I would invite all the gay warblers of spring to nestle in your blooming bosom. Had I not wasted years in deliberating, after I ceased to doubt, how I ought to have acted—I might now be useful and happy. For my sake, warned by my example, always appear what you are, and you will not pass through existence without enjoying its genuine blessings, love and respect.

"Born in one of the most romantic parts of England, an enthusiastic fondness for the varying charms of nature is the first sentiment I recollect; or rather it was the first consciousness of pleasure that employed and formed my imagination.

"My father had been a captain of a man of war; but, disgusted with the service, on account of the preferment of men whose chief merit was their family connections or borough interest, he retired into the country; and, not knowing what to do with himself—married. In his family, to regain his lost consequence, he determined to keep up the same passive obedience as in the vessels in which he had commanded. His orders were not to be disputed; and the whole house was expected to fly, at the word of command, as if to man the shrouds, or mount aloft in an elemental strife, big with life or death. He was to be instantaneously obeyed, especially by my mother, whom he very benevolently married for love; but took care to remind her of the obligation, when she dared, in the slightest instance, to question his absolute authority. My eldest brother, it is true, as he grew up, was treated with more respect by my father; and became in due form the deputy tyrant of the house. The representative of my father, a being privileged by nature—a boy, and the darling of my mother, he did not fail to act like an heir apparent. Such indeed was my mother's extravagant partiality that, in comparison with her affection for him, she might be said not to love the rest of her children. Yet none of the children seemed to have so little affection for her. Extreme indulgence had rendered him so selfish that he only thought of himself; and from tormenting insects and animals, he became the despot of his brothers, and still more of his sisters.

"It is perhaps difficult to give you an idea of the petty cares which obscured the morning of my life; continual restraint in the most trivial matters; unconditional submission to orders, which, as a mere child, I soon discovered to be unreasonable, because inconsistent and contradictory. Thus are we destined to experience a mixture of bitterness, with the recollection of our most innocent enjoyments.

"The circumstances which, during my childhood, occurred to fashion my mind, were various; yet, as it would probably afford me more pleasure to revive the fading remembrance of newborn delight, than you, my child, could feel in the perusal, I will not entice you to stray with me into the verdant meadow, to search for the flowers that youthful hopes scatter in every path; though, as I write, I almost scent the fresh green of spring—of that spring which never returns!

"I had two sisters, and one brother, younger than myself; my brother Robert was two years older, and might truly be termed the idol of his parents, and the torment of the rest of the family. Such indeed is the force of prejudice that what was called spirit and wit in him was cruelly repressed as forwardness in me.

"My mother had an indolence of character which prevented her from paying much attention to our education. But the healthy breeze of a neighboring heath, on which we bounded at pleasure, volatilized the humors that improper food might have generated. And to enjoy open air and freedom was paradise after the unnatural restraint of our fireside, where we were often obliged to sit three or four hours together, without daring to utter a word, when my father was out of humor, from want of employment, or of a variety of boisterous amusement. I had however one advantage, an instructor, the brother of my father, who, intended for the church, had of course received a liberal education. But, becoming attached to a young lady of great beauty and large fortune, and acquiring in the world some opinions not consonant with the profession for which he was designed, he accepted, with the most sanguine expectations of success, the offer of a nobleman to accompany him to India, as his confidential secretary.

"A correspondence was regularly kept up with the object of his affection; and the intricacies of business, peculiarly wearisome to a man of a romantic turn of mind, contributed, with a forced absence, to increase his attachment. Every other passion was lost in this master one, and only served to swell the torrent. Her relations, such were his waking dreams, who had despised him, would court in their turn his alliance, and all the blandishments of taste would grace the triumph of love. While he basked in the warm sunshine of love, friendship also promised to shed its dewy freshness; for a friend, whom he loved next to his mistress, was the confidant, who forwarded the letters from one to the other, to elude the observation of prying relations. A friend false in similar circumstances, is, my dearest girl, an old tale; yet, let not this example, or the frigid caution of coldblooded moralists, make you endeavor to stifle hopes, which are the buds that naturally unfold themselves during the spring of life! Whilst your own heart is sincere, always expect to meet one glowing with the same sentiments; for to fly from pleasure, is not to avoid pain!

"My uncle realized, by good luck, rather than management, a handsome fortune; and returning on the wings of love, lost in the most enchanting reveries, to England, to share it with his mistress and his friend, he found them—united.

"There were some circumstances, not necessary for me to recite, which aggravated the guilt of the friend beyond measure, and the deception, that had been carried on to the last moment, was so base, it produced the most violent effect on my uncle's health and spirits. His native country, the world! lately a garden of blooming sweets, blasted by treachery, seemed changed into a parched desert, the abode of hissing serpents. Disappointment rankled in his heart; and, brooding over his wrongs, he was attacked by a raging fever, followed by a derangement of mind, which only gave place to habitual melancholy as he recovered more strength of body.

"Declaring an intention never to marry, his relations were ever clustering about him, paying the grossest adulation to a man, who, disgusted with mankind, received them with scorn, or bitter sarcasms. Something in my countenance pleased him, when I began to prattle. Since his return, he appeared dead to affection; but I soon, by showing him innocent fondness, became a favorite; and endeavoring to enlarge and strengthen my mind, I grew dear to him in proportion as I imbibed his sentiments. He had a forcible manner of speaking, rendered more so by a certain impressive wildness of look and gesture, calculated to engage the attention of a young and ardent mind. It is not then surprising that I quickly adopted his opinions in preference, and reverenced him as one of a superior order of beings. He inculcated, with great warmth, self-respect, and a lofty consciousness of acting right, independent of the censure or applause of the world; nay, he almost taught me to brave, and even despise its censure, when convinced of the rectitude of my own intentions.

"Endeavoring to prove to me that nothing which deserved the name of love or friendship existed in the world, he drew such animated pictures of his own feelings, rendered permanent by disappointment, as imprinted the sentiments strongly on my heart, and animated my imagination. These remarks are necessary to elucidate some peculiarities in my character, which by the world are indefinitely termed romantic.

"My uncle's increasing affection led him to visit me often. Still, unable to rest in any place, he did not remain long in the country to soften domestic tyranny; but he brought me books, for which I had a passion, and they conspired with his conversation to make me form an ideal picture of life. I shall pass over the tyranny of my father, much as I suffered from it; but it is necessary to notice that it undermined my mother's health; and that her temper, continually irritated by domestic bickering, became intolerably peevish.

"My eldest brother was articled to a neighboring attorney, the shrewdest, and, I may add, the most unprincipled man in that part of the country. As my brother generally came home every Saturday, to astonish my mother by exhibiting his attainments, he gradually assumed a right of directing the whole family, not excepting my father. He seemed to take a peculiar pleasure in tormenting and humbling me; and if I ever ventured to complain of this treatment to either my father or mother, I was rudely rebuffed for presuming to judge of the conduct of my eldest brother.

"About this period a merchant's family came to settle in our neighborhood. A mansionhouse in the village, lately purchased, had been preparing the whole spring, and the sight of the costly furniture, sent from London, had excited my mother's envy, and roused my father's pride. My sensations were very different, and all of a pleasurable kind. I longed to see new characters, to break the tedious monotony of my life; and to find a friend, such as fancy had portrayed. I cannot then describe the emotion I felt, the Sunday they made their appearance at church. My eyes were riveted on the pillar round which I expected first to catch a glimpse of them, and darted forth to meet a servant who hastily preceded a group of ladies, whose white robes and waving plumes seemed to stream along the gloomy aisle, diffusing the light by which I contemplated their figures.

"We visited them in form; and I quickly selected the eldest daughter for my friend. The second son, George, paid me particular attention, and finding his attainments and manners superior to those of the young men of the village, I began to imagine him superior to the rest of mankind. Had my home been more comfortable, or my previous acquaintance more numerous, I should not probably have been so eager to open my heart to new affections.

"Mr. Venables, the merchant, had acquired a large fortune by unremitting attention to business; but his health declining rapidly, he was obliged to retire, before his son, George, had acquired sufficient experience to enable him to conduct their affairs on the same prudential plan his father had invariably pursued. Indeed, he had labored to throw off his authority, having despised his narrow plans and cautious speculation. The eldest son could not be prevailed on to enter the firm; and, to oblige his wife, and have peace in the house, Mr. Venables had purchased a commission for him in the guards.

"I am now alluding to circumstances which came to my knowledge long after; but it is necessary, my dearest child, that you should know the character of your father, to prevent your despising your mother; the only parent inclined to discharge a parent's duty. In London, George had acquired habits of libertinism, which he carefully concealed from his father and his commercial connections. The mask he wore was so complete a covering of his real visage that the praise his father lavished on his conduct, and, poor mistaken man! on his principles, contrasted with his brother's, rendered the notice he took of me peculiarly flattering. Without any fixed design, as I am now convinced, he continued to single me out at the dance, press my hand at parting, and utter expressions of unmeaning passion, to which I gave a meaning naturally suggested by the romantic turn of my thoughts. His stay in the country was short; his manners did not entirely please me; but, when he left us, the coloring of my picture became more vivid—Whither did not my imagination lead me? In short, I fancied myself in love—in love with the disinterestedness, fortitude, generosity, dignity, and humanity, with which I had invested the hero I dubbed. A circumstance which soon after occurred rendered all these

virtues palpable. [The incident is perhaps worth relating on
other accounts, and therefore I shall describe it distinctly.]

"I had a great affection for my nurse, old Mary, for whom
I used often to work, to spare her eyes. Mary had a younger
sister, married to a sailor, while she was suckling me; for
my mother only suckled my eldest brother, which might be
the cause of her extraordinary partiality. Peggy, Mary's
sister, lived with her, till her husband, becoming a mate in
a West Indian trader, got a little before-hand in the world.
He wrote to his wife from the first port in the Channel, after
his most successful voyage, to request her to come to London
to meet him; he even wished her to determine on living
there for the future, to save him the trouble of coming to her
the moment he came on shore; and to turn a penny by
keeping a greenstall. It was too much to set out on a journey
the moment he had finished a voyage, and fifty miles by
land was worse than a thousand leagues by sea.

"She packed up her alls, and came to London—but did not
meet honest Daniel. A common misfortune prevented her,
and the poor are bound to suffer for the good of their country—
he was pressed in the river—and never came on shore.

"Peggy was miserable in London, not knowing, as she
said, 'the face of any living soul.' Besides, her imagination
had been employed, anticipating a month or six weeks' happiness with her husband. Daniel was to have gone with her
to Sadler's Wells and Westminster Abbey, and to many
sights, which he knew she never heard of in the country.
Peggy too was thrifty, and how could she manage to put his
plan in execution alone? He had acquaintance; but she did
not know the very name of their places of abode. His letters
were made up of—How do you does, and God bless yous—
information was reserved for the hour of meeting.

"She too had her portion of information, near at heart.
Molly and Jacky were grown such little darlings, she was
almost angry that daddy did not see their tricks. She had
not half the pleasure she should have had from their prattle,
could she have recounted to him each night the pretty
speeches of the day. Some stories, however, were stored
up—and Jacky could say papa with such a sweet voice, it
must delight his heart. Yet when she came, and found no
Daniel to greet her, when Jacky called papa, she wept,
bidding 'God bless his innocent soul, that did not know what
sorrow was.' But more sorrow was in store for Peggy, inno-

cent as she was. Daniel was killed in the first engagement, and then the *papa* was agony, sounding to the heart.

"She had lived sparingly on his wages, while there was any hope of his return; but, that gone, she returned with a breaking heart to the country, to a little market town nearly three miles from our village. She did not like to go to service, to be snubbed about, after being her own mistress. To put her children out to nurse was impossible: how far would her wages go? and to send them to her husband's parish, a distant one, was to lose her husband twice over.

"I had heard all from Mary, and made my uncle furnish a little cottage for her, to enable her to sell—so sacred was poor Daniel's advice, now he was dead and gone—a little fruit, toys, and cakes. The minding of the shop did not require her whole time, nor even the keeping her children clean, and she loved to see them clean; so she took in washing, and altogether made a shift to earn bread for her children, still weeping for Daniel, when Jacky's arch looks made her think of his father. It was pleasant to work for her children. 'Yes; from morning till night, could she have had a kiss from their father, God rest his soul! Yes; had it pleased Providence to have let him come back without a leg or an arm, it would have been the same thing to her—for she did not love him because he maintained them—no; she had hands of her own.'

"The country people were honest, and Peggy left her linen out to dry very late. A recruiting party, as she supposed, passing through, made free with a large wash; for it was all swept away, including her own and her children's little stock.

"This was a dreadful blow; two dozen of shirts, stocks, and handkerchiefs. She gave the money which she had laid by for half a year's rent, and promised to pay two shillings a week till all was cleared; so she did not lose her employment. This two shillings a week, and the buying a few necessaries for the children, drove her so hard, that she had not a penny to pay her rent with, when a twelvemonth's became due.

"She was now with Mary, and had just told her tale, which Mary instantly repeated—it was intended for my ear. Many houses in this town, producing a borough-interest, were included in the estate purchased by Mr. Venables, and the attorney with whom my brother lived, was appointed his agent, to collect and raise the rents.

"He demanded Peggy's, and, in spite of her entreaties, her poor goods had been seized and sold. So that she had not, and what was worse her children, 'for she had known sorrow enough,' a bed to lie on. She knew that I was good-natured—right charitable, yet not liking to ask for more than needs must, she scorned to petition while people could anyhow be made to wait. But now, should she be turned out of doors, she must expect nothing less than to lose all her customers, and then she must beg or starve—and what would become of her children?—'had Daniel not been pressed—but God knows best—all this could not have happened.'

"I had two mattresses on my bed; what did I want with two, when such a worthy creature must lie on the ground? My mother would be angry, but I could conceal it till my uncle came down; and then I would tell him all the whole truth, and if he absolved me, heaven would.

"I begged the housemaid to come upstairs with me (servants always feel for the distresses of poverty, and so would the rich if they knew what it was). She assisted me to tie up the mattress; I discovering, at the same time, that one blanket would serve me till winter, could I persuade my sister, who slept with me, to keep my secret. She entering in the midst of the package, I gave her some new feathers, to silence her. We got the mattress down the back stairs, unperceived, and I helped to carry it, taking with me all the money I had, and what I could borrow from my sister.

"When I got to the cottage, Peggy declared that she would not take what I had brought secretly; but when, with all the eager eloquence inspired by a decided purpose, I grasped her hand with weeping eyes, assuring her that my uncle would screen me from blame, when he was once more in the country, describing, at the same time, what she would suffer in parting with her children, after keeping them so long from being thrown on the parish, she reluctantly consented.

"My project of usefulness ended not here; I determined to speak to the attorney; he frequently paid me compliments. His character did not intimidate me; but, imagining that Peggy must be mistaken, and that no man could turn a deaf ear to such a tale of complicated distress, I determined to walk to the town with Mary the next morning, and request him to wait for the rent, and keep my secret, till my uncle's return.

"My repose was sweet; and, waking with the first dawn of

day, I bounded to Mary's cottage. What charms do not a light heart spread over nature! Every bird that twittered in a bush, every flower that enlivened the hedge, seemed placed there to awaken me to rapture—yes, to rapture. The present moment was full-fraught with happiness; and on futurity I bestowed not a thought, excepting to anticipate my success with the attorney.

"This man of the world, with rosy face and simpering features, received me politely, nay kindly; listened with complacency to my remonstrances, though he scarcely heeded Mary's tears. I did not then suspect that my eloquence was in my complexion, the blush of seventeen, or that, in a world where humanity to women is the characteristic of advancing civilization, the beauty of a young girl was so much more interesting than the distress of an old one. Pressing my hand, he promised to let Peggy remain in the house as long as I wished. I more than returned the pressure—I was so grateful and so happy. Emboldened by my innocent warmth, he then kissed me—and I did not draw back—I took it for a kiss of charity.

"Gay as a lark, I went to dine at Mr. Venables'. I had previously obtained five shillings from my father, towards reclothing the poor children of my care, and prevailed on my mother to take one of the girls into the house, whom I determined to teach to work and read.

"After dinner, when the younger part of the circle retired to the music room, I recounted with energy my tale; that is, I mentioned Peggy's distress, without hinting at the steps I had taken to relieve her. Miss Venables gave me half a crown; the heir five shillings; but George sat unmoved. I was cruelly distressed by the disappointment—I scarcely could remain on my chair; and, could I have got out of the room unperceived, I should have flown home, as if to run away from myself. After several vain attempts to rise, I leaned my head against the marble chimney-piece, and gazing on the evergreens that filled the fireplace, moralized on the vanity of human expectations; regardless of the company. I was roused by a gentle tap on my shoulder from behind Charlotte's chair. I turned my head, and George slid a guinea into my hand, putting his finger to his mouth, to enjoin me silence.

"What a revolution took place, not only in my train of thoughts, but feelings! I trembled with emotion—now, indeed, I was in love. Such delicacy, too, to enhance his benev-

olence! I felt in my pocket every five minutes, only to feel
the guinea; and its magic touch invested my hero with more
than mortal beauty. My fancy had found a basis to erect its
model of perfection on; and quickly went to work, with all
the happy credulity of youth, to consider that heart as devoted to virtue, which had only obeyed a virtuous impulse.
The bitter experience was yet to come that has taught me
how very distinct are the principles of virtue from the casual feelings from which they germinate.

CHAPTER 8

"I have perhaps dwelt too long on a circumstance which is
only of importance as it marks the progress of a deception
that has been so fatal to my peace; and introduces to your
notice a poor girl, whom, intending to serve, I led to ruin.
Still it is probable that I was not entirely the victim of
mistake; and that your father, gradually fashioned by the
world, did not quickly become what I hesitate to call him—
out of respect to my daughter.

"But, to hasten to the more busy scenes of my life. Mr.
Venables and my mother died the same summer; and, wholly
engrossed by my attention to her, I thought of little else.
The neglect of her darling, my brother Robert, had a violent
effect on her weakened mind; for, though boys may be reckoned the pillars of the house without doors, girls are often
the only comfort within. They but too frequently waste their
health and spirits attending a dying patient, who leaves
them in comparative poverty. After closing, with filial piety,
a father's eyes, they are chased from the paternal roof, to
make room for the first-born, the son, who is to carry the
empty family name down to posterity; though, occupied with
his own pleasures, he scarcely thought of discharging, in the
decline of his parent's life, the debt contracted in his childhood. My mother's conduct led me to make these reflections.
Great as was the fatigue I endured, and the affection my
unceasing solicitude evinced, of which my mother seemed
perfectly sensible, still, when my brother, whom I could
hardly persuade to remain a quarter of an hour in her
chamber, was with her alone, a short time before her death,

she gave him a little hoard, which she had been some years accumulating.

"During my mother's illness, I was obliged to manage my father's temper, who, from the lingering nature of her malady, began to imagine that it was merely fancy. At this period, an artful kind of upper servant attracted my father's attention, and the neighbors made many remakrs on the finery, not honestly got, exhibited at evening service. But I was too much occupied with my mother to observe any change in her dress or behavior, or to listen to the whisper of scandal.

"I shall not dwell on the deathbed scene, lively as is the remembrance, or on the emotion produced by the last grasp of my mother's cold hand; when blessing me, she added, 'A little patience, and all will be over!' Ah! my child, how often have those words rung mournfully in my ears—and I have exclaimed—'A little more patience, and I too shall be at rest!'

"My father was violently affected by her death, recollected instances of his unkindness, and wept like a child.

"My mother had solemnly recommended my sisters to my care, and bid me be a mother to them. They, indeed, became more dear to me as they became more forlorn; for, during my mother's illness, I discovered the ruined state of my father's circumstances, and that he had only been able to keep up appearances by the sums which he borrowed of my uncle.

"My father's grief, and consequent tenderness to his children, quickly abated, the house grew still more gloomy or riotous; and my refuge from care was again at Mr. Venables'; the young 'squire having taken his father's place, and allowing, for the present, his sister to preside at his table. George, though dissatisfied with his portion of the fortune, which had till lately been all in trade, visited the family as usual. He was now full of speculations in trade, and his brow became clouded by care. He seemed to relax in his attention to me, when the presence of my uncle gave a new turn to his behavior. I was too unsuspecting, too disinterested, to trace these changes to their source.

My home every day became more and more disagreeable to me; my liberty was unnecessarily abridged, and my books, on the pretext that they made me idle, taken from me. My father's mistress was with child, and he, doting on her, allowed or overlooked her vulgar manner of tyrannizing over us. I was indignant, especially when I saw her endeavoring to attract, shall I say seduce? my younger brother. By allowing women but one way of rising in the world, the fostering the libertinism of men, society makes monsters of them, and then their ignoble vices are brought forward as a proof of inferiority of intellect.

The wearisomeness of my situation can scarcely be described. Though my life had not passed in the most even tenor with my mother, it was paradise to that I was destined to endure with my father's mistress, jealous of her illegitimate authority. My father's former occasional tenderness, in spite of his violence of temper, had been soothing to me; but now he only met me with reproofs or portentous frowns. The housekeeper, as she was now termed, was the vulgar despot of the family; and assuming the new character of a fine lady, she could never forgive the contempt which was sometimes visible in my countenance, when she uttered with pomposity her bad English, or affected to be well-bred.

To my uncle I ventured to open my heart; and he, with his wonted benevolence, began to consider in what manner he could extricate me out of my present irksome situation. In spite of his own disappointment, or, most probably, actuated by the feelings that had been petrified, not cooled, in all their sanguine fervor, like a boiling torrent of lava suddenly dashing into the sea, he thought a marriage of mutual inclination (would envious stars permit it) the only chance for happiness in this disastrous world. George Venables had the reputation of being attentive to business, and my father's example gave great weight to this circumstance; for habits of order in business would, he conceived, extend to the regulation of the affections in domestic life. George seldom spoke in my uncle's company, except to utter a short, judicious question, or to make a pertinent remark, with all due deference to his superior judgment; so that my uncle seldom left his company without observing that the young man had more in him than people supposed.

In this opinion he was not singular; yet, believe me, and I am not swayed by resentment, these speeches so justly poised, this silent deference, when the animal spirits of other young people were throwing off youthful ebullitions, were not the effect of thought or humility, but sheer barrenness of mind, and want of imagination. A colt of mettle will curvet and show his paces. Yes, my dear girl, these prudent young men want all the fire necessary to ferment their faculties, and

are characterized as wise only because they are not foolish.
It is true that George was by no means so great a favorite of
mine as during the first year of our acquaintance; still, as
he often coincided in opinion with me, and echoed my sentiments, and having myself no other attachment, I heard with
pleasure my uncle's proposal, but thought more of obtaining
my freedom than of my lover. But, when George, seemingly
anxious for my happiness, pressed me to quit my present
painful situation, my heart swelled with gratitude—I knew
not that my uncle had promised him five thousand pounds.

Had this truly generous man mentioned his intention to
me, I should have insisted on a thousand pounds being settled
on each of my sisters; George would have contested; I should
have seen his selfish soul; and—gracious God! have been
spared the misery of discovering, when too late, that I was
united to a heartless, unprincipled wretch. All my schemes
of usefulness would not have been blasted. The tenderness
of my heart would not have heated my imagination with
visions of the ineffable delight of happy love; nor would the
sweet duty of a mother have been so cruelly interrupted.

But I must not suffer the fortitude I have so hardly acquired to be undermined by unavailing regret. Let me hasten forward to describe the turbid stream in which I had to
wade—but let me exultingly declare that it is passed—my
soul holds fellowship with him no more. He cut the Gordian
knot, which my principles, mistaken ones, respected; he
dissolved the tie, the fetters rather, that ate into my very
vitals—and I should rejoice, conscious that my mind is freed,
though confined in hell itself; the only place that even fancy
can imagine more dreadful than my present abode.

These varying emotions will not allow me to proceed. I
heave sigh after sigh; yet my heart is still oppressed. For
what am I reserved? Why was I not born a man, or why was
I born at all?

CHAPTER 9

"I resume my pen to fly from thought. I was married; and
we hastened to London. I had purposed taking one of my
sisters with me; for a strong motive for marrying was the
desire of having a home at which I could receive them, now

their own grew so uncomfortable as not to deserve the cheering appellation. An objection was made to her accompanying me that appeared plausible; and I reluctantly acquiesced. I was, however, willingly allowed to take with me Molly, poor Peggy's daughter. London and preferment are ideas commonly associated in the country; and, as blooming as May, she bade adieu to Peggy with weeping eyes. I did not even feel hurt at the refusal in relation to my sister, till hearing what my uncle had done for me, I had the simplicity to request, speaking with warmth of their situation, that he would give them a thousand pounds apiece, which seemed to me but justice. He asked me, giving me a kiss, 'If I had lost my senses?' I started back, as if I had found a wasp in a rosebush. I expostulated. He sneered: and the demon of discord entered our paradise, to poison with his pestiferous breath every opening joy.

"I had sometimes observed defects in my husband's understanding; but, led astray by a prevailing opinion that goodness of disposition is of the first importance in the relative situations of life, in proportion as I perceived the narrowness of his understanding, fancy enlarged the boundary of his heart. Fatal error! How quickly is the so much vaunted milkiness of nature turned into gall by an intercourse with the world, if more generous juices do not sustain the vital source of virtue!

"One trait in my character was extreme credulity; but, when my eyes were once opened, I saw but too clearly all I had before overlooked. My husband was sunk in my esteem; still there are youthful emotions, which, for a while, fill up the chasm of love and friendship. Besides, it required some time to enable me to see his whole character in a just light, or rather to allow it to become fixed. While circumstances were ripening my faculties, and cultivating my taste, commerce and gross relaxations were shutting his against any possibility of improvement, till, by stifling every spark of virtue in himself, he began to imagine that it nowhere existed.

"Do not let me lead you astray, my child, I do not mean to assert that any human being is entirely incapable of feeling the generous emotions, which are the foundation of every true principle of virtue; but they are frequently, I fear, so feeble, that, like the inflammable quality which more or less lurks in all bodies, they often lie forever dormant; the circumstances never occurring, necessary to call them into action.

"I discovered, however, by chance, that, in consequence of some losses in trade, the natural effect of his gambling desire to start suddenly into riches, the five thousand pounds given me by my uncle had been paid very opportunely. This discovery, strange as you may think the assertion, gave me pleasure; my husband's embarrassments endeared him to me. I was glad to find an excuse for his conduct to my sisters, and my mind became calmer.

"My uncle introduced me to some literary society; and the theatres were a never-failing source of amusement to me. My delighted eye followed Mrs. Siddons, when, with dignified delicacy, she played Calista; and I involuntarily repeated after her, in the same tone, and with a long-drawn sigh,

'Hearts like ours were pair'd—not match'd.'*

"These were, at first, spontaneous emotions, though, becoming acquainted with men of wit and polished manners, I could not sometimes help regretting my early marriage; and that, in my haste to escape from a temporary dependence, and expand my newly fledged wings in an unknown sky, I had been caught in a trap, and caged for life. Still the novelty of London, and the attentive fondness of my husband, for he had some personal regard for me, made several months glide away. Yet, not forgetting the situation of my sisters, who were still very young, I prevailed on my uncle to settle a thousand pounds on each; and to place them in a school near town, where I could frequently visit, as well as have them at home with me.

"I now tried to improve my husband's taste, but we had few subjects in common; indeed he soon appeared to have little relish for my society, unless he was hinting to me the use he could make of my uncle's wealth. When we had company, I was disgusted by an ostentatious display of riches, and I have often quitted the room to avoid listening to exaggerated tales of money obtained by lucky hits.

"With all my attention and affectionate interest, I perceived that I could not become the friend or confidante of my husband. Everything I learned relative to his affairs I gath-

*Calista is the heroine of Nicholas Rowe's *The Fair Penitent* (1703). Like Maria, as the line she quotes indicates, Calista marries for family reasons. Her true love is for the dissolute Lothario, whose name became a synonym for "seducer."

ered up by accident; and I vainly endeavored to establish, at our fireside, that social converse which often renders people of different characters dear to each other. Returning from the theater, or any amusing party, I frequently began to relate what I had seen and highly relished; but with sullen taciturnity he soon silenced me. I seemed therefore gradually to lose, in his society, the soul, the energies of which had just been in action. To such a degree, in fact, did his cold, reserved manner affect me that, after spending some days with him alone, I have imagined myself the most stupid creature in the world, till the abilities of some casual visitor convinced me that I had some dormant animation, and sentiments above the dust in which I had been groveling. The very countenance of my husband changed; his complexion became sallow, and all the charms of youth were vanishing with its vivacity.

"I give you one view of the subject; but these experiments and alterations took up the space of five years, during which period, I had most reluctantly extorted several sums from my uncle, to save my husband, to use his own words, from destruction. At first it was to prevent bills being noted, to the injury of his credit; then to bail him; and afterwards to prevent an execution from entering the house. I began at last to conclude that he would have made more exertions of his own to extricate himself had he not relied on mine, cruel as was the task he imposed on me; and I firmly determined that I would make use of no more pretexts.

"From the moment I pronounced this determination, indifference on his part was changed into rudeness, or something worse.

"He now seldom dined at home, and continually returned at a late hour, drunk, to bed. I retired to another apartment; I was glad, I own, to escape from his; for personal intimacy without affection seemed to me the most degrading, as well as the most painful, state in which a woman of any taste, not to speak of the peculiar delicacy of fostered sensibility, could be placed. But my husband's fondness for women was of the grossest kind, and imagination was so wholly out of the question, as to render his indulgences of this sort entirely promiscuous, and of the most brutal nature. My health suffered, before my heart was entirely estranged by the loathsome information; could I then have returned to his sullied arms, but as a victim to the prejudices of mankind, who have made women the property of their husbands? I discovered even, by his conversation, when intoxicated that his favorites were wantons of the lowest class, who could by their vulgar, indecent mirth, which he called nature, rouse his sluggish spirits. Meretricious ornaments and manners were necessary to attract his attention. He seldom looked twice at a modest woman, and sat silent in their company; and the charms of youth and beauty had not the slightest effect on his senses, unless the possessors were initiated in vice. His intimacy with profligate women, and his habits of thinking, gave him a contempt for female endowments; and he would repeat, when wine had loosed his tongue, most of the commonplace sarcasms leveled at them by men who do not allow them to have minds, because mind would be an impediment to gross enjoyment. Men who are inferior to their fellow men are always most anxious to establish their superiority over women. But where are these reflections leading me?

"Women who have lost their husband's affection are justly reproved for neglecting their persons, and not taking the same pains to keep as to gain a heart; but who thinks of giving the same advice to men, though women are continually stigmatized for being attached to fops; and from the nature of their education are more susceptible of disgust? Yet why a woman should be expected to endure a sloven with more patience than a man, and magnanimously to govern herself, I cannot conceive; unless it be supposed arrogant in her to look for respect as well as a maintenance. It is not easy to be pleased, because, after promising to love, in different circumstances, we are told that it is our duty. I cannot, I am sure (though, when attending the sick, I never felt disgust), forget my own sensations, when rising with health and spirit, and after scenting the sweet morning, I have met my husband at the breakfast table. The active attention I had been giving to domestic regulations, which were generally settled before he rose, or a walk, gave a glow to my countenance that contrasted with his squalid appearance. The squeamishness of stomach alone, produced by the last night's intemperance, which he took no pains to conceal, destroyed my appetite. I think I now see him lolling in an armchair, in a dirty powdering gown, soiled linen, ungartered stockings, and tangled hair, yawning and stretching himself. The newspaper was immediately called for, if not brought in on the tea-board, from which he would scarcely lift his eyes while I poured out the tea, excepting to ask for some brandy to put into it, or to declare that he could not eat. In answer to any question, in his best humor, it was a drawling 'What do you say, child?' But if I demanded money for the house expenses, which I put off till the last moment, his customary reply, often prefaced with an oath, was 'Do you think me, madam, made of money?'—The butcher, the baker, must wait; and, what was worse, I was often obliged to witness his surly dismissal of tradesmen, who were in want of their money, and whom I sometimes paid with the presents my uncle gave me for my own use.

At this juncture my father's mistress, by terrifying his conscience, prevailed on him to marry her; he was already become a Methodist; and my brother, who now practiced for himself, had discovered a flaw in the settlement made on my mother's children, which set it aside, and he allowed my father, whose distress made him submit to anything, a tithe of his own, or rather our fortune.

My sisters had left school, but were unable to endure home, which my father's wife rendered as disagreeable as possible, to get rid of girls whom she regarded as spies on her conduct. They were accomplished, yet you can (may you never be reduced to the same destitute state!) scarcely conceive the trouble I had to place them in the situation of governesses, the only one in which even a well-educated woman, with more than ordinary talents, can struggle for a subsistence; and even this is a dependence next to menial. Is it then surprising that so many forlorn women, with human passions and feelings, take refuge in infamy? Alone in large mansions, I say alone, because they had no companions with whom they could converse on equal terms, or from whom they could expect the endearments of affection, they grew melancholy, and the sound of joy made them sad; and the youngest, having a more delicate frame, fell into a decline. It was with great difficulty that I, who now almost supported the house by loans from my uncle, could prevail on the *master* of it to allow her a room to die in. I watched her sickbed for some months, and then closed her eyes, gentle spirit! forever. She was pretty, with very engaging manners; yet had never an opportunity to marry, excepting to a very old man. She had abilities sufficient to have shown in any profession, had there been any professions for women, though she shrunk at the name of milliner or mantua-maker as degrading to a gentlewoman. I would not term this feeling false pride to any one but you, my child, whom I fondly hope to see (yes; I will indulge the hope for a moment!) possessed of that energy of character which gives dignity to any situation; and with that clear, firm spirit that will enable you to choose a situation for yourself, or submit to be classed in the lowest, if it be the only one in which you can be the mistress of your own actions.

"Soon after the death of my sister, an incident occurred, to prove to me that the heart of a libertine is dead to natural affection; and to convince me that the being who has appeared all tenderness, to gratify a selfish passion, is as regardless of the innocent fruit of it as of the object, when the fit is over. I had casually observed an old, mean-looking woman, who called on my husband every two or three months to receive some money. One day entering the passage of his little countinghouse, as she was going out, I heard her say, 'The child is very weak; she cannot live long, she will soon die out of your way, so you need not grudge her a little physic.'

" 'So much the better,' he replied, 'and pray mind your own business, good woman.'

"I was struck by his unfeeling, inhuman tone of voice, and drew back, determined when the woman came again to try to speak to her, not out of curiosity, I had heard enough, but with the hope of being useful to a poor, outcast girl.

"A month or two elapsed before I saw this woman again; and then she had a child in her hand that tottered along, scarcely able to sustain her own weight. They were going away, to return at the hour Mr. Venables was expected; he was now from home. I desired the woman to walk into the parlor. She hesitated, yet obeyed. I assured her that I should not mention to my husband (the word seemed to weigh on my respiration) that I had seen her, or his child. The woman stared at me with astonishment; and I turned my eyes on the squalid object [that accompanied her]. She could hardly support herself, her complexion was sallow, and her eyes inflamed, with an indescribable look of cunning, mixed with the wrinkles produced by the peevishness of pain.

" 'Poor child!' I exclaimed. 'Ah! You may well say poor child,' replied the woman. 'I brought her here to see whether he would have the heart to look at her, and not get some advice. I do not know what they deserve who nursed her. Why, her legs bent under her like a bow when she came to me, and she has never been well since; but, if they were no better paid than I am, it is not to be wondered at, sure enough.'

"On further inquiry I was informed that this miserable spectacle was the daughter of a servant, a country girl, who caught Mr. Venables' eye, and whom he seduced. On his marriage he sent her away, her situation being too visible. After her delivery, she was thrown on the town; and died in an hospital within the year. The babe was sent to a parish nurse, and afterwards to this woman, who did not seem much better; but what was to be expected from such a close bargain? She was only paid three shillings a week for board and washing.

"The woman begged me to give her some old clothes for the child, assuring me, that she was almost afraid to ask master for money to buy even a pair of shoes.

"I grew sick at heart. And, fearing Mr. Venables might enter, and oblige me to express my abhorrence, I hastily inquired where she lived, promised to pay her two shillings a week more, and to call on her in a day or two; putting a trifle into her hand as a proof of my good intention.

"If the state of this child affected me, what were my feelings at a discovery I made respecting Peggy———?*

CHAPTER 10

"My father's situation was now so distressing, that I prevailed on my uncle to accompany me to visit him, and to lend me his assistance, to prevent the whole property of the family from becoming the prey of my brother's rapacity; for, to extricate himself out of present difficulties, my father was totally regardless of futurity. I took down with me some presents for my stepmother; it did not require an effort for me to treat her with civility, or to forget the past.

"This was the first time I had visited my native village since my marriage. But with what different emotions did I return from the busy world, with a heavy weight of experience benumbing my imagination, to scenes that whispered recollections of joy and hope most eloquently to my heart! The first scent of the wild flowers from the heath thrilled through my veins, awakening every sense to pleasure. The

*Peggy's story is never completed. EDITOR.

icy hand of despair seemed to be removed from my bosom;
and—forgetting my husband—the nurtured visions of a romantic mind, bursting on me with all their original wildness and gay exuberance, were again hailed as sweet realities.
I forgot, with equal facility, that I ever felt sorrow or knew
care in the country; while a transient rainbow stole athwart
the cloudy sky of despondency. The picturesque form of
several favorite trees, and the porches of rude cottages, with
their smiling hedges, were recognized with the gladsome
playfulness of childish vivacity. I could have kissed the
chickens that pecked on the common; and longed to pat the
cows, and frolic with the dogs that sported on it. I gazed
with delight on the windmill, and thought it lucky that it
should be in motion, at the moment I passed by; and entering the dear green lane, which led directly to the village,
the sound of the well-known rookery gave that sentimental
tinge to the varying sensations of my active soul, which only
served to heighten the luster of the luxuriant scenery. But,
spying, as I advanced, the spire peeping over the withered
tops of the aged elms that composed the rookery, my thoughts
flew immediately to the churchyard, and tears of affection,
such was the effect of my imagination, bedewed my mother's
grave! Sorrow gave place to devotional feelings. I wandered
through the church in fancy, as I used sometimes to do
on Saturday evening. I recollected with what fervor I
addressed the God of my youth: and once more with rapturous
love looked above my sorrows to the Father of nature. I
pause——feeling forcibly all the emotions I am describing;
and (reminded, as I register my sorrows, of the sublime calm
I have felt, when in some tremendous solitude, my soul rested
on itself, and seemed to fill the universe) I insensibly breathe
soft, hushing every wayward emotion, as if fearing to sully
with a sigh, a contentment so ecstatic.

"Having settled my father's affairs, and, by my exertions
in his favor, made my brother my sworn foe, I returned to
London. My husband's conduct was now changed; I had
during my absence, received several affectionate, peniten-
tial letters from him; and he seemed on my arrival to wish
by his behavior to prove his sincerity. I could not then
conceive why he acted thus; and, when the suspicion darted
into my head, that it might arise from observing my increasing influence with my uncle, I almost despised myself
for imagining that such a degree of debasing selfishness
could exist.

"He became, unaccountable as was the change, tender and attentive; and, attacking my weak side, made a confession of his follies, and lamented the embarrassments in which I, who merited a far different fate, might be involved. He besought me to aid him with my counsel, praised my understanding, and appealed to the tenderness of my heart.

"This conduct only inspired me with compassion. I wished to be his friend; but love had spread his rosy pinions and fled far, far away; and had not (like some exquisite perfumes, the fine spirit of which is continually mingling with the air) left a fragrance behind, to mark where he had shook his wings. My husband's renewed caresses then became hateful to me; his brutality was tolerable, compared to his distasteful fondness. Still, compassion, and the fear of insulting his supposed feelings by a want of sympathy made me dissemble, and do violence to my delicacy. What a task!

"Those who support a system of what I term false refinement, and will not allow great part of love in the female, as well as male breast, to spring in some respects involuntarily, may not admit that charms are as necessary to feed the passion, as virtues to convert the mellowing spirit into friendship. To such observers I have nothing to say, any more than to the moralists, who insist that women ought to and can love their husbands, because it is their duty. To you, my child, I may add, with a heart tremblingly alive to your future conduct, some observations, dictated by my present feelings, on calmly reviewing this period of my life. When novelists or moralists praise as a virtue a woman's coldness of constitution, and want of passion; and make her yield to the ardor of her lover out of sheer compassion, or to promote a frigid plan of future comfort, I am disgusted. They may be good women, in the ordinary acceptation of the phrase, and do no harm; but they appear to me not to have those 'finely fashioned nerves,' which render the senses exquisite. They may possess tenderness; but they want that fire of the imagination which produces *active* sensibility, and *positive* virtue. How does the woman deserve to be characterized, who marries one man, with a heart and imagination devoted to another? Is she not an object of pity or contempt, when thus sacrilegiously violating the purity of her own feelings? Nay, it is as indelicate, when she is indifferent, unless she be constitutionally insensible; then indeed it is a mere affair of barter; and I have nothing to do with the secrets of trade. Yes; eagerly as I wish you to possess true rectitude of mind, and purity of affection, I must insist that a heartless conduct is the contrary of virtuous. Truth is the only basis of virtue; and we cannot, without depraving our minds, endeavor to please a lover or husband, but in proportion as he pleases us. Men, more effectually to enslave us, may inculcate this partial morality, and lose sight of virtue in subdividing it into the duties of particular stations; but let us not blush for nature without a cause!

"After these remarks, I am ashamed to own that I was pregnant. The greatest sacrifice of my principles in my whole life was the allowing my husband again to be familiar with my person, though to this cruel act of self-denial, when I wished the earth to open and swallow me, you owe your birth; and I the unutterable pleasure of being a mother. There was something of delicacy in my husband's bridal attentions; but now his tainted breath, pimpled face, and bloodshot eyes were not more repugnant to my senses than his gross manners and loveless familiarity to my taste.

"A man would only be expected to maintain, yes, barely grant a subsistence to, a woman rendered odious by habitual intoxication; but who would expect him or think it possible to love her? And unless 'youth, and genial years were flown,' it would be thought equally unreasonable to insist, [under penalty of] forfeiting almost everything reckoned valuable in life, that he should not love another: whilst woman, weak in reason, impotent in will, is required to moralize, sentimentalize herself to stone, and pine her life away, laboring to reform her embruted mate. He may even spend in dissipation and intemperance, the very intemperance which renders him so hateful, her property, and by stinting her expenses, not permit her to beguile in society, a wearisome, joyless life; for over their mutual fortune she has no power, it must all pass through his hand. And if she be a mother, and in the present state of women, it is a great misfortune to be prevented from discharging the duties, and cultivating the affections of one, what has she not to endure?—But I have suffered the tenderness of one to lead me into reflections that I did not think of making, to interrupt my narrative—yet the full heart will overflow.

"Mr. Venables' embarrassments did not now endear him to me; still, anxious to befriend him, I endeavored to prevail on him to retrench his expenses; but he had always some plausible excuse to give to justify his not following my advice. Humanity, compassion, and the interest produced by a habit of living together, made me try to relieve, and sympathize with him; but, when I recollected that I was bound to live with such a being forever—my heart died within me; my desire of improvement became languid, and baleful, corroding melancholy took possession of my soul. Marriage had bastilled me for life. I discovered in myself a capacity for the enjoyment of the various pleasures existence affords; yet, fettered by the partial laws of society, this fair globe was to me an universal blank.

"When I exhorted my husband to economy, I referred to himself. I was obliged to practice the most rigid, or contract debts, which I had too much reason to fear would never be paid. I despised this paltry privilege of a wife, which can only be of use to the vicious or inconsiderate, and determined not to increase the torrent that was bearing him down. I was then ignorant of the extent of his fraudulent speculations, whom I was bound to honor and obey.

"A woman neglected by her husband, or whose manners form a striking contrast with his, will always have men on the watch to soothe and flatter her. Besides, the forlorn state of a neglected woman, not destitute of personal charms, is particularly interesting, and rouses that species of pity, which is so near akin, it easily slides into love. A man of feeling thinks not of seducing, he is himself seduced by all the noblest emotions of his soul. He figures to himself all the sacrifices a woman of sensibility must make, and every situation in which his imagination places her touches his heart and fires his passions. Longing to take to his bosom the shorn lamb, and bid the drooping buds of hope revive, benevolence changes into passion: and should he then discover that he is beloved, honor binds him fast, though foreseeing that he may afterwards be obliged to pay severe damages to the man, who never appeared to value his wife's society, till he found that there was a chance of his being indemnified for the loss of it.

"Such are the partial laws enacted by men; for, only to lay a stress on the dependent state of a woman in the grand question of the comforts arising from the possession of property, she is [even in this article] much more injured by the loss of the husband's affection than he by that of his wife; yet where is she, condemned to the solitude of a deserted home, to look for a compensation from the woman who seduces him from her? She cannot drive an unfaithful husband from his house, nor separate, or tear, his children from him, however culpable he may be; and he, still the master of his own fate, enjoys the smiles of a world that would brand her with infamy, did she, seeking consolation, venture to retaliate.

"These remarks are not dictated by experience; but merely by the compassion I feel for many amiable women, the *outlaws* of the world. For myself, never encouraging any of the advances that were made to me, my lovers dropped off like the untimely shoots of spring. I did not even coquet with them, because I found, on examining myself, I could not coquet with a man without loving him a little; and I perceived that I should not be able to stop at the line of what are termed *innocent freedoms*, did I suffer any. My reserve was then the consequence of delicacy. Freedom of conduct has emancipated many women's minds; but my conduct has most rigidly been governed by my principles, till the improvement of my understanding has enabled me to discern the fallacy of prejudices at war with nature and reason.

"Shortly after the change I have mentioned in my husband's conduct, my uncle was compelled by his declining health to seek the succor of a milder climate, and embark for Lisbon. He left his will in the hands of a friend, an eminent solicitor; he had previously questioned me relative to my situation and state of mind, and declared very freely that he could place no reliance on the stability of my husband's professions. He had been deceived in the unfolding of his character; he now thought it fixed in a train of actions that would inevitably lead to ruin and disgrace.

"The evening before his departure, which we spent alone together, he folded me to his heart, uttering the endearing appellation of 'child.'—My more than father! why was I not permitted to perform the last duties of one, and smooth the pillow of death? He seemed by his manner to be convinced that he should never see me more; yet requested me, most earnestly, to come to him, should I be obliged to leave my husband. He had before expressed his sorrow at hearing of my pregnancy, having determined to prevail on me to accompany him, till I informed him of that circumstance. He expressed himself unfeignedly sorry that any new tie should bind me to a man whom he thought so incapable of estimating my value; such was the kind language of affection.

"I must repeat his own words; they made an indelible impression on my mind:

" 'The marriage state is certainly that in which women, generally speaking, can be most useful; but I am far from thinking that a woman, once married, ought to consider the engagement as indissoluble (especially if there be no children to reward her for sacrificing her feelings) in case her husband merits neither her love nor esteem. Esteem will often supply the place of love; and prevent a woman from being wretched, though it may not make her happy. The magnitude of a sacrifice ought always to bear some proportion to the utility in view; and for a woman to live with a man for whom she can cherish neither affection nor esteem, or even be of any use to him, excepting in the light of a housekeeper, is an abjectness of condition, the enduring of which no concurrence of circumstances can ever make a duty in the sight of God or just men. If indeed she submits to it merely to be maintained in idleness, she has no right to complain bitterly of her fate; or to act, as a person of independent character might, as if she had a title to disregard general rules.

" 'But the misfortune is that many women only submit in appearance, and forfeit their own respect to secure their reputation in the world. The situation of a woman separated from her husband is undoubtedly very different from that of a man who has left his wife. He, with lordly dignity, has shaken off a clog; and the allowing her food and raiment is thought sufficient to secure his reputation from taint. And, should she have been inconsiderate, he will be celebrated for his generosity and forbearance. Such is the respect paid to the master-key of property! A woman, on the contrary, resigning what is termed her natural protector (though he never was so, but in name) is despised and shunned for asserting the independence of mind distinctive of a rational being, and spurning at slavery.'

"During the remainder of the evening, my uncle's tenderness led him frequently to revert to the subject, and utter, with increasing warmth, sentiments to the same purport. At length it was necessary to say 'Farewell!'—and we parted—gracious God! to meet no more.

CHAPTER 11

"A gentleman of large fortune and of polished manners had lately visited very frequently at our house, and treated me, if possible, with more respect than Mr. Venables paid him; my pregnancy was not yet visible, his society was a great relief to me, as I had for some time past, to avoid expense, confined myself very much at home. I ever disdained unnecessary, perhaps even prudent concealments; and my husband, with great ease, discovered the amount of my uncle's parting present. A copy of a writ was the stale pretext to extort it from me; and I had soon reason to believe that it was fabricated for the purpose. I acknowledge my folly in thus suffering myself to be continually imposed on. I had adhered to my resolution not to apply to my uncle, on the part of my husband, any more; yet, when I had received a sum sufficient to supply my own wants, and to enable me to pursue a plan I had in view, to settle my younger brother in a respectable employment, I allowed myself to be duped by Mr. Venables' shallow pretenses, and hypocritical professions.

"Thus did he pillage me and my family, thus frustrate all my plans of usefulness. Yet this was the man I was bound to respect and esteem: as if respect and esteem depended on an arbitrary will of our own! But a wife being as much a man's property as his horse, or his ass, she has nothing she can call her own. He may use any means to get at what the law considers as his, the moment his wife is in possession of it, even to the forcing of a lock, as Mr. Venables did, to search for notes in my writing desk—and all this is done with a show of equity, because, forsooth, he is responsible for her maintenance.

"The tender mother cannot *lawfully* snatch from the grip of the gambling spendthrift, or beastly drunkard, unmindful of his offspring, the fortune which falls to her by chance; or (so flagrant is the injustice) what she earns by her own exertions. No; he can rob her with impunity, even to waste publicly on a courtesan; and the laws of her country—if women have a country—afford her no protection or redress from the oppressor, unless she have the plea of bodily fear;

yet how many ways are there of goading the soul almost to madness, equally unmanly, though not so mean? When such laws were framed, should not impartial lawgivers have first decreed, in the style of a great assembly, who recognized the existence of an *être suprême*, to fix the national belief that the husband should always be wiser and more virtuous than his wife, in order to entitle him, with a show of justice, to keep this idiot, or perpetual minor, forever in bondage. But I must have done—on this subject, my indignation continually runs away with me.

"The company of the gentleman I have already mentioned, who had a general acquaintance with literature and subjects of taste, was grateful to me; my countenance brightened up as he approached, and I unaffectedly expressed the pleasure I felt. The amusement his conversation afforded me made it easy to comply with my husband's request to endeavor to render our house agreeable to him.

"His attentions became more pointed; but, as I was not of the number of women whose virtue, as it is termed, immediately takes alarm, I endeavored, rather by raillery than serious expostulation, to give a different turn to his conversation. He assumed a new mode of attack, and I was, for a while, the dupe of his pretended friendship.

"I had, merely in the style of *badinage*, boasted of my conquest, and repeated his loverlike compliments to my husband. But he begged me, for God's sake, not to affront his friend, or I should destroy all his projects, and be his ruin. Had I had more affection for my husband, I should have expressed my contempt of this time-serving politeness: now I imagined that I only felt pity; yet it would have puzzled a casuist to point out in what the exact difference consisted.

"This friend began now, in confidence, to discover to me the real state of my husband's affairs. 'Necessity,' said Mr. S——; why should I reveal his name? for he affected to palliate the conduct he could not excuse, 'had led him to take such steps, by accommodation bills, buying goods on credit, to sell them for ready money, and similar transactions, that his character in the commercial world was gone. He was considered,' he added, lowering his voice, 'on 'Change as a swindler.'

"I felt at that moment the first maternal pang. Aware of the evils my sex have to struggle with, I still wished, for my own consolation, to be the mother of a daughter; and I could not bear to think, that the *sins* of her father's entailed disgrace, should be added to the ills to which woman is heir.

"So completely was I deceived by these shows of friendship (nay, I believe, according to his interpretation, Mr. S—— really was my friend) that I began to consult him respecting the best mode of retrieving my husband's character: it is the good name of a woman only that sets to rise no more. I knew not that he had been drawn into a whirlpool, out of which he had not the energy to attempt to escape. He seemed indeed destitute of the power of employing his faculties in any regular pursuit. His principles of action were so loose, and his mind so uncultivated, that everything like order appeared to him in the shape of restraint; and, like men in the savage state, he required the strong stimulus of hope or fear, produced by wild speculations, in which the interests of others went for nothing, to keep his spirits awake. He one time professed patriotism, but he knew not what it was to feel honest indignation; and pretended to be an advocate for liberty, when, with as little affection for the human race as for individuals, he thought of nothing but his own gratification. He was just such a citizen as a father. The sums he adroitly obtained by a violation of the laws of his country, as well as those of humanity, he would allow a mistress to squander; though she was, with the same *sang froid*, consigned, as were his children, to poverty, when another proved more attractive.

"On various pretenses, his friend continued to visit me; and, observing my want of money, he tried to induce me to accept of pecuniary aid; but this offer I absolutely rejected, though it was made with such delicacy I could not be displeased.

"One day he came, as I thought accidentally, to dinner. My husband was very much engaged in business, and quitted the room soon after the cloth was removed. We conversed as usual, till confidential advice led again to love. I was extremely mortified. I had a sincere regard for him, and hoped that he had an equal friendship for me. I therefore began mildly to expostulate with him. This gentleness he mistook for coy encouragement; and he would not be diverted from the subject. Perceiving his mistake, I seriously asked him how, using such language to me, he could profess to be my husband's friend? A significant sneer excited my curiosity, and he, supposing this to be my only scruple, took a letter deliberately out of his pocket, saying, 'Your husband's honor is not inflexible. How could you, with your discernment, think it so? Why, he left the room this very day on purpose to give me an opportunity to explain myself; *he* thought me too timid—too tardy.'

"I snatched the letter with indescribable emotion. The purport of it was to invite him to dinner, and to ridicule his chivalrous respect for me. He assured him 'that every woman had her price, and, with gross indecency, hinted, that he should be glad to have the duty of a husband taken off his hands. These he termed *liberal sentiments*. He advised him not to shock my romantic notions, but to attack my credulous generosity, and weak pity; and concluded with requesting him to lend him five hundred pounds for a month or six weeks.' I read this letter twice over; and the firm purpose it inspired, calmed the rising tumult of my soul. I rose deliberately, requested Mr. S—— to wait a moment, and instantly going into the countinghouse, desired Mr. Venables to return with me to the dining parlor.

"He laid down his pen, and entered with me, without observing any change in my countenance. I shut the door, and, giving him the letter, simply asked 'whether he wrote it, or was it a forgery?'

"Nothing could equal the confusion. His friend's eye met his, and he muttered something about a joke—But I interrupted him.—'It is sufficient—We part forever.'

"I continued, with solemnity, 'I have borne with your tyranny and infidelities. I disdain to utter what I have borne with. I thought you unprincipled, but not so decidedly vicious. I formed a tie, in the sight of heaven—I have held it sacred; even when men, more conformable to my taste, have made me feel—I despise all subterfuge!—that I was not dead to love. Neglected by you, I have resolutely stifled the enticing emotions, and respected the plighted faith you outraged. And you dare now to insult me, by selling me to prostitution! —Yes—equally lost to delicacy and principle—you dared sacrilegiously to barter the honor of the mother of your child.'

"Then, turning to Mr. S——, I added, 'I call on you, sir, to witness,' and I lifted my hands and eyes to heaven, 'that, as solemnly as I took his name, I now abjure it,' I pulled off my ring, and put it on the table; 'and that I mean immediately to quit his house, never to enter it more. I will provide for myself and child. I leave him as free as I am determined to be myself—he shall be answerable for no debts of mine.'

"Astonishment closed their lips, till Mr. Venables, gently pushing his friend, with a forced smile, out of the room, nature for a moment prevailed, and, appearing like himself, he turned round, burning with rage, to me: but there was no terror in the frown, excepting when contrasted with the malignant smile which preceded it. He bade me 'leave the house at my peril; told me he despised my threats; I had no resource; I could not swear the peace against him!—I was not afraid of my life!—he had never struck me!'

"He threw the letter in the fire, which I had incautiously left in his hands; and, quitting the room, locked the door on me.

"When left alone, I was a moment or two before I could recollect myself—One scene had succeeded another with such rapidity, I almost doubted whether I was reflecting on a real event. 'Was it possible? Was I, indeed, free?'—Yes; free I termed myself, when I decidedly perceived the conduct I ought to adopt. How had I panted for liberty—liberty, that I would have purchased at any price, but that of my own esteem! I rose, and shook myself; opened the window, and methought the air never smelled so sweet. The face of heaven grew fairer as I viewed it, and the clouds seemed to flit away obedient to my wishes, to give my soul room to expand. I was all soul, and (wild as it may appear) felt as if I could have dissolved in the soft balmy gale that kissed my cheek, or have glided below the horizon on the glowing, descending beams. A seraphic satisfaction animated, without agitating my spirits; and my imagination collected, in visions sublimely terrible, or soothingly beautiful, an immense variety of the endless images, which nature affords, and fancy combines, of the grand and fair. The luster of these bright picturesque sketches faded with the setting sun; but I was still alive to the calm delight they had diffused through my heart.

"There may be advocates for matrimonial obedience, who, making distinction between the duty of a wife and of a human being, may blame my conduct. To them I write not—my feelings are not for them to analyze; and may you, my child, never be able to ascertain, by heartrending experience, what your mother felt before the present emancipation of her mind!

"I began to write a letter to my father, after closing one to my uncle; not to ask advice, but to signify my determination; when I was interrupted by the entrance of Mr. Venables. His manner was changed. His views on my uncle's fortune made him averse to my quitting his house, or he would, I am convinced, have been glad to have shaken off even the slight restraint my presence imposed on him; the restraint of showing me some respect. So far from having an affection for me, he really hated me, because he was convinced that I must despise him.

"He told me, that, 'As I now had had time to cool and reflect, he did not doubt but that my prudence, and nice sense of propriety, would lead me to overlook what was passed.'

" 'Reflection,' I replied, 'had only confirmed my purpose, and no power on earth could divert me from it.'

"Endeavoring to assume a soothing voice and look, when he would willingly have tortured me, to force me to feel his power, his countenance had an infernal expression, when he desired me, 'Not to expose myself to the servants, by obliging him to confine me in my apartment; if then I would give my promise not to quit the house precipitately, I should be free—and—.' I declared, interrupting him, 'that I would promise nothing. I had no measures to keep with him—I was resolved, and would not condescend to subterfuge.'

"He muttered, 'that I should soon repent of these preposterous airs'; and, ordering tea to be carried into my little study, which had a communication with my bedchamber, he once more locked the door upon me, and left me to my own meditations. I had passively followed him up stairs, not wishing to fatigue myself with unavailing exertion.

"Nothing calms the mind like a fixed purpose. I felt as if I had heaved a thousandweight from my heart; the atmosphere seemed lightened; and, if I execrated the institutions of society, which thus enabled men to tyrannize over women, it was almost a disinterested sentiment. I disregarded present inconveniences, when my mind had done struggling with itself, when reason and inclination had shaken hands and were at peace. I had no longer the cruel task before me, in endless perspective, aye, during the tedious forever of life, of laboring to overcome my repugnance—of laboring to extinguish the hopes, the maybes of a lively imagination. Death I had hailed as my only chance for deliverance; but, while existence had still so many charms, and life promised happiness, I shrunk from the icy arms of an unknown tyrant, though far more inviting than those of the man, to whom I supposed myself bound without any other alternative; and was content to linger a little longer, waiting for I knew not what, rather than leave 'the warm precincts of the cheerful day,' and all the unenjoyed affection of my nature.

"My present situation gave a new turn to my reflection; and I wondered (now the film seemed to be withdrawn, that obscured the piercing sight of reason) how I could, previously to the deciding outrage, have considered myself as everlastingly united to vice and folly! 'Had an evil genius cast a spell at my birth; or a demon stalked out of chaos, to perplex my understanding, and enchain my will, with delusive prejudices?'

"I pursued this train of thinking; it led me out of myself, to expatiate on the misery peculiar to my sex. 'Are not,' I thought, 'the despots forever stigmatized, who, in the wantonness of power, commanded even the most atrocious criminals to be chained to dead bodies? though surely those laws are much more inhuman, which forge adamantine fetters to bind minds together, that never can mingle in social communion! What indeed can equal the wretchedness of that state, in which there is no alternative, but to extinguish the affections, or encounter infamy?'

CHAPTER 12

"Towards midnight Mr. Venables entered my chamber; and, with calm audacity preparing to go to bed, he bade me make haste, 'for that was the best place for husbands and wives to end their differences.' He had been drinking plentifully to aid his courage.

"I did not at first deign to reply. But perceiving that he affected to take my silence for consent, I told him that, 'If he would not go to another bed, or allow me, I should sit up in my study all night.' He attempted to pull me into the chamber, half-joking. But I resisted; and, as he had determined not to give me any reason for saying that he used violence, after a few more efforts, he retired, cursing my obstinacy, to bed.

"I sat musing some time longer; then, throwing my cloak around me, prepared for sleep on a sofa. And, so fortunate

seemed my deliverance, so sacred the pleasure of being thus
wrapped up in myself, that I slept profoundly, and woke
with a mind composed to encounter the struggles of the day.
Mr. Venables did not wake till some hours after; and then
he came to me half-dressed, yawning and stretching, with
haggard eyes, as if he scarcely recollected what had passed
the preceding evening. He fixed his eyes on me for a moment, then, calling me a fool, asked 'How long I intended to
continue this pretty farce? For his part, he was devilish sick
of it; but this was the plague of marrying women who
pretended to know something.'

"I made no other reply to this harangue, than to say,
'That he ought to be glad to get rid of a woman so unfit to be
his companion—and that any change in my conduct would be
mean dissimulation; for maturer reflection only gave the
sacred seal of reason to my first resolution.'

"He looked as if he could have stamped with impatience,
at being obliged to stifle his rage; but, conquering his anger
(for weak people, whose passions seem the most ungovern-
able, restrain them with the greatest ease, when they have
a sufficient motive), he exclaimed, 'Very pretty, upon my
soul! very pretty, theatrical flourishes! Pray, fair Roxana,
stoop from your altitudes, and remember that you are acting
a part in real life.'

"He uttered this speech with a self-satisfied air, and went
down stairs to dress.

"In about an hour he came to me again; and in the same
tone said, 'That he came as a gentleman-usher to hand me
down to breakfast.'

" 'Of the black rod?' asked I.

"This question, and the tone in which I asked it, a little
disconcerted him. To say the truth, I now felt no resentment; my firm resolution to free myself from my ignoble
thraldom, had absorbed the various emotions which, during
six years, had racked my soul. The duty pointed out by my
principles seemed clear; and not one tender feeling intruded
to make me swerve: The dislike which my husband had
inspired was strong; but it only led me to wish to avoid, to
wish to let him drop out of my memory; there was no
misery, no torture that I would not deliberately have chosen, rather than renew my lease of servitude.

"During the breakfast, he attempted to reason with me on
the folly of romantic sentiments; for this was the indiscriminate epithet he gave to every mode of conduct or thinking

superior to his own. He asserted, 'that all the world were governed by their own interest; those who pretended to be actuated by different motives were only deeper knaves, or fools crazed by books, who took for gospel all the rodomontade nonsense written by men who knew nothing of the world. For his part, he thanked God, he was no hypocrite; and, if he stretched a point sometimes, it was always with an intention of paying every man his own.'

"He then artfully insinuated, 'that he daily expected a vessel to arrive, a successful speculation, that would make him easy for the present, and that he had served other schemes actually depending, that could not fail. He had no doubt of becoming rich in a few years, though he had been thrown back by some unlucky adventures at the setting out.'

"I mildly replied, 'That I wished he might not involve himself still deeper.'

"He had no notion that I was governed by a decision of judgment, not to be compared with a mere spurt of resentment. He knew not what it was to feel indignation against vice, and often boasted of his placable temper, and readiness to forgive injuries. True; for he only considered the being deceived, as an effort of skill he had not guarded against; and then, with a cant of candor, would observe, 'that he did not know how he might himself have been tempted to act in the same circumstances.' And, as his heart never opened to friendship, it never was wounded by disappointment. Every new acquaintance he protested, it is true, was 'the cleverest fellow in the world'; and he really thought so, till the novelty of his conversation or manners ceased to have any effect on his sluggish spirits. His respect for rank or fortune was more permanent, though he chanced to have no design of availing himself of the influence of either to promote his own views.

"After a prefatory conversation—my blood (I thought it had been cooler) flushed over my whole countenance as he spoke—he alluded to my situation. He desired me to reflect—'and act like a prudent woman, as the best proof of my superior understanding; for he must own I had sense, did I know how to use it. I was not,' he laid a stress on his words, 'without my passions; and a husband was a convenient cloak. —He was liberal in his way of thinking; and why might not we, like many other married people, who were above vulgar prejudices, tacitly consent to let each other follow their own inclination?—He meant nothing more, in the letter I made the ground of complaint; and the pleasure which I seemed to take in Mr. S.'s company led him to conclude that he was not disagreeable to me.'

"A clerk brought in the letters of the day, and I, as I often did, while he was discussing subjects of business, went to the pianoforte, and began to play a favorite air to restore myself, as it were, to nature, and drive the sophisticated sentiments I had just been obliged to listen to out of my soul.

"They had excited sensations similar to those I have felt in viewing the squalid inhabitants of some of the lanes and back streets of the metropolis, mortified at being compelled to consider them as my fellow creatures, as if an ape had claimed kindred with me. Or, as when surrounded by a mephitical fog, I have wished to have a volley of cannon fired, to clear the encumbered atmosphere, and give me room to breathe and move.

"My spirits were all in arms, and I played a kind of extempory prelude. The cadence was probably wild and impassioned, while, lost in thought, I made the sounds a kind of echo to my train of thinking.

"Pausing for a moment, I met Mr. Venables' eyes. He was observing me with an air of conceited satisfaction, as much as to say—'My last insinuation has done the business—she begins to know her own interest.' Then gathering up his letters, he said, 'That he hoped he should hear no more romantic stuff, well enough in a miss just come from boarding school'; and went, as was his custom, to the counting-house. I still continued playing; and, turning to a sprightly lesson, I executed it with uncommon vivacity. I heard footsteps approach the door, and was soon convinced that Mr. Venables was listening; the consciousness only gave more animation to my fingers. He went down into the kitchen, and the cook, probably by his desire, came to me, to know what I would please to order for dinner. Mr. Venables came into the parlor again, with apparent carelessness. I perceived that the cunning man was overreaching himself; and I gave my directions as usual, and left the room.

"While I was making some alteration in my dress, Mr. Venables peeped in, and, begging my pardon for interrupting me, disappeared. I took up some work (I could not read), and two or three messages were sent to me, probably for no other purpose, but to enable Mr. Venables to ascertain what I was about.

"I listened whenever I heard the streetdoor open; at last I imagined I could distinguish Mr. Venables' step, going out. I laid aside my work; my heart palpitated; still I was afraid hastily to inquire; and I waited a long half-hour, before I ventured to ask the boy whether his master was in the countinghouse?

"Being answered in the negative, I bade him call me a coach, and collecting a few necessaries hastily together, with a little parcel of letters and papers which I had collected the preceding evening, I hurried into it, desiring the coachman to drive to a distant part of the town.

"I almost feared that the coach would break down before I got out of the street; and, when I turned the corner, I seemed to breathe a freer air. I was ready to imagine that I was rising above the thick atmosphere of earth; or I felt, as wearied souls might be supposed to feel on entering another state of existence.

"I stopped at one or two stands of coaches to elude pursuit, and then drove round the skirts of the town to seek for an obscure lodging, where I wished to remain concealed till I could avail myself of my uncle's protection. I had resolved to assume my own name immediately, and openly to avow my determination, without any formal vindication, the moment I had found a home in which I could rest free from the daily alarm of expecting to see Mr. Venables enter.

"I looked at several lodgings; but finding that I could not, without a reference to some acquaintance, who might inform my tyrant, get admittance into a decent apartment—men have not all this trouble—I thought of a woman whom I had assisted to furnish a little haberdasher's shop, and who I knew had a first floor to let.

"I went to her, and though I could not persuade her that the quarrel between me and Mr. Venables would never be made up, still she agreed to conceal me for the present; yet assuring me at the same time, shaking her head, that, when a woman was once married, she must bear everything. Her pale face, on which appeared a thousand haggard lines and delving wrinkles, produced by what is emphatically termed fretting, enforced her remark; and I had afterwards an opportunity of observing the treatment she had to endure, which grizzled her into patience. She toiled from morning till night; yet her husband would rob the till, and take away the money reserved for paying bills; and, returning home drunk, he would beat her if she chanced to offend him, though she had a child at the breast.

"These scenes awoke me at night; and, in the morning, I heard her, as usual, talk to her dear Johnny—he, forsooth, was her master; no slave in the West Indies had one more despotic; but fortunately she was of the true Russian breed of wives.

"My mind, during the few past days, seemed, as it were, disengaged from my body; but, now the struggle was over, I felt very forcibly the effect which perturbation of spirits produces on a woman in my situation.

"The apprehension of a miscarriage obliged me to confine myself to my apartment near a fortnight; but I wrote to my uncle's friend for money, promising 'to call on him, and explain my situation, when I was well enough to go out; meantime I earnestly entreated him not to mention my place of abode to anyone, lest my husband—such the law considered him—should disturb the mind he could not conquer. I mentioned my intention of setting out for Lisbon, to claim my uncle's protection, the moment my health would permit.'

"The tranquility however, which I was recovering, was soon interrupted. My landlady came up to me one day, with eyes swollen with weeping, unable to utter what she was commanded to say. She declared, 'That she was never so miserable in her life; that she must appear an ungrateful monster; and that she would readily go down on her knees to me, to entreat me to forgive her, as she had done to her husband to spare her the cruel task.' Sobs prevented her from proceeding, or answering my impatient inquiries, to know what she meant.

"When she became a little more composed, she took a newspaper out of her pocket, declaring, 'that her heart smote her, but what could she do?—she must obey her husband.' I snatched the paper from her. An advertisement quickly met my eye, purporting, that 'Maria Venables had, without any assignable cause, absconded from her husband; and any person harboring her was menaced with the utmost severity of the law.'

"Perfectly acquainted with Mr. Venables' meanness of soul, this step did not excite my surprise, and scarcely my contempt. Resentment in my breast never survived love. I bade the poor woman, in a kind tone, wipe her eyes, and request her husband to come up and speak to me himself.

"My manner awed him. He respected a lady, though not a woman; and began to mutter out an apology.

" 'Mr. Venables was a rich gentleman; he wished to oblige me, but he had suffered enough by the law already, to tremble at the thought; besides, for certain, we should come together again, and then even I should not thank him for being accessory to keeping us asunder. A husband and wife were, God knows, just as one, and all would come round at last.' He uttered a drawling 'Hem!' and then with an arch look, added—'Master might have had his little frolics—but—Lord bless your heart!—men would be men while the world stands.'

"To argue with this privileged firstborn of reason, I perceived, would be vain. I therefore only requested him to let me remain another day at his house, while I sought for a lodging; and not to inform Mr. Venables that I had ever been sheltered there.

"He consented, because he had not the courage to refuse a person for whom he had an habitual respect; but I heard the pent-up choler burst forth in curses, when he met his wife, who was waiting impatiently at the foot of the stairs, to know what effect my expostulations would have on him.

"Without wasting any time in the fruitless indulgence of vexation, I once more set out in search of an abode in which I could hide myself for a few weeks.

"Agreeing to pay an exorbitant price, I hired an apartment, without any reference being required relative to my character: indeed, a glance at my shape seemed to say that my motive for concealment was sufficiently obvious. Thus was I obliged to shroud my head in infamy.

"To avoid all danger of detection—I use the appropriate word, my child, for I was hunted out like a felon—I determined to take possession of my new lodgings that very evening.

"I did not inform my landlady where I was going. I knew that she had a sincere affection for me, and would willingly have run any risk to show her gratitude; yet I was fully convinced that a few kind words from Johnny would have found the woman in her, and her dear benefactress, as she termed me in an agony of tears, would have been sacrificed, to recompense her tyrant for condescending to treat her like an equal. He could be kind-hearted, as she expressed it, when he pleased. And this thawed sternness, contrasted with his habitual brutality, was the more acceptable, and could not be purchased at too dear a rate.

"The sight of the advertisement made me desirous of taking refuge with my uncle, let what would be the consequence; and I repaired in a hackney coach (afraid of meeting some person who might chance to know me, had I walked) to the chambers of my uncle's friend.

"He received me with great politeness (my uncle had already prepossessed him in my favor), and listened, with interest, to my explanation of the motives which had induced me to fly from home, and skulk in obscurity, with all the timidity of fear that ought only to be the companion of guilt. He lamented, with rather more gallantry than, in my situation, I thought delicate, that such a woman should be thrown away on a man insensible to the charms of beauty or grace. He seemed at a loss what to advise me to do, to evade my husband's search, without hastening to my uncle, whom, he hesitating said, I might not find alive. He uttered this intelligence with visible regret; requested me, at least, to wait for the arrival of the next packet; offered me what money I wanted, and promised to visit me.

"He kept his word; still no letter arrived to put an end to my painful state of suspense. I procured some books and music, to beguile the tedious solitary days.

'Come, ever smiling Liberty,
'And with thee bring thy jocund train:'

I sung—and sung till, saddened by the strain of joy, I bitterly lamented the fate that deprived me of all social pleasure. Comparative liberty indeed I had possessed myself of; but the jocund train lagged far behind!

CHAPTER 13

"By watching my only visitor, my uncle's friend, or by some other means, Mr. Venables discovered my residence, and came to inquire for me. The maidservant assured him there was no such person in the house. A bustle ensued—I caught the alarm—listened—distinguished his voice, and immediately locked the door. They suddenly grew still; and I waited near a quarter of an hour, before I heard him open the parlor door, and mount the stairs with the mistress of the house, who obsequiously declared that she knew nothing of me.

"Finding my door locked, she requested me to 'open it, and prepare to go home with my husband, poor gentleman! to whom I had already occasioned sufficient vexation.' I made no reply. Mr. Venables then, in an assumed tone of softness, entreated me, 'to consider what he suffered, and my own reputation, and get the better of childish resentment.' He ran on in the same strain, pretending to address me, but evidently adapting his discourse to the capacity of the landlady; who, at every pause, uttered an exclamation of pity; or 'Yes, to be sure—Very true, sir.'

"Sick of the farce, and perceiving that I could not avoid the hated interview, I opened the door, and he entered. Advancing with easy assurance to take my hand, I shrunk from his touch, with an involuntary start, as I should have done from the noisome reptile, with more disgust than terror. His conductress was retiring, to give us, as she said, an opportunity to accommodate matters. But I bade her come in, or I would go out; and curiosity impelled her to obey me.

"Mr. Venables began to expostulate; and this woman, proud of his confidence, to second him. But I calmly silenced her, in the midst of a vulgar harangue, and turning to him, asked, 'Why he vainly tormented me? declaring that no power on earth should force me back to his house.'

"After a long altercation, the particulars of which it would be to no purpose to repeat, he left the room. Some time was spent in loud conversation in the parlor below, and I discovered that he had brought his friend, an attorney, with him.

The tumult on the landing place brought out a gentleman who had recently taken apartments in the house; he inquired why I was thus assailed? The voluble attorney instantly repeated the trite tale. The stranger turned to me, observing, with the most soothing politeness and manly interest, that 'my countenance told a very different story.' He added, 'that I should not be insulted, or forced out of the house, by anybody.'

" 'Not by her husband?' asked the attorney.

" 'No, sir, not by her husband.' Mr. Venables advanced towards him—But there was a decision in his attitude, that so well seconded that of his voice,* They left the house: at the same time protesting that anyone that should dare to protect me should be prosecuted with the utmost rigor.

"They were scarcely out of the house when my landlady came up to me again, and begged my pardon, in a very different tone. For, though Mr. Venables had bid her, at her peril, harbor me, he had not attended, I found, to her broad hints, to discharge the lodging. I instantly promised to pay her, and make her a present to compensate for my abrupt departure, if she would procure me another lodging, at a sufficient distance; and she, in return, repeating Mr. Venables' plausible tale, I raised her indignation, and excited her sympathy, by telling her briefly the truth.

"She expressed her commiseration with such honest warmth that I felt soothed; for I have none of that fastidious sensitiveness which a vulgar accent or gesture can alarm to the disregard of real kindness. I was ever glad to perceive in others the humane feelings I delighted to exercise; and the recollection of some ridiculous characteristic circumstances, which have occurred in a moment of emotion, has convulsed me with laughter, though at the instant I should have thought it sacrilegious to have smiled. Your improvement, my dearest girl, being ever present to me while I write, I note these feelings, because women, more accustomed to observe manners than actions, are too much alive to ridicule. So much so that their boasted sensibility is often stifled by false delicacy. True sensibility, the sensibility which is the auxiliary of virtue, and the soul of genius, is in society so occupied with the feelings of others as scarcely to regard its own sensations. With what reverence have I looked up at my uncle, the dear parent of my mind! when I have seen the sense of his own sufferings, of mind and body, absorbed in a desire to comfort those, whose misfortunes were comparatively trivial. He would have been ashamed of being as indulgent to himself, as he was to others. 'Genuine fortitude,' he would assert, 'consisted in governing our own emotions, and making allowance for the weaknesses in our friends, that we would not tolerate in ourselves.' But where is my fond regret leading me!

" 'Women must be submissive,' said my landlady. 'Indeed what could most women do? Who had they to maintain

---

*Godwin notes that two and a half lines of asterisks appear here in the original.

them, but their husbands? Every woman, and especially a lady, could not go through rough and smooth, as she had done, to earn a little bread.'

"She was in a talking mood, and proceeded to inform me how she had been used in the world. 'She knew what it was to have a bad husband, or she did not know who should.' I perceived that she would be very much mortified, were I not to attend to her tale, and I did not attempt to interrupt her, though I wished her, as soon as possible, to go out in search of a new abode for me, where I could once more hide my head.

"She began by telling me, 'That she had saved a little money in service; and was overpersuaded (we must all be in love once in our lives) to marry a likely man, a footman in the family, not worth a groat. My plan,' she continued, 'was to take a house, and let out lodgings; and all went on well, till my husband got acquainted with an impudent slut, who chose to live on other people's means—and then all went to rack and ruin. He ran in debt to buy her fine clothes, such clothes as I never thought of wearing myself, and—would you believe it?—he signed an execution on my very goods, bought with the money I worked so hard to get; and they came and took my bed from under me, before I heard a word of the matter. Aye, madam, these are misfortunes that you gentle-folks know nothing of—but sorrow is sorrow, let it come which way it will.

" 'I sought for a service again—very hard, after having a house of my own!—but he used to follow me, and kick up such a riot when he was drunk, that I could not keep a place; nay, he even stole my clothes, and pawned them; and when I went to the pawnbroker's, and offered to take my oath that they were not bought with a farthing of his money, they said, 'It was all as one, my husband had a right to whatever I had.'

" 'At last he listed for a soldier, and I took a house, making an agreement to pay for the furniture by degrees; and I almost starved myself, till I once more got before-hand in the world.

" 'After an absence of six years (God forgive me! I thought he was dead) my husband returned, found me out, and came with such a penitent face, I forgave him, and clothed him from head to foot. But he had not been a week in the house before some of his creditors arrested him; and, he selling my goods, I found myself once more reduced to beggary, for I was not as well able to work, go to bed late, and rise early, as when I quitted service; and then I thought it hard enough. He was soon tired of me, when there was nothing more to be had, and left me again.

" 'I will not tell you how I was buffeted about, till, hearing for certain that he had died in an hospital abroad, I once more returned to my old occupation; but have not yet been able to get my head above water: so, madam, you must not be angry if I am afraid to run any risk, when I know so well that women have always the worst of it, when law is to decide.'

"After uttering a few more complaints, I prevailed on my landlady to go out in quest of a lodging; and, to be more secure, I condescended to the mean shift of changing my name.

"But why should I dwell on similar incidents!—I was hunted, like an infected beast, from three different apartments, and should not have been allowed to rest in any, had not Mr. Venables, informed of my uncle's dangerous state of health, been inspired with the fear of hurrying me out of the world as I advanced in my pregnancy, by thus tormenting and obliging me to take sudden journeys to avoid him; and then his speculations on my uncle's fortune must prove abortive.

"One day, when he had pursued me to an inn, I fainted, hurrying from him; and, falling down, the sight of my blood alarmed him, and obtained a respite for me. It is strange that he should have retained any hope, after observing my unwavering determination; but, from the mildness of my behavior, when I found all my endeavors to change his disposition unavailing, he formed an erroneous opinion of my character, imagining that, were we once more together, I should part with the money he could not legally force from me, with the same facility as formerly. My forbearance and occasional sympathy he had mistaken for weakness of character; and, because he perceived that I disliked resistance, he thought my indulgence and compassion mere selfishness, and never discovered that the fear of being unjust, or of unnecessarily wounding the feelings of another, was much more painful to me than anything I could have to endure myself. Perhaps it was pride which made me imagine that I could bear what I dreaded to inflict; and that it was often easier to suffer than to see the sufferings of others.

"I forgot to mention that, during this persecution, I received a letter from my uncle, informing me, 'that he only found relief from continual change of air; and that he intended to return when the spring was a little more advanced (it was now the middle of February), and then we would plan a journey to Italy, leaving the fogs and cares of England far behind.' He approved of my conduct, promised to adopt my child, and seemed to have no doubt of obliging Mr. Venables to hear reason. He wrote to his friend, by the same post, desiring him to call on Mr. Venables in his name; and, in consequence of the remonstrances he dictated, I was permitted to lie-in tranquilly.

"The two or three weeks previous, I had been allowed to rest in peace; but, so accustomed was I to pursuit and alarm, that I seldom closed my eyes without being haunted by Mr. Venables' image, who seemed to assume terrific or hateful forms to torment me, wherever I turned—sometimes a wild cat, a roaring bull, or hideous assassin, whom I vainly attempted to fly; at others he was a demon, hurrying me to the brink of a precipice, plunging me into dark waves, or horrid gulfs; and I woke, in violent fits of trembling anxiety, to assure myself that it was all a dream, and to endeavor to lure my waking thoughts to wander to the delightful Italian vales, I hoped soon to visit; or to picture some august ruins, where I reclined in fancy on a moldering column, and escaped, in the contemplation of the heart-enlarging virtues of antiquity, from the turmoil of cares that had depressed all the daring purposes of my soul. But I was not long allowed to calm my mind by the exercise of my imagination; for the third day after your birth, my child, I was surprised by a visit from my elder brother, who came in the most abrupt manner, to inform me of the death of my uncle. He had left the greater part of his fortune to my child, appointing me its guardian; in short, every step was taken to enable me to be mistress of his fortune, without putting any part of it in Mr. Venables' power. My brother came to vent his rage on me, for having, as he expressed himself, 'deprived him, my uncle's eldest nephew, of his inheritance'; though my uncle's property, the fruit of his own exertion, being all in the funds, or on landed securities, there was not a shadow of justice in the charge.

"As I sincerely loved my uncle, this intelligence brought on a fever, which I struggled to conquer with all the energy of my mind; for, in my desolate state, I had it very much at heart to suckle you, my poor babe. You seemed my only tie to life, a cherub, to whom I wished to be a father, as well as a mother; and the double duty appeared to me to produce a proportionate increase of affection. But the pleasure I felt, while sustaining you, snatched from the wreck of hope, was cruelly damped by melancholy reflections on my widowed state—widowed by the death of my uncle. Of Mr. Venables I thought not, even when I thought of the felicity of loving your father, and how a mother's pleasure might be exalted, and her care softened by a husband's tenderness.—'Ought to be!' I exclaimed; and I endeavored to drive away the tenderness that suffocated me; but my spirits were weak, and the unbidden tears would flow. 'Why was I,' I would ask thee, but thou didst not heed me—'cut off from the participation of the sweetest pleasure of life?' I imagined with what ecstasy, after the pains of childbed, I should have presented my little stranger, whom I had so long wished to view, to a respectable father, and with what maternal fondness I should have pressed them both to my heart!—Now I kissed her with less delight, though with the most endearing compassion, poor helpless one! when I perceived a slight resemblance of him, to whom she owed her existence; or, if any gesture reminded me of him, even in his best days, my heart heaved, and I pressed the innocent to my bosom, as if to purify it—yes, I blushed to think that its purity had been sullied, by allowing such a man to be its father.

"After my recovery, I began to think of taking a house in the country, or of making an excursion on the continent, to avoid Mr. Venables; and to open my heart to new pleasures and affection. The spring was melting into summer, and you, my little companion, began to smile—that smile made hope bud out afresh, assuring me the world was not a desert. Your gestures were ever present to my fancy; and I dwelt on the joy I should feel when you would begin to walk and lisp. Watching your wakening mind, and shielding from every rude blast my tender blossom, I recovered my spirits—I dreamed not of the frost—'the killing frost,' to which you were destined to be exposed.—But I lose all patience—and execrate the injustice of the world—folly! ignorance!—I should rather call it; but, shut up from a free circulation of thought, and always pondering on the same griefs, I writhe under the torturing apprehensions, which ought to excite only honest indignation, or active compassion; and would, could I view them as the natural consequence of things. But, born a woman—and born to suffer, in endeavoring to repress my own emotions, I feel more acutely the various ills my sex are fated to bear—I feel that the evils they are subject to endure, degrade them so far below their oppressors, as almost to justify their tyranny; leading at the same time superficial reasoners to term that weakness the cause, which is only the consequence of shortsighted despotism.

CHAPTER 14

"As my mind grew calmer, the visions of Italy again returned with their former glow of coloring; and I resolved on quitting the kingdom for a time, in search of the cheerfulness, that naturally results from a change of scene, unless we carry the barbed arrow with us, and only see what we feel.

"During the period necessary to prepare for a long absence, I sent a supply to pay my father's debts, and settled my brothers in eligible situations; but my attention was not wholly engrossed by my family, though I do not think it necessary to enumerate the common exertions of humanity. The manner in which my uncle's property was settled, prevented me from making the addition to the fortune of my surviving sister that I could have wished; but I had prevailed on him to bequeath her two thousand pounds, and she determined to marry a lover to whom she had been some time attached. Had it not been for this engagement, I should have invited her to accompany me in my tour; and I might have escaped the pit, so artfully dug in my path, when I was the least aware of danger.

"I had thought of remaining in England, till I weaned my child; but this state of freedom was too peaceful to last, and I had soon reason to wish to hasten my departure. A friend of Mr. Venables, the same attorney who had accompanied him in several excursions to hunt me from my hiding places, waited on me to propose a reconciliation. On my refusal, he indirectly advised me to make over to my husband—for husband he would term him—the greater part of the property I had at command, menacing me with continual persecution unless I complied, and that, as a last resort, he would claim the child. I did not, though intimidated by the last insinuation, scruple to declare that I would not allow him to squander the money left to me for far different purposes, but offered him five hundred pounds, if he would sign a bond not to torment me any more. My maternal anxiety made me thus appear to waver from my first determination, and probably suggested to him, or his diabolical agent, the infernal plot, which has succeeded but too well.

"The bond was executed; still I was impatient to leave England. Mischief hung in the air when we breathed the same; I wanted seas to divide us, and waters to roll between, till he had forgotten that I had the means of helping him through a new scheme. Disturbed by the late occurrences, I instantly prepared for my departure. My only delay was waiting for a maidservant, who spoke French fluently, and had been warmly recommended to me. A valet I was advised to hire, when I fixed on my place of residence for any time.

"My God, with what a light heart did I set out for Dover! —It was not my country, but my cares, that I was leaving behind. My heart seemed to bound with the wheels, or rather appeared the center on which they twirled. I clasped you to my bosom, exclaiming 'And you will be safe—quite safe—when—we are once on board the packet.—Would we were there!' I smiled at my idle fears, as the natural effect of continual alarm; and I scarcely owned to myself that I dreaded Mr. Venables' cunning, or was conscious of the horrid delight he would feel, at forming stratagem after stratagem to circumvent me. I was already in the snare—I never reached the packet—I never saw thee more.—I grow breathless. I have scarcely patience to write down the details. The maid—the plausible woman I had hired—put, doubtless, some stupefying potion in what I ate or drank, the morning I left town. All I know is that she must have quitted the chaise, shameless wretch! and taken (from my breast) my babe with her. How could a creature in a female form see me caress thee, and steal thee from my arms! I must stop, stop to repress a mother's anguish; lest, in bitterness of soul, I imprecate the wrath of heaven on this tiger, who tore my only comfort from me.

"How long I slept I know not; certainly many hours, for I woke at the close of day, in a strange confusion of thought. I was probably roused to recollection by someone thundering at a huge, unwieldly gate. Attempting to ask where I was, my voice died away, and I tried to raise it in vain, as I have done in a dream. I looked for my babe with affright; feared that it had fallen out of my lap, while I had so strangely forgotten her; and, such was the vague intoxication, I can give it no other name, in which I was plunged, I could not recollect when or where I last saw you; but I sighed, as if my heart wanted room to clear my head.

"The gates opened heavily, and the sullen sound of many locks and bolts drawn back, grated on my very soul, before I was appalled by the creaking of the dismal hinges, as they closed after me. The gloomy pile was before me, half in ruins; some of the aged trees of the avenue were cut down, and left to rot where they fell; and as we approached some moldering steps, a monstrous dog darted forwards to the length of his chain, and barked and growled infernally.

"The door was opened slowly, and a murderous visage peeped out, with a lantern. 'Hush!' he uttered, in a threatening tone, and the affrighted animal stole back to his kennel. The door of the chaise flew back, the stranger put down the lantern, and clasped his dreadful arms around me. It was certainly the effect of the soporific draught, for, instead of exerting my strength, I sunk without motion, though not without sense, on his shoulder, my limbs refusing to obey my will. I was carried up the steps into a close-shut hall. A candle flaring in the socket, scarcely dispersed the darkness, though it displayed to me the ferocious countenance of the wretch who held me.

"He mounted a wide staircase. Large figures painted on the walls seemed to start on me, and glaring eyes to meet me at every turn. Entering a long gallery, a dismal shriek made me spring out of my conductor's arms, with I know not what mysterious emotion of terror; but I fell on the floor, unable to sustain myself.

"A strange-looking female started out of one of the recesses, and observed me with more curiosity than interest; till, sternly bid retire, she flitted back like a shadow. Other faces, strongly marked, or distorted, peeped through the half-opened doors, and I heard some incoherent sounds. I had no distinct idea where I could be—I looked on all sides, and almost doubted whether I was alive or dead.

"Thrown on a bed, I immediately sunk into insensibility again; and next day, gradually recovering the use of reason, I began, starting affrighted from the conviction, to discover where I was confined—I insisted on seeing the master of the mansion—I saw him—and perceived that I was buried alive.

"Such, my child, are the events of thy mother's life to this dreadful moment—Should she ever escape from the fangs of

her enemies, she will add the secrets of her prison-house—
and—"

Some lines were here crossed out, and the memoirs broke
off abruptly with the names of Jemima and Darnford.

CHAPTER 15

Darnford returned the memoirs to Maria, with a most
affectionate letter, in which he reasoned on "the absurdity
of the laws respecting matrimony, which, till divorces could
be more easily obtained, was," he declared, "the most insuf-
ferable bondage. Ties of this nature could not bind minds
governed by superior principles; and such beings were privileged to act above the dictates of laws they had no voice in
framing, if they had sufficient strength of mind to endure
the natural consequence. In her case, to talk of duty was a
farce, excepting what was due to herself. Delicacy, as well
as reason, forbade her ever to think of returning to her
husband: was she then to restrain her charming sensibility
through mere prejudice? These arguments were not absolutely impartial, for he disdained to conceal, that, when he
appealed to her reason, he felt that he had some interest in
her heart.—The conviction was not more transporting, than
sacred—a thousand times a day, he asked himself how he
had merited such happiness?—and as often he determined
to purify the heart she deigned to inhabit—He entreated to
be again admitted to her presence."

He was; and the tear which glistened in his eye, when he
respectfully pressed her to his bosom, rendered him peculiarly dear to the unfortunate mother. Grief had stilled the
transports of love, only to render their mutual tenderness
more touching. In former interviews, Darnford had contrived,
by a hundred little pretexts, to sit near her, to take her
hand, or to meet her eyes—now it was all soothing affection,
and esteem seemed to have rivaled love. He adverted to her
narrative, and spoke with warmth of the oppression she
had endured. His eyes, glowing with a lambent flame, told
her how much he wished to restore her to liberty and love;
but he kissed her hand, as if it had been that of a saint; and
spoke of the loss of her child, as if it had been his own.
—What could have been more flattering to Maria? Every

instance of self-denial was registered in her heart, and she loved him, for loving her too well to give way to the transports of passion.

They met again and again; and Darnford declared, while passion suffused his cheeks, that he never before knew what it was to love.

One morning Jemima informed Maria that her master intended to wait on her, and speak to her without witnesses. He came, and brought a letter with him, pretending that he was ignorant of its contents, though he insisted on having it returned to him. It was from the attorney already mentioned, who informed her of the death of her child, and hinted, "that she could not now have a legitimate heir, and that, would she make over the half of her fortune during life, she should be conveyed to Dover, and permitted to pursue her plan of traveling."

Maria answered with warmth, "That she had no terms to make with the murderer of her babe, nor would she purchase liberty at the price of her own respect."

She began to expostulate with her jailor; but he sternly bade her, "Be silent—he had not gone so far, not to go further."

Darnford came in the evening. Jemima was obliged to be absent, and she, as usual, locked the door on them, to prevent interruption or discovery. The lovers were, at first, embarrassed; but fell insensibly into confidential discourse. Darnford represented, "that they might soon be parted," and wished her "to put it out of the power of fate to separate them."

As her husband she now received him, and he solemnly pledged himself as her protector—and eternal friend.

There was one peculiarity in Maria's mind: she was more anxious not to deceive than to guard against deception; and had rather trust without sufficient reason, than be forever the prey of doubt. Besides, what are we, when the mind has, from reflection, a certain kind of elevation, which exalts the contemplation above the little concerns of prudence! We see what we wish, and make a world of our own—and, though reality may sometimes open a door to misery, yet the moments of happiness procured by the imagination, may, without a paradox, be reckoned among the solid comforts of life. Maria now, imagining that she had found a being of celestial mold—was happy—nor was she deceived.—He was then plastic in her impassioned hand—and reflected all the sentiments which animated and warmed her.

CHAPTER 16

One morning confusion seemed to reign in the house, and Jemima came in terror, to inform Maria, "that her master had left it, with a determination, she was assured (and too many circumstances corroborated the opinion, to leave a doubt of its truth) of never returning. I am prepared then," said Jemima, "to accompany you in your flight."

Maria started up, her eyes darting towards the door, as if afraid that some one should fasten it on her for ever.

Jemima continued, "I have perhaps no right now to expect the performance of your promise; but on you it depends to reconcile me with the human race."

"But Darnford!"—exclaimed Maria, mournfully—sitting down again, and crossing her arms—"I have no child to go to, and liberty has lost its sweets."

"I am much mistaken, if Darnford is not the cause of my master's flight—his keepers assure me that they have promised to confine him two days longer, and then he will be free—you cannot see him; but they will give a letter to him the moment he is free. In that inform him where he may find you in London; fix on some hotel. Give me your clothes; I will send them out of the house with mine, and we will slip out at the garden gate. Write your letter while I make these arrangements, but lose no time!"

In an agitation of spirit, not to be calmed, Maria began to write to Darnford. She called him by the sacred name of "husband," and bade him "hasten to her, to share her fortune, or she would return to him." An hotel in the Adelphi was the place of rendezvous.

The letter was sealed and given in charge; and with light footsteps, yet terrified at the sound of them, she descended, scarcely breathing, and with an indistinct fear that she should never get out at the garden gate. Jemima went first.

A being, with a visage that would have suited one possessed with a devil, crossed the path, and seized Maria by the arm. Maria had no fear but of being detained—"Who are you? what are you?" for the form was scarcely human. "If you are made of flesh and blood," his ghastly eyes glared at her, "do not stop me!"

"Woman," interrupted a sepulchral voice, "what have I to do with thee?"—Still he grasped her hand, muttering a curse.

"No, no; you have nothing to do with me," she exclaimed, "this is a moment of life and death!"—

With supernatural force she broke from him, and, throwing her arms round Jemima, cried, "Save me!" The being, from whose grasp she had loosed herself, took up a stone as they opened the door, and with a kind of hellish sport threw it after them. They were out of his reach.

When Maria arrived in town, she drove to the hotel already fixed on. But she could not sit still—her child was ever before her; and all that had passed during her confinement appeared to be a dream. She went to the house in the suburbs where, as she now discovered, her babe had been sent. The moment she entered, her heart grew sick; but she wondered not that it had proved its grave. She made the necessary inquiries, and the churchyard was pointed out, in which it rested under a turf. A little frock which the nurse's child wore (Maria had made it herself) caught her eye. The nurse was glad to sell it for a half a guinea, and Maria hastened away with the relic, and, reentering the hackney coach which waited for her, gazed on it, till she reached her hotel.

She then waited on the attorney who had made her uncle's will, and explained to him her situation. He readily advanced her some of the money which still remained in his hands, and promised to take the whole of the case into consideration. Maria only wished to be permitted to remain in quiet—She found that several bills, apparently with her signature, had been presented to her agent, nor was she for a moment at a loss to guess by whom they had been forged; yet, equally averse to threaten or entreat, she requested her friend [the solicitor] to call on Mr. Venables. He was not to be found at home; but at length his agent, the attorney, offered a conditional promise to Maria, to leave her in peace, as long as she behaved with propriety, if she would give up the notes. Maria inconsiderately consented—Darnford was arrived, and she wished to be only alive to love; she wished to forget the anguish she felt whenever she thought of her child.

They took a ready furnished lodging together, for she was above disguise; Jemima insisting on being considered as her housekeeper, and to receive the customary stipend. On no other terms would she remain with her friend.

Darnford was indefatigable in tracing the mysterious circumstances of his confinement. The cause was simply that a relation, a very distant one, to whom he was heir, had died intestate, leaving a considerable fortune. On the news of Darnford's arrival [in England, a person, entrusted with the management of the property and who had the writings in his possession determining, by one bold stroke, to strip Darnford of the succession], had planned his confinement; and [as soon as he had taken the measures he judged most conducive to his object, this ruffian, together with his instrument], the keeper of the private madhouse, left the kingdom. Darnford, who still pursued his inquiries, at last discovered that they had fixed their place of refuge at Paris.

Maria and he determined, therefore, with the faithful Jemima, to visit that metropolis, and accordingly were preparing for the journey, when they were informed that Mr. Venables had commenced an action against Darnford for seduction and adultery. The indignation Maria felt cannot be explained; she repented of the forbearance she had exercised in giving up the notes. Darnford could not put off his journey without risking the loss of his property: Maria therefore furnished him with money for his expedition, and determined to remain in London till the termination of this affair.

She visited some ladies with whom she had formerly been intimate, but was refused admittance; and at the opera, or Ranelagh, they could not recollect her. Among these ladies there were some, not her most intimate acquaintance, who were generally supposed to avail themselves of the cloak of marriage to conceal a mode of conduct that would forever have damned their fame, had they been innocent, seduced girls. These particularly stood aloof. Had she remained with her husband, practicing insincerity and neglecting her child to manage an intrigue, she would still have been visited and respected. If, instead of openly living with her lover, she could have condescended to call into play a thousand arts, which, degrading her own mind, might have allowed the people who were not deceived to pretend to be so, she would have been caressed and treated like an honorable woman. "And Brutus is an honorable man!" said Mark Antony with equal sincerity.

With Darnford she did not taste uninterrupted felicity; there was a volatility in his manner which often distressed her; but love gladdened the scene; besides, he was the most

tender, sympathizing creature in the world. A fondness for
the sex often gives an appearance of humanity to the behavior of men, who have small pretensions to the reality; and
they seem to love others, when they are only pursuing their
own gratification. Darnford appeared ever willing to avail
himself of her taste and acquirements, while she endeavored
to profit by his decision of character, and to eradicate some
of the romantic notions, which had taken root in her mind,
while in adversity she had brooded over visions of unattain-
able bliss.

The real affections of life, when they are allowed to burst
forth, are buds pregnant with joy and all the sweet emotions
of the soul; yet they branch out with wild ease, unlike the
artificial forms of felicity, sketched by an imagination painful alive. The substantial happiness, which enlarges and
civilizes the mind, may be compared to the pleasure experienced in roving through nature at large, inhaling the sweet
gale natural to the clime; while the reveries of a feverish
imagination continually sport themselves in gardens full of
aromatic shrubs, which cloy while they delight, and weaken
the sense of pleasure they gratify. The heaven of fancy,
below or beyond the stars, in this life, or in those ever
smiling regions surrounded by the unmarked ocean of futurity, have an insipid uniformity which palls. Poets have
imagined scenes of bliss; but fencing out sorrow, all the
ecstatic emotions of the soul, and even its grandeur, seem to
be equally excluded. We doze over the unruffled lake, and
long to scale the rocks which fence the happy valley of
contentment, though serpents hiss in the pathless desert, and
danger lurks in the unexplored wiles. Maria found herself
more indulgent as she was happier, and discovered virtues
in characters she had before disregarded, while chasing the
phantoms of elegance and excellence, which sported in the
meteors that exhale in the marshes of misfortune. The heart
is often shut by romance against social pleasure; and,
fostering a sickly sensibility, grows callous to the soft touches
of humanity.

To part with Darnford was indeed cruel. It was to feel
most painfully alone; but she rejoiced to think that she
should spare him the care and perplexity of the suit, and
meet him again, all his own. Marriage, as at present constituted, she considered as leading to immorality—yet, as the
odium of society impedes usefulness, she wished to avow her
affection to Darnford by becoming his wife according to

established rules; not to be confounded with women who act from very different motives, though her conduct would be just the same without the ceremony as with it, and her expectations from him not less firm. The being summoned to defend herself from a charge which she was determined to plead guilty to, was still galling, as it roused bitter reflections on the situation of women in society.

CHAPTER 17

Such was her state of mind when the dogs of law were let loose on her. Maria took the task of conducting Darnford's defense upon herself. She instructed his counsel to plead guilty to the charge of adultery; but to deny that of seduction.

The counsel for the plaintiff opened the cause by observing, "that his client had ever been an indulgent husband, and had borne with several defects of temper, while he had nothing criminal to lay to the charge of his wife. But that she left his house without assigning any cause. He could not assert that she was then acquainted with the defendant; yet, when he was once endeavoring to bring her back to her home, this man put the peace officers to flight, and took her he knew not whither. After the birth of her child, her conduct was so strange, and a melancholy malady having afflicted one of the family, which delicacy forbade the dwelling on, it was necessary to confine her. By some means the defendant enabled her to make her escape, and they had lived together, in despite of all sense of order and decorum. The adultery was allowed, it was not necessary to bring any witnesses to prove it; but the seduction, though highly probable from the circumstances which he had the honor to state, could not be so clearly proved.—It was of the most atrocious kind, as decency was set at defiance, and respect for reputation, which shows internal compunction, utterly disregarded."

A strong sense of injustice had silenced every motion, which a mixture of true and false delicacy might otherwise have excited in Maria's bosom. She only felt in earnest to insist on the privilege of her nature. The sarcasms of society, and the condemnations of a mistaken world, were nothing to her, compared with acting contrary to those feelings which were the foundation of her principles. [She therefore eagerly put herself forward, instead of desiring to be absent, on this memorable occasion.]

Convinced that the subterfuges of the law were disgraceful, she wrote a paper, which she expressly desired might be read in court:

"Married when scarcely able to distinguish the nature of the engagement, I yet submitted to the rigid laws which enslave women, and obeyed the man whom I could no longer love. Whether the duties of the state are reciprocal, I mean not to discuss; but I can prove repeated infidelities which I overlooked or pardoned. Witnesses are not wanting to establish these facts. I at present maintain the child of a maid-servant, sworn to him, and born after our marriage. I am ready to allow that education and circumstances lead men to think and act with less delicacy than the preservation of order in society demands from women; but surely I may without assumption declare that, though I could excuse the birth, I could not the desertion of this unfortunate babe:—and, while I despised the man, it was not easy to venerate the husband. With proper restrictions, however, I revere the institution which fraternizes the world. I exclaim against the laws which throw the whole weight of the yoke on the weaker shoulders, and force women, when they claim protectorship as mothers, to sign a contract which renders them dependent on the caprice of the tyrant, whom choice or necessity has appointed to reign over them. Various are the cases in which a woman ought to separate herself from her husband; and mine, I may be allowed emphatically to insist, comes under the description of the most aggravated.

"I will not enlarge on those provocations which only the individual can estimate; but will bring forward such charges only, the truth of which is an insult upon humanity. In order to promote certain destructive speculations, Mr. Venables prevailed on me to borrow certain sums of a wealthy relation; and, when I refused further compliance, he thought of bartering my person; and not only allowed opportunities to, but urged, a friend from whom he borrowed money, to seduce me. On the discovery of this act of atrocity, I determined to leave him, and in the most decided manner, for ever. I consider all obligations as made void by his conduct; and hold, that schisms which proceed from want of principles, can never be healed.

"He received a fortune with me to the amount of five thousand pounds. On the death of my uncle, convinced that

I could provide for my child, I destroyed the settlement of that fortune. I required none of my property to be returned to me, nor shall enumerate the sums extorted from me during six years that we lived together.

"After leaving what the law considers as my home, I was hunted like a criminal from place to place, though I contracted no debts, and demanded no maintenance—yet, as the laws sanction such proceeding, and make women the property of their husbands, I forbear to animadvert. After the birth of my daughter, and the death of my uncle, who left a very considerable property to myself and child, I was exposed to new persecution; and, because I had, before arriving at what is termed years of discretion, pledged my faith, I was treated by the world as bound forever to a man whose vices were notorious. Yet what are the vices generally known, to the various miseries that a woman may be subject to, which, though deeply felt, eating into the soul, elude description, and may be glossed over! A false morality is even established, which makes all the virtue of women consist in chastity, submission, and the forgiveness of injuries.

"I pardon my oppressor—bitterly as I lament the loss of my child, torn from me in the most violent manner. But nature revolts, and my soul sickens at the bare supposition, that it could ever be a duty to pretend affection, when a separation is necessary to prevent my feeling hourly aversion.

"To force me to give my fortune, I was imprisoned—yes; in a private madhouse.—There, in the heart of misery, I met the man charged with seducing me. We became attached—I deemed, and ever shall deem, myself free. The death of my babe dissolved the only tie which subsisted between me and my, what is termed, lawful husband.

"To this person, thus encountered, I voluntarily gave myself, never considering myself as any more bound to transgress the laws of moral purity, because the will of my husband might be pleaded in my excuse, than to transgress those laws to which [the policy of artificial society has] annexed [positive] punishments.—While no command of a husband can prevent a woman from suffering for certain crimes, she must be allowed to consult her conscience, and regulate her conduct, in some degree, by her own sense of right. The respect I owe to myself, demanded my strict adherence to my determination of never viewing Mr. Venables in the light of a husband, nor could it forbid me from encouraging another. If I am unfortunately united to an unprincipled man, am I forever to be shut out from fulfilling the duties of a wife and mother?—I wish my country to approve of my conduct; but, if laws exist, made by the strong to oppress the weak, I appeal to my own sense of justice, and declare that I will not live with the individual, who has violated every moral obligation which binds man to man.

"I protest equally against any charge being brought to criminate the man whom I consider as my husband. I was six-and-twenty when I left Mr. Venables' roof; if ever I am to be supposed to arrive at an age to direct my own actions, I must by that time have arrived at it.—I acted with deliberation.—Mr. Darnford found me a forlorn and oppressed woman, and promised the protection women in the present state of society want.—But the man who now claims me—was he deprived of my society by this conduct? The question is an insult to common sense, considering where Mr. Darnford met me.—Mr. Venables' door was indeed open to me—nay, threats and entreaties were used to induce me to return; but why? Was affection or honor the motive?—I cannot, it is true, dive into the recesses of the human heart—yet I presume to assert, [borne out as I am by a variety of circumstances,] that he was merely influenced by the most rapacious avarice.

"I claim then a divorce, and the liberty of enjoying, free from molestation, the fortune left to me by a relation, who was well aware of the character of the man with whom I had to contend.—I appeal to the justice and humanity of the jury—a body of men, whose private judgment must be allowed to modify laws, that must be unjust, because definite rules can never apply to indefinite circumstances—and I deprecate punishment upon the man of my choice, freeing him, as I solemnly do, from the charge of seduction.

"I did not put myself into a situation to justify a charge of adultery till I had, from conviction, shaken off the fetters which bound me to Mr. Venables.—While I lived with him, I defy the voice of calumny to sully what is termed the fair fame of woman.—Neglected by my husband, I never encouraged a lover; and preserved with scrupulous care what is termed my honor, at the expense of my peace, till he, who should have been its guardian, laid traps to ensnare me. From that moment I believed myself, in the sight of heaven, free—and no power on earth shall force me to renounce my resolution."

The judge, in summing up the evidence, alluded to "the fallacy of letting women plead their feelings, as an excuse for the violation of the marriage vow. For his part, he had always determined to oppose all innovation, and the new-fangled notions which encroached on the good old rules of conduct. We did not want French principles in public or private life—and, if women were allowed to plead their feelings, as an excuse or palliation of infidelity, it was opening a floodgate for immorality. What virtuous woman thought of her feelings?—It was her duty to love and obey the man chosen by her parents and relations, who were qualified by their experience to judge better for her, than she could for herself. As to the charges brought against the husband, they were vague, supported by no witnesses, excepting that of imprisonment in a private madhouse. The proofs of an insanity in the family, might render that, however, a prudent measure; and indeed the conduct of the lady did not appear that of a person of sane mind. Still such a mode of proceeding could not be justified, and might perhaps entitle the lady [in another court] to a sentence of separation from bed and board, during the joint lives of the parties; but he hoped that no Englishman would legalize adultery, by enabling the adulteress to enrich her seducer. Too many restrictions could not be thrown in the way of divorces, if we wished to maintain the sanctity of marriage; and, though they might bear a little hard on a few, very few individuals, it was evidently for the good of the whole."

CONCLUSION

. . . .

I

"Darnford's letters were affectionate; but circumstances occasioned delays, and the miscarriage of some letters rendered the reception of wished-for answers doubtful: his return was necessary to calm Maria's mind."

II

"As Darnford had informed her that his business was settled, his delaying to return seemed extraordinary; but love to excess excludes fear or suspicion."

. . . .

I

"Trial for adultery—Maria defends herself—A separation from bed and board is the consequence—Her fortune is thrown into chancery—Darnford obtains a part of his property—Maria goes into the country."

II

"A prosecution for adultery commenced—Trial—Darnford sets out for France—Letters—Once more pregnant—He returns—Mysterious behavior—Visit—Expectation—Discovery—Interview—Consequence."

III

"Sued by her husband—Damages awarded to him—Separation from bed and board—Darnford goes abroad—Maria into the country—Provides for her father—Is shunned—Returns to London—Expects to see her lover—The rack of expectation—Finds herself again with Child—Delighted—A discovery—A visit—A miscarriage—Conclusion."

. . . .

IV

"Divorced by her husband—Her lover unfaithful—Pregnancy—Miscarriage—Suicide."

. . . .

THE END

"She swallowed the laudanum; her soul was calm—the tempest had subsided—and nothing remained but an eager longing to forget herself—to fly from the anguish she endured to escape from thought—from this hell of disappointment.

"Still her eyes closed not—one remembrance with frightful velocity followed another—All the incidents of her life were in arms, embodied to assail her, and prevent her sinking into the sleep of death.—Her murdered child again appeared to her, mourning for the babe of which she was the tomb.—'And could it have a nobler?—Surely it is better to die with me, than to enter on life without a mother's care!—I cannot live!—but could I have deserted my child the moment it was born?—thrown it on the troubled wave of life, without a hand to support it?'—She looked up: 'What have I not suffered!—may I find a father where I am going!'—Her head turned; a stupor ensued: a faintness—'Have a little patience,' said Maria, holding her swimming head (she thought of her mother), 'this cannot last long; and what is a little bodily pain to the pangs I have endured?'

"A new vision swam before her. Jemima seemed to enter—leading a little creature, that, with tottering footsteps, approached the bed. The voice of Jemima sounding as at a distance, called her—she tried to listen, to speak, to look!

" 'Behold your child!' exclaimed Jemima. Maria started off the bed, and fainted.—Violent vomiting followed.

"When she was restored to life, Jemima addressed her with great solemnity: '——— led me to suspect, that your husband and brother had deceived you, and secreted the child. I would not torment you with doubtful hopes, and I left you (at a fatal moment) to search for the child!—I snatched her from misery—and (now she is alive again) would you leave her alone in the world, to endure what I have endured?'

"Maria gazed wildly at her, her whole frame was convulsed with emotion; when the child, whom Jemima had been tutoring all the journey, uttered the word 'Mamma!' she caught her to her bosom, and burst into a passion of tears—then, resting the child gently on the bed, as if afraid of killing it, she put her hand to her eyes, to conceal as it were the agonizing struggle of her soul. She remained silent for five minutes, crossing her arms over her bosom, and reclining her head, then exclaimed: 'The conflict is over!—I will live for my child!' "

. . . .

ON SOCIETY
AND
HUMAN RIGHTS

A Vindication of the Rights of Men

IN HER FIRST *Vindication*, her answer to Edmund Burke's *Reflections on the Revolution in France*, Wollstonecraft sets herself up as the voice of reason against Burke's emotionalism, but her own emotions often permeate her argument; she condemns Burke's personal attack on her mentor, the liberal Dr. Richard Price, while attacking Burke's character in the defense. Such inconsistencies undermine Wollstonecraft's authority in debate, but the very vigor of her tone compels attention. A strong and impulsive personality makes itself felt in *A Vindication of the Rights of Men*: like its author, the work "glow[s] with indignation."

The energy which this hastily written pamphlet exudes has many sources. Her portrait of Dr. Price, drawn from life, has a sentimental power, but her description also contains satiric barbs aimed at Burke. She pictures her aging friend "tottering on the verge of the grave . . . and, if a glimpse of the glad dawn of liberty rekindled the fire of youth in his veins, you, who could not stand the fascinating glance of a *great* Lady's eyes when neither virtue nor sense beamed in them, might have pardoned his unseemly transport—if such it must be deemed." That "*great* Lady" (the French queen) is the heroine of the central passage in which Burke sums up the virtues of tradition in a rapturous tribute to French royalty. Writing with horror of October 6, 1789, when the Parisian mob marched the royal family from Versailles to the Tuileries, he had described the vision of light that Marie Antoinette had seemed to be when he saw her years ago, as dauphiness, at Versailles, "glittering like the morning star, full of life, and splendor and joy." (In her own book on the French Revolution, Wollstonecraft was to offer a counter-portrait of Marie Antoinette; where Burke saw the morning star, she saw Lucifer.)

Wollstonecraft frequently resorts to italics in the *Vindication*, when she quotes directly from Burke or describes attitudes of his which she particularly scorns. Burke's ennoblement of family life as the symbol of civilized order (and raised to its highest embodiment by the Bourbon dynasty) inflames Wollstonecraft, for she had felt too keenly the indignities produced by the system that sacrificed younger children to the eldest son and "female morals" to "family convenience." Property, she says, corrupts all human relationships. She challenges Burke for protecting a system in which only the property of the wealthy is secure, and supplies powerful evidence to dispute Burke's complacent justification of those whom she considers selfish and privileged. Poor men are impressed for naval service, put to death for the theft of a few pounds or for poaching the deer of the rich.

This ex-governess, who had seen Eton up close and knew the flaws of educational establishments, derides Burke's praise of the role of the clergy in training the minds of gentlemen. As ever, she views early training as the key to character. In one of the many original comparisons that make the *Vindication* so vibrant, Wollstonecraft seems to recall her own sense of "the little respect paid, in great houses, to tutors and chaplains ... sometimes only modern substitutes for the jesters of Gothic memory." Rather than enhance their respect for religious principles, the tutorial clergy, servile employees of the wealthy, make their charges contemptuous of religion. In her indictment of the clergy's failure to provide aristocrats with a truly Christian education, she asks whether true Christians would support the slave trade as many such clergymen did. Like the American feminists who followed and were influenced by her work, Wollstonecraft heartily despised the institution of slavery.

In such pungent illustrations of the injustice tolerated by conservatives, Wollstonecraft reiterates her belief in progress and heralds the innovations fashioned by the French National Assembly. But her anger at Burke stems not only from his treatment of the French Revolution and Dr. Price. She criticizes Burke's second book, *A Philosophical Inquiry into the Origin of Our Ideas of the Sublime and Beautiful*, written in 1757, upbraiding him for inconsistency and vanity. These critical remarks launched her on a subject close to her heart, and anticipate *The Vindication of the Rights of Woman*. She partly blames Burke's *Inquiry* for the superficial and immoral quality of "civilized" women's lives. In his earlier work, as he defined beautiful women, Burke recommended to them a state of ornamental mindlessness. His advice, Wollstonecraft infers, is based on Burke's assumption "that one half of the human species, at least, have not souls." Speaking out for the poor, the oppressed, and the degraded of either sex, all of whom Wollstonecraft includes in the generic "men," she would, through her literary powers, teach Edmund Burke, as she taught her pupils, that whoever respects "the rights of men . . . fears God and loves his fellow creatures."

A
VINDICATION
OF THE
RIGHTS OF MEN,
IN A
LETTER
TO THE RIGHT HONORABLE
EDMUND BURKE;
OCCASIONED BY
HIS REFLECTIONS
ON THE
REVOLUTION IN FRANCE

. . . .

I glow with indignation when I attempt, methodically, to unravel your slavish paradoxes, in which I can find no fixed first principle to refute; I shall not, therefore, condescend to show where you affirm in one page what you deny in another; and how frequently you draw conclusions without any previous premises: it would be something like cowardice to fight with a man who had never exercised the weapons with which his opponent chose to combat, and irksome to refute sentence after sentence in which the latent spirit of tyranny appeared.

I perceive, from the whole tenor of your Reflections, that you have a mortal antipathy to reason; but, if there is anything like argument, or first principles, in your wild declamation, behold the result: that we are to reverence the rust of antiquity, and term the unnatural customs, which ignorance and mistaken self-interest have consolidated, the sage fruit of experience: nay, that, if we do discover some errors, our *feelings* should lead us to excuse, with blind love or unprincipled filial affection, the venerable vestiges of ancient days. These are gothic notions of beauty—the ivy is beautiful, but when it insidiously destroys the trunk from which it receives support, who would not grub it up?

Further, that we ought cautiously to remain forever in frozen inactivity, because a thaw, whilst it nourishes the soil, spreads a temporary inundation; and the fear of risking any personal present convenience should prevent a struggle for the most estimable advantages. This is sound reasoning, I grant, in the mouth of the rich and short-sighted.

Yes, sir, the strong gained riches, the few have sacrificed the many to their vices; and, to be able to pamper their appetites, and supinely exist without exercising mind or body, they have ceased to be men. Lost to the relish of true pleasure, such beings would, indeed, deserve compassion, if injustice was not softened by the tyrant's plea—necessity; if prescription was not raised as an immortal boundary against innovation. Their minds, in fact, instead of being cultivated, have been so warped by education that it may require some ages to bring them back to nature, and enable them to see their true interest, with that degree of conviction which is necessary to influence their conduct.

The civilization which has taken place in Europe has been very partial, and, like every custom that an arbitrary point of honor has established, refines the manners at the expense of morals, by making sentiments and opinions current in conversation that have no root in the heart, or weight in the cooler resolves of the mind. And what has stopped its progress? Hereditary property—hereditary honors. The man has been changed into an artificial monster by the station in which he was born, and the consequent homage that benumbed his faculties like the torpedo's touch; or a being, with a capacity of reasoning, would not have failed to discover, as his faculties unfolded, that true happiness arose from the friendship and intimacy which can only be enjoyed by equals; and that charity is not a condescending distribution of alms, but an intercourse of good offices and mutual benefits, founded on respect for justice and humanity.

. . . .

The imperfection of all modern governments must, without waiting to repeat the trite remark that all human institutions are unavoidably imperfect, in a great measure have arisen from this simple circumstance, that the constitution, if such an heterogeneous mass deserve that name, was settled in the dark days of ignorance, when the minds of men were shackled by the grossest prejudices and most immoral superstition. And do you, sir, a sagacious philosopher, recommend night as the fittest time to analyze a ray of light?

Are we to seek for the rights of men in the ages when a few marks were the only penalty imposed for the life of a man, and death for death when the property of the rich was touched? when—I blush to discover the depravity of our nature—when a deer was killed! Are these the laws that it is natural to love, and sacrilegious to invade?—Were the rights of men understood when the law authorized or tolerated murder?—or is power and right the same in your creed?

But, in fact, all your declamation leads so directly to this conclusion that I beseech you to ask your own heart, when you call yourself a friend of liberty, whether it would not be more consistent to style yourself the champion of property, the adorer of the golden image which power has set up? . . .

. . . .

It is necessary emphatically to repeat that there are rights which men inherit at their birth, as rational creatures, who were raised above the brute creation by their improvable faculties; and that, in receiving these, not from their forefathers but from God, prescription can never undermine natural rights.

A father may dissipate his property without his child having any right to complain; but should he attempt to sell him for a slave, or fetter him with laws contrary to reason, nature, in enabling him to discern good from evil, teaches him to break the ignoble chain. . . .

There is no end to this implicit submission to authority—somewhere it must stop, or we return to barbarism; and the capacity of improvement, which gives us a natural scepter on earth, is a cheat, an ignis-fatuus, that leads us from inviting meadows into bogs and dunghills. . . .

But on what principle Mr. Burke could defend American independence, I cannot conceive; for the whole tenor of his plausible arguments settles slavery on an everlasting foundation. Allowing his servile reverence for antiquity, and prudent attention to self-interest, to have the force which he insists on, the slave trade ought never to be abolished; and, because our ignorant forefathers, not understanding the native dignity of man, sanctioned a traffic that outrages every suggestion of reason and religion, we are to submit to the inhuman custom, and term an atrocious insult to humanity the love of our country, and a proper submission to the laws by which our property is secured. Security of property! Behold, in a few words, the definition of English liberty. And to this selfish principle every nobler one is sacrificed. . . . But softly—it is only the property of the rich that is secure; the man who lives by the sweat of his brow has no asylum from oppression; the strong man may enter—when was the castle of the poor sacred?—and the base informer steal him from the family that depend on his industry for subsistence.

Fully sensible as you must be of the baneful consequences that inevitably follow this notorious infringement on the dearest rights of men, and that it is an infernal blot on the very face of our immaculate constitution, I cannot avoid expressing my surprise that when you recommended our form of government as a model, you did not caution the French against the arbitrary custom of pressing men for the sea service. You should have hinted to them that property in England is much more secure than liberty, and not have concealed that the liberty of an honest mechanic—his all—is often sacrificed to secure the property of the rich. For it is a farce to pretend that a man fights *for his country, his hearth, or his altars*, when he has neither liberty nor property. His property is in his nervous arms—and they are compelled to pull a strange rope at the surly command of a tyrannic boy, who probably obtained his rank on account of his family connections, or the prostituted vote of his father, whose interest in a borough, or voice as a senator, was acceptable to the minister.

Our penal laws punish with death the thief who steals a few pounds; but to take by violence, or trepan, a man, is no such heinous offence.—For who shall dare to complain of the venerable vestige of the law that rendered the life of a deer more sacred than that of a man? But it was the poor man with only his native dignity who was thus oppressed—and only metaphysical sophists and cold mathematicians can discern this insubstantial form; it is a work of abstraction—

and a *gentleman* of lively imagination must borrow some drapery from fancy before he can love or pity a *man*. Misery, to reach your heart, I perceive, must have its cap and bells; your tears are reserved, very *naturally* considering your character, for the declamation of the theater, or for the downfall of queens, whose rank alters the nature of folly, and throws a graceful veil over vices that degrade humanity; whilst the distress of many industrious mothers, whose *helpmates* have been torn from them, and the hungry cry of helpless babes, were vulgar sorrows that could not move your commiseration, though they might extort an alms . . .

. . . .

A government that acts in this manner cannot be called a good parent, nor inspire natural (habitual is the proper word) affection, in the breasts of children who are thus disregarded.

The game laws are almost as oppressive to the peasantry as press warrants to the mechanic. In this land of liberty what is to secure the property of the poor farmer when his noble landlord chooses to plant a decoy field near his little property? Game devour the fruit of his labor; but fines and imprisonment await him if he dare to kill any—or lift up his hand to interrupt the pleasure of his lord. How many families have been plunged, in the *sporting* countries, into misery and vice for some paltry transgression of these coercive laws, by the natural consequence of that anger which a man feels when he sees the reward of his industry laid waste by unfeeling luxury?—when his children's bread is given to dogs!

. . . .

In reprobating Dr. Price's opinions you might have spared the man; and if you had had but half as much reverence for the gray hairs of virtue as for the accidental distinctions of rank, you would not have treated with such indecent familiarity and supercilious contempt a member of the community whose talents and modest virtues place him high in the scale of moral excellence. I am not accustomed to look up with vulgar awe, even when mental superiority exalts a man above his fellows; but still the sight of a man whose habits are fixed by piety and reason, and whose virtues are consolidated into goodness, commands my homage—and I should touch his errors with a tender hand when I made a parade of my sensibility. Granting, for a moment, that Dr. Price's political opinions are Utopian reveries, and that the world is not yet sufficiently civilized to adopt such a sublime system of morality; they could, however, only be the reveries of a benevolent mind. Tottering on the verge of the grave, that worthy man in his whole life never dreamt of struggling for power or riches; and, if a glimpse of the glad dawn of liberty rekindled the fire of youth in his veins, you, who could not stand the fascinating glance of a *great* Lady's eyes, when neither virtue nor sense beamed in them, might have pardoned his unseemly transport—if such it must be deemed.

I could almost fancy that I now see this respectable old man, in his pulpit, with hands clasped, and eyes devoutly fixed, praying with all the simple energy of unaffected piety; or, when more erect, inculcating the dignity of virtue, and enforcing the doctrines his life adorns; benevolence animated each feature, and persuasion attuned his accents; the preacher grew eloquent, who only labored to be clear; and the respect that he extorted seemed only the respect due to personified virtue and matured wisdom. Is this the man you brand with so many opprobrious epithets? he whose private life will stand the test of the strictest inquiry—away with such unmanly sarcasms and puerile conceits. . . .

. . . .

Man has been termed, with strict propriety, a microcosm, a little world in himself. He is so—yet must, however, be reckoned an ephemera, or, to adopt your figure of rhetoric, a summer's fly. The perpetuation of property in our families is one of the privileges you most warmly contend for; yet it would not be very difficult to prove that the mind must have a very limited range that thus confines its benevolence to such a narrow circle, which, with great propriety, may be included in the sordid calculations of blind self-love.

A brutal attachment to children has appeared most conspicuous in parents who have treated them like slaves, and demanded due homage for all the property they transferred to them during their lives. It has led them to force their children to break the most sacred ties; to do violence to a natural impulse, and run into legal prostitution to increase wealth or shun poverty; and, still worse, the dread of paren-

tal malediction has made many weak characters violate
truth in the face of Heaven; and, to avoid a father's angry
curse, the most sacred promises have been broken. It appears to be a natural suggestion of reason that a man should
be freed from implicit obedience to parents and private punishments when he is of an age to be subject to the jurisdic-
tion of the laws of his country; and that the barbarous
cruelty of allowing parents to imprison their children, to
prevent their contaminating their noble blood by following
the dictates of nature when they choose to marry, or for any
misdemeanor that does not come under the cognizance of
public justice, is one of the most arbitrary violations of
liberty.

Who can recount all the unnatural crimes which the *laudable, interesting* desire of perpetuating a name has produced?
The younger children have been sacrificed to the eldest son;
sent into exile, or confined in convents, that they might not
encroach on what was called, with shameful falsehood, the
family estate. Will Mr. Burke call this parental affection
reasonable or virtuous? No; it is the spurious offspring of
overweening, mistaken pride—and not that first source of
civilization, natural parental affection, that makes no difference between child and child, but what reason justifies by
pointing out superior merit.

Another pernicious consequence which unavoidably arises
from this artificial affection is the insuperable bar which it
puts in the way of early marriages. It would be difficult to
determine whether the minds or bodies of our youth are
most injured by this impediment. Our young men become
selfish coxcombs, and gallantry with modest women, and
intrigues with those of another description, weaken both
mind and body, before either has arrived at maturity. The
character of a master of a family, a husband, and a father,
forms the citizen imperceptibly, by producing a sober man-
liness of thought, and orderly behavior; but, from the lax
morals and depraved affections of the libertine, what results—
a cynical man of taste, who is only anxious to secure his
own private gratifications, and to maintain his rank in
society.

The same system has an equally pernicious effect on female morals. Girls are sacrificed to family convenience, or
else marry to settle themselves in a superior rank, and
coquet, without restraint, with the fine gentleman whom I

have already described. And to such lengths has this vanity, this desire of shining, carried them, that it is not now necessary to guard girls against imprudent love matches; for if some widows did not now and then *fall* in love, Love and Hymen would seldom meet, unless at a village church.

I do not intend to be sarcastically paradoxical when I say that women of fashion take husbands that they may have it in their power to coquet, the grand business of genteel life, with a number of admirers, and thus flutter the spring of life away, without laying up any store for the winter of age, or being of any use to society. Affection in the marriage state can only be founded on respect—and are these weak beings respectable? Children are neglected for lovers, and we express surprise that adulteries are so common! A woman never forgets to adorn herself to make an impression on the senses of the other sex, and to extort the homage which it is gallant to pay, and yet we wonder that they have such confined understandings!

Have ye not heard that we cannot serve two masters? an immoderate desire to please contracts the faculties, and immerses, to borrow the idea of a great philosopher, the soul in matter, till it becomes unable to mount on the wing of contemplation.

It would be an arduous task to trace all the vice and misery that arise in society from the middle class of people aping the manners of the great. All are aiming to procure respect on account of their property; and most places are considered as sinecures that enable men to start into notice. The grand concern of three parts out of four is to contrive to live above their equals, and to appear to be richer than they are. How much domestic comfort and private satisfaction is sacrificed to this irrational ambition! It is a destructive mildew that blights the fairest virtues; benevolence, friendship, generosity, and all those endearing charities which bind human hearts together, and the pursuits which raise the mind to higher contemplations, all that were not cankered in the bud by the false notions that "grew with its growth and strengthened with its strength," are crushed by the iron hand of property!

Property, I do not scruple to aver it, should be fluctuating, which would be the case if it were more equally divided amongst all the children of a family; else it is an everlasting rampart, in consequence of a barbarous feudal institution, that enables the elder son to overpower talents and depress virtue.

Besides, an unmanly servility, most inimical to true dignity of character is, by this means, fostered in society. Men of some abilities play on the follies of the rich, and mounting to fortune as they degrade themselves, they stand in the way of men of superior talents, who cannot advance in such crooked paths, or wade through the filth which *parasites* never boggle at. Pursuing their way straight forward, their spirit is either bent or broken by the rich man's contumelies, or the difficulties they have to encounter.

The only security of property that nature authorizes and reason sanctions is the right a man has to enjoy the acquisitions which his talents and industry have acquired; and to bequeath them to whom he chooses. Happy would it be for the world if there were no other road to wealth or honor; if pride, in the shape of parental affection, did not absorb the man, and prevent friendship from having the same weight as relationship. Luxury and effeminacy would not then introduce so much idiotism into the noble families which form one of the pillars of our state: the ground would not lie fallow, nor would undirected activity of mind spread the contagion of restless idleness, and its concomitant, vice, through the whole mass of society.

Instead of gaming they might nourish a virtuous ambition, and love might take place of the gallantry which you, with knightly fealty, venerate. Women would probably then act like mothers, and the fine lady, become a rational woman, might think it necessary to superintend her family and suckle her children, in order to fulfill her part of the social compact. But vain is the hope, whilst great masses of property are hedged round by hereditary honors; for numberless vices, forced in the hotbed of wealth, assume a sightly form to dazzle the senses and cloud the understanding. The respect paid to rank and fortune damps every generous purpose of the soul, and stifles the natural affections on which human contentment ought to be built. . . .

. . . .

In what respect are we superior to the brute creation, if intellect is not allowed to be the guide of passion? Brutes hope and fear, love and hate; but, without a capacity to improve, a power of turning these passions to good or evil, they neither acquire virtue nor wisdom. Why? Because the Creator has not given them reason.

But the cultivation of reason is an arduous task, and men of lively fancy, finding it easier to follow the impulse of passion, endeavor to persuade themselves and others that it is most *natural*. And happy is it for those who indolently let that heaven-lighted spark rest like the ancient lamps in sepulchers, that some virtuous habits, with which the reason of others shackled them, supplies its place. Affection for parents, reverence for superiors or antiquity, notions of honor, or that worldly self-interest that shrewdly shows them that honesty is the best policy: all proceed from the reason for which they serve as substitutes; but it is reason at second-hand.

Children are born ignorant, consequently innocent; the passions are neither good nor evil dispositions till they receive a direction, and either bound over the feeble barrier raised by a faint glimmering of unexercised reason called conscience, or strengthen her wavering dictates till sound principles are deeply rooted, and able to cope with the head-strong passions that often assume her awful form. What moral purpose can be answered by extolling good dispositions, as they are called, when these good dispositions are described as instincts: for instinct moves in a direct line to its ultimate end, and asks not for guide or support. But if virtue is to be acquired by experience, or taught by example, reason, perfected by reflection, must be the director of the whole host of passions, which produce a fructifying heat, but no light, that you would exalt into her place. She must hold the rudder, or, let the wind blow which way it list, the vessel will never advance smoothly to its destined port; for the time lost in tacking about would dreadfully impede its progress.

. . . .

You observe that "our education is so formed as to confirm and fix . . . respect for the religious establishment; and that our education is in a manner wholly in the hands of ecclesiastics, and in all stages from infancy to manhood." Far from agreeing with you, sir, that these regulations render the clergy a more useful and respectable body, experience convinces me that the very contrary is the fact. In schools and colleges they may, in some degree, support their dignity

within the monastic walls; but, in paying due respect to the
parents of the young nobility under their tutorage, they do
not forget, obsequiously, to respect their noble patrons. The
little respect paid, in great houses, to tutors and chaplains
proves, sir, the fallacy of your reasoning. It would be almost
invidious to remark that they sometimes are only modern
substitutes for the jesters of Gothic memory, and serve as
whetstones for the blunt wit of the noble peer who patron-
izes them; and what respect a boy can imbibe for a *butt*, at
which the shaft of ridicule is daily glanced, I leave those to
determine who can distinguish depravity of morals under
the specious mask of refined manners.

Besides, the custom of sending clergymen to travel with
their noble pupils as humble companions, instead of exalt-
ing, tends inevitably to degrade the clerical character: it is
notorious that they meanly submit to the most servile dependence, and gloss over the most capricious follies, to use a
soft phrase, of the boys to whom they look up for preferment. An airy miter dances before them, and they wrap
their sheep's clothing more closely about them, and make
their spirits bend till it is prudent to claim the rights of men
and the honest freedom of speech of an Englishman. How,
indeed, could they venture to reprove for his vices their
patron: the clergy only give the true feudal emphasis to this
word. It has been observed, by men who have not superfi-
cially investigated the human heart, that when a man makes
his spirit bend to any power but reason, his character is
soon degraded, and his mind shackled by the very prejudices
to which he submits with reluctance. The observations of
experience have been carried still further; and the servility
to superiors, and tyranny to inferiors, said to characterize
our clergy, have rationally been supposed to arise naturally
from their associating with the nobility. Among unequals
there can be no society; giving a manly meaning to the
term; from such intimacies friendship can never grow; if the
basis of friendship is mutual respect, and not a commercial
treaty. Taken thus out of their sphere, and enjoying their
tithes at a distance from their flocks, is it not natural for
them to become courtly parasites, and intriguing dependents
on great patrons, or the treasury? Observing all this—for
these things have not been transacted in the dark—our
young men of fashion, by a common, though erroneous,
association of ideas, have conceived a contempt for religion,
as they sucked in with their milk a contempt for the clergy.

Time only will show whether the general censure, which you afterwards qualify, if not contradict, and the unmerited contempt that you have ostentatiously displayed of the National Assembly, be founded on reason, the offspring of conviction, or the spawn of envy. Time may show that this obscure throng knew more of the human heart and of legislation than the profligates of rank, emasculated by hereditary effeminacy.

It is not, perhaps, of very great consequence who were the founders of a state; savages, thieves, curates, or practitioners in the law. It is true, you might sarcastically remark, that the Romans had always a *smack* of the old leaven, and that the private robbers, supposing the tradition to be true, only became public depredators. You might have added that their civilization must have been very partial, and had more influence on the manners than morals of the people; or the amusements of the amphitheater would not have remained an everlasting blot not only on their humanity, but on their refinement, if a vicious elegance of behavior and luxurious mode of life is not a prostitution of the term. However, the thundering censures which you have cast with a ponderous arm, and the more playful bushfiring of ridicule, are not arguments that will ever depreciate the National Assembly, for applying to their understanding rather than to their imagination, when they met to settle the newly acquired liberty of the state on a solid foundation.

If you had given the same advice to a young history painter of abilities, I should have admired your judgment, and reechoed your sentiments. Study, you might have said, the noble models of antiquity, till your imagination is inflamed; and, rising above the vulgar practice of the hour, you may imitate without copying those great originals. A glowing picture, of some interesting moment, would probably have been produced by these natural means; particularly if one little circumstance is not overlooked, that the painter had noble models to revert to, calculated to excite admiration and stimulate exertion.

But, in settling a constitution that involved the happiness of millions, that stretch beyond the computation of science, it was, perhaps, necessary for the Assembly to have a higher model in view than the *imagined* virtues of their forefathers; and wise to deduce their respect for themselves from the only legitimate source, respect for justice. Why was it a duty to repair an ancient castle, built in barbarous ages, of Gothic materials? Why were the legislators obliged to rake amongst heterogeneous ruins; to rebuild old walls, whose foundations could scarcely be explored, when a simple structure might be raised on the foundation of experience, the only valuable inheritance our forefathers could bequeath? Yet of this bequest we can make little use till we have gained a stock of our own; and even then, their inherited experience would rather serve as lighthouses, to warn us against dangerous rocks or sandbanks, than as fingerposts that stand at every turning to point out the right road.

Nor was it absolutely necessary that they should be diffident of themselves when they were dissatisfied with, or could not discern "the *almost obliterated* constitution of their ancestors." They should first have been convinced that our constitution was not only the best modern, but the best possible one; and that our social compact was the surest foundation of all the *possible* liberty a mass of men could enjoy, that the human understanding could form. They should have been certain that our representation answered all the purposes of representation; and that an established inequality of rank and property secured the liberty of the whole community, instead of rendering it a sounding epithet of subjection, when applied to the nation at large. They should have had the same respect for our House of Commons that you, vauntingly, intrude on us, though your conduct throughout life has spoken a very different language; before they made a point of not deviating from the model which first engaged their attention.

That the British House of Commons is filled with everything illustrious in rank, in descent, in hereditary, and acquired opulence, may be true—but that it contains everything respectable in talents, in military, civil, naval, and political distinction, is very problematical. Arguing from natural causes, the very contrary would appear to the speculatist to be the fact; and let experience say whether these speculations are built on sure ground.

. . . .

. . . Is it among the list of possibilities that a man of rank and fortune *can* have received a good education? How can he discover that he is a man, when all his wants are instantly supplied, and invention is never sharpened by necessity? Will he labor, for everything valuable must be the fruit of laborious exertions, to attain knowledge and virtue, in order to merit the affection of his equals, when the flattering attention of sycophants is a more luscious cordial?

Health can only be secured by temperance; but is it easy to persuade a man to live on plain food even to recover his health, who has been accustomed to fare sumptuously every day? Can a man relish the simple food of friendship, who has been habitually pampered by flattery? And when the blood boils, and the senses meet allurements on every side, will knowledge be pursued on account of its abstract beauty? No; it is well known that talents are only to be unfolded by industry, and that we must have made some advances, led by an inferior motive, before we discover that they are their own reward.

But *full-blown* talents *may*, according to your system, be hereditary, and as independent of ripening judgment, as the inbred feelings that, rising above reason, naturally guard Englishmen from error. Noble franchises! what a groveling mind must that man have who can pardon his stepdame Nature for not having made him at least a lord?

And who will, after your description of senatorial virtues, dare to say that our House of Commons has often resembled a bear garden, and appeared rather like a committee of *ways and means* than a dignified legislative body, though the concentrated wisdom and virtue of the whole nation blazed in one superb constellation? That it contains a dead weight of benumbing opulence I readily allow, and of ignoble ambition; nor is there anything surpassing belief in a supposition that the raw recruits, when properly drilled by the minister, would gladly march to the Upper House to unite hereditary honors to fortune. But talents, knowledge, and virtue must be a part of the man, and cannot be put, as robes of state often are, on a servant or a block, to render a pageant more magnificent.

. . . .

Reading your Reflections warily over, it has continually and forcibly struck me that had you been a Frenchman, you would have been, in spite of your respect for rank and antiquity, a violent revolutionist; and deceived, as you now probably are, by the passions that cloud your reason, have termed your romantic enthusiasm an enlightened love of your country, a benevolent respect for the rights of men. Your imagination would have taken fire, and have found arguments, full as ingenious as those you now offer, to prove that the constitution, of which so few pillars remained, that constitution which time had almost obliterated, was not a model sufficiently noble to deserve close adherence. And, for the English constitution, you might not have had such a profound veneration as you have lately acquired; nay, it is not impossible that you might have entertained the same opinion of the English Parliament that you professed to have during the American war.

Another observation which, by frequently occurring, has almost grown into a conviction, is simply this, that had the English in general reprobated the French revolution, you would have stood forth alone, and been the avowed Goliath of liberty. But, not liking to see so many brothers near the throne of fame, you have turned the current of your passions, and consequently of your reasoning, another way. Had Dr. Price's sermon not lighted some sparks very like envy in your bosom, I shrewdly suspect that he would have been treated with more candor; nor is it charitable to suppose that anything but personal pique and hurt vanity could have dictated such bitter sarcasms and reiterated expressions of contempt as occur in your Reflections.

But without fixed principles even goodness of heart is no security from inconsistency, and mild affectionate sensibility only renders a man more ingeniously cruel, when the pangs of hurt vanity are mistaken for virtuous indignation, and the gall of bitterness for the milk of Christian charity.

Where is the dignity, the infallibility of sensibility, in the fair ladies, whom, if the voice of rumor is to be credited, the captive negroes curse in all the agony of bodily pain, for the unheard of tortures they invent? It is probable that some of them, after the sight of a flagellation, compose their ruffled spirits and exercise their tender feelings by the perusal of the last imported novel. How true these tears are to nature, I leave you to determine. But these ladies may have read your *Inquiry into the Origin of Our Ideas of the Sublime and Beautiful*, and, convinced by your arguments, may have labored to be pretty, by counterfeiting weakness.

You may have convinced them that *littleness* and *weakness* are the very essence of beauty; and that the Supreme

Being, in giving women beauty in the most supereminent degree, seemed to command them, by the powerful voice of Nature, not to cultivate the moral virtues that might chance to excite respect, and interfere with the pleasing sensations they were created to inspire. Thus confining truth, fortitude, and humanity within the rigid pale of manly morals, they might justly argue that to be loved—woman's high end and great distinction—they should "learn to lisp, to totter in their walk, and nickname God's creatures." Never, they might repeat after you, was any man, much less a woman, rendered amiable by the force of those exalted qualities, fortitude, justice, wisdom, and truth; and thus forewarned of the sacrifice they must make to those austere, unnatural virtues, they would be authorized to turn all their attention to their persons, systematically neglecting morals to secure beauty. Some rational old woman indeed might chance to stumble at this doctrine, and hint that in avoiding atheism you had not steered clear of the Moslem's creed; but you could readily exculpate yourself by turning the charge on Nature, who made our idea of beauty independent of reason. Nor would it be necessary for you to recollect that if virtue has any other foundation than worldly utility, you have clearly proved that one half of the human species, at least, have not souls; and that Nature, by making women *little, smooth, delicate, fair* creatures, never designed that they should exercise their reason to acquire the virtues that produce opposite, if not contradictory, feelings. The affection they excite, to be uniform and perfect, should not be tinctured with the respect which moral virtues inspire, lest pain should be blended with pleasure, and admiration disturb the soft intimacy of love. This laxity of morals in the female world is certainly more captivating to a libertine imagination than the cold arguments of reason, that give no sex to virtue. If beautiful weakness be interwoven in a woman's frame, if the chief business of her life be (as you insinuate) to inspire love, and Nature has made an eternal distinction between the qualities that dignify a rational being and this animal perfection, her duty and happiness in this life must clash with any preparation for a more exalted state. So that Plato and Milton were grossly mistaken in asserting that human love led to heavenly, and was only an exaltation of the same affection; for the love of the Deity, which is mixed with the most profound reverence, must be love of perfection, and not compassion for weakness.

To say the truth, I not only tremble for the souls of women, but for the good-natured man, whom everyone loves. The *amiable* weakness of his mind is a strong argument against its immateriality, and seems to prove that beauty relaxes the *solids* of the soul as well as the body.

It follows then immediately, from your own reasoning, that respect and love are antagonist principles; and that, if we really wish to render men more virtuous, we must endeavor to banish all enervating modifications of beauty from civil society. We must, to carry your argument a little further, return to the Spartan regulations, and settle the virtues of men on the stern foundation of mortification and self-denial; for any attempt to civilize the heart, to make it humane by implanting reasonable principles, is a mere philosophic dream. If refinement inevitably lessens respect for virtue, by rendering beauty, the grand tempter, more seductive; if these relaxing feelings are incompatible with the nervous exertions of morality, the sun of Europe is not set; it begins to dawn, when cold metaphysicians try to make the head give laws to the heart.

But should experience prove that there is a beauty in virtue, a charm in order, which necessarily implies exertion, a depraved sensual taste may give way to a more manly one—and *melting* feelings to rational satisfactions. Both may be equally natural to man; the test is their moral difference, and that point reason alone can decide.

. . . .

You find it very difficult to separate policy from justice: in the political world they have frequently been separated with shameful dexterity. To mention a recent instance: according to the limited views of timid, or interested politicians, an abolition of the infernal slave trade would not only be unsound policy, but a flagrant infringement of the laws (which are allowed to have been infamous) that induced the planters to purchase their estates. But is it not consonant with justice, with the common principles of humanity, not to mention Christianity, to abolish this abominable mischief? There is not one argument, one invective, leveled by you at the confiscators of the church revenue, which could not, with the strictest propriety, be applied by the planters and negro-drivers to our Parliament, if it gloriously dared to show the world that British senators were men: if the natural feelings of humanity silenced the cold cautions of timidity, till this stigma on our nature was wiped off, and all men were allowed to enjoy their birthright—liberty, till by their crimes they had authorized society to deprive them of the blessing they had abused.

. . . .

. . . A transient view of society will further illustrate arguments which appear so obvious that I am almost ashamed to produce illustrations. How many children have been taught economy, and many other virtues, by the extravagant thoughtlessness of their parents; yet a good education is allowed to be an inestimable blessing. The tenderest mothers are often the most unhappy wives; but can the good that accrues from the private distress that produces a sober dignity of mind justify the inflictor? Right or wrong may be estimated according to the point of sight, and other adventitious circumstances; but, to discover its real nature, the inquiry must go deeper than the surface, and beyond the local consequences that confound good and evil together. The rich and weak, a numerous train, will certainly applaud your system, and loudly celebrate your pious reverence for authority and establishments—they find it pleasanter to enjoy than to think; to justify oppression than correct abuses. *The rights of men* are grating sounds that set their teeth on edge; the impertinent inquiry of philosophic meddling innovation.

. . . .

It may be confidently asserted that no man chooses evil because it is evil; he only mistakes it for happiness, the good he seeks. And the desire of rectifying these mistakes is the noble ambition of an enlightened understanding, the impulse of feelings that Philosophy invigorates. To endeavor to make unhappy men resigned to their fate is the tender endeavor of shortsighted benevolence, of transient yearnings of humanity; but to labor to increase human happiness by extirpating error is a masculine godlike affection. This remark may be carried still further. Men who possess uncommon sensibility, whose quick emotions show how closely the eye and heart are connected, soon forget the most forcible sensations. Not tarrying long enough in the brain to be subject to reflection, the next sensations, of course, obliterate them. Memory, however, treasures up these proofs of native goodness; and the being who is not spurred on to any virtuous act, still thinks itself of consequence, and boasts of its feelings. Why? Because the sight of distress, or an affecting narrative, made its blood flow with more velocity, and the heart, literally speaking, beat with sympathetic emotion. We ought to beware of confounding mechanical instinctive sensations with emotions that reason deepens, and justly terms the feelings of *humanity*. This word discriminates the active exertions of virtue from the vague declamation of sensibility.

. . . .

. . . It is, sir, *possible* to render the poor happier in this world, without depriving them of the consolation which you gratuitously grant them in the next. They have a right to more comfort than they at present enjoy; and more comfort might be afforded them, without encroaching on the pleasures of the rich: not now waiting to inquire whether the rich have any right to exclusive pleasures. What do I say?— encroaching! No; if an intercourse were established between them, it would impart the only true pleasure that can be snatched in this land of shadows, this hard school of moral discipline.

I know, indeed, that there is often something disgusting in the distresses of poverty, at which the imagination revolts, and starts back to exercise itself in the more attractive Arcadia of fiction. The rich man builds a house; art and taste give it the highest finish. His gardens are planted, and the trees grow to re-create the fancy of the planter, though the temperature of the climate may rather force him to avoid the dangerous damps they exhale, than seek the umbrageous retreat. Everything on the estate is cherished but man; yet to contribute to the happiness of man is the most sublime of all enjoyments. But if, instead of sweeping pleasure-grounds, obelisks, temples, and elegant cottages, as *objects* for the eye, the heart was allowed to beat true to nature, decent farms would be scattered over the estate, and plenty smile around. Instead of the poor being subject to the griping hand of an avaricious steward, they would be watched over with fatherly solicitude by the man whose duty and pleasure it was to guard their happiness, and shield from rapacity the beings who, by the sweat of their brow, exalted him above his fellows.

I could almost imagine I see a man thus gathering blessings as he mounted the hill of life; or consolation, in those days when the spirits lag, and the tired heart finds no pleasure in them. It is not by squandering alms that the poor can be relieved, or improved—it is the fostering sun of kindness, the wisdom that finds them employments calculated to give them habits of virtue, that meliorates their condition. Love is only the fruit of love; condescension and authority may produce the obedience you applaud; but he has lost his heart of flesh who can see a fellow creature humbled before him, and trembling at the frown of a being, whose heart is supplied by the same vital current, and whose pride ought to be checked by a consciousness of having the same infirmities.

What salutary dews might not be shed to refresh this thirsty land, if men were more *enlightened!* Smiles and premiums might encourage cleanliness, industry, and emulation. A garden more inviting than Eden would then meet the eye, and springs of joy murmur on every side. The clergyman would superintend his own flock, the shepherd would then love the sheep he daily tended; the school might rear its decent head, and the buzzing tribe, let loose to play, impart a portion of their vivacious spirits to the heart that longed to open their minds, and lead them to taste the pleasures of men. Domestic comfort, the civilizing relations of husband, brother, and father, would soften labor, and render life contented.

. . . .

In this great city that proudly rears its head and boasts of its population and commerce, how much misery lurks in pestilential corners, whilst idle mendicants assail, on every side, the man who hates to encourage imposters, or repress, with angry frown, the plaints of the poor! How many mechanics, by a flux of trade or fashion, lose their employment; whom misfortunes, not to be warded off, lead to the idleness that vitiates their character and renders them afterwards averse to honest labor! Where is the eye that marks these evils, more gigantic than any of the infringements of property, which you piously deprecate? Are these remediless evils? And is the humane heart satisfied with turning the poor over to *another* world, to receive the blessings this could afford? If society was regulated on a more enlarged plan; if man was contented to be the friend of man, and did not seek to bury the sympathies of humanity in the servile appellation of master; if, turning his eyes from ideal regions of taste and elegance, he labored to give the earth he inhabited all the beauty it is capable of receiving, and was ever on the watch to shed abroad all the happiness which human nature can enjoy; he who, respecting the rights of men, wishes to convince or persuade society that this is true happiness and dignity, is not the cruel *oppressor* of the poor, nor a short-sighted philosopher. He fears God and loves his fellow creatures. Behold the whole duty of man—the citizen who acts differently is a sophisticated being.

Surveying civilized life and seeing, with undazzled eye, the polished vices of the rich, their insincerity, want of natural affections, with all the specious train that luxury introduces, I have turned impatiently to the poor, to look for man undebauched by riches or power—but, alas! what did I see? a being scarcely above the brutes, over which he tyrannized; a broken spirit, worn-out body, and all those gross vices which the example of the rich, rudely copied, could produce. Envy built a wall of separation, that made the poor hate, whilst they bent to their superiors; who, on their part, stepped aside to avoid the loathsome sight of human misery.

What were the outrages of a day* to these continual miseries? Let those sorrows hide their diminished head before the tremendous mountain of woe that thus defaces our globe! Man preys on man; and you mourn for the idle tapestry that decorated a Gothic pile, and the dronish bell that summoned the fat priest to prayer. You mourn for the empty pageant of a name, when slavery flaps her wing, and the sick heart retires to die in lonely wilds, far from the abodes of men. Did the pangs you felt for insulted nobility, the anguish that rent your heart when the gorgeous robes were torn off the idol human weakness had set up, deserve to be compared with the long-drawn sigh of melancholy reflection, when misery and vice are thus seen to haunt our steps, and swim on the top of every cheering prospect? Why is our fancy to be appalled by terrific perspectives of a hell beyond the grave? Hell stalks abroad; the lash resounds on the slave's naked sides; and the sick wretch, who can no longer earn the sour bread of unremitting labor, steals to a ditch to

*The 6th of October, 1789, when the mob drove the royal family from Versailles to Paris.

bid the world a long good night—or, neglected in some ostentatious hospital, breathes his last amidst the laugh of mercenary attendants.

Such misery demands more than tears—I pause to recollect myself; and smother the contempt I feel rising for your rhetorical flourishes and infantine sensibility. . . .

A Vindication of the
Rights of Woman

FIVE AND A HALF YEARS of writing professionally about
flaws in female conduct and character and the oppression from
which they seemed to spring inevitably led Wollstonecraft
to analyze their ultimate source. In working on *A Vindication of the Rights of Men*, she traced the roots of oppression
to the unfair distribution of property, ridiculing the pampered upper classes who claimed to represent an elevated
mode of civilization while they exploited the classes beneath
them in order to realize financial or social gains that were
rarely attainable through their own abilities. Writing late
in 1791 at the midpoint of her literary career, she again
asked the classic question: Who profits from the present
state of social relationships? In answering that question, she
produced the work that is as central to her thought as it is
to her chronology and that remains even today one of the
central feminist texts: *A Vindication of the Rights of Woman*,
published in 1792.

Who profits? Men. To conduct her audit of profit and loss,
she goes back to the precept she seems to have held intuitively all her life—that education and social ideals make us
what we are—and dissects the causes of the inferior education available to females, as she had already catalogued its
effects. Thus *A Vindication of the Rights of Woman* is a
political document, but it is not propaganda. Wollstonecraft
never claims that women are "better" than men. She acknowledges gender distinctions and endorses the dignity of
women's domestic role. She does assail men who want to
make more than is right of whatever natural advantages
they may have—as she had assailed them for their exploita-
tion of the poor in her first *Vindication*—although she grants
males' physical superiority.

Wollstonecraft's investigation of the economic motives that
repress all people extends in the *Rights of Woman* to the
peculiarly sexual economy that governs the relations of men

and women. Her analysis of male-female relationships in economic rather than romantic terms is startlingly modern. She proclaims that so long as men want to keep women as voluptuous toys, the masculine advantage is apparently served if their wives and daughters can never function independently. But if women continue to be trained to limit their thinking, they must remain inferior companions for men; likewise, if they realize themselves only through marriage, they can be loved only as "trusty servant[s]" might be. Wollstonecraft criticizes the double standard that condones male promiscuity but demands absolute chastity from women even while it ties them to men they cannot love. "The two sexes mutually corrupt and improve each other," Wollstonecraft insists, and she demonstrates that ignoring this mutuality consigns the women who are brought up to please men to being "house slaves."

These insights, still applicable today and still capable of shocking certain audiences, are the more remarkable because Wollstonecraft's tone in this *Vindication* is nowhere as scathing or contemptuous as she allowed herself to be in addressing Edmund Burke. If anything, she is even more eager here to envisage a finer world for all humanity, providing that the term be understood to include females as it often did not when used in the context of social and political discussions. To the extent that women have suffered more than men under the patriarchally skewed systems of laws, education, and morality that she describes, it is only just that women receive fuller redress. But to the extent that men as well as women have lost more than they have gained, to the extent that their profit has been at best illusory, Wollstonecraft argues that teaching women as men are taught will work toward the masculine advantage:

> Would men but generously snap our chains, and be content with rational fellowship instead of slavish obedience, they would find us more observant daughters, more affectionate sisters, more faithful wives, more reasonable mothers—in a word, better citizens. We should then love them with true affection, because we should learn to respect ourselves; and the peace of mind of a worthy man would not be interrupted by the idle vanity of his wife, nor the babes sent to nestle in a strange bosom, having never found a home in their mother's.

A Vindication of the Rights of Woman, the most contro-
versial of Wollstonecraft's books, was quickly translated and
published abroad, and became one of the most influential
documents ever written by a woman.

Unfortunately, Godwin's *Memoirs*, publicizing her private
history, her scandalous affair with Imlay and the illegitimacy of her first child, fueled the attacks on her work. One
of the early critics of the *Rights of Woman*, Horace Walpole,
dubbed her a "hyena in petticoats," and later antagonists
found it easier to dismiss her feminism because of her notorious life and her advocacy of divorce in *The Wrongs of
Woman*. Even her excruciatingly female death of an infection resulting from childbirth was vengefully interpreted as
serving her right.

It is a cruel irony that Wollstonecraft's anatomy should
have proved her destiny, but her book, however excoriated,
did not die. More than seventy years after it was first published, *A Vindication of the Rights of Woman* reappeared in
serial form in Susan B. Anthony's newspaper, *The Revolution*. It has taken almost another hundred years for Wollstonecraft's key work to attain general circulation, but it is
unlikely to fade from public view again. It has become a
cornerstone of feminist thought, a foundation for all women
to build upon.

A VINDICATION OF THE
RIGHTS OF WOMAN

INTRODUCTION

After considering the historic page, and viewing the living world with anxious solicitude, the most melancholy emotions of sorrowful indignation have depressed my spirits, and I have sighed when obliged to confess that either nature has made a great difference between man and man or that the civilization which has hitherto taken place in the world has been very partial. I have turned over various books written on the subject of education, and patiently observed the conduct of parents and the management of schools; but what has been the result?—a profound conviction that the neglected education of my fellow creatures is the grand source of the misery I deplore; and that women, in particular, are rendered weak and wretched by a variety of concurring causes, originating from one hasty conclusion. The conduct and manners of women, in fact, evidently prove that their minds are not in a healthy state; for, like the flowers which are planted in too rich a soil, strength and usefulness are sacrificed to beauty; and the flaunting leaves, after having pleased a fastidious eye, fade, disregarded on the stalk, long before the season when they ought to have arrived at maturity. One cause of this barren blooming I attribute to a false system of education, gathered from the books written on this subject by men who, considering females rather as women than human creatures, have been more anxious to make them alluring mistresses than affectionate wives and rational mothers; and the understanding of the sex has been so bubbled by this specious homage that the civilized women of the present century, with a few exceptions, are only anxious to inspire love, when they ought to cherish a nobler ambition, and by their abilities and virtues exact respect.

In a treatise, therefore, on female rights and manners, the works which have been particularly written for their improvement must not be overlooked; especially when it is asserted, in direct terms, that the minds of women are enfeebled by false refinement; that the books of instruction, written by men of genius, have had the same tendency as more frivolous productions; and that, in the true style of Mohammedanism, they are treated as a kind of subordinate beings, and not as a part of the human species, when improvable reason is allowed to be the dignified distinction which raises men above the brute creation, and puts a natural scepter in a feeble hand.

Yet, because I am a woman, I would not lead my readers to suppose that I mean violently to agitate the contested question respecting the equality or inferiority of the sex; but as the subject lies in my way, and I cannot pass it over without subjecting the main tendency of my reasoning to misconstruction, I shall stop a moment to deliver, in a few words, my opinion. In the government of the physical world it is observable that the female in point of strength is, in general, inferior to the male. This is the law of nature; and it does not appear to be suspended or abrogated in favor of woman. A degree of physical superiority cannot, therefore, be denied—and it is a noble prerogative! But not content with this natural preeminence, men endeavor to sink us still lower, merely to render us alluring objects for a moment; and women, intoxicated by the adoration which men, under the influence of their senses, pay them, do not seek to obtain a durable interest in their hearts, or to become the friends of the fellow creatures who find amusement in their society.

I am aware of an obvious inference: from every quarter have I heard exclamations against masculine women; but where are they to be found? If by this appellation men mean to inveigh against their ardor in hunting, shooting, and gaming, I shall most cordially join in the cry; but if it be against the imitation of manly virtues, or, more properly speaking, the attainment of those talents and virtues, the exercise of which ennobles the human character, and which raise females in the scale of animal being, when they are comprehensively termed mankind; all those who view them with a philosophic eye must, I should think, wish with me that they may every day grow more and more masculine.

This discussion naturally divides the subject. I shall first consider women in the grand light of human creatures, who, in common with men, are placed on this earth to unfold their faculties; and afterwards I shall more particularly point out their peculiar designation.

I wish also to steer clear of an error which many respectable writers have fallen into; for the instruction which has hitherto been addressed to women has rather been applicable to *ladies*, if the little indirect advice that is scattered through Sandford and Merton* be excepted; but, addressing my sex in a firmer tone, I pay particular attention to those in the middle class, because they appear to be in the most natural state. Perhaps the seeds of false refinement, immorality, and vanity, have ever been shed by the great. Weak, artificial beings, raised above the common wants and affections of their race, in a premature unnatural manner, undermine the very foundation of virtue, and spread corruption through the whole mass of society! As a class of mankind they have the strongest claim to pity; the education of the rich tends to render them vain and helpless, and the unfolding mind is not strengthened by the practice of those duties which dignify the human character. They only live to amuse themselves, and by the same law which in nature invariably produces certain effects, they soon only afford barren amusement.

But as I purpose taking a separate view of the different ranks of society, and of the moral character of women, in each, this hint is, for the present, sufficient; and I have only alluded to the subject, because it appears to me to be the very essence of an introduction to give a cursory account of the contents of the work it introduces.

My own sex, I hope, will excuse me, if I treat them like rational creatures, instead of flattering their *fascinating* graces, and viewing them as if they were in a state of perpetual childhood, unable to stand alone. I earnestly wish to point out in what true dignity and human happiness consists—I wish to persuade women to endeavor to acquire strength, both of mind and body, and to convince them that the soft phrases, susceptibility of heart, delicacy of senti-

The History of Sandford and Merton: A Work Intended for the Use of Children (3 vols. 1783–89), by Thomas Day.

ment, and refinement of taste, are almost synonymous with epithets of weakness, and that those beings who are only the objects of pity and that kind of love, which has been termed its sister, will soon become objects of contempt.

Dismissing then those pretty feminine phrases which the men condescendingly use to soften our slavish dependence, and despising that weak elegancy of mind, exquisite sensibility, and sweet docility of manners supposed to be the sexual characteristics of the weaker vessel, I wish to show that elegance is inferior to virtue, that the first object of laudable ambition is to obtain a character as a human being, regardless of the distinction of sex; and that secondary views should be brought to this simple touchstone.

This is a rough sketch of my plan; and should I express my conviction with the energetic emotions that I feel whenever I think of the subject, the dictates of experience and reflection will be felt by some of my readers. Animated by this important object, I shall disdain to cull my phrases or polish my style; I aim at being useful, and sincerity will render me unaffected; for, wishing rather to persuade by the force of my arguments, than dazzle by the elegance of my language, I shall not waste my time in rounding periods, or in fabricating the turgid bombast of artificial feelings, which, coming from the head, never reach the heart. I shall be employed about things, not words—and, anxious to render my sex more respectable members of society, I shall try to avoid that flowery diction which has slided from essays into novels, and from novels into familiar letters and conversation.

These pretty superlatives, dropping glibly from the tongue, vitiate the taste, and create a kind of sickly delicacy that turns away from simple unadorned truth; and a deluge of false sentiments and overstretched feelings, stifling the natural emotions of the heart, render the domestic pleasures insipid, that ought to sweeten the exercise of those severe duties, which educate a rational and immortal being for a nobler field of action.

The education of women has, of late, been more attended to than formerly; yet they are still reckoned a frivolous sex, and ridiculed or pitied by the writers who endeavor by satire or instruction to improve them. It is acknowledged that they spend many of the first years of their lives in acquiring a smattering of accomplishments; meanwhile strength of body and mind are sacrificed to libertine notions of beauty, to the desire of establishing themselves—the only way women can rise in the world—by marriage. And this desire making mere animals of them, when they marry they act as such children may be expected to act: they dress, they paint,* and nickname God's creatures. Surely these weak beings are only fit for a seraglio! Can they be expected to govern a family with judgment, or take care of the poor babes whom they bring into the world?

If then it can be fairly deduced from the present conduct of the sex, from the prevalent fondness for pleasure which takes place of ambition and those nobler passions that open and enlarge the soul, that the instruction which women have hitherto received has only tended, with the constitution of civil society, to render them insignificant objects of desire—mere propagators of fools—if it can be proved that in aiming to accomplish them, without cultivating their understandings, they are taken out of their sphere of duties, and made ridiculous and useless when the short-lived blood of beauty is over,† I presume that *rational* men will excuse me for endeavoring to persuade them to become more masculine and respectable.

Indeed the word *masculine* is only a bugbear: there is little reason to fear that women will acquire too much courage or fortitude; for their apparent inferiority with respect to bodily strength must render them, in some degree, dependent on men in the various relations of life; but why should it be increased by prejudices that give a sex to virtue, and confound simple truths with sensual reveries?

Women are, in fact, so much degraded by mistaken notions of female excellence that I do not mean to add a paradox when I assert that this artificial weakness produces a propensity to tyrannize, and gives birth to cunning, the natural opponent of strength, which leads them to play off those contemptible infantine airs that undermine esteem even whilst they excite desire. Let men become more chaste and modest, and if women do not grow wiser in the same ratio, it will be clear that they have weaker understandings. It seems scarcely necessary to say that I now speak of the sex in general. Many individuals have more sense than their male relatives; and, as nothing preponderates where

*They apply paint (makeup) to their faces.
†"A lively writer, I cannot recollect his name, asks what business women turned of forty have to do in the world?" (Wollstonecraft's note).

there is a constant struggle for an equilibrium, without it has naturally more gravity, some women govern their husbands without degrading themselves, because intellect will always govern.

. . . .

THE PREVAILING OPINION OF A SEXUAL CHARACTER DISCUSSED

To account for, and excuse the tyranny of man, many ingenious arguments have been brought forward to prove that the two sexes, in the acquirement of virtue, ought to aim at attaining a very different character: or, to speak explicitly, women are not allowed to have sufficient strength of mind to acquire what really deserves the name of virtue. Yet it should seem, allowing them to have souls, that there is but one way appointed by Providence to lead *mankind* to either virtue or happiness.

If then women are not a swarm of ephemeron triflers, why should they be kept in ignorance under the specious name of innocence? Men complain, and with reason, of the follies and caprices of our sex, when they do not keenly satirize our headstrong passions and groveling vices. Behold, I should answer, the natural effect of ignorance! The mind will ever be unstable that has only prejudices to rest on, and the current will run with destructive fury when there are no barriers to break its force. Women are told from their infancy, and taught by the example of their mothers, that a little knowledge of human weakness, justly termed cunning, softness of temper, *outward* obedience, and a scrupulous attention to a puerile kind of propriety, will obtain for them the protection of man; and should they be beautiful, everything else is needless for at least twenty years of their lives.

Thus Milton describes our first frail mother; though when he tells us that women are formed for softness and sweet attractive grace, I cannot comprehend his meaning, unless, in the true Mohammedan strain, he meant to deprive us of souls, and insinuate that we were beings only designed by sweet attractive grace, and docile blind obedience, to gratify the senses of man when he can no longer soar on the wing of contemplation.

How grossly do they insult us who thus advise us only to render ourselves gentle, domestic brutes! For instance, the winning softness so warmly, and frequently, recommended, that governs by obeying. What childish expressions, and how insignificant is the being—can it be an immortal one? who will condescend to govern by such sinister methods! "Certainly," says Lord Bacon, "man is of kin to the beasts by his body; and if he be not of kin to God by his spirit, he is a base and ignoble creature!" Men, indeed, appear to me to act in a very unphilosophical manner when they try to secure the good conduct of women by attempting to keep them always in a state of childhood. Rousseau was more consistent when he wished to stop the progress of reason in both sexes, for if men eat of the tree of knowledge, women will come in for a taste; but, from the imperfect cultivation which their understandings now receive, they only attain a knowledge of evil.

Children, I grant, should be innocent; but when the epithet is applied to men, or women, it is but a civil term for weakness. For if it be allowed that women were destined by Providence to acquire human virtues, and by the exercise of their understandings, that stability of character which is the firmest ground to rest our future hopes upon, they must be permitted to turn to the fountain of light, and not forced to shape their course by the twinkling of a mere satellite. Milton, I grant, was of a very different opinion; for he only bends to the indefeasible right of beauty, though it would be difficult to render two passages which I now mean to contrast, consistent. But into similar inconsistencies are great men often led by their senses.

> To whom thus Eve with *perfect beauty* adorn'd.
> My Author and Disposer, what thou bidst
> *Unargued* I obey; So God ordains;
> God is *thy law, thou mine*: to know no more
> Is Woman's *happiest* knowledge and her *praise*.*

These are exactly the arguments that I have used to children; but I have added, your reason is now gaining strength, and, till it arrives at some degree of maturity, you

*Wollstonecraft's italics; *Paradise Lost IV*. 634–38

must look up to me for advice—then you ought to *think*, and only rely on God.

Yet in the following lines Milton seems to coincide with me; when he makes Adam thus expostulate with his Maker.

> Hast thou not made me here thy substitute,
> And these inferior far beneath me set?
> Among *unequals* what society
> Can sort, what harmony or true delight?
> Which must be mutual, in proportion due
> Giv'n and receiv'd; but in *disparity*
> The one intense, the other still remiss
> Cannot well suit with either, but soon prove
> Tedious alike: of *fellowship* I speak
> Such as I seek, fit to participate
> All rational delight—*

In treating, therefore, of the manners of women, let us, disregarding sensual arguments, trace what we should endeavor to make them in order to cooperate, if the expression be not too bold, with the supreme Being.

By individual education, I mean, for the sense of the word is not precisely defined, such an attention to a child as will slowly sharpen the senses, form the temper, regulate the passions as they begin to ferment, and set the understanding to work before the body arrives at maturity; so that the man may only have to proceed, not to begin, the important task of learning to think and reason.

To prevent any misconstruction, I must add that I do not believe that a private education can work the wonders which some sanguine writers have attributed to it. Men and women must be educated, in a great degree, by the opinions and manners of the society they live in. In every age there has been a stream of popular opinion that has carried all before it, and given a family character, as it were, to the century. It may then fairly be inferred that, till society be differently constituted, much cannot be expected from education. It is, however, sufficient for my present purpose to assert that, whatever effect circumstances have on the abilities, every being may become virtuous by the exercise of its own reason; for if but one being was created with vicious inclinations, that is positively bad, what can save us from atheism? or if we worship a God, is not that God a devil?

*Wollstonecraft's italics; *Paradise Lost* VIII, 381–92.

Consequently, the most perfect education, in my opinion, is such an exercise of the understanding as is best calculated to strengthen the body and form the heart. Or, in other words, to enable the individual to attain such habits of virtue as will render it independent. In fact, it is a farce to call any being virtuous whose virtues do not result from the exercise of its own reason. This was Rousseau's opinion respecting men: I extend it to women, and confidently assert that they have been drawn out of their sphere by false refinement, and not by an endeavor to acquire masculine qualities. Still the regal homage which they receive is so intoxicating that till the manners of the times are changed, and formed on more reasonable principles, it may be impossible to convince them that the illegitimate power which they obtain by degrading themselves is a curse, and that they must return to nature and equality, if they wish to secure the placid satisfaction that unsophisticated affections impart. But for this epoch we must wait—wait, perhaps, till kings and nobles, enlightened by reason, and, preferring the real dignity of man to childish state, throw off their gaudy hereditary trappings: and if then women do not resign the arbitrary power of beauty—they will prove that they have *less* mind than man.

I may be accused of arrogance; still I must declare what I firmly believe, that all the writers who have written on the subject of female education and manners, from Rousseau to Dr. Gregory,* have contributed to render women more artificial, weak characters than they would otherwise have been; and, consequently, more useless members of society. I might have expressed this conviction in a lower key; but I am afraid it would have been the whine of affectation, and not the faithful expression of my feelings, of the clear result, which experience and reflection have led me to draw. When I come to that division of the subject I shall advert to the passages that I more particularly disapprove of, in the works of the authors I have just alluded to; but it is first necessary to observe that my objection extends to the whole purport of those books, which tend, in my opinion, to degrade one-half of the human species, and render women pleasing at the expense of every solid virtue.

*Jean-Jacques Rousseau, author of *Émile* (1762), and Dr. John Gregory, author of *A Father's Legacy to His Daughters* (1774).

Though, to reason on Rousseau's ground, if man did attain a degree of perfection of mind when his body arrived at maturity, it might be proper, in order to make a man and his wife *one*, that she should rely entirely on his understanding; and the graceful ivy, clasping the oak that supported it, would form a whole in which strength and beauty would be equally conspicuous. But, alas! husbands, as well as their helpmates, are often only overgrown children; nay, thanks to early debauchery, scarcely men in their outward form—and if the blind lead the blind, one need not come from heaven to tell us the consequence.

Many are the causes that, in the present corrupt state of society, contribute to enslave women by cramping their understandings and sharpening their senses. One, perhaps, that silently does more mischief than all the rest, is their disregard of order.

To do everything in an orderly manner is a most important precept, which women, who, generally speaking, receive only a disorderly kind of education, seldom attend to with that degree of exactness that men, who from their infancy are broken into method, observe. This negligent kind of guesswork, for what other epithet can be used to point out the random exertions of a sort of instinctive common sense, never brought to the test of reason? prevents their generalizing matters of fact—so they do today, what they did yesterday, merely because they did it yesterday.

This contempt of the understanding in early life has more baneful consequences than is commonly supposed; for the little knowledge which women of strong minds attain is, from various circumstances, of a more desultory kind than the knowledge of men, and it is acquired more by sheer observations on real life than from comparing what has been individually observed with the results of experience generalized by speculation. Led by their dependent situation and domestic employments more into society, what they learn is rather by snatches; and as learning is with them, in general, only a secondary thing, they do not pursue any one branch with that persevering ardor necessary to give vigor to the faculties and clearness to the judgment. In the present state of society, a little learning is required to support the character of a gentleman; and boys are obliged to submit to a few years of discipline. But in the education of women, the cultivation of the understanding is always subordinate to the acquirement of some corporeal accomplishment; even while enervated by confinement and false notions of modesty, the body is prevented from attaining that grace and beauty which relaxed half-formed limbs never exhibit. Besides, in youth their faculties are not brought forward by emulation; and having no serious scientific study, if they have natural sagacity it is turned too soon on life and manners. They dwell on effects, and modifications, without tracing them back to causes; and complicated rules to adjust behavior are a weak substitute for simple principles.

As a proof that education gives this appearance of weakness to females, we may instance the example of military men, who are, like them, sent into the world before their minds have been stored with knowledge or fortified by principles. The consequences are similar; soldiers acquire a little superficial knowledge, snatched from the muddy current of conversation, and, from continually mixing with society, they gain what is termed a knowledge of the world; and this acquaintance with manners and customs has frequently been confounded with a knowledge of the human heart. But can the crude fruit of casual observation, never brought to the test of judgment, formed by comparing speculation and experience, deserve such a distinction? Soldiers, as well as women, practice the minor virtues with punctilious politeness. Where is then the sexual difference when the education has been the same? All the difference that I can discern arises from the superior advantage of liberty, which enables the former to see more of life.

It is wandering from my present subject, perhaps, to make a political remark; but, as it was produced naturally by the train of my reflections, I shall not pass it silently over.

Standing armies can never consist of resolute, robust men; they may be well-disciplined machines, but they will seldom contain men under the influence of strong passions, or with very vigorous faculties. And as for any depth of understanding, I will venture to affirm that it is as rarely to be found in the army as amongst women; and the cause, I maintain, is the same. It may be further observed that officers are also particularly attentive to their persons, fond of dancing, crowded rooms, adventures, and ridicule.* Like the *fair* sex,

---

*"Why should women be censured with petulant acrimony, because they seem to have a passion for a scarlet coat? Has not education placed them more on a level with soldiers than any other class of men?" (Wollstonecraft's note)

the business of their lives is gallantry. They were taught to please, and they only live to please. Yet they do not lose their rank in the distinction of sexes, for they are still reckoned superior to women, though in what their superiority consists, beyond what I have just mentioned, it is difficult to discover.

The great misfortune is this, that they both acquire manners before morals, and a knowledge of life before they have, from reflection, any acquaintance with the grand ideal outline of human nature. The consequence is natural; satisfied with common nature, they become a prey to prejudices, and taking all their opinions on credit, they blindly submit to authority. So that, if they have any sense, it is a kind of instinctive glance that catches proportions, and decides with respect to manners; but fails when arguments are to be pursued before the surface, or opinions analyzed.

May not the same remark be applied to women? Nay, the argument may be carried still further, for they are both thrown out of a useful station by the unnatural distinctions established in civilized life. Riches and hereditary honors have made ciphers of women to give consequence to the numerical figure; and idleness has produced a mixture of gallantry and despotism into society, which leads the very men who are the slaves of their mistresses to tyrannize over their sisters, wives, and daughters. This is only keeping them in rank and file, it is true. Strengthen the female mind by enlarging it, and there will be an end to blind obedience; but, as blind obedience is ever sought for by power, tyrants and sensualists are in the right when they endeavor to keep women in the dark, because the former only want slaves, and the latter a plaything. The sensualist, indeed, has been the most dangerous of tyrants, and women have been duped by their lovers, as princes by their ministers, whilst dreaming that they reigned over them.

I now principally allude to Rousseau, for his character of Sophia* is, undoubtedly, a captivating one, though it appears to me grossly unnatural; however, it is not the superstructure, but the foundation of her character, the principles on which her education was built, that I mean to attack; nay, warmly as I admire the genius of that able writer, whose opinions I shall often have occasion to cite, indignation always takes place of admiration, and the rigid frown of

*In *Emile*, Book V.

insulted virtue effaces the smile of complacency, which his
eloquent periods are wont to raise, when I read his voluptuous reveries. Is this the man who, in his ardor for virtue,
would banish all the soft arts of peace, and almost carry us
back to Spartan discipline? Is this the man who delights to
paint the useful struggles of passion, the triumphs of good
dispositions, and the heroic flights which carry the glowing
soul out of itself? How are these mighty sentiments lowered
when he describes the pretty foot and enticing airs of his
little favorite! But, for the present, I waive the subject, and,
instead of severely reprehending the transient effusions of
overweening sensibility, I shall only observe that whoever
has cast a benevolent eye on society must often have been
gratified by the sight of a humble mutual love, not dignified
by sentiment, or strengthened by a union in intellectual
pursuits. The domestic trifles of the day have afforded matters for cheerful converse, and innocent caresses have softened toils which did not require great exercise of mind or
stretch of thought: yet, has not the sight of this moderate
felicity excited more tenderness than respect? An emotion
similar to what we feel when children are playing, or animals sporting* whilst the contemplation of the noble struggles of suffering merit has raised admiration, and carried
our thoughts to that world where sensation will give place
to reason.

Women are, therefore, to be considered either as moral
beings, or so weak that they must be entirely subjected to
the superior faculties of men.

Let us examine this question. Rousseau declares that a
woman should never for a moment feel herself independent,
that she should be governed by fear to exercise her natural
cunning, and made a coquetish slave in order to render her
a more alluring object of desire, a *sweeter* companion to
man, whenever he chooses to relax himself. He carries the

---

*"Similar feelings has Milton's pleasing picture of paradisiacal hap-
piness ever raised in my mind; yet, instead of envying the lovely
pair, I have, with conscious dignity, or Satanic pride, turned to hell
for sublimer objects. In the same style, when viewing some noble
monument of human art, I have traced the emanation of the Deity
in the order I admired, till, descending from that giddy height, I
have caught myself contemplating the grandest of all human sights;
for fancy quickly placed, in some solitary recess, an outcast of
fortune, rising superior to passion and discontent." (Wollstonecraft's
note)

arguments, which he pretends to draw from the indications of nature, still further, and insinuates that truth and fortitude, the cornerstones of all human virtue, should be cultivated with certain restrictions, because, with respect to the female character, obedience is the grand lesson which ought to be impressed with unrelenting rigor.

What nonsense! When will a great man arise with sufficient strength of mind to puff away the fumes which pride and sensuality have thus spread over the subject! If women are by nature inferior to men, their virtues must be the same in quality, if not in degree, or virtue is a relative idea; consequently, their conduct should be founded on the same principles, and have the same aim.

Connected with man as daughters, wives, and mothers, their moral character may be estimated by their manner of fulfilling those simple duties; but the end, the grand end of their exertions, should be to unfold their own faculties and acquire the dignity of conscious virtue. They may try to render their road pleasant; but ought never to forget, in common with man, that life yields not the felicity which can satisfy an immortal soul. I do not mean to insinuate that either sex should be so lost in abstract reflections or distant views as to forget the affections and duties that lie before them, and are, in truth, the means appointed to produce the fruit of life; on the contrary, I would warmly recommend them, even while I assert that they afford most satisfaction when they are considered in their true, sober light.

Probably the prevailing opinion that woman was created for man may have taken its rise from Moses's poetical story; yet, as very few, it is presumed, who have bestowed any serious thought on the subject, ever supposed that Eve was, literally speaking, one of Adam's ribs, the deduction must be allowed to fall to the ground; or, only be so far admitted as it proves that man, from the remotest antiquity, found it convenient to exert his strength to subjugate his companion, and his invention to show that she ought to have her neck bent under the yoke, because the whole creation was only created for his convenience or pleasure.

Let it not be concluded that I wish to invert the order of things; I have already granted that, from the constitution of their bodies, men seem to be designed by Providence to attain a greater degree of virtue. I speak collectively of the whole sex; but I see not the shadow of a reason to conclude that their virtues should differ in respect to their nature. In fact, how can they, if virtue has only one eternal standard? I must therefore, if I reason consequentially, as strenuously maintain that they have the same simple direction, as that there is a God.

It follows then that cunning should not be opposed to wisdom, little cares to great exertions, or insipid softness, varnished over with the name of gentleness, to that fortitude which grand views alone can inspire.

I shall be told that woman would then lose many of her peculiar graces, and the opinion of a well-known poet might be quoted to refute my unqualified assertion. For Pope has said, in the name of the whole male sex,

> Yet ne'er so sure our passion to create,
> As when she touch'd the brink of all we hate.*

In what light this sally places men and women, I shall leave to the judicious to determine; meanwhile I shall content myself with observing that I cannot discover why, unless they are mortal, females should always be degraded by being made subservient to love or lust.

To speak disrespectfully of love is, I know, high treason against sentiment and fine feelings; but I wish to speak the simple language of truth, and rather to address the head than the heart. To endeavor to reason love out of the world would be to out-Quixote Cervantes, and equally offend against common sense: but an endeavor to restrain this tumultuous passion, and to prove that it should not be allowed to dethrone superior powers, or to usurp the scepter which the understanding should ever coolly wield, appears less wild.

Youth is the season for love in both sexes; but in those days of thoughtless enjoyment provision should be made for the more important years of life, when reflection takes place of sensation. But Rousseau, and most of the male writers who have followed his steps, have warmly inculcated that the whole tendency of female education ought to be directed to one point: to render them pleasing.

Let me reason with the supporters of this opinion who have any knowledge of human nature; do they imagine that marriage can eradicate the habitude of life? The woman who has only been taught to please will soon find that her charms are oblique sunbeams, and that they cannot have

*Alexander Pope, *Moral Essays* II, 51–52.

much effect on her husband's heart when they are seen every day, when the summer is passed and gone. Will she then have sufficient native energy to look into herself for comfort, and cultivate her dormant faculties? or, is it not more rational to expect that she will try to please other men; and, in the emotions raised by the expectation of new conquests, endeavor to forget the mortification her love or pride has received? When the husband ceases to be a lover—and the time will inevitably come—her desire of pleasing will then grow languid, or become a spring of bitterness; and love, perhaps, the most evanescent of all passions, gives place to jealousy or vanity.

I now speak of women who are restrained by principle or prejudice; such women, though they would shrink from an intrigue with real abhorrence, yet nevertheless wish to be convinced by the homage of gallantry that they are cruelly neglected by their husbands; or, days and weeks are spent in dreaming of the happiness enjoyed by congenial souls till their health is undermined and their spirits broken by discontent. How then can the great art of pleasing be such a necessary study? it is only useful to a mistress; the chaste wife and serious mother should only consider her power to please as the polish of her virtues, and the affection of her husband as one of the comforts that render her task less difficult and her life happier. But, whether she be loved or neglected, her first wish should be to make herself respectable, and not to rely for all her happiness on a being subject to like infirmities with herself.

The worthy Dr. Gregory fell into a similar error. I respect his heart; but entirely disapprove of his celebrated Legacy to his Daughters.

He advises them to cultivate a fondness for dress, because a fondness for dress, he asserts, is natural to them. I am unable to comprehend what either he or Rousseau mean, when they frequently use this indefinite term. If they told us that in a preexistent state the soul was fond of dress, and brought this inclination with it into a new body, I should listen to them with a half-smile, as I often do when I hear a rant about innate elegance. But if he only meant to say that the exercise of the faculties will produce this fondness, I deny it. It is not natural, but arises, like false ambition in men, from a love of power.

Dr. Gregory goes much further; he actually recommends dissimulation, and advises an innocent girl to give the lie to her feelings, and not dance with spirit, when gaiety of heart would make her feel eloquent without making her gestures immodest. In the name of truth and common sense, why should not one woman acknowledge that she can take more exercise than another? or, in other words, that she has a sound constitution; and why, to damp innocent vivacity, is she darkly to be told that men will draw conclusions which she little thinks of? Let the libertine draw what inference he pleases; but I hope that no sensible mother will restrain the natural frankness of youth by instilling such indecent cautions. Out of the abundance of the heart the mouth speaketh; and a wiser than Solomon hath said that the heart should be made clean, and not trivial ceremonies observed, which it is not very difficult to fulfill with scrupulous exactness when vice reigns in the heart.

Women ought to endeavor to purify their heart; but can they do so when their uncultivated understandings make them entirely dependent on their senses for employment and amusement, when no noble pursuit sets them above the little vanities of the day, or enables them to curb the wild emotions that agitate a reed over which every passing breeze has power? To gain the affections of a virtuous man, is affectation necessary? Nature has given woman a weaker frame than man; but, to ensure her husband's affections, must a wife, who by the exercise of her mind and body whilst she was discharging the duties of a daughter, wife, and mother, has allowed her constitution to retain its natural strength, and her nerves a healthy tone, is she, I say, to condescend to use art and feign a sickly delicacy in order to secure her husband's affection? Weakness may excite tenderness, and gratify the arrogant pride of man; but the lordly caresses of a protector will not gratify a noble mind that pants for, and deserves to be respected. Fondness is a poor substitute for friendship!

In a seraglio, I grant, that all these arts are necessary; the epicure must have his palate tickled, or he will sink into apathy; but have women so little ambition as to be satisfied with such a condition? Can they supinely dream life away in the lap of pleasure, or the languor of weariness, rather than assert their claim to pursue reasonable pleasures and render themselves conspicuous by practising the virtues which dignify mankind? Surely she has not an immortal soul who can loiter life away merely employed to adorn her person, that she may amuse the languid hours, and soften the cares of a fellow creature who is willing to be enlivened by her smiles and tricks, when the serious business of life is over.

Besides, the woman who strengthens her body and exercises her mind will, by managing her family and practising various virtues, become the friend, and not the humble dependent of her husband; and if she, by possessing such substantial qualities, merit his regard, she will not find it necessary to conceal her affection, nor to pretend to an unnatural coldness of constitution to excite her husband's passions. In fact, if we revert to history, we shall find that the women who have distinguished themselves have neither been the most beautiful nor the most gentle of their sex.

Of the same complexion is Dr. Gregory's advice respecting delicacy of sentiment, which he advises a woman not to acquire, if she have determined to marry. This determination, however, perfectly consistent with his former advice, he calls *indelicate*, and earnestly persuades his daughters to conceal it, though it may govern their conduct; as if it were indelicate to have the common appetites of human nature.

Noble morality! and consistent with the cautious prudence of a little soul that cannot extend its views beyond the present minute division of existence. If all the faculties of woman's mind are only to be cultivated as they respect her dependence on man; if, when a husband be obtained, she have arrived at her goal, and meanly proud rests satisfied with such a paltry crown, let her grovel contentedly, scarcely raised by her employments above the animal kingdom; but, if, struggling for the prize of her high calling, she look beyond the present scene, let her cultivate her understanding without stopping to consider what character the husband may have whom she is destined to marry. Let her only determine, without being too anxious about present happiness, to acquire the qualities that ennoble a rational being, and a rough inelegant husband may shock her taste without destroying her peace of mind. She will not model her soul to suit the frailties of her companion, but to bear with them: his character may be a trial, but not an impediment to virtue.

If Dr. Gregory confined his remark to romantic expectations of constant love and congenial feelings, he should have recollected that experience will banish what advice can never make us cease to wish for, when the imagination is kept alive at the expense of reason.

I own it frequently happens that women who have fostered a romantic unnatural delicacy of feeling waste their* lives in *imagining* how happy they should have been with a husband who could love them with a fervid increasing affection every day, and all day. But they might as well pine married as single—and would not be a jot more unhappy with a bad husband than longing for a good one. That a proper education, or, to speak with more precision, a well-stored mind, would enable a woman to support a single life with dignity, I grant; but that she should avoid cultivating her taste, lest her husband should occasionally shock it, is quitting a substance for a shadow. To say the truth, I do not know of what use is an improved taste, if the individual be not rendered more independent of the casualties of life; if new sources of enjoyment, only dependent on the solitary operations of the mind, are not opened. People of taste, married or single, without distinction, will ever be disgusted by various things that touch not less observing minds. On this conclusion the argument must not be allowed to hinge; but in the whole sum of enjoyment is taste to be denominated a blessing?

The question is, whether it procures most pain or pleasure? The answer will decide the propriety of Dr. Gregory's advice, and show how absurd and tyrannic it is thus to lay down a system of slavery; or to attempt to educate moral beings by any other rules than those deduced from pure reason, which apply to the whole species.

Gentleness of manners, forbearance, and long-suffering are such amiable Godlike qualities, that in sublime poetic strains the Deity has been invested with them; and, perhaps, no representation of his goodness so strongly fastens on the human affections as those that represent him abundant in mercy and willing to pardon. Gentleness, considered in this point of view, bears on its front all the characteristics of grandeur, combined with the winning graces of condescension; but what a different aspect it assumes when it is the submissive demeanor of dependence, the support of weakness that loves, because it wants protection; and is forbearing because it must silently endure injuries; smiling under the lash at which it dare not snarl. Abject as this picture appears, it is the portrait of an accomplished woman, according to the received opinion of female excellence, sepa-

*"For example, the herd of novelists." (Wollstonecraft's note)

rated by specious reasoners from human excellence. Or, they* kindly restore the rib, and make one moral being of a man and woman; not forgetting to give her all the "submissive charms."

How women are to exist in that state where there is to be neither marrying nor giving in marriage, we are not told. For though moralists have agreed that the tenor of life seems to prove that *man* is prepared by various circumstances for a future state, they constantly concur in advising *woman* only to provide for the present. Gentleness, docility, and a spaniel-like affection are, on this ground, consistently recommended as the cardinal virtues of the sex; and, disregarding the arbitrary economy of nature, one writer has declared that it is masculine for a woman to be melancholy. She was created to be the toy of man, his rattle, and it must jingle in his ears whenever, dismissing reason, he chooses to be amused.

To recommend gentleness, indeed, on a broad basis is strictly philosophical. A frail being should labor to be gentle. But when forbearance confounds right and wrong, it ceases to be a virtue; and, however convenient it may be found in a companion, that companion will ever be considered as an inferior, and only inspire a vapid tenderness, which easily degenerates into contempt. Still, if advice could really make a being gentle, whose natural disposition admitted not of such a fine polish, something towards the advancement of order would be attained; but if, as might quickly be demonstrated, only affectation be produced by this indiscriminate counsel, which throws a stumbling block in the way of gradual improvement, and true melioration of temper, the sex is not much benefited by sacrificing solid virtues to the attainment of superficial graces, though for a few years they may procure the individual's regal sway.

As a philosopher, I read with indignation the plausible epithets which men use to soften their insults; and, as a moralist, I ask what is meant by such heterogeneous associations, as fair defects, amiable weakness, etc.? If there be but one criterion of morals, but one archetype for man, women appear to be suspended by destiny, according to the vulgar tale of Mohammed's coffin; they have neither the unerring instinct of brutes, nor are allowed to fix the eye of reason on a perfect model. They were made to be loved, and

---

*"Vide Rousseau, and Swedenborg." (Wollstonecraft's note)

must not aim at respect, lest they should be hunted out of
society as masculine.

But to view the subject in another point of view. Do
passive indolent women make the best wives? Confining our
discussion to the present moment of existence, let us see
how such weak creatures perform their part? Do the women
who, by the attainment of a few superficial accomplishments,
have strengthened the prevailing prejudice, merely contribute to the happiness of their husbands? Do they display
their charms merely to amuse them? And have women, who
have early imbibed notions of passive obedience, sufficient
character to manage a family or educate children? So far
from it that, after surveying the history of woman, I cannot
help agreeing with the severest satirist, considering the sex
as the weakest as well as the most oppressed half of the
species. What does history disclose but marks of inferiority,
and how few women have emancipated themselves from the
galling yoke of sovereign man? So few, that the exceptions
remind me of an ingenious conjecture respecting Newton:
that he was probably a being of a superior order, accidentally caged in a human body. Following the same train of
thinking, I have been led to imagine that the few extraordinary women who have rushed in eccentrical directions out
of the orbit prescribed to their sex were *male* spirits, confined by mistake in female frames. But if it be not philosophical to think of sex when the soul is mentioned, the
inferiority must depend on the organs; or the heavenly fire,
which is to ferment the clay, is not given in equal portions.

But avoiding, as I have hitherto done, any direct comparison of the two sexes collectively, or frankly acknowledging
the inferiority of woman, according to the present appearance of things, I shall only insist that men have increased
that inferiority till women are almost sunk below the standard of rational creatures. Let their faculties have room to
unfold, and their virtues to gain strength, and then determine where the whole sex must stand in the intellectual
scale. Yet let it be remembered that for a small number of
distinguished women I do not ask a place.

It is difficult for us purblind mortals to say to what height
human discoveries and improvements may arrive when the
gloom of despotism subsides, which makes us stumble at
every step; but, when morality shall be settled on a more
solid basis, then, without being gifted with a prophetic spirit, I will venture to predict that woman will be either the

friend or slave of man. We shall not, as at present, doubt whether she is a moral agent, or the link which unites man with brutes. But, should it then appear that like the brutes they were principally created for the use of man, he will let them patiently bite the bridle, and not mock them with empty praise; or, should their rationality be proved, he will not impede their improvement merely to gratify his sensual appetites. He will not, with all the graces of rhetoric, advise them to submit implicitly their understanding to the guidance of man. He will not, when he treats of the education of women, assert that they ought never to have the free use of reason, nor would he recommend cunning and dissimulation to beings who are acquiring, in like manner as himself, the virtues of humanity.

Surely there can be but one rule of right, if morality has an eternal foundation, and whoever sacrifices virtue, strictly so called, to present convenience, or whose *duty* it is to act in such a manner, lives only for the passing day, and cannot be an accountable creature.

The poet then should have dropped his sneer when he says,

> If weak women go astray,
> The stars are more in fault than they.

For that they are bound by the adamantine chain of destiny is most certain, if it be proved that they are never to exercise their own reason, never to be independent, never to rise above opinion, or to feel the dignity of a rational will that only bows to God, and often forgets that the universe contains any being but itself and the model of perfection to which its ardent gaze is turned, to adore attributes that, softened into virtues, may be imitated in kind, though the degree overwhelms the enraptured mind.

If, I say, for I would not impress by declamation when Reason offers her sober light, if they be really capable of acting like rational creatures, let them not be treated like slaves; or, like the brutes who are dependent on the reason of man when they associate with him; but cultivate their minds, give them the salutary, sublime curb of principle, and let them attain conscious dignity by feeling themselves only dependent on God. Teach them, in common with man, to submit to necessity, instead of giving, to render them more pleasing, a sex to morals.

Further, should experience prove that they cannot attain the same degree of strength of mind, perseverance, and fortitude, let their virtues be the same in kind, though they may vainly struggle for the same degree; and the superiority of man will be equally clear, if not clearer; and truth, as it is a simple principle, which admits of no modification, would be common to both. Nay, the order of society as it is at present regulated would not be inverted, for woman would then only have the rank that reason assigned her, and arts could not be practiced to bring the balance even, much less to turn it.

These may be termed Utopian dreams. Thanks to that Being who impressed them on my soul, and gave me sufficient strength of mind to dare to exert my own reason, till, becoming dependent only on him for the support of my virtue, I view with indignation the mistaken notions that enslave my sex.

I love man as my fellow; but his scepter, real or usurped, extends not to me, unless the reason of an individual demands my homage; and even then the submission is to reason, and not to man. In fact, the conduct of an accountable being must be regulated by the operations of its own reason; or on what foundation rests the throne of God?

It appears to me necessary to dwell on these obvious truths, because females have been insulated, as it were; and, while they have been stripped of the virtues that should clothe humanity, they have been decked with artificial graces that enable them to exercise a short-lived tyranny. Love, in their bosoms taking place of every nobler passion, their sole ambition is to be fair, to raise emotion instead of inspiring respect; and this ignoble desire, like the servility in absolute monarchies, destroys all strength of character. Liberty is the mother of virtue, and if women be, by their very constitution, slaves, and not allowed to breathe the sharp invigorating air of freedom, they must ever languish like exotics, and be reckoned beautiful flaws in nature.

As to the argument respecting the subjection in which the sex has ever been held, it retorts on man. The many have always been enthralled by the few; and monsters, who scarcely have shown any discernment of human excellence, have tyrannized over thousands of their fellow creatures. Why have men of superior endowments submitted to such degradation? For, is it not universally acknowledged that kings, viewed collectively, have ever been inferior, in abilities and virtue, to the same number of men taken from the common mass of mankind—yet, have they not, and are they not still treated with a degree of reverence that is an insult to reason? China is not the only country where a living man has been made a God. *Men* have submitted to superior strength to enjoy with impunity the pleasure of the moment—*women* have only done the same; and therefore till it is proved that the courtier, who servilely resigns the birthright of a man, is not a moral agent, it cannot be demonstrated that woman is essentially inferior to man because she has always been subjugated.

Brutal force has hitherto governed the world and that the science of politics is in its infancy is evident from philosophers scrupling to give the knowledge most useful to man that determinate distinction.

I shall not pursue this argument any further than to establish an obvious inference, that as sound politics diffuse liberty, mankind, including woman, will become more wise and virtuous.

THE SAME SUBJECT CONTINUED

Bodily strength from being the distinction of heroes is now sunk into such unmerited contempt that men as well as women seem to think it unnecessary: the latter, as it takes from their feminine graces, and from that lovely weakness the source of their undue power; and the former, because it appears inimical to the character of a gentleman.

. . . .

But, if strength of body be, with some show of reason, the boast of men, why are women so infatuated as to be proud of a defect? Rousseau has furnished them with a plausible excuse, which could only have occurred to a man, whose imagination had been allowed to run wild, and refine on the impressions made by exquisite senses—that they might, forsooth, have a pretext for yielding to a natural appetite without violating a romantic species of modesty, which gratifies the pride and libertinism of man.

Women, deluded by these sentiments, sometimes boast of their weakness, cunningly obtaining power by playing on the *weakness* of men; and they may well glory in their illicit sway, for, like Turkish bashaws, they have more real power than their masters: but virtue is sacrificed to temporary gratifications, and the respectability of life to the triumph of an hour.

Women, as well as despots, have now, perhaps, more power than they would have if the world, divided and subdivided into kingdoms and families, were governed by laws deduced from the exercise of reason; but in obtaining it, to carry on the comparison, their character is degraded, and licentiousness spread through the whole aggregate of society. The many become pedestal to the few. I, therefore, will venture to assert that till women are more rationally educated, the progress of human virtue and improvement in knowledge must receive continual checks. And if it be granted that woman was not created merely to gratify the appetite of man, or to be the upper servant, who provides his meals and takes care of his linen, it must follow that the first care of those mothers or fathers who really attend to the education of females should be, if not to strengthen the body, at least not to destroy the constitution by mistaken notions of beauty and female excellence; nor should girls ever be allowed to imbibe the pernicious notion that a defect can, by any chemical process of reasoning, become an excellence. In this respect, I am happy to find that the author of one of the most instructive books that our country has produced for children coincides with me in opinion; I shall quote his pertinent remarks to give the force of his respectable authority to reason.*

*"A respectable old man gives the following sensible account of the method he pursued when educating his daughter. 'I endeavored to give both to her mind and body a degree of vigor, which is seldom found in the female sex. As soon as she was sufficiently advanced in strength to be capable of the lighter labors of husbandry and gardening, I employed her as my constant companion. Selene, for that was her name, soon acquired a dexterity in all these rustic employments, which I considered with equal pleasure and admiration. If women are in general feeble both in body and mind, it arises less from nature than from education. We encourage a vicious indolence and inactivity, which we falsely call delicacy; instead of hardening their minds by the severer principles of reason and philosophy, we breed them to useless arts, which terminate in vanity and sensuality. In most of the countries which I had visited, they are taught nothing of an higher nature than a few modula-

But should it be proved that woman is naturally weaker than man, whence does it follow that it is natural for her to labor to become still weaker than nature intended her to be? Arguments of this cast are an insult to common sense, and savor of passion. The *divine right* of husbands, like the divine right of kings, may, it is to be hoped, in this enlightened age, be contested without danger, and, though conviction may not silence many boisterous disputants, yet, when any prevailing prejudice is attacked, the wise will consider, and leave the narrow-minded to rail with thoughtless vehemence at innovation.

The mother who wishes to give true dignity of character to her daughter must, regardless of the sneers of ignorance, proceed on a plan diametrically opposite to that which Rousseau has recommended with all the deluding charms of eloquence and philosophical sophistry: for his eloquence renders absurdities plausible, and his dogmatic conclusions puzzle, without convincing, those who have not ability to refute them.

Throughout the whole animal kingdom every young creature requires almost continual exercise, and the infancy of children, conformable to this intimation, should be passed in harmless gambols that exercise the feet and hands, without requiring very minute direction from the head, or the constant attention of a nurse. In fact, the care necessary for

---

tions of the voice, or useless postures of the body; their time is consumed in sloth or trifles, and trifles become the only pursuits capable of interesting them. We seem to forget that it is upon the qualities of the female sex that our own domestic comforts and the education of our children must depend. And what are the comforts or the education which a race of beings, corrupted from their infancy, and unacquainted with all the duties of life, are fitted to bestow? To touch a musical instrument with useless skill, to exhibit their natural or affected graces to the eyes of indolent and debauched young men, to dissipate their husband's patrimony in riotous and unnecessary expenses, these are the only arts cultivated by women in most of the polished nations I had seen. And the consequences are uniformly such as may be expected to proceed from such polluted sources, private misery and public servitude.

" 'But Selene's education was regulated by different views, and conducted upon severer principles; if that can be called severity which opens the mind to a sense of moral and religious duties, and most effectually arms it against the inevitable evils of life.' Mr. Day's *Sandford and Merton*, Vol III." (Wollstonecraft's note)

self-preservation is the first natural exercise of the understanding, as little inventions to amuse the present moment
unfold the imagination. But these wise designs of nature are
counteracted by mistaken fondness or blind zeal. The child
is not left a moment to its own direction, particularly a girl,
and thus rendered dependent—dependence is called natural.

To preserve personal beauty, woman's glory, the limbs
and faculties are cramped with worse than Chinese bands,
and the sedentary life which they are condemned to live,
whilst boys frolic in the open air, weakens the muscles and
relaxes the nerves. As for Rousseau's remarks, which have
since been echoed by several writers, that they have naturally, that is from their birth, independent of education, a
fondness for dolls, dressing, and talking—they are so puerile
as not to merit a serious refutation. That a girl, condemned
to sit for hours together listening to the idle chat of weak
nurses, or to attend at her mother's toilet, will endeavor to
join the conversation, is, indeed, very natural; and that she
will imitate her mother or aunts, and amuse herself by
adorning her lifeless doll, as they do in dressing her, poor
innocent babe, is undoubtedly a most natural consequence.
For men of the greatest abilities have seldom had sufficient
strength to rise above the surrounding atmosphere; and, if
the page of genius have always been blurred by the prejudices of the age, some allowance should be made for a sex,
who, like kings, always see things through a false medium.

Pursuing these reflections, the fondness for dress, conspicuous in women, may be easily accounted for, without
supposing it the result of a desire to please the sex on which
they are dependent. The absurdity, in short, of supposing
that a girl is naturally a coquette, and that a desire connected with the impulse of nature to propagate the species,
should appear even before an improper education has, by
heating the imagination, called it forth prematurely, is so
unphilosophical, that such a sagacious observer as Rousseau
would not have adopted it, if he had not been accustomed to
make reason give way to his desire of singularity, and truth
to a favorite paradox.

Yet thus to give a sex to mind was not very consistent
with the principles of a man who argued so warmly, and so
well, for the immortality of the soul. But what a weak
barrier is truth when it stands in the way of an hypothesis!
Rousseau respected—almost adored—virtue and yet he allowed himself to love with sensual fondness. His imagina-

tion constantly prepared inflammable fuel for his inflammable senses; but, in order to reconcile his respect for self-denial, fortitude, and those heroic virtues, which a mind like his could not coolly admire, he labors to invert the law of nature, and broaches a doctrine pregnant with mischief and derogatory to the character of supreme wisdom.

His ridiculous stories, which tend to prove that girls are *naturally* attentive to their persons, without laying any stress on daily example, are below contempt. And that a little miss should have such a correct taste as to neglect the pleasing amusement of making O's, merely because she perceived that it was an ungraceful attitude, should be selected with the anecdotes of the learned pig.*

I have, probably, had an opportunity of observing more girls in their infancy than J. J. Rousseau—I can recollect my own feelings, and I have looked steadily around me; yet, so far from coinciding with him in opinion respecting the first dawn of the female character, I will venture to affirm that a girl whose spirits have not been damped by inactivity, or innocence tainted by false shame, will always be a romp, and the doll will never excite attention unless confinement allows her no alternative. Girls and boys, in short, would play harmlessly together, if the distinction of sex was not inculcated long before nature makes any difference. I will go further, and affirm, as an indisputable fact, that most of the women in the circle of my observation who have acted like rational creatures, or shown any vigor of intellect, have accidentally been allowed to run wild—as some of the elegant formers of the fair sex would insinuate.

The baneful consequences which flow from inattention to health during infancy and youth extend further than is supposed—dependence of body naturally produces dependence

*" 'I once knew a young person who learned to write before she learned to read, and began to write with her needle before she could use a pen. At first, indeed, she took it into her head to make no other letter than the *O*: this letter she was constantly making of all sizes, and always the wrong way. Unluckily, one day, as she was intent on this employment, she happened to see herself in the looking-glass; when, taking a dislike to the constrained attitude in which she sat while writing, she threw away her pen, like another Pallas, and determined against making the *O* any more. Her brother was also equally averse to writing: it was the confinement, however, and not the constrained attitude, that most disgusted him.' Rousseau's *Emilius*." (Wollstonecraft's note)

of mind; and how can she be a good wife or mother, the greater part of whose time is employed to guard against or endure sickness? Nor can it be expected that a woman will resolutely endeavor to strengthen her constitution and abstain from enervating indulgencies if artificial notions of beauty and false descriptions of sensibility have been early entangled with her motives of action. Most men are sometimes obliged to bear with bodily inconveniencies, and to endure, occasionally, the inclemency of the elements; but genteel women are, literally speaking, slaves to their bodies, and glory in their subjection.

I once knew a weak woman of fashion who was more than commonly proud of her delicacy and sensibility. She thought a distinguishing taste and puny appetite the height of all human perfection, and acted accordingly. I have seen this weak sophisticated being neglect all the duties of life, yet recline with self-complacency on a sofa, and boast of her want of appetite as a proof of delicacy that extended to, or, perhaps, arose from, her exquisite sensibility: for it is difficult to render intelligible such ridiculous jargon. Yet, at the moment, I have seen her insult a worthy old gentlewoman whom unexpected misfortunes had made dependent on her ostentatious bounty, and who, in better days, had claims on her gratitude. Is it possible that a human creature could have become such a weak and depraved being, if, like the Sybarites, dissolved in luxury, everything like virtue had not been worn away, or never impressed by precept, a poor substitute, it is true, for cultivation of mind, though it serves as a fence against vice?

Such a woman is not a more irrational monster than some of the Roman emperors, who were depraved by lawless power. Yet, since kings have been more under the restraint of law, and the curb, however weak, of honor, the records of history are not filled with such unnatural instances of folly and cruelty, nor does the despotism that kills virtue and genius in the bud, hover over Europe with that destructive blast which desolates Turkey,* and renders the men, as well as the soil, unfruitful.

Women are everywhere in this deplorable state; for, in order to preserve their innocence, as ignorance is courteously termed, truth is hidden from them, and they are made to assume an artificial character before their faculties have

*The strong, hot, sand-laden wind known as the *simoom* or *samiel*.

acquired any strength. Taught from their infancy that beauty
is woman's scepter, the mind shapes itself to the body and,
roaming round its gilt cage, only seeks to adorn its prison.
Men have various employments and pursuits which engage
their attention and give a character to the opening mind;
but women, confined to one, and having their thoughts constantly directed to the most insignificant part of themselves,
seldom extend their views beyond the triumph of the hour.
But were their understanding once emancipated from the
slavery to which the pride and sensuality of man and their
shortsighted desire, like that of dominion in tyrants, of
present sway, has subjected them, we should probably read
of their weaknesses with surprise. I must be allowed to
pursue the argument a little farther.

Perhaps, if the existence of an evil being were allowed,
who, in the allegorical language of scripture, went about
seeking whom he should devour, he could not more effectually degrade the human character than by giving a man
absolute power.

This argument branches into various ramifications. Birth,
riches, and every extrinsic advantage that exalt a man above
his fellows without any mental exertion sink him in reality
below them. In proportion to his weakness, he is played
upon by designing men, till the bloated monster has lost all
traces of humanity. And that tribes of men, like flocks of
sheep, should quietly follow such a leader is a solecism that
only a desire of present enjoyment and narrowness of understanding can solve. Educated in slavish dependence, and
enervated by luxury and sloth, where shall we find men who
will stand forth to assert the rights of man—or claim the
privilege of moral beings, who should have but one road to
excellence? Slavery to monarchs and ministers, which the
world will be long in freeing itself from, and whose deadly
grasp stops the progress of the human mind, is not yet
abolished.

Let not men, then, in the pride of power, use the same
arguments that tyrannic kings and venal ministers have
used, and fallaciously assert that woman ought to be subjected because she has always been so. But, when man,
governed by reasonable laws, enjoys his natural freedom, let
him despise woman, if she do not share it with him; and, till
that glorious period arrives, in descanting on the folly of the
sex, let him not overlook his own.

Women, it is true, obtaining power by unjust means, by

practicing or fostering vice, evidently lose the rank which reason would assign them, and they become either abject slaves or capricious tyrants. They lose all simplicity, all dignity of mind, in acquiring power, and act as men are observed to act when they have been exalted by the same means.

It is time to effect a revolution in female manners—time to restore to them their lost dignity—and make them, as a part of the human species, labor by reforming themselves to reform the world. It is time to separate unchangeable morals from local manners. If men be demigods—why let us serve them! And if the dignity of the female soul be as disputable as that of animals—if their reason does not afford sufficient light to direct their conduct whilst unerring instinct is denied—they are surely of all creatures the most miserable, and, bent beneath the iron hand of destiny, must submit to be a *fair defect* in creation. But to justify the ways of Providence respecting them, by pointing out some irrefragable reason for thus making such a large portion of mankind accountable and not accountable, would puzzle the subtilest casuist.

. . . .

Besides, if women be educated for dependence, that is, to act according to the will of another fallible being, and submit, right or wrong, to power, where are we to stop? Are they to be considered as viceregents allowed to reign over a small domain, and answerable for their conduct to a higher tribunal, liable to error?

It will not be difficult to prove that such delegates will act like men subjected by fear, and make their children and servants endure their tyrannical oppression. As they submit without reason, they will, having no fixed rules to square their conduct by, be kind, or cruel, just as the whim of the moment directs; and we ought not to wonder if sometimes, galled by their heavy yoke, they take a malignant pleasure in resting it on weaker shoulders.

But, supposing a woman trained up to obedience be married to a sensible man, who directs her judgment without making her feel the servility of her subjection, to act with as much propriety by this reflected light as can be expected when reason is taken at second hand, yet she cannot insure the life of her protector; he may die and leave her with a large family.

A double duty devolves on her; to educate them in the character of both father and mother; to form their principles and secure their property. But, alas, she has never thought, much less acted for herself. She has only learned to please* men, to depend gracefully on them; yet, encumbered with children, how is she to obtain another protector—a husband to supply the place of reason? A rational man, for we are not treading on romantic ground, though he may think her a pleasing docile creature, will not choose to marry a *family* for love, when the world contains many more pretty creatures. What is then to become of her? She either falls an easy prey to some mean fortune hunter, who defrauds her children of their paternal inheritance and renders her miserable; or becomes the victim of discontent and blind indulgence. Unable to educate her sons, or impress them with respect—for it is not a play on words to assert that people are never respected, though filling an important station, who are not respectable—she pines under the anguish of

---

*" 'In the union of the sexes, both pursue one common object, but not in the same manner. From their diversity in this particular, arises the first determinate difference between the moral relations of each. The one should be active and strong, the other passive and weak: it is necessary the one should have both the power and the will, and that the other should make little resistance.

" 'This principle being established, it follows that woman is expressly formed to please the man: if the obligation be reciprocal also, and the man ought to please in his turn, it is not so immediately necessary: his great merit is in his power, and he pleases merely because he is strong. This, I must confess, is not one of the refined maxims of love; it is, however, one of the laws of nature, prior to love itself.

" 'If woman be formed to please and be subjected to man, it is her place, doubtless, to render herself agreeable to him, instead of challenging his passion. The violence of his desires depends on her charms; it is by means of these she should urge him to the exertion of those powers which nature hath given him. The most successful method of exciting them, is, to render such exertion necessary by resistance; as, in that case, self-love is added to desire, and the one triumphs in the victory which the other obliged to acquire. Hence arise the various modes of attack and defence between the sexes; the boldness of one sex and the timidity of the other; and, in a word, that bashfulness and modesty with which nature hath armed the weak, in order to subdue the strong.' Rousseau's *Emilius*. I shall make no other comment on this ingenious passage, than just to observe, that it is the philosophy of lasciviousness." (Wollstonecraft's note)

unavailing impotent regret. The serpent's tooth enters into her very soul, and the vices of licentious youth bring her with sorrow, if not with poverty also, to the grave.

This is not an overcharged picture; on the contrary, it is a very possible case, and something similar must have fallen under every attentive eye.

I have, however, taken it for granted, that she was well-disposed, though experience shows that the blind may as easily be led into a ditch as along the beaten road. But supposing, no very improbable conjecture, that a being only taught to please must still find her happiness in pleasing; what an example of folly, not to say vice, will she be to her innocent daughters! The mother will be lost in the coquette, and, instead of making friends of her daughters, view them with eyes askance, for they are rivals—rivals more cruel than any other, because they invite a comparison, and drive her from the throne of her beauty, who has never thought of a seat on the bench of reason.

It does not require a lively pencil, or the discriminating outline of a caricature, to sketch the domestic miseries and petty vices which such a mistress of a family diffuses. Still she only acts as a woman ought to act, brought up according to Rousseau's system. She can never be reproached for being masculine, or turning out of her sphere; nay, she may observe another of his grand rules, and, cautiously preserving her reputation free from spot, be reckoned a good kind of woman. Yet in what respect can she be termed good? She abstains, it is true, without any great struggle, from committing gross crimes; but how does she fulfill her duties? Duties!—in truth she has enough to think of to adorn her body and nurse a weak constitution.

With respect to religion, she never presumed to judge for herself; but conformed, as a dependent creature should, to the ceremonies of the church which she was brought up in, piously believing that wiser heads than her own have settled that business: and not to doubt is her point of perfection. She therefore pays her tithe of mint and cumin—and thanks her God that she is not as other women are. These are the blessed effects of a good education! These the virtues of man's helpmate.*

***

* "'O how lovely,' exclaims Rousseau, speaking of Sophia, 'is her ignorance! Happy is he who is destined to instruct her! She will never pretend to be the tutor of her husband, but will be content to be his pupil. Far from attempting to subject him to her taste, she

I must relieve myself by drawing a different picture.

Let fancy now present a woman with a tolerable understanding, for I do not wish to leave the line of mediocrity, whose constitution, strengthened by exercise, has allowed her body to acquire its full vigor; her mind, at the same time, gradually expanding itself to comprehend the moral duties of life, and in what human virtue and dignity consist.

Formed thus by the discharge of the relative duties of her station, she marries from affection, without losing sight of prudence, and looking beyond matrimonial felicity, she secures her husband's respect before it is necessary to exert mean arts to please him and feed a dying flame, which nature doomed to expire when the object became familiar, when friendship and forbearance take place of a more ardent affection. This is the natural death of love, and domestic peace is not destroyed by struggles to prevent its extinction. I also suppose the husband to be virtuous; or she is still more in want of independent principles.

Fate, however, breaks this tie. She is left a widow, perhaps, without a sufficient provision; but she is not desolate! The pang of nature is felt; but after time has softened sorrow into melancholy resignation, her heart turns to her children with redoubled fondness, and anxious to provide for them, affection gives a sacred heroic cast to her maternal duties. She thinks that not only the eye sees her virtuous efforts from whom all her comfort now must flow, and whose approbation is life; but her imagination, a little abstracted and exalted by grief, dwells on the fond hope that the eyes which her trembling hand closed may still see how she subdues every wayward passion to fulfill the double duty of being the father as well as the mother of her children. Raised to heroism by misfortunes, she represses the first faint dawning of a natural inclination, before it ripens into love, and in the bloom of life forgets her sex— forgets the pleasure of an awakening passion, which might again have been inspired and returned. She no longer thinks of pleasing, and conscious dignity prevents her from priding herself

---

will accommodate herself to his. She will be more estimable to him, than if she was learned: he will have a pleasure in instructing her.' Rousseau's *Emilius*. I shall content myself with simply asking, how friendship can subsist, when love expires, between the master and his pupil?" (Wollstonecraft's note)

on account of the praise which her conduct demands. Her children have her love, and her brightest hopes are beyond the grave, where her imagination often strays.

I think I see her surrounded by her children, reaping the reward of her care. The intelligent eye meets hers, whilst health and innocence smile on their chubby cheeks, and as they grow up the cares of life are lessened by their grateful attention. She lives to see the virtues which she endeavored to plant on principles fixed into habits, to see her children attain a strength of character sufficient to enable them to endure adversity without forgetting their mother's example.

The task of life thus fulfilled, she calmly waits for the sleep of death, and rising from the grave, may say—Behold, thou gavest me a talent—and here are five talents.

I wish to sum up what I have said in a few words, for I here throw down my gauntlet, and deny the existence of sexual virtues, not excepting modesty. For man and woman, truth, if I understand the meaning of the word, must be the same; yet the fanciful female character, so prettily drawn by poets and novelists, demanding the sacrifice of truth and sincerity, virtue becomes a relative idea, having no other foundation than utility, and of that utility men pretend arbitrarily to judge, shaping it to their own convenience.

Women, I allow, may have different duties to fulfill: but they are *human* duties, and the principles that should regulate the discharge of them, I sturdily maintain, must be the same.

To become respectable, the exercise of their understanding is necessary, there is no other foundation for independence of character; I mean explicitly to say that they must only bow to the authority of reason, instead of being the *modest* slaves of opinion.

In the superior ranks of life how seldom do we meet with a man of superior abilities, or even common acquirements? The reason appears to me clear: the state they are born in was an unnatural one. The human character has ever been formed by the employments the individual, or class, pursues; and if the faculties are not sharpened by necessity, they must remain obtuse. The argument may fairly be extended to women; for, seldom occupied by serious business, the pursuit of pleasure gives that insignificancy to their character which renders the society of the *great* so insipid. The same want of firmness, produced by a similar cause, forces them both to fly from themselves to noisy pleasures, and artificial passions, till vanity takes place of every social affection, and the characteristics of humanity can scarcely be discerned. Such are the blessings of civil governments, as they are at present organized, that wealth and female softness equally tend to debase mankind, and are produced by the same cause; but allowing women to be rational creatures, they should be incited to acquire virtues which they may call their own, for how can a rational being be ennobled by anything that is not obtained by its *own* exertions?

OBSERVATIONS ON THE STATE OF DEGRADATION TO WHICH WOMAN IS REDUCED BY VARIOUS CAUSES

That woman is naturally weak, or degraded by a concurrence of circumstances, is, I think, clear. But this position I shall simply contrast with a conclusion, which I have frequently heard fall from sensible men in favor of an aristocracy: that the mass of mankind cannot be anything, or the obsequious slaves, who patiently allow themselves to be driven forward, would feel their own consequence, and spurn their chains. Men, they further observe, submit everywhere to oppression, when they have only to lift up their heads to throw off the yoke; yet, instead of asserting their birthright, they quietly lick the dust, and say, let us eat and drink, for tomorrow we die. Women, I argue from analogy, are degraded by the same propensity to enjoy the present moment; and, at last, despise the freedom which they have not sufficient virtue to struggle to attain. But I must be more explicit.

With respect to the culture of the heart, it is unanimously allowed that sex is out of the question; but the line of subordination in the mental powers is never to be passed over.* Only "absolute in loveliness," the portion of rational-

---

*"Into what inconsistencies do men fall when they argue without the compass of principles. Women, weak women, are compared with angels; yet, a superior order of beings should be supposed to possess more intellect than man; or, in what does their superiority consist? In the same strain, to drop the sneer, they are allowed to possess more goodness of heart, piety, and benevolence. I doubt

ity granted to woman, is, indeed, very scanty; for, denying her genius and judgment, it is scarcely possible to divine what remains to characterize intellect.

The stamen of immortality, if I may be allowed the phrase, is the perfectibility of human reason; for, were man created perfect, or did a flood of knowledge break in upon him, when he arrived at maturity, that precluded error, I should doubt whether his existence would be continued after the dissolution of the body. But, in the present state of things, every difficulty in morals that escapes from human discussion, and equally baffles the investigation of profound thinking, and the lightning glance of genius, is an argument on which I build my belief of the immortality of the soul. Reason is, consequentially, the simple power of improvement; or, more properly speaking, of discerning truth. Every individual is in this respect a world in itself. More or less may be conspicuous in one being than another; but the nature of reason must be the same in all, if it be an emanation of divinity, the tie that connects the creature with the Creator; for, can that soul be stamped with the heavenly image, that is not perfected by the exercise of its own reason?* Yet outwardly ornamented with elaborate care, and so adorned to delight man, "that with honor he may love,"† the soul of woman is not allowed to have this distinction, and man, ever placed between her and reason, she is always represented as only created to see through a gross medium, and to take things on trust. But dismissing these fanciful theories, and considering woman as a whole, let it be what it will, instead of a part of man, the inquiry is whether she have reason or not. If she have, which, for a moment, I will take for granted, she was not created merely to be the solace of man, and the sexual should not destroy the human character.

---

the fact, though it be courteously brought forward, unless ignorance be allowed to be the mother of devotion; for I am firmly persuaded that, on an average, the proportion between virtue and knowledge, is more upon a par than is commonly granted." (Wollstonecraft's note)

*" 'The brutes,' says Lord Monboddo, 'remain in the state in which nature has placed them, except in so far as their natural instinct is improved by the culture *we* bestow upon them.' " (Wollstonecraft's note). [James Burnett, Lord Monboddo, *Of the Origin and Progress of Language*, 1774.]

†"Vide Milton." (Wollstonecraft's note)

Into this error men have, probably, been led by viewing education in a false light; not considering it as the first step to form a being advancing gradually towards perfection;* but only as preparation for life. On this sensual error, for I must call it so, has the false system of female manners been reared, which robs the whole sex of its dignity, and classes the brown and fair with the smiling flowers that only adorn the land. This has ever been the language of men, and the fear of departing from a supposed sexual character, has made even women of superior sense adopt the same sentiments.† Thus understanding, strictly speaking, has been denied to woman; and instinct, sublimated into wit and cunning, for the purposes of life, has been substituted in its stead.

The power of generalizing ideas, of drawing comprehensive conclusions from individual observations, is the only acquirement for an immortal being that really deserves the name of knowledge. Merely to observe, without endeavoring

---

*"This word is not strictly just, but I cannot find a better." (Wollstonecraft's note)

†" 'Pleasure's the portion of th' *inferior* kind;/But glory, virtue, Heaven for *man* design'd.' After writing these lines, how could Mrs. Barbauld write the following ignoble comparison?

To a Lady, with some painted flowers.

Flowers to the fair: to you these flowers I bring,
And strive to greet you with an earlier spring.
Flowers SWEET, *and gay, and* DELICATE LIKE YOU:
Emblems of innocence, and beauty too.
With flowers the Graces bind their yellow hair,
And flowery wreaths consenting lovers wear.
Flowers, the sole luxury which nature knew,
In Eden's pure and guiltless garden grew.
To loftier forms are rougher tasks assign'd;
The sheltering oak resists the stormy wind,
The tougher yew repels invading foes,
And the tall pine for future navies grows;
But this soft family, to cares unknown,
Were born for pleasure and delight ALONE.
Gay without toil, and lovely without art,
They spring to CHEER *the sense, and* GLAD *the heart.*
Nor blush, my fair, to own you copy these;
Your BEST, *your* SWEETEST *empire is*—TO PLEASE.'

So the men tell us; but virtue, says reason, must be acquired by *rough* toils, and useful struggles with worldly *cares*." (Wollstonecraft's note)

to account for anything, may (in a very incomplete manner) serve as the common sense of life; but where is the store laid up that is to clothe the soul when it leaves the body?

This power has not only been denied to women; but writers have insisted that it is inconsistent, with a few exceptions, with their sexual character. Let men prove this, and I shall grant that woman only exists for man. I must, however, previously remark that the power of generalizing ideas, to any great extent, is not very common amongst men or women. But this exercise is the true cultivation of the understanding; and everything conspires to render the cultivation of the understanding more difficult in the female than the male world.

I am naturally led by this assertion to the main subject of the present chapter, and shall now attempt to point out some of the causes that degrade the sex, and prevent women from generalizing their observations.

I shall not go back to the remote annals of antiquity to trace the history of woman; it is sufficient to allow that she has always been either a slave, or a despot, and to remark that each of these situations equally retards the progress of reason. The grand source of female folly and vice has ever appeared to me to arise from narrowness of mind; and the very constitution of civil governments has put almost insuperable obstacles in the way to prevent the cultivation of the female understanding—yet virtue can be built on no other foundation! The same obstacles are thrown in the way of the rich, and the same consequences ensue.

Necessity has been proverbially termed the mother of invention—the aphorism may be extended to virtue. It is an acquirement, and an acquirement of which pleasure must be sacrificed—and who sacrifices pleasure when it is within the grasp, whose mind has not been opened and strengthened by adversity, or the pursuit of knowledge goaded on by necessity? Happy is it when people have the cares of life to struggle with; for these struggles prevent their becoming a prey to enervating vices, merely from idleness! But, if from their birth men and women be placed in a torrid zone, with the meridian sun of pleasure darting directly upon them, how can they sufficiently brace their minds to discharge the duties of life, or even to relish the affections that carry them out of themselves?

Pleasure is the business of woman's life, according to the present modification of society, and while it continues to be so, little can be expected from such weak beings. Inheriting, in a lineal descent from the first fair defect in nature, the sovereignty of beauty, they have, to maintain their power, resigned the natural rights which the exercise of reason might have procured them, and chosen rather to be short-lived queens than labor to obtain the sober pleasures that arise from equality. Exalted by their inferiority (this sounds like a contradiction), they constantly demand homage as women, though experience should teach them that the men who pride themselves upon paying this arbitrary insolent respect to the sex, with the most scrupulous exactness, are most inclined to tyrannize over, and despise, the very weakness they cherish. . . .

Ah! why do women, I write with affectionate solicitude, condescend to receive a degree of attention and respect from strangers, different from that reciprocation of civility which the dictates of humanity and the politeness of civilization authorize between man and man? And, why do they not discover, when "in the noon of beauty's power," that they are treated like queens only to be deluded by hollow respect, till they are led to resign, or not assume, their natural prerogatives? Confined then in cages like the feathered race, they have nothing to do but to plume themselves, and stalk with mock majesty from perch to perch. It is true they are provided with food and raiment, for which they neither toil nor spin, but health, liberty, and virtue are given in exchange. But where, amongst mankind, has been found sufficient strength of mind to enable a being to resign these adventitious prerogatives; one who, rising with the calm dignity of reason above opinion, dared to be proud of the privileges inherent in man? And it is vain to expect it whilst hereditary power chokes the affections and nips reason in the bud.

The passions of men have thus placed women on thrones, and, till mankind become more reasonable, it is to be feared that women will avail themselves of the power which they attain with the least exertion, and which is the most indisputable. They will smile—yes, they will smile, though told that—

> In beauty's empire is no mean,
> And woman, either slave or queen,
> Is quickly scorn'd when not ador'd.*

*Anna Barbauld "Song V," 16–18

But the adoration comes first, and the scorn is not anticipated.
. . . .

I lament that women are systematically degraded by receiving the trivial attentions which men think it manly to pay to the sex, when, in fact, they are insultingly supporting their own superiority. It is not condescension to bow to an inferior. So ludicrous, in fact, do these ceremonies appear to me that I scarcely am able to govern my muscles when I see a man start with eager and serious solicitude to lift a handkerchief, or shut a door, when the *lady* could have done it herself, had she only moved a pace or two.

A wild wish has just flown from my heart to my head, and I will not stifle it though it may excite a horselaugh. I do earnestly wish to see the distinction of sex confounded in society, unless where love animates the behavior. For this distinction is, I am firmly persuaded, the foundation of the weakness of character ascribed to woman; is the cause why the understanding is neglected, whilst accomplishments are acquired with sedulous care: and the same cause accounts for their preferring the graceful before the heroic virtues.

Mankind, including every description, wish to be loved and respected by *something*; and the common herd will always take the nearest road to the completion of their wishes. The respect paid to wealth and beauty is the most certain, and unequivocal; and, of course, will always attract the vulgar eye of common minds. Abilities and virtues are absolutely necessary to raise men from the middle rank of life into notice; and the natural consequence is notorious: the middle rank contains most virtue and abilities. Men have thus, in one station, at least an opportunity of exerting themselves with dignity, and of rising by the exertions which really improve a rational creature; but the whole female sex are, till their character is formed, in the same condition as the rich: for they are born—I now speak of a state of civilization—with certain sexual privileges, and whilst they are gratuitously granted them, few will ever think of works of supererogation to obtain the esteem of a small number of superior people.

When do we hear of women who, starting out of obscurity, boldly claim respect on account of their great abilities or daring virtues? Where are they to be found? "To be observed, to be attended to, to be taken notice of with sympathy, complacency, and approbation, are all the advantages

which they seek."* True! my male readers will probably exclaim; but let them before they draw any conclusion, recollect that this was not written originally as descriptive of
women, but of the rich. In Dr. Smith's *Theory of Moral
Sentiments* I have found a general character of people of
rank and fortune that, in my opinion, might with the greatest propriety be applied to the female sex. I refer the sagacious reader to the whole comparison; but must be allowed
to quote a passage to enforce an argument that I mean to
insist on, as the one most conclusive against a sexual character. For if, excepting warriors, no great men, of any denomination, have ever appeared amongst the nobility, may
it not be fairly inferred that their local situation swallowed
up the man, and produced a character similar to that of
women, who are *localized*, if I may be allowed the word, by
the rank they are placed in, by *courtesy*? Women, commonly
called Ladies, are not to be contradicted in company, are not
allowed to exert any manual strength; and from them the
negative virtues only are expected, when any virtues are
expected: patience, docility, good humor, and flexibility;
virtues incompatible with any vigorous exertion of intellect.
Besides, by living more with each other, and being seldom
absolutely alone, they are more under the influence of sentiments than passions. Solitude and reflection are necessary
to give to wishes the force of passions, and to enable the
imagination to enlarge the object, and make it the most
desirable. The same may be said of the rich; they do not
sufficiently deal in general ideas, collected by impassioned
thinking, or calm investigation, to acquire that strength of
character on which great resolves are built. . . .

. . . .

   In the middle rank of life . . . men, in their youth, are
prepared for professions, and marriage is not considered as
the grand feature in their lives; whilst women, on the contrary, have no other scheme to sharpen their faculties. It is
not business, extensive plans, or any of the excursive flights
of ambition, that engross their attention; no, their thoughts
are not employed in rearing such noble structures. To rise in
the world, and have the liberty of running from pleasure to
pleasure, they must marry advantageously, and to this object their time is sacrificed, and their persons often legally

*Adam Smith, *The Theory of Moral Sentiments* (1756).

prostituted. A man when he enters any profession has his eye steadily fixed on some future advantage (and the mind gains great strength by having all its efforts directed to one point), and, full of his business, pleasure is considered as mere relaxation; whilst women seek for pleasure as the main purpose of existence. In fact, from the education, which they receive from society, the love of pleasure may be said to govern them all; but does this prove that there is a sex in souls? It would be just as rational to declare that the courtiers in France, when a destructive system of despotism had formed their character, were not men, because liberty, virtue, and humanity were sacrificed to pleasure and vanity— fatal passions, which have ever domineered over the *whole* race!

The same love of pleasure, fostered by the whole tendency of their education, gives a trifling turn to the conduct of women in most circumstances: for instance, they are ever anxious about secondary things; and on the watch for adventures, instead of being occupied by duties.

A man, when he undertakes a journey, has, in general, the end in view; a woman thinks more of the incidental occurrences, the strange things that may possibly occur on the road; the impression that she may make on her fellow travelers; and, above all, she is anxiously intent on the care of the finery that she carries with her, which is more than ever a part of herself, when going to figure on a new scene; when, to use an apt French turn of expression, she is going to produce a sensation. Can dignity of mind exist with such trivial cares?

In short, women, in general, as well as the rich of both sexes, have acquired all the follies and vices of civilization, and missed the useful fruit. It is not necessary for me always to premise that I speak of the condition of the whole sex, leaving exceptions out of the question. Their senses are inflamed, and their understandings neglected; consequently they become the prey of their senses, delicately termed sensibility, and are blown about by every momentary gust of feeling. Civilized women are, therefore, so weakened by false refinement, that, respecting morals, their condition is much below what it would be were they left in a state nearer to nature. Ever restless and anxious, their overexercised sensibility not only renders them uncomfortable themselves, but troublesome, to use a soft phrase, to others. All their thoughts turn on things calculated to excite emotion;

and feeling, when they should reason, their conduct is unstable, and their opinions are wavering—not the wavering produced by deliberation or progressive views, but by contradictory emotions. By fits and starts they are warm in many pursuits; yet this warmth, never concentrated into perseverance, soon exhausts itself; exhaled by its own heat, or meeting with some other fleeting passion, to which reason has never given any specific gravity, neutrality ensues. Miserable, indeed, must be that being whose cultivation of mind has only tended to inflame its passions! A distinction should be made between inflaming and strengthening them. The passions thus pampered, whilst the judgment is left unformed, what can be expected to ensue? Undoubtedly, a mixture of madness and folly!

This observation should not be confined to the *fair* sex; however, at present, I only mean to apply it to them.

Novels, music, poetry, and gallantry, all tend to make women the creatures of sensation, and their character is thus formed in the mold of folly during the time they are acquiring accomplishments, the only improvement they are excited, by their station in society, to acquire. This overstretched sensibility naturally relaxes the other powers of the mind, and prevents intellect from attaining that sovereignty which it ought to attain to render a rational creature useful to others, and content with its own station: for the exercise of the understanding, as life advances, is the only method pointed out by nature to calm the passions.

Satiety has a very different effect, and I have often been forcibly struck by an emphatical description of damnation: when the spirit is represented as continually hovering with abortive eagerness round the defiled body, unable to enjoy any thing without the organs of sense. Yet, to their senses are women made slaves, because it is by their sensibility that they obtain present power.

And will moralists pretend to assert that this is the condition in which one-half of the human race should be encouraged to remain with listless inactivity and stupid acquiescence? Kind instructors! what were we created for? To remain, it may be said, innocent; they mean in a state of childhood. We might as well never have been born, unless it were necessary that we should be created to enable man to acquire the noble privilege of reason, the power of discerning good from evil, whilst we lie down in the dust from whence we were taken, never to rise again.

It would be an endless task to trace the variety of meannesses, cares, and sorrows into which women are plunged by the prevailing opinion, that they were created rather to feel than reason, and that all the power they obtain, must be obtained by their charms and weakness:

Fine by defect, and amiably weak!*

And, made by this amiable weakness entirely dependent, excepting what they gain by illicit sway on man, not only for protection, but advice, is it surprising that, neglecting the duties that reason alone points out, and shrinking from trials calculated to strengthen their minds, they only exert themselves to give their defects a graceful covering, which may serve to heighten their charms in the eye of the voluptuary, though it sink them below the scale of moral excellence?

Fragile in every sense of the word, they are obliged to look up to man for every comfort. In the most trifling dangers they cling to their support, with parasitical tenacity, piteously demanding succour; and their *natural* protector extends his arm, or lifts up his voice, to guard the lovely trembler—from what? Perhaps the frown of an old cow, or the jump of a mouse; a rat would be a serious danger. In the name of reason, and even common sense, what can save such beings from contempt; even though they be soft and fair?

These fears, when not affected, may produce some pretty attitudes; but they show a degree of imbecility which degrades a rational creature in a way women are not aware of—for love and esteem are very distinct things.

I am fully persuaded that we should hear of none of these infantine airs, if girls were allowed to take sufficient exercise, and not confined in close rooms till their muscles are relaxed, and their powers of digestion destroyed. To carry the remark still further, if fear in girls, instead of being cherished, perhaps created, were treated in the same manner as cowardice in boys, we should quickly see women with more dignified aspects. It is true they could not then with equal propriety be termed the sweet flowers that smile in the walk of man; but they would be more respectable members of society, and discharge the important duties of life by the light of their own reason. "Educate women like men,"

*Alexander Pope, *Moral Essays* II, 44.

says Rousseau, "and the more they resemble our sex the less power will they have over us."* This is the very point I aim at. I do not wish them to have power over men; but over themselves.

In the same strain have I heard men argue against instructing the poor; for many are the forms that aristocracy assumes. "Teach them to read and write," say they, "and you take them out of the station assigned them by nature." An eloquent Frenchman has answered them; I will borrow his sentiments. But they know not, when they make man a brute, that they may expect every instant to see him transformed into a ferocious beast. Without knowledge there can be no morality!

Ignorance is a frail base for virtue! Yet, that it is the condition for which woman was organized, has been insisted upon by the writers who have most vehemently argued in favor of the superiority of man; a superiority not in degree, but essence; though, to soften the argument, they have labored to prove, with chivalrous generosity, that the sexes ought not to be compared; man was made to reason, woman to feel: and that together, flesh and spirit, they make the most perfect whole, by blending happily reason and sensibility into one character.

And what is sensibility? "Quickness of sensation; quickness of perception; delicacy." Thus it is defined by Dr. Johnson, and the definition gives me no other idea than of the most exquisitely polished instinct. I discern not a trace of the image of God in either sensation or matter. Refined seventy times seven, they are still material; intellect dwells not there; nor will fire ever make lead gold!

I come round to my old argument; if woman be allowed to have an immortal soul, she must have, as the employment of life, an understanding to improve. And when, to render the present state more complete, though everything proves it to be but a fraction of a mighty sum, she is incited by present gratification to forget her grand destination, nature is counteracted, or she was born only to procreate and rot. Or, granting brutes of every description a soul, though not a reasonable one, the exercise of instinct and sensibility may be the step, which they are to take, in this life, towards the attainment of reason in the next; so that through all eter-

*Rousseau's point is to warn women against losing their feminine advantage by demanding a masculine education.

nity they will lag behind man, who, why we cannot tell, had the power given him of attaining reason in his first mode of existence.

When I treat of the peculiar duties of women, as I should treat of the peculiar duties of a citizen or father, it will be found that I do not mean to insinuate that they should be taken out of their families, speaking of the majority. "He that hath wife and children," says Lord Bacon, "hath given hostages to fortune; for they are impediments to great enterprises, either of virtue or mischief. Certainly the best works, and of greatest merit for the public, have proceeded from the unmarried or childless men.* I say the same of women. But the welfare of society is not built on extraordinary exertions; and were it more reasonably organized, there would be still less need of great abilities, or heroic virtues.

In the regulation of a family, in the education of children, understanding, in an unsophisticated sense, is particularly required: strength both of body and mind; yet the men who, by their writings, have most earnestly labored to domesticate women have endeavored, by arguments dictated by a gross appetite, which satiety had rendered fastidious, to weaken their bodies and cramp their minds. But if even by these sinister methods they really *persuaded* women, by working on their feelings, to stay at home, and fulfill the duties of a mother and mistress of a family, I should cautiously oppose opinions that led women to right conduct, by prevailing on them to make the discharge of such important duties the main business of life, though reason were insulted. Yet, and I appeal to experience, if by neglecting the understanding they be as much, nay, more detached from these domestic employments, than they could be by the most serious intellectual pursuit, though it may be observed, that the mass of mankind will never vigorously pursue an intellectual object,† I may be allowed to infer that reason is absolutely necessary to enable a woman to perform any duty properly, and I must again repeat that sensibility is not reason.

The comparison with the rich still occurs to me; for, when men neglect the duties of humanity, women will follow their example; a common stream hurries them both along with

---

*Francis Bacon, Essay VIII, "Of Marriage and the Single Life.
†"The mass of mankind are rather the slaves of their appetites than of their passions." (Wollstonecraft's note)

thoughtless celerity. Riches and honors prevent a man from enlarging his understanding, and enervate all his powers by reversing the order of nature, which has ever made true pleasure the reward of labor. Pleasure—enervating pleasure—is, likewise, within women's reach without earning it. But, till hereditary possessions are spread abroad, how can we expect men to be proud of virtue? And, till they are, women will govern them by the most direct means, neglecting their dull domestic duties to catch the pleasure that sits lightly on the wing of time.

"The power of the woman," says some author, "is her sensibility," and men, not aware of the consequence, do all they can to make this power swallow up every other. Those who constantly employ their sensibility will have most: for example, poets, painters, and composers.* Yet, when the sensibility is thus increased at the expense of reason, and even the imagination, why do philosophical men complain of their fickleness? The sexual attention of man particularly acts on female sensibility, and this sympathy has been exercised from their youth up. A husband cannot long pay those attentions with the passion necessary to excite lively emotions, and the heart, accustomed to lively emotions, turns to a new lover, or pines in secret, the prey of virtue or prudence. I mean when the heart has really been rendered susceptible, and the taste formed; for I am apt to conclude, from what I have seen in fashionable life, that vanity is oftener fostered than sensibility by the mode of education, and the intercourse between the sexes, which I have reprobated; and that coquetry more frequently proceeds from vanity than from that inconstancy, which overstrained sensibility naturally produces.

Another argument that has had great weight with me must, I think, have some force with every considerate benevolent heart. Girls who have been thus weakly educated, are often cruelly left by their parents without any provision; and, of course, are dependent on not only the reason but the bounty of their brothers. These brothers are, to view the fairest side of the question, good sort of men, and give as a favor what children of the same parents had an equal right to.

*"Men of these descriptions pour it into their compositions, to amalgamate the gross materials; and, molding them with passion, give to the inert body a soul; but, in woman's imagination, love alone concentrates these ethereal beams." (Wollstonecraft's note)

In this equivocal humiliating situation, a docile female may remain some time, with a tolerable degree of comfort. But, when the brother marries, a probable circumstance, from being considered as the mistress of the family she is viewed with averted looks as an intruder, an unnecessary burden on the benevolence of the master of the house and his new partner.

Who can recount the misery which many unfortunate beings, whose minds and bodies are equally weak, suffer in such situations—unable to work and ashamed to beg? The wife, a cold-hearted, narrow-minded, woman, and this is not an unfair supposition, for the present mode of education does not tend to enlarge the heart any more than the understanding, is jealous of the little kindness which her husband shows to his relations; and her sensibility not rising to humanity, she is displeased at seeing the property of *her* children lavished on an helpless sister.

These are matters of fact which have come under my eye again and again. The consequence is obvious: the wife has recourse to cunning to undermine the habitual affection, which she is afraid openly to oppose; and neither tears nor caresses are spared till the spy is worked out of her home, and thrown on the world, unprepared for its difficulties; or sent, as a great effort of generosity, or from some regard to propriety, with a small stipend, and an uncultivated mind, into joyless solitude.

These two women may be much upon a par, with respect to reason and humanity; and, changing situations, might have acted just the same selfish part; but had they been differently educated, the case would also have been very different. The wife would not have had that sensibility, of which self is the center, and reason might have taught her not to expect, and not even to be flattered by, the affection of her husband, if it led him to violate prior duties. She would wish not to love him merely because he loved her, but on account of his virtues; and the sister might have been able to struggle for herself instead of eating the bitter bread of dependence.

I am, indeed, persuaded that the heart, as well as the understanding, is opened by cultivation; and by, which may not appear so clear, strengthening the organs; I am not now talking of momentary flashes of sensibility, but of affections. And, perhaps, in the education of both sexes, the most difficult task is so to adjust instruction as not to narrow the understanding, whilst the heart is warmed by the generous juices of spring, just raised by the electric fermentation of the season; nor to dry up the feelings by employing the mind in investigations remote from life.

With respect to women, when they receive a careful education, they are either made fine ladies, brimful of sensibility, and teeming with capricious fancies; or mere notable women.* The latter are often friendly, honest creatures, and have a shrewd kind of good sense joined with worldly prudence, that often render them more useful members of society than the fine sentimental lady, though they possess neither greatness of mind nor taste. The intellectual world is shut against them; take them out of their family or neighborhood, and they stand still; the mind finding no employment, for literature affords a fund of amusement which they have never sought to relish, but frequently to despise. The sentiments and taste of more cultivated minds appear ridiculous, even in those whom chance and family connections have led them to love; but in mere acquaintance they think it all affectation.

A man of sense can only love such a woman on account of her sex, and respect her because she is a trusty servant. He lets her, to preserve his own peace, scold the servants, and go to church in clothes made of the very best materials. A man of her own size of understanding would, probably, not agree so well with her; for he might wish to encroach on her prerogative, and manage some domestic concerns himself. Yet women whose minds are not enlarged by cultivation, or the natural selfishness of sensibility expanded by reflection, are very unfit to manage a family; for, by an undue stretch of power, they are always tyrannizing to support a superiority that only rests on the arbitrary distinction of fortune. The evil is sometimes more serious, and domestics are deprived of innocent indulgences, and made to work beyond their strength, in order to enable the notable woman to keep a better table, and outshine her neighbors in finery and parade. If she attend to her children, it is, in general, to dress them in a costly manner—and, whether this attention arise from vanity or fondness, it is equally pernicious.

Besides, how many women of this description pass their days; or, at least, their evenings, discontentedly. Their husbands acknowledge that they are good managers, and chaste

*"Notable" women are energetic, capable housewives.

wives; but leave home to seek for more agreeable, may I be allowed to use a significant French word, *piquant* society; and the patient drudge, who fulfils her task like a blind horse in a mill, is defrauded of her just reward; for the wages due to her are the caresses of her husband; and women who have so few resources in themselves, do not very patiently bear this privation of a natural right.

. . . .

The female understanding has often been spoken of with contempt, as arriving sooner at maturity than the male. I shall not answer this argument by alluding to the early proofs of reason, as well as genius, in Cowley, Milton, and Pope,* but only appeal to experience to decide whether young men, who are early introduced into company (and examples now abound), do not acquire the same precocity. So notorious is this fact that the bare mentioning of it must bring before people who at all mix in the world the idea of a number of swaggering apes of men, whose understandings are narrowed by being brought into the society of men when they ought to have been spinning a top or twirling a hoop.

It has also been asserted by some naturalists that men do not attain their full growth and strength till thirty; but that women arrive at maturity by twenty. I apprehend that they reason on false ground, led astray by the male prejudice, which deems beauty the perfection of woman—mere beauty of features and complexion, the vulgar acceptation of the word, whilst male beauty is allowed to have some connection with the mind. Strength of body, and that character of countenance which the French term a *physionomie,* women do not acquire before thirty, any more than men. The little artless tricks of children, it is true, are particularly pleasing and attractive; yet, when the pretty freshness of youth is worn off, these artless graces become studied airs, and disgust every person of taste. In the countenance of girls we only look for vivacity and bashful modesty; but, the spring tide of life over, we look for soberer sense in the face, and for traces of passion, instead of the dimples of animal spirits, expecting to see individuality of character, the only fastener

*"Many other names might be added." (Wollstonecraft's note) Abraham Cowley, John Milton, and Alexander Pope all began writing poetry as children.

of the affections.* We then wish to converse, not to fondle, to give scope to our imaginations as well as to the sensations of our hearts.

At twenty the beauty of both sexes is equal; but the libertinism of man leads him to make the distinction, and superannuated coquettes are commonly of the same opinion; for, when they can no longer inspire love, they pay for the vigor and vivacity of youth. The French, who admit more of mind into their notions of beauty, give the preference to women of thirty. I mean to say that they allow women to be in their most perfect state, when vivacity gives place to reason, and to that majestic seriousness of character which marks maturity—or, the resting point. In youth, till twenty, the body shoots out, till thirty the solids are attaining a degree of density; and the flexible muscles, growing daily more rigid, give character to the countenance; that is, they trace the operations of the mind with the iron pen of fate, and tell us not only what powers are within, but how they have been employed.

. . . .

. . . When a man seduces a woman, it should, I think, be termed a *left-handed* marriage, and the man should be *legally* obliged to maintain the woman and her children, unless adultery, a natural divorcement, abrogated the law. And this law should remain in force as long as the weakness of women caused the word seduction to be used as an excuse for their frailty and want of principle; nay, while they depend on man for a subsistence instead of earning it by the exertion of their own hands or heads. But these women should not, in the full meaning of the relationship, be termed wives, or the very purpose of marriage would be subverted, and all those endearing charities that flow from personal fidelity, and give a sanctity to the tie, when neither love nor friendship unites the hearts, would melt into selfishness. The woman who is faithful to the father of her children demands respect, and should not be treated like a prostitute; though I readily grant that if it be necessary for a man and woman to live together in order to bring up their offspring,

*"The strength of an affection is, generally, in the same proportion as the character of the species in the object beloved, is lost in that of the individual." (Wollstonecraft's note)

nature never intended that a man should have more than one wife.

Still, highly as I respect marriage, as the foundation of almost every social virtue, I cannot avoid feeling the most lively compassion for those unfortunate females who are broken off from society, and by one error torn from all those affections and relationships that improve the heart and mind. It does not frequently even deserve the name of error, for many innocent girls become the dupes of a sincere, affectionate heart, and still more are, as it may emphatically be termed, *ruined* before they know the difference between virtue and vice—and thus prepared by their education for infamy, they become infamous. Asylums and Magdalenes* are not the proper remedies for these abuses. It is justice, not charity, that is wanting in the world!

A woman who has lost her honor imagines that she cannot fall lower, and as for recovering her former station, it is impossible; no exertion can wash this stain away. Losing thus every spur, and having no other means of support, prostitution becomes her only refuge, and the character is quickly depraved by circumstances over which the poor wretch has little power, unless she possesses an uncommon portion of sense and loftiness of spirit. Necessity never makes prostitution the business of men's lives; though numberless are the women who are thus rendered systematically vicious. This, however, arises, in a great degree from the state of idleness in which women are educated, who are always taught to look up to man for a maintenance, and to consider their persons as the proper return for his exertions to support them. Meretricious airs, and the whole science of wantonness, have then a more powerful stimulus than either appetite or vanity; and this remark gives force to the prevailing opinion, that with chastity all is lost that is respectable in woman. Her character depends on the observance of one virtue, though the only passion fostered in her heart is love. Nay, the honor of a woman is not made even to depend on her will.

When Richardson† makes Clarissa tell Lovelace that he had robbed her of her honor, he must have had strange

---

*Institutions for rehabilitating prostitutes.
†"Dr. Young supports the same opinion, in his plays, when he talks of the misfortune that shunned the light of day." (Wollstonecraft's note); Samuel Richardson, *Clarissa* (1747–48).

notions of honor and virtue. For miserable beyond all names
of misery is the condition of a being who could be degraded
without its own consent! . . .

. . . .

Women have seldom sufficient serious employment to silence their feelings; a round of little cares, or vain pursuits
frittering away all strength of mind and organs, they become naturally only objects of sense. In short, the whole
tenor of female education (the education of society) tends to
render the best disposed romantic and inconstant, and the
remainder vain and mean. In the present state of society
this evil can scarcely be remedied, I am afraid, in the slightest degree; should a more laudable ambition ever gain ground
they may be brought nearer to nature and reason, and
become more virtuous and useful as they grow more respectable.

But I will venture to assert that their reason will never
acquire sufficient strength to enable it to regulate their
conduct, whilst the making an appearance in the world is
the first wish of the majority of mankind. To this weak wish
the natural affections and the most useful virtues are sacrificed. Girls marry merely to *better themselves,* to borrow a
significant vulgar phrase, and have such perfect power over
their hearts as not to permit themselves to *fall in love* till a
man with a superior fortune offers. On this subject I mean
to enlarge in a future chapter; it is only necessary to drop a
hint at present, because women are so often degraded by
suffering the selfish prudence of age to chill the ardor of
youth.

From the same source* flows an opinion that young girls
ought to dedicate great part of their time to needlework; yet,
this employment contracts their faculties more than any
other that could have been chosen for them, by confining
their thoughts to their persons. Men order their clothes to
be made, and have done with the subject; women make their
own clothes, necessary or ornamental, and are continually
talking about them; and their thoughts follow their hands.
It is not indeed the making of necessaries that weakens the
mind, but the frippery of dress. For when a woman in the
lower rank of life makes her husband's and children's clothes,
she does her duty; this is her part of the family business; but

*Rousseau's *Émile.*

when women work only to dress better than they could otherwise afford, it is worse than sheer loss of time. To render the poor virtuous they must be employed, and women in the middle rank of life, did they not ape the fashions of the nobility, without catching their ease, might employ them, whilst they themselves managed their families, instructed their children, and exercised their own minds. Gardening, experimental philosophy, and literature would afford them subjects to think of and matter for conversation that in some degree would exercise their understandings. The conversation of French women, who are not so rigidly nailed to their chairs to twist lappets and knot ribands, is frequently superficial; but I contend that it is not half so insipid as that of those English women whose time is spent in making caps, bonnets, and the whole mischief of trimmings, not to mention shopping, bargain hunting, etc. etc.; and it is the decent, prudent women who are most degraded by these practices, for their motive is simply vanity. The wanton who exercises her taste to render her passion alluring has something more in view.

These observations all branch out of a general one which I have before made, and which cannot be too often insisted upon, for, speaking of men, women, or professions, it will be found that the employment of the thoughts shapes the character both generally and individually. The thoughts of women ever hover round their persons, and is it surprising that their persons are reckoned most valuable? Yet some degree of liberty of mind is necessary even to form the person; and this may be one reason why some gentle wives have so few attractions beside that of sex. Add to this, sedentary employments render the majority of women sickly—and false notions of female excellence make them proud of this delicacy, though it be another fetter that, by calling the attention continually to the body, cramps the activity of the mind.

Women of quality seldom do any of the manual part of their dress; consequently only their taste is exercised, and they acquire, by thinking less of the finery, when the business of their toilet is over, that ease which seldom appears in the deportment of women who dress merely for the sake of dressing. In fact, the observation with respect to the middle rank, the one in which talents thrive best, extends not to women; for those of the superior class, by catching at least a smattering of literature, and conversing more with men on general topics, acquire more knowledge than the women who ape their fashions and faults without sharing their advantages. With respect to virtue, to use the word in a comprehensive sense, I have seen most in low life. Many poor women maintain their children by the sweat of their brow, and keep together families that the vices of the fathers would have scattered abroad; but gentlewomen are too indolent to be actively virtuous, and are softened rather than refined by civilization. Indeed, the good sense which I have met with, among the poor women who have had few advantages of education, and yet have acted heroically, strongly confirmed me in the opinion that trifling employments have rendered woman a trifler. Man taking her* body, the mind is left to rust; so that while physical love enervates man, as being his favorite recreation, he will endeavor to enslave woman—and, who can tell how many generations may be necessary to give vigor to the virtue and talents of the freed posterity of abject slaves?†

In tracing the causes that, in my opinion, have degraded woman, I have confined my observations to such as universally act upon the morals and manners of the whole sex, and to me it appears clear that they all spring from want of understanding. Whether this arise from a physical or accidental weakness of faculties, time alone can determine; for I shall not lay any great stress on the example of a few women‡ who, from having received a masculine education, have acquired courage and resolution; I only contend that the men who have been placed in similar situations have acquired a similar character—I speak of bodies of men, and that men of genius and talents have started out of a class in which women have never yet been placed.

---

*" 'I take her body,' says Ranger." (Wollstonecraft's note): Ranger is a character in Benjamin Hoadly's *The Suspicious Husband* (1747).
†'Supposing that women are voluntary slaves—slavery of any kind is unfavorable to human happiness and improvement.' *Knox's Essays."* (Wollstonecraft's note)
‡"Sappho, Eloisa, Mrs. Macaulay, the Empress of Russia, Madame d'Eon, etc. These, and many more, may be reckoned exceptions; and, are not all heroes, as well as heroines, exceptions to general rules? I wish to see women neither heroines nor brutes; but reasonable creatures." (Wollstonecraft's note)

ANIMADVERSIONS ON SOME OF THE WRITERS WHO HAVE RENDERED WOMEN OBJECTS OF PITY, BORDERING ON CONTEMPT

The opinions speciously supported in some modern publications on the female character and education which have given the tone to most of the observations made, in a more cursory manner, on the sex, remain now to be examined.

SECTION I

The pernicious tendency of those books in which the writers insidiously degrade the sex whilst they are prostrate before their personal charms cannot be too often or too severely exposed.

Let us, my dear contemporaries, arise above such narrow prejudices! If wisdom be desirable on its own account, if virtue, to deserve the name, must be founded on knowledge; let us endeavor to strengthen our minds by reflection, till our heads become a balance for our hearts; let us not confine all our thoughts to the petty occurrences of the day, or our knowledge to an acquaintance with our lovers' or husbands' hearts; but let the practice of every duty be subordinate to the grand one of improving our minds, and preparing our affections for a more exalted state!

Beware then, my friends, of suffering the heart to be moved by every trivial incident: the reed is shaken by a breeze, and annually dies, but the oak stands firm, and for ages braves the storm!

Were we, indeed, only created to flutter our hour out and die—why let us then indulge sensibility, and laugh at the severity of reason. Yet, alas! even then we should want strength of body and mind, and life would be lost in feverish pleasures or wearisome languor.

But the system of education, which I earnestly wish to see exploded, seems to presuppose what ought never to be taken for granted, that virtue shields us from the casualties of life;

and that fortune, slipping off her bandage, will smile on a well-educated female, and bring in her hand an Emilius or a Telemachus. Whilst, on the contrary, the reward which virtue promises to her votaries is confined, it seems clear, to their own bosoms; and often must they contend with the most vexatious worldly cares, and bear with the vices and humors of relations for whom they can never feel a friendship.

There have been many women in the world who, instead of being supported by the reason and virtue of their fathers and brothers, have strengthened their own minds by struggling with their vices and follies, yet have never met with a hero in the shape of a husband who, paying the debt that mankind owed them, might chance to bring back their reason to its natural dependent state, and restore the usurped prerogative of rising above opinion to man.

SECTION II

Dr. Fordyce's sermons have long made a part of a young woman's library; nay, girls at school are allowed to read them; but I should instantly dismiss them from my pupil's, if I wished to strengthen her understanding, by leading her to form sound principles on a broad basis; or, were I only anxious to cultivate her taste; though they must be allowed to contain many sensible observations.*

Dr. Fordyce may have had a very laudable end in view; but these discourses are written in such an affected style that were it only on that account, and had I nothing to object against his *mellifluous* precepts, I should not allow girls to peruse them unless I designed to hunt every spark of nature out of their composition, melting every human quality into female meekness and artificial grace. I say artificial, for true grace arises from some kind of independence of mind.

. . . .

I particularly object to the loverlike phrases of pumped-up passion which are everywhere interspersed. If women be ever allowed to walk without leading strings, why must they be cajoled into virtue by artful flattery and sexual compliments? Speak to them the language of truth and soberness,

*Dr. James Fordyce, *Sermons to Young Women* (1765).

and away with the lullaby strains of condescending endearment! Let them be taught to respect themselves as rational creatures, and not led to have a passion for their own insipid persons. It moves my gall to hear a preacher descanting on dress and needlework; and still more, to hear him address the *British fair, the fairest of the fair,* as if they had only feelings.

Even recommending piety he uses the following argument. "Never, perhaps, does a fine woman strike more deeply, than when, composed into pious recollection, and possessed with the noblest considerations, she assumes, without knowing it, superior dignity and new graces; so that the beauties of holiness seem to radiate about her, and the by-standers are almost induced to fancy her already worshipping amongst her kindred angels!" Why are women to be thus bred up with a desire of conquest? The very word, used in this sense, gives me a sickly qualm! Do religion and virtue offer no stronger motives, no brighter reward? Must they always be debased by being made to consider the sex of their companions? Must they be taught always to be pleasing? And when leveling their small artillery at the heart of man, is it necessary to tell them that a little sense is sufficient to render their attention *incredibly soothing?* "As a small degree of knowledge entertains in a woman, so from a woman, though for a different reason, a small expression of kindness delights, particularly if she have beauty!" I should have supposed for the same reason.

Why are girls to be told that they resemble angels, but to sink them below women? Or that a gentle innocent female is an object that comes nearer to the idea which we have formed of angels than any other. Yet they are told, at the same time, that they are only like angels when they are young and beautiful; consequently, it is their persons, not their virtues, that procure them this homage.

Idle empty words! What can such delusive flattery lead to but vanity and folly? The lover, it is true, has a poetic licence to exalt his mistress; his reason is the bubble of his passion, and he does not utter a falsehood when he borrows the language of adoration. His imagination may raise the idol of his heart, unblamed, above humanity; and happy would it be for women if they were only flattered by the men who loved them; I mean, who love the individual, not the sex; but should a grave preacher interlard his discourses with such fooleries?

In sermons or novels, however, voluptuousness is always true to its text. Men are allowed by moralists to cultivate, as Nature directs, different qualities, and assume the different characters that the same passions, modified almost to infinity, give to each individual. A virtuous man may have a choleric or a sanguine constitution, be gay or grave, unreproved; be firm till he is almost overbearing, or, weakly submissive, have no will or opinion of his own; but all women are to be leveled, by meekness and docility, into one character of yielding softness and gentle compliance.

I will use the preacher's own words. "Let it be observed, that in your sex manly exercises are never graceful; that in them a tone and figure, as well as an air and deportment of the masculine kind, are always forbidding; and that men of sensibility desire in every woman soft features, and a flowing voice, a form, not robust, and demeanor delicate and gentle."

Is not the following portrait the portrait of a house slave? "I am astonished at the folly of many women, who are still reproaching their husbands for leaving them alone, for preferring this or that company to theirs, for treating them with this and the other mark of disregard or indifference; when, to speak the truth, they have themselves in a great measure to blame. Not that I would justify the men in anything wrong on their part. But had you behaved to them with more *respectful observance,* and a more *equal tenderness; studying their humors, overlooking their mistakes, submitting to their opinions* in matters indifferent, passing by little instances of unevenness, caprice, or passion, giving *soft* answers to hasty words, complaining as seldom as possible, and making it your daily care to relieve their anxieties and prevent their wishes, to enliven the hour of dullness, and call up the ideas of felicity: had you pursued this conduct, I doubt not but you would have maintained and even increased their esteem, so far as to have secured every degree of influence that could conduce to their virtue, or your mutual satisfaction; and your house might at this day have been the abode of domestic bliss." Such a woman ought to be an angel—or she is an ass—for I discern not a trace of the human character, neither reason nor passion in this domestic drudge, whose being is absorbed in that of a tyrant's.

Still Dr. Fordyce must have very little acquaintance with the human heart, if he really supposed that such conduct would bring back wandering love, instead of exciting contempt. No, beauty, gentleness, etc., etc. may gain a heart; but esteem, the only lasting affection, can alone be obtained by virtue supported by reason. It is respect for the understanding that keeps alive tenderness for the person.

As these volumes are so frequently put into the hands of young people, I have taken more notice of them than, strictly speaking, they deserve; but as they have contributed to vitiate the taste and enervate the understanding of many of my fellow creatures, I could not pass them silently over.

SECTION III

Such paternal solicitude pervades Dr. Gregory's Legacy to his Daughters that I enter on the task of criticism with affectionate respect* but as this little volume has many attractions to recommend it to the notice of the most respectable part of my sex, I cannot silently pass over arguments that so speciously support opinions which, I think, have had the most baneful effect on the morals and manners of the female world.

. . . .

Besides, having two objects in view, he seldom adhered steadily to either; for wishing to make his daughters amiable, and fearing lest unhappiness should only be the consequence of instilling sentiments that might draw them out of the track of common life without enabling them to act with consonant independence and dignity, he checks the natural flow of his thoughts, and neither advises one thing nor the other.

. . . .

Why, for instance, should the following caution be given when art of every kind must contaminate the mind; and why entangle the grand motives of action, which reason and religion equally combine to enforce, with pitiful worldly shifts and slight-of-hand tricks to gain the applause of gaping tasteless fools? "Be even cautious in displaying your good sense.† It will be thought you assume a superiority

---

*Dr. John Gregory, *A Father's Legacy to His Daughters* (1774).
†"Let women once acquire good sense—and if it deserve the name, it will teach them; or, of what use will it be?" (Wollstonecraft's note)

over the rest of the company. But if you happen to have
any learning, keep it a profound secret, especially from the
men who generally look with a jealous and malignant eye
on a woman of great parts, and a cultivated understanding."
If men of real merit, as he afterwards observes, be superior
to this meanness, where is the necessity that the behavior of
the whole sex should be modulated to please fools, or men,
who having little claim to respect as individuals, choose to
keep close in their phalanx. Men, indeed, who insist on their
common superiority, having only this sexual superiority,
are certainly very excusable.

. . . .

Surely it would have been wiser to have advised women to
improve themselves till they rose above the fumes of vanity;
and then to let the public opinion come round—for where
are rules of accommodation to stop? The narrow path of
truth and virtue inclines neither to the right nor left—it is a
straightforward business, and they who are earnestly pursuing their road may bound over many decorous prejudices,
without leaving modesty behind. Make the heart clean, and
give the head employment, and I will venture to predict that
there will be nothing offensive in the behavior.

The air of fashion which many young people are so eager
to attain always strikes me like the studied attitudes of
some modern pictures, copied with tasteless servility after
the antiques; the soul is left out, and none of the parts are
tied together by what may properly be termed character.
This varnish of fashion, which seldom sticks very close to
sense, may dazzle the weak; but leave nature to itself, and it
will seldom disgust the wise. Besides, when a woman has
sufficient sense not to pretend to anything which she does
not understand in some degree, there is no need of determining to hide her talents under a bushel. Let things take
their natural course, and all will be well.

It is this system of dissimulation, throughout the volume,
that I despise. Women are always to *seem* to be this and
that—yet virtue might apostrophize them, in the words of
Hamlet—Seems! I know not seems!—Have that within that
passeth show!

. . . .

THE EFFECT WHICH AN EARLY
ASSOCIATION OF IDEAS HAS UPON THE
CHARACTER

Educated in the enervating style recommended by the writers on whom I have been animadverting, and not having a chance, from their subordinate state in society, to recover their lost ground, is it surprising that women everywhere appear a defect in nature? Is it surprising, when we consider what a determinate effect an early association of ideas has on the character, that they neglect their understandings, and turn all their attention to their persons?

. . . .

. . . The generality of people cannot see or feel poetically; they want fancy, and therefore fly from solitude in search of sensible objects; but when an author lends them his eyes they can see as he saw, and be amused by images they could not select, though lying before them.

Education thus only supplies the man of genius with knowledge to give variety and contrast to his associations; but there is an habitual association of ideas, that grows "with our growth," which has a great effect on the moral character of mankind; and by which a turn is given to the mind that commonly remains throughout life. So ductile is the understanding, and yet so stubborn, that the associations which depend on adventitious circumstances, during the period that the body takes to arrive at maturity, can seldom be disentangled by reason. One idea calls up another, its old associate, and memory, faithful to the first impressions, particularly when the intellectual powers are not employed to cool our sensations, retraces them with mechanical exactness.

This habitual slavery to first impressions has a more baneful effect on the female than the male character, because business and other dry employments of the understanding tend to deaden the feelings and break associations that do violence to reason. But females, who are made women of when they are mere children, and brought back to childhood when they ought to leave the go-cart forever, have not sufficient strength of mind to efface the superinductions of art that have smothered nature.

Everything that they see or hear serves to fix impressions, call forth emotions, and associate ideas that give a sexual character to the mind. False notions of beauty and delicacy stop the growth of their limbs and produce a sickly soreness, rather than delicacy of organs; and thus weakened by being employed in unfolding instead of examining the first associations, forced on them by every surrounding object, how can they attain the vigor necessary to enable them to throw off their factitious character? where find strength to recur to reason and rise superior to a system of oppression, that blasts the fair promises of spring? This cruel association of ideas, which everything conspires to twist into all their habits of thinking, or, to speak with more precision, of feeling, receives new force when they begin to act a little for themselves; for they then perceive that it is only through their address to excite emotions in men, that pleasure and power are to be obtained. Besides, the books professedly written for their instruction, which make the first impression on their minds, all inculcate the same opinions. Educated then in worse than Egyptian bondage, it is unreasonable, as well as cruel, to upbraid them with faults that can scarcely be avoided, unless a degree of native vigor be supposed, that falls to the lot of very few amongst mankind.

For instance, the severest sarcasms have been levelled against the sex, and they have been ridiculed for repeating "a set of phrases learnt by rote,"* when nothing could be more natural, considering the education they receive, and that their "highest praise is to obey, unargued"†—the will of man. If they be not allowed to have reason sufficient to govern their own conduct—why, all they learn—must be learned by rote! And when all their ingenuity is called forth to adjust their dress, "a passion for a scarlet coat"‡ is so natural that it never surprised me; and, allowing Pope's summary of their character to be just, "that every woman is at heart a rake,"§ why should they be bitterly censured for seeking a congenial mind, and preferring a rake to a man of sense?

*Jonathan Swift, "The Furniture of a Woman's Mind."
†*Paradise Lost* IV, 636–38.
‡"The Furniture of a Woman's Mind."
§Pope, *Moral Essays* II, 215–16.

Rakes know how to work on their sensibility, whilst the modest merit of reasonable men has, of course, less effect on their feelings, and they cannot reach the heart by the way of the understanding, because they have few sentiments in common.

It seems a little absurd to expect women to be more reasonable than men in their *likings,* and still to deny them the uncontrolled use of reason. When do men *fall in love* with sense? When do they, with their superior powers and advantages, turn from the person to the mind? And how can they then expect women, who are only taught to observe behavior, and acquire manners rather than morals, to despise what they have been all their lives laboring to attain? Where are they suddenly to find judgment enough to weigh patiently the sense of an awkward virtuous man, when his manners, of which they are made critical judges, are rebuffing, and his conversation cold and dull, because it does not consist of pretty repartees, or well-turned compliments? In order to admire or esteem anything for a continuance, we must, at least, have our curiosity excited by knowing, in some degree, what we admire; for we are unable to estimate the value of qualities and virtues above our comprehension. Such a respect, when it is felt, may be very sublime; and the confused consciousness of humility may render the dependent creature an interesting object, in some points of view; but human love must have grosser ingredients; and the person very naturally will come in for its share—and, an ample share it mostly has!

Love is, in a great degree, an arbitrary passion, and will reign, like some other stalking mischiefs, by its own authority, without deigning to reason; and it may also be easily distinguished from esteem, the foundation of friendship, because it is often excited by evanescent beauties and graces, though, to give an energy to the sentiment, something more solid must deepen their impression and set the imagination to work, to make the most fair—the first good.

Common passions are excited by common qualities. Men look for beauty and the simper of good-humored docility: women are captivated by easy manners; a gentlemanlike man seldom fails to please them, and their thirsty ears eagerly drink the insinuating nothings of politeness, whilst they turn from the unintelligible sounds of the charmer—reason, charm he never so wisely. With respect to superficial accomplishments, the rake certainly has the advantage;

and of these females can form an opinion, for it is their own
ground. Rendered gay and giddy by the whole tenor of their
lives, the very aspect of wisdom, or the severe graces of
virtue, must have a lugubrious appearance to them; and
produce a kind of restraint from which they and love, sport-
ive child, naturally revolt. Without taste, excepting of the
lighter kind, for taste is the offspring of judgment, how can
they discover that true beauty and grace must arise from
the play of the mind and how can they be expected to relish
in a lover what they do not, or very imperfectly, possess
themselves? The sympathy that unites hearts, and invites
to confidence, in them is so very faint, that it cannot take
fire, and thus mount to passion. No, I repeat it, the love
cherished by such minds must have grosser fuel!

The inference is obvious; till women are led to exercise
their understandings, they should not be satirized for their
attachment to rakes; or even for being rakes at heart, when
it appears to be the inevitable consequence of their education.
They who live to please—must find their enjoyments, their
happiness, in pleasure! It is a trite, yet true remark, that we
never do anything well, unless we love it for its own sake.

Supposing, however, for a moment, that women were, in
some future revolution of time, to become what I sincerely
wish them to be, even love would acquire more serious
dignity, and be purified in its own fires; and virtue giving
true delicacy to their affections, they would turn with disgust from a rake. Reasoning then, as well as feeling, the
only province of woman at present, they might easily guard
against exterior graces, and quickly learn to despise the
sensibility that had been excited and hackneyed in the ways
of women, whose trade was vice; and allurements, wanton
airs. They would recollect that the flame, one must use
appropriated expressions, which they wished to light up,
had been exhausted by lust, and that the sated appetite,
losing all relish for pure and simple pleasures, could only be
roused by licentious arts or variety. What satisfaction could
a woman of delicacy promise herself in a union with such a
man, when the very artlessness of her affection might appear insipid? Thus does Dryden describe the situation.

Where love is duty, on the female side,
On theirs mere sensual gust, and sought with surly
    pride.

*John Dryden, *Palamon and Arcite12 III, 231–32.*

But one grand truth women have yet to learn, though much it imports them to act accordingly. In the choice of a husband, they should not be led astray by the qualities of a lover—for a lover the husband, even supposing him to be wise and virtuous, cannot long remain.

Were women more rationally educated, could they take a more comprehensive view of things, they would be contented to love but once in their lives; and after marriage calmly let passion subside into friendship—into that tender intimacy which is the best refuge from care; yet is built on such pure, still affections, that idle jealousies would not be allowed to disturb the discharge of the sober duties of life, or to engross the thoughts that ought to be otherwise employed. This is a state in which many men live; but few, very few women. And the difference may easily be accounted for, without recurring to a sexual character. Men, for whom we are told women were made, have too much occupied the thoughts of women; and this association has so entangled love with all their motives of action; and, to harp a little on an old string, having been solely employed either to prepare themselves to excite love, or actually putting their lessons in practice, they cannot live without love. But, when a sense of duty, or fear of shame, obliges them to restrain this pampered desire of pleasing beyond certain lengths, too far for delicacy, it is true, though far from criminality, they obstinately determine to love, I speak of the passion, their husbands to the end of the chapter—and then acting the part which they foolishly exacted from their lovers, they become abject woers, and fond slaves.

Men of wit and fancy are often rakes; and fancy is the food of love. Such men will inspire passion. Half the sex, in its present infantine state, would pine for a Lovelace,* a man so witty, so graceful, and so valiant: and can they *deserve* blame for acting according to principles so constantly inculcated? They want a lover, and protector; and behold him kneeling before them—bravery prostrate to beauty! The virtues of a husband are thus thrown by love into the background, and gay hopes, or lively emotions, banish reflection till the day of reckoning comes; and come it surely will, to turn the sprightly lover into a surly suspicious tyrant, who contemptuously insults the very weakness he fostered. Or, supposing the rake reformed, he cannot quickly get rid of

*Robert Lovelace in Samuel Richardson's *Clarissa* (1747–1748).

old habits. When a man of abilities is first carried away by his passions, it is necessary that sentiment and taste varnish the enormities of vice, and give a zest to brutal indulgences; but when the gloss of novelty is worn off, and pleasure palls upon the sense, lasciviousness becomes barefaced, and enjoyment only the desperate effort of weakness flying from reflection as from a legion of devils. Oh! virtue, thou art not an empty name! All that life can give—thou givest!

If much comfort cannot be expected from the friendship of a reformed rake of superior abilities, what is the consequence when he lacketh sense, as well as principles? Verily misery, in its most hideous shape. When the habits of weak people are consolidated by time, a reformation is barely possible; and actually makes the beings miserable who have not sufficient mind to be amused by innocent pleasure; like the tradesman who retires from the hurry of business, nature presents to them only a universal blank. . . .

MORALITY UNDERMINED BY SEXUAL NOTIONS OF THE IMPORTANCE OF A GOOD REPUTATION

The greater number of people take their opinions on trust to avoid the trouble of exercising their own minds, and these indolent beings naturally adhere to the letter, rather than the spirit of a law, divine or human. "Women," says some author, I cannot recollect who, "mind not what only heaven sees." Why, indeed, should they? It is the eye of man that they have been taught to dread—and if they can lull their Argus* to sleep, they seldom think of heaven or themselves, because their reputation is safe; and it is reputation, not chastity and all its fair train, that they are employed to keep free from spot, not as a virtue, but to preserve their station in the world.

To prove the truth of this remark, I need only advert to the intrigues of married women, particularly in high life, and in countries where women are suitably married, accord-

*Greek mythology: a monster with one hundred eyes.

ing to their respective ranks, by their parents. If an innocent girl become a prey to love, she is degraded forever,
though her mind was not polluted by the arts which married
women, under the convenient cloak of marriage, practice;
nor has she violated any duty—but the duty of respecting
herself. The married woman, on the contrary, breaks a most
sacred engagement, and becomes a cruel mother when she is
a false and faithless wife. If her husband have still an
affection for her, the arts which she must practice to deceive
him will render her the most contemptible of human beings;
and, at any rate, the contrivances necessary to preserve
appearances will keep her mind in that childish, or vicious,
tumult, which destroys all its energy. Besides, in time, like
those people who habitually take cordials to raise their
spirits, she will want an intrigue to give life to her thoughts,
having lost all relish for pleasures that are not highly sea-
soned by hope or fear.

Sometimes married women act still more audaciously; I
will mention an instance.

A woman of quality, notorious for her gallantries, though
as she still lived with her husband, nobody chose to place her
in the class where she ought to have been placed, made a
point of treating with the most insulting contempt a poor
timid creature, abashed by a sense of her former weakness,
whom a neighboring gentleman had seduced and afterwards
married. This woman had actually confounded virtue with
reputation; and, I do believe, valued herself on the propriety
of her behavior before marriage, though when once settled
to the satisfaction of her family, she and her lord were
equally faithless—so that the half-alive heir to an immense
estate came from heaven knows where!

To view this subject in another light.

I have known a number of women who, if they did not
love their husbands, loved nobody else, give themselves entirely up to vanity and dissipation, neglecting every domestic duty; nay, even squandering away all the money which
should have been saved for their helpless younger children,
yet have plumed themselves on their unsullied reputation,
as if the whole compass of their duty as wives and mothers
was only to preserve it. Whilst other indolent women, neglecting every personal duty, have thought that they deserved their husbands' affection, because, forsooth, they acted
in this respect with propriety.

Weak minds are always fond of resting in the ceremonials

of duty, but morality offers much simpler motives; and it were to be wished that superficial moralists had said less respecting behavior, and outward observances, for unless virtue of any kind be built on knowledge, it will only produce a kind of insipid decency. Respect for the opinion of the world, has, however, been termed the principal duty of woman in the most express words, for Rousseau declares, "that reputation is no less indispensable than chastity." "A man," adds he, "secure in his own good conduct, depends only on himself, and may brave the public opinion: but a woman, in behaving well, performs but half her duty; as what is thought of her, is as important to her as what she really is. It follows hence, that the system of a woman's education should, in this respect, be directly contrary to that of ours. Opinion is the grave of virtue among the men; but its throne among women." It is strictly logical to infer that the virtue that rests on opinion is merely worldly, and that it is the virtue of a being to whom reason has been denied. But, even with respect to the opinion of the world, I am convinced that this class of reasoners are mistaken.

This regard for reputation, independent of its being one of the natural rewards of virtue, however, took its rise from a cause that I have already deplored as the grand source of female depravity, the impossibility of regaining respectability by a return to virtue, though men preserve theirs during the indulgence of vice. It was natural for women then to endeavor to preserve what once lost—was lost forever, till this care swallowing up every other care, reputation for chastity became the one thing needful to the sex. But vain is the scrupulosity of ignorance, for neither religion nor virtue, when they reside in the heart, require such a puerile attention to mere ceremonies, because the behavior must, upon the whole, be proper, when the motive is pure.

. . . .

The leading principles which run through all my disquisitions would render it unnecessary to enlarge on this subject, if a constant attention to keep the varnish of the character fresh, and in good condition, were not often inculcated as the sum total of female duty; if rules to regulate the behavior, and to preserve the reputation, did not too frequently supersede moral obligations. But, with respect to reputation, the attention is confined to a single virtue—chastity. If the honor of a woman, as it is absurdly called, be safe, she

may neglect every social duty; nay, ruin her family by
gaming and extravagance; yet still present a shameless
front—for truly she is an honorable woman!

. . . .

But, in proportion as this regard for the reputation of
chastity is prized by women, it is despised by men: and the
two extremes are equally destructive to morality.

. . . .

I have before observed that men ought to maintain the
women whom they have seduced; this would be one means
of reforming female manners, and stopping an abuse that
has an equally fatal effect on population and morals. Another, no less obvious, would be to turn the attention of woman
to the real virtue of chastity; for to little respect has that
woman a claim, on the score of modesty, though her reputation may be white as the driven snow, who smiles on the
libertine whilst she spurns the victims of his lawless appetites and their own folly.

Besides, she has a taint of the same folly, pure as she
esteems herself, when she studiously adorns her person only
to be seen by men, to excite respectful sighs, and all the idle
homage of what is called innocent gallantry. Did women
really respect virtue for its own sake they would not seek for
a compensation in vanity, for the self-denial which they are
obliged to practice to preserve their reputation, nor would
they associate with men who set reputation at defiance.

The two sexes mutually corrupt and improve each other.
This I believe to be an indisputable truth, extending it to
every virtue. Chastity, modesty, public spirit, and all the
noble train of virtues on which social virtue and happiness
are built should be understood and cultivated by all mankind, or they will be cultivated to little effect. And, instead
of furnishing the vicious or idle with a pretext for violating
some sacred duty, by terming it a sexual one, it would be
wiser to show that nature has not made any difference, for
that the unchaste man doubly defeats the purpose of nature,
by rendering women barren, and destroying his own constitution, though he avoids the shame that pursues the crime
in the other sex. These are the physical consequences; the
moral are still more alarming: for virtue is only a nominal
distinction when the duties of citizens, husbands, wives,

fathers, mothers, and directors of families, become merely the selfish ties of convenience.

Why then do philosophers look for public spirit? Public spirit must be nurtured by private virtue, or it will resemble the factitious sentiment which makes women careful to preserve their reputation, and men their honor, a sentiment that often exists unsupported by virtue, unsupported by that sublime morality which makes the habitual breach of one duty a breach of the whole moral law.

OF THE PERNICIOUS EFFECTS WHICH ARISE FROM THE UNNATURAL DISTINCTIONS ESTABLISHED IN SOCIETY

. . . .

It is vain to expect virtue from women till they are, in some degree, independent of men; nay, it is vain to expect that strength of natural affection which would make them good wives and mothers. Whilst they are absolutely dependent on their husbands they will be cunning, mean, and selfish, and the men who can be gratified by the fawning fondness of spaniel-like affection have not much delicacy, for love is not to be bought, in any sense of the words, its silken wings are instantly shriveled up when anything beside a return in kind is sought. Yet whilst wealth enervates men; and women live, as it were, by their personal charms, how can we expect them to discharge those ennobling duties which equally require exertion and self-denial? Hereditary property sophisticates* the mind, and the unfortunate victims to it, if I may so express myself, swathed from their birth, seldom exert the locomotive faculty of body or mind; and, thus viewing everything through one medium, and that a false one, they are unable to discern in what true merit and happiness consist. False, indeed, must be the light when the drapery of situation hides the man, and makes him stalk in masquerade, dragging from one scene of dissipation to another the nerveless limbs that hang with stupid listlessness, and rolling round the vacant eye which plainly tells us that there is no mind at home.

*Corrupts.

I mean, therefore, to infer that the society is not properly organized which does not compel men and women to discharge their respective duties, by making it the only way to acquire that countenance from their fellow creatures which every human being wishes some way to attain. The respect, consequently, which is paid to wealth and mere personal charms is a true northeast blast that blights the tender blossoms of affection and virtue. Nature has wisely attached affections to duties to sweeten toil and to give that vigor to the exertions of reason which only the heart can give. But the affection which is put on merely because it is the appropriated insignia of a certain character, when its duties are not fulfilled, is one of the empty compliments which vice and folly are obliged to pay to virtue and the real nature of things.

To illustrate my opinion, I need only observe that when a woman is admired for her beauty, and suffers herself to be so far intoxicated by the admiration she receives as to neglect to discharge the indispensable duty of a mother, she sins against herself by neglecting to cultivate an affection that would equally tend to make her useful and happy. True happiness, I mean all the contentment and virtuous satisfaction that can be snatched in this imperfect state, must arise from well-regulated affections; and an affection includes a duty. Men are not aware of the misery they cause, and the vicious weakness they cherish, by only inciting women to render themselves pleasing; they do not consider that they thus make natural and artificial duties clash, by sacrificing the comfort and respectability of a woman's life to voluptuous notions of beauty, when in nature they all harmonize.

Cold would be the heart of a husband were he not rendered unnatural by early debauchery, who did not feel more delight at seeing his child suckled by its mother, than the most artful wanton tricks could ever raise; yet this natural way of cementing the matrimonial tie, and twisting esteem with fonder recollections, wealth leads women to spurn.* To preserve their beauty, and wear the flowery crown of the day, which gives them a kind of right to reign for a short time over the sex, they neglect to stamp impressions on their husbands' hearts that would be remembered with more tenderness when the snow on the head began to chill the

*Frequently, wealthy women hired wet-nurses to breast-feed their infants.

bosom than even their virgin charms. The maternal solicitude of a reasonable affectionate woman is very interesting, and the chastened dignity with which a mother returns the caresses that she and her child receive from a father who has been fulfilling the serious duties of his station is not only a respectable but a beautiful sight. So singular, indeed, are my feelings, and I have endeavored not to catch factitious ones, that after having been fatigued with the sight of insipid grandeur and the slavish ceremonies that with cumberous pomp supplied the place of domestic affections, I have turned to some other scene to relieve my eye by resting it on the refreshing green everywhere scattered by nature. I have then viewed with pleasure a woman nursing her children, and discharging the duties of her station with, perhaps, merely a servant maid to take off her hands the servile part of the household business. I have seen her prepare herself and children, with only the luxury of cleanliness, to receive her husband, who returning weary home in the evening found smiling babes and a clean hearth. My heart has loitered in the midst of the group, and has even throbbed with sympathetic emotion, when the scraping of the well-known foot has raised a pleasing tumult.

Whilst my benevolence has been gratified by contemplating this artless picture, I have thought that a couple of this description, equally necessary and independent of each other, because each fulfilled the respective duties of their station, possessed all that life could give: raised sufficiently above abject poverty not to be obliged to weigh the consequence of every farthing they spend, and having sufficient to prevent their attending to a frigid system of economy, which narrows both heart and mind. I declare, so vulgar are my conceptions, that I know not what is wanted to render this the happiest as well as the most respectable situation in the world, but a taste for literature, to throw a little variety and interest into social converse, and some superfluous money to give to the needy and to buy books. For it is not pleasant when the heart is opened by compassion and the head active in arranging plans of usefulness, to have a prim urchin continually twitching back the elbow to prevent the hand from drawing out an almost empty purse, whispering at the same time some prudential maxim about the priority of justice.

Destructive, however, as riches and inherited honors are to the human character, women are more debased and cramped, if possible, by them, than men, because men may still, in some degree, unfold their faculties by becoming soldiers and statesmen.

. . . .

The preposterous distinctions of rank, which render civilization a curse, by dividing the world between voluptuous tyrants and cunning envious dependents, corrupt, almost equally, every class of people, because respectability is not attached to the discharge of the relative duties of life, but to the station, and when the duties are not fulfilled the affections cannot gain sufficient strength to fortify the virtue of which they are the natural reward. Still there are some loopholes out of which a man may creep, and dare to think and act for himself; but for a woman it is an herculean task, because she has difficulties peculiar to her sex to overcome, which require almost superhuman powers.

A truly benevolent legislator always endeavors to make it the interest of each individual to be virtuous; and thus private virtue becoming the cement of public happiness, an orderly whole is consolidated by the tendency of all the parts towards a common center. But, the private or public virtue of woman is very problematical; for Rousseau, and a numerous list of male writers, insist that she should all her life be subjected to a severe restraint, that of propriety. Why subject her to propriety blind propriety, if she be capable of acting from a nobler spring, if she be an heir of immortality? Is sugar always to be produced by vital blood? Is one-half of the human species, like the poor African slaves, to be subject to prejudices that brutalize them, when principles would be a surer guard, only to sweeten the cup of man? Is not this indirectly to deny woman reason, for a gift is a mockery, if it be unfit for use.

Women are, in common with men, rendered weak and luxurious by the relaxing pleasures which wealth procures; but added to this they are made slaves to their persons, and must render them alluring that man may lend them his reason to guide their tottering steps aright. Or should they be ambitious, they must govern their tyrants by sinister tricks, for without rights there cannot be any incumbent duties. The laws respecting woman, which I mean to discuss in a future part, make an absurd unit of a man and his wife;* and then, by the easy transition of only considering him as responsible, she is reduced to a mere cipher.

The being who discharges the duties of its station is independent; and, speaking of women at large, their first duty is to themselves as rational creatures, and the next, in point of importance, as citizens, is that, which includes so many, of a mother. The rank in life which dispenses with their fulfilling this duty necessarily degrades them by making them mere dolls. Or, should they turn to something more important than merely fitting drapery upon a smooth block, their minds are only occupied by some soft platonic attachment; or the actual management of an intrigue may keep their thoughts in motion; for when they neglect domestic duties, they have it not in their power to take the field and march and countermarch like soldiers, or wrangle in the senate to keep their faculties from rusting.

I know that, as a proof of the inferiority of the sex, Rousseau has exultingly exclaimed, How can they leave the nursery for the camp! And the camp has by some moralists been termed the school of the most heroic virtues; though, I think, it would puzzle a keen casuist to prove the reasonableness of the greater number of wars that have dubbed heroes. I do not mean to consider this question critically; because, having frequently viewed these freaks of ambition as the first natural mode of civilization, when the ground must be torn up, and the woods cleared by fire and sword, I do not choose to call them pests; but surely the present system of war has little connection with virtue of any denomination, being rather the school of *finesse* and effeminacy, than of fortitude.

Yet, if defensive war, the only justifiable war, in the present advanced state of society, where virtue can show its face and ripen amidst the rigors which purify the air on the mountain's top, were alone to be adopted as just and glorious, the true heroism of antiquity might again animate female bosoms. But fair and softly, gentle reader, male or female, do not alarm thyself, for though I have compared the character of a modern soldier with that of a civilized woman, I am not going to advise them to turn their distaff into a musket, though I sincerely wish to see the bayonet converted into a pruning hook. I only recreated an imagination, fatigued by contemplating the vices and follies which

*Once married, a woman's legal identity was that of her husband.

all proceed from a feculent stream of wealth that has muddied the pure rills of natural affection, by supposing that society will some time or other be so constituted that man must necessarily fulfill the duties of a citizen or be despised, and that while he was employed in any of the departments of civil life, his wife, also an active citizen, should be equally intent to manage her family, educate her children, and assist her neighbors.

But, to render her really virtuous and useful, she must not, if she discharge her civil duties, want, individually, the protection of civil laws; she must not be dependent on her husband's bounty for her subsistence during his life, or support after his death—for how can a being be generous who has nothing of its own, or, virtuous, who is not free? The wife, in the present state of things, who is faithful to her husband, and neither suckles nor educates her children, scarcely deserves the name of a wife, and has no right to that of a citizen. But take away natural rights, and duties become null.

Women then must be considered as only the wanton solace of men, when they become so weak in mind and body that they cannot exert themselves, unless to pursue some frothy pleasure, or to invent some frivolous fashion. What can be a more melancholy sight to a thinking mind, than to look into the numerous carriages that drive helter-skelter about this metropolis in a morning full of pale-faced creatures who are flying from themselves. I have often wished, with Dr. Johnson, to place some of them in a little shop with half a dozen children looking up to their languid countenances for support. I am much mistaken, if some latent vigor would not soon give health and spirit to their eyes, and some lines drawn by the exercise of reason on the blank cheeks, which before were only undulated by dimples, might restore lost dignity to the character, or rather enable it to attain the true dignity of its nature. Virtue is not to be acquired even by speculation, much less by the negative supineness that wealth naturally generates.

Besides, when poverty is more disgraceful than even vice, is not morality cut to the quick? Still to avoid misconstruction, though I consider that women in the common walks of life are called to fulfill the duties of wives and mothers, by religion and reason, I cannot help lamenting that women of a superior cast have not a road open by which they can pursue more extensive plans of usefulness and independence.

I may excite laughter by dropping an hint, which I mean to pursue some future time, for I really think that women ought to have representatives, instead of being arbitrarily governed without having any direct share allowed them in the deliberations of government.

But, as the whole system of representation is now, in this country, only a convenient handle for despotism, they need not complain, for they are as well represented as a numerous class of hard-working mechanics, who pay for the support of royalty when they can scarcely stop their children's mouths with bread. How are they represented whose very sweat supports the splendid stud of an heir apparent, or varnishes the chariot of some female favorite who looks down on shame? Taxes on the very necessaries of life enable an endless tribe of idle princes and princesses to pass with stupid pomp before a gaping crowd, who almost worship the very parade which costs them so dear. This is mere Gothic grandeur, something like the barbarous useless parade of having sentinels on horseback at Whitehall, which I could never view without a mixture of contempt and indignation.

How strangely must the mind be sophisticated when this sort of state impresses it! But, till these monuments of folly are leveled by virtue, similar follies will leaven the whole mass. For the same character, in some degree, will prevail in the aggregate of society: and the refinements of luxury, or the vicious repinings of envious poverty, will equally banish virtue from society, considered as the characteristic of that society, or only allow it to appear as one of the stripes of the harlequin coat, worn by the civilized man.

In the superior ranks of life, every duty is done by deputies, as if duties could ever be waived, and the vain pleasures which consequent idleness forces the rich to pursue appear so enticing to the next rank that the numerous scramblers for wealth sacrifice everything to tread on their heels. The most sacred trusts are then considered as sinecures, because they were procured by interest, and only sought to enable a man to keep *good company*. Women, in particular, all want to be ladies: which is simply to have nothing to do, but listlessly to go they scarcely care where, for they cannot tell what.

But what have women to do in society? I may be asked, but to loiter with easy grace; surely you would not condemn them all to suckle fools and chronicle small beer! No. Women might certainly study the art of healing, and be physicians as well as nurses. And midwifery, decency seems to allot to them, though I am afraid the word midwife, in our dictionaries, will soon give place to *accoucheur*,* and one proof of the former delicacy of the sex be effaced from the language.

They might, also, study politics, and settle their benevolence on the broadest basis; for the reading of history will scarcely be more useful than the perusal of romances, if read as mere biography; if the character of the times, the political improvements, arts, etc., be not observed. In short, if it be not considered as the history of man; and not of particular men, who filled a niche in the temple of fame, and dropped into the black rolling stream of time, that silently sweeps all before it, into the shapeless void called—eternity. For shape, can it be called, "that shape hath none?"

Business of various kinds they might likewise pursue, if they were educated in a more orderly manner, which might save many from common and legal prostitution. Women would not then marry for a support, as men accept of places under government, and neglect the implied duties; nor would an attempt to earn their own subsistence, a most laudable one! sink them almost to the level of those poor abandoned creatures who live by prostitution. For are not milliners and mantuamakers reckoned the next class? The few employments open to women, so far from being liberal, are menial; and when a superior education enables them to take charge of the education of children as governesses, they are not treated like the tutors of sons, though even clerical tutors are not always treated in a manner calculated to render them respectable in the eyes of their pupils, to say nothing of the private comfort of the individual. But as women educated like gentlewomen are never designed for the humiliating situation which necessity sometimes forces them to fill, these situations are considered in the light of a degradation; and they know little of the human heart, who need to be told, that nothing so painfully sharpens sensibility as such a fall in life.

Some of these women might be restrained from marrying by a proper spirit or delicacy, and others may not have had it in their power to escape in this pitiful way from servitude; is not that government then very defective, and very unmindful of the happiness of one-half of its members, that does not provide for honest, independent women by encour-

*A male physician who delivered babies.

aging them to fill respectable stations? But in order to render their private virtue a public benefit, they must have a civil existence in the state, married or single; else we shall continually see some worthy woman, whose sensibility has been rendered painfully acute by undeserved contempt, droop like "the lily broken down by a plow-share."

It is a melancholy truth; yet such is the blessed effect of civilization! the most respectable women are the most oppressed; and, unless they have understandings far superior to the common run of understandings, taking in both sexes, they must, from being treated like contemptible beings, become contemptible. How many women thus waste life away the prey of discontent, who might have practiced as physicians, regulated a farm, managed a shop, and stood erect, supported by their own industry, instead of hanging their heads surcharged with the dew of sensibility that consumes the beauty to which it at first gave luster; nay, I doubt whether pity and love are so near akin as poets feign, for I have seldom seen much compassion excited by the helplessness of females, unless they were fair; then, perhaps, pity was the soft handmaid of love, or the harbinger of lust.

How much more respectable is the woman who earns her own bread by fulfilling any duty than the most accomplished beauty—beauty did I say—so sensible am I of the beauty of moral loveliness, or the harmonious propriety that attunes the passions of a well-regulated mind, that I blush at making the comparison; yet I sigh to think how few women aim at attaining this respectability by withdrawing from the giddy whirl of pleasure, or the indolent calm that stupefies the good sort of women it sucks in.

Proud of their weakness, however, they must always be protected, guarded from care, and all the rough toils that dignify the mind. If this be the fiat of fate, if they will make themselves insignificant and contemptible, sweetly to waste life away, let them not expect to be valued when their beauty fades, for it is the fate of the fairest flowers to be admired and pulled to pieces by the careless hand that plucked them. In how many ways do I wish, from the purest benevolence, to impress this truth on my sex; yet I fear that they will not listen to a truth that dear-bought experience has brought home to many an agitated bosom, nor willingly resign the privileges of rank and sex for the privileges of humanity, to which those have no claim who do not discharge its duties.

Those writers are particularly useful, in my opinion, who make man feel for man, independent of the station he fills, or the drapery of factitious sentiments. I then would fain convince reasonable men of the importance of some of my remarks, and prevail on them to weigh dispassionately the whole tenor of my observations. I appeal to their understandings; and, as a fellow creature, claim, in the name of my sex, some interest in their hearts. I entreat them to assist to emancipate their companion, to make her a *helpmeet* for them!

Would men but generously snap our chains, and be content with rational fellowship instead of slavish obedience, they would find us more observant daughters, more affectionate sisters, more faithful wives, more reasonable mothers—in a word, better citizens. We should then love them with true affection, because we should learn to respect ourselves; and the peace of mind of a worthy man would not be interrupted by the idle vanity of his wife, nor the babes sent to nestle in a strange bosom, having never found a home in their mother's.

PARENTAL AFFECTION

As the care of children in their infancy is one of the grand duties annexed to the female character by nature, this duty would afford many forcible arguments for strengthening the female understanding, if it were properly considered.

The formation of the mind must be begun very early, and the temper, in particular, requires the most judicious attention—an attention which women cannot pay who only love their children because they are their children, and seek no further for the foundation of their duty than in the feelings of the moment. It is this want of reason in their affections which makes women so often run into extremes, and either be the most fond or most careless and unnatural mothers.

To be a good mother a woman must have sense, and that independence of mind which few women possess who are taught to depend entirely on their husbands. Meek wives are, in general, foolish mothers; wanting their children to love them best, and take their part, in secret, against the father, who is held up as a scarecrow. When chastisement is necessary, though they have offended the mother, the father must inflict the punishment; he must be the judge in all disputes: but I shall more fully discuss this subject when I treat of private education. I now only mean to insist that unless the understanding of woman be enlarged, and her character rendered more firm by being allowed to govern her own conduct, she will never have sufficient sense or command of temper to manage her children properly. Her parental affection, indeed, scarcely deserves the name, when it does not lead her to suckle her children, because the discharge of this duty is equally calculated to inspire maternal and filial affection: and it is the indispensable duty of men and women to fulfill the duties which give birth to affections that are the surest preservatives against vice. Natural affection, as it is termed, I believe to be a very faint tie; affections must grow out of the habitual exercise of a mutual sympathy; and what sympathy does a mother exercise who sends her babe to a nurse, and only takes it from a nurse to send it to a school?

In the exercise of their maternal feelings providence has furnished women with a natural substitute for love, when the lover becomes only a friend, and mutual confidence takes place of overstrained admiration—a child then gently twists the relaxing cord, and a mutual care produces a new mutual sympathy. But a child, though a pledge of affection, will not enliven it, if both father and mother be content to transfer the charge to hirelings; for they who do their duty by proxy should not murmur if they miss the reward of duty—parental affection produces filial duty.

DUTY TO PARENTS

. . . .

Females, it is true, in all countries, are too much under the dominion of their parents; and few parents think of addressing their children in the following manner, though it is in this reasonable way that Heaven seems to command the whole human race. It is your interest to obey me till you can judge for yourself; and the Almighty Father of all has implanted an affection in me to serve as a guard to you whilst your reason is unfolding; but when your mind arrives at maturity, you must only obey me, or rather respect my opinions, so far as they coincide with the light that is breaking in on your own mind.

A slavish bondage to parents cramps every faculty of the mind; and Mr. Locke very judiciously observes that "if the mind be curbed and humbled too much in children; if their spirits be abased and broken much by too strict an hand over them; they lose all their vigor and industry."* This strict hand may in some degree account for the weakness of women; for girls, from various causes, are more kept down by their parents, in every sense of the word, than boys. The duty expected from them is, like all the duties arbitrarily imposed on women, more from a sense of propriety, more out of respect for decorum than reason; and thus taught slavishly to submit to their parents, they are prepared for the slavery of marriage. I may be told that a number of women are not slaves in the marriage state. True, but they then become tyrants; for it is not rational freedom, but a lawless kind of power resembling the authority exercised by the favorites of absolute monarchs, which they obtain by debasing means. I do not, likewise, dream of insinuating that either boys or girls are always slaves; I only insist that when they are obliged to submit to authority blindly, their faculties are weakened, and their tempers rendered imperious or abject. I also lament that parents, indolently availing themselves of a supposed privilege, damp the first faint glimmering of reason, rendering at the same time the duty, which they are so anxious to enforce, an empty name; because they will not let it rest on the only basis on which a duty can rest securely: for unless it be founded on knowledge, it cannot gain sufficient strength to resist the squalls of passion, or the silent sapping of self-love. But it is not the parents who have given the surest proof of their affection for their children, or, to speak more properly, who by fulfilling their duty, have allowed a natural parental affection to take root in their hearts, the child of exercised sympathy and reason, and not the overweening offspring of selfish pride, who most vehemently insist on their children submitting to their will merely because it is their will. On the contrary,

*John Locke, *Some Thoughts Concerning Education* (1693).

the parent who sets a good example patiently lets that example work; and it seldom fails to produce its natural effect—filial reverence.

. . . .

It is the irregular exercise of parental authority that first injures the mind, and to these irregularities girls are more subject than boys. The will of those who never allow their will to be disputed, unless they happen to be in a good humor, when they relax proportionally, is almost always unreasonable. To elude this arbitrary authority girls very early learn the lessons which they afterwards practice on their husbands; for I have frequently seen a little sharp-faced miss rule a whole family, excepting that now and then mamma's angry will burst out of some accidental cloud; either her hair was ill dressed,* or she had lost more money at cards, the night before, than she was willing to own to her husband; or some such moral cause of anger.

After observing sallies of this kind, I have been led into a melancholy train of reflection respecting females, concluding that when their first affection must lead them astray, or make their duties clash till they rest on mere whims and customs, little can be expected from them as they advance in life. How indeed can an instructor remedy this evil? for to teach them virtue on any solid principle is to teach them to despise their parents. Children cannot, ought not, to be taught to make allowance for the faults of their parents, because every such allowance weakens the force of reason in their minds, and makes them still more indulgent to their own. It is one of the most sublime virtues of maturity that leads us to be severe with respect to ourselves, and forbearing to others; but children should only be taught the simple virtues, for if they begin too early to make allowance for human passions and manners, they wear off the fine edge of the criterion by which they should regulate their own, and become unjust in the same proportion as they grow indulgent.

The affections of children, and weak people, are always selfish; they love their relatives, because they are beloved

---

*"I myself heard a little girl once say to a servant, 'My mama has been scolding me finely this morning, because her hair was not dressed to please her.' Though this remark was pert, it was just. And what respect could a girl acquire for such a parent without doing violence to reason?" (Wollstonecraft's note).

by them, and not on account of their virtues. Yet, till esteem and love are blended together in the first affection, and reason made the foundation of the first duty, morality will stumble at the threshold. But, till society is very differently constituted, parents, I fear, will still insist on being obeyed, because they will be obeyed, and constantly endeavor to settle that power on a Divine right which will not bear the investigation of reason.

ON NATIONAL EDUCATION

. . . .

I have already animadverted on the bad habits which females acquire when they are shut up together; and I think that the observation may fairly be extended to the other sex, till the natural inference is drawn which I have had in view throughout—that to improve both sexes they ought, not only in private families, but in public schools, to be educated together. If marriage be the cement of society, mankind should all be educated after the same model, or the intercourse of the sexes will never deserve the name of fellowship, nor will women ever fulfill the peculiar duties of their sex, till they become enlightened citizens, till they become free by being enabled to earn their own subsistence, independent of men; in the same manner, I mean, to prevent misconstruction, as one man is independent of another. Nay, marriage will never be held sacred till women, by being brought up with men, are prepared to be their companions rather than their mistresses; for the mean doublings of cunning will ever render them contemptible, whilst oppression renders them timid. So convinced am I of this truth that I will venture to predict that virtue will never prevail in society till the virtues of both sexes are founded on reason; and, till the affections common to both are allowed to gain their due strength by the discharge of mutual duties.

Were boys and girls permitted to pursue the same studies together, those graceful decencies might early be inculcated which produce modesty without those sexual distinctions that taint the mind. Lessons of politeness, and that formulary of decorum which treads on the heels of falsehood would be rendered useless by habitual propriety of behavior. Not, indeed, put on for visitors like the courtly robe of politeness, but the sober effect of cleanliness of mind. Would not this simple elegance of sincerity be a chaste homage paid to domestic affections, far surpassing the meretricious compliments that shine with false luster in the heartless intercourse of fashionable life? But, till more understanding preponderates in society, there will ever be a want of heart and taste, and the harlot's *rouge* will supply the place of that celestial suffusion which only virtuous affections can give to the face. Gallantry, and what is called love, may subsist without simplicity of character; but the main pillars of friendship are respect and confidence—esteem is never founded on it cannot tell what!

. . . .

To render this practicable, day schools, for particular ages should be established by government, in which boys and girls might be educated together. The school for the younger children, from five to nine years of age, ought to be absolutely free and open to all classes.* A sufficient number of masters should also be chosen by a select committee, in each parish, to whom any complaint of negligence, etc., might be made, if signed by six of the children's parents.

Ushers would then be unnecessary; for I believe experience will ever prove that this kind of subordinate authority is particularly injurious to the morals of youth. What, indeed, can tend to deprave the character more than outward submission and inward contempt? Yet how can boys be expected to treat an usher with respect, when the master seems to consider him in the light of a servant, and almost to countenance the ridicule which becomes the chief amusement of the boys during the play hours?

But nothing of this kind could occur in an elementary day school, where boys and girls, the rich and poor, should meet together. And to prevent any of the distinctions of vanity, they should be dressed alike, and all obliged to submit to the same discipline, or leave the school. The schoolroom

---

*"Treating this part of the subject, I have borrowed some hints from a very sensible pamphlet, written by the late bishop of Autun on Public Education." (Wollstonecraft's note). She is referring to Charles Maurice de Talleyrand's *Rapport sur L' Instruction Publique* (Paris, 1791).

ought to be surrounded by a large piece of ground, in which the children might be usefully exercised, for at this age they should not be confined to any sedentary employment for more than an hour at a time. But these relaxations might all be rendered a part of elementary education, for many things improve and amuse the senses when introduced as a kind of show, to the principles of which, dryly laid down, children would turn a deaf ear, for instance: botany, mechanics, and astronomy. Reading, writing, arithmetic, natural history, and some simple experiments in natural philosophy might fill up the day; but these pursuits should never encroach on gymnastic plays in the open air. The elements of religion, history, the history of man, and politics might also be taught by conversations, in the socratic form.

After the age of nine, girls and boys intended for domestic employments or mechanical trades ought to be removed to other schools, and receive instruction, in some measure appropriated to the destination of each individual, the two sexes being still together in the morning; but in the afternoon, the girls should attend a school, where plain-work, mantua making, millinery, etc., would be their employment.

The young people of superior abilities, or fortune, might now be taught, in another school, the dead and living languages, the elements of science, and continue the study of history and politics, on a more extensive scale, which would not exclude polite literature.

Girls and boys still together? I hear some readers ask: yes. And I should not fear any other consequence than that some early attachment might take place, which, whilst it had the best effect on the moral character of the young people, might not perfectly agree with the views of the parents, for it will be a long time, I fear, before the world will be so far enlightened that parents, only anxious to render their children virtuous, shall allow them to choose companions for life themselves.

Besides, this would be a sure way to promote early marriages, and from early marriages the most salutary physical and moral effects naturally flow. What a different character does a married citizen assume from the selfish coxcomb, who lives but for himself, and who is often afraid to marry lest he should not be able to live in a certain style. Great emergencies excepted, which would rarely occur in a society of which equality was the basis, a man can only be prepared to discharge the duties of public life by the habitual practice of those inferior ones which form the man.

In this plan of education the constitution of boys would not be ruined by the early debaucheries which now make men so selfish, or girls rendered weak and vain by indolence, and frivolous pursuits. But I presuppose that such a degree of equality should be established between the sexes as would shut out gallantry and coquetry, yet allow friendship and love to temper the heart for the discharge of higher duties.

These would be schools of morality—and the happiness of man, allowed to flow from the pure springs of duty and affection, what advances might not the human mind make? Society can only be happy and free in proportion as it is virtuous; but the present distinctions, established in society, corrode all private, and blast all public virtue.

I have already inveighed against the custom of confining girls to their needle, and shutting them out from all political and civil employments; for by thus narrowing their minds they are rendered unfit to fulfill the peculiar duties which nature has assigned them.

Only employed about the little incidents of the day, they necessarily grow up cunning. My very soul has often sickened at observing the sly tricks practiced by women to gain some foolish thing on which their silly hearts were set. Not allowed to dispose of money, or call anything their own, they learn to turn the market penny; or, should a husband offend by staying from home, or give rise to some emotions of jealousy—a new gown, or any pretty bauble, smooths Juno's angry brow.

But these *littlenesses* would not degrade their character if women were led to respect themselves, if political and moral subjects were opened to them; and, I will venture to affirm, that this is the only way to make them properly attentive to their domestic duties. An active mind embraces the whole circle of its duties, and finds time enough for all. It is not, I assert, a bold attempt to emulate masculine virtues; it is not the enchantment of literary pursuits or the steady investigation of scientific subjects that leads women astray from duty. No, it is indolence and vanity—the love of pleasure and the love of sway, that will reign paramount in an empty mind. I say empty emphatically, because the education which women now receive scarcely deserves the name. For the little knowledge that they are led to acquire during the important years of youth is merely relative to accomplishments; and accomplishments without a bottom, for unless the understanding be cultivated, superficial and monotonous is every grace. Like the charms of a made-up face, they only strike the senses in a crowd; but at home, wanting mind, they want variety. The consequence is obvious; in gay scenes of dissipation we meet the artificial mind and face, for those who fly from solitude dread, next to solitude, the domestic circle; not having it in their power to amuse or interest, they feel their own insignificance, or find nothing to amuse or interest themselves.

Besides, what can be more indelicate than a girl's *coming out* in the fashionable world? Which, in other words, is to bring to market a marriageable miss, whose person is taken from one public place to another, richly caparisoned. Yet, mixing in the giddy circle under restraint, these butterflies long to flutter at large, for the first affection of their souls is their own persons, to which their attention has been called with the most sedulous care whilst they were preparing for the period that decides their fate for life. Instead of pursuing this idle routine, sighing for tasteless show, and heartless state, with what dignity would the youths of both sexes form attachments in the schools that I have cursorily pointed out; in which, as life advanced, dancing, music, and drawing might be admitted as relaxations, for at these schools young people of fortune ought to remain, more or less, till they were of age. Those who were designed for particular professions might attend, three or four mornings in the week, the schools appropriated for their immediate instruction.

I only drop these observations at present, as hints; rather, indeed, as an outline of the plan I mean, than a digested one; but I must add, that I highly approve of one regulation mentioned in the pamphlet* already alluded to, that of making the children and youths independent of the masters respecting punishments. They should be tried by their peers, which would be an admirable method of fixing sound principles of justice in the mind, and might have the happiest effect on the temper, which is very early soured or irritated by tyranny, till it becomes peevishly cunning, or ferociously overbearing.

My imagination darts forward with benevolent fervor to

*"The Bishop of Autun's." (Wollstonecraft's note)

greet these amiable and respectable groups, in spite of the sneering of cold hearts, who are at liberty to utter, with frigid self-importance, the damning epithet—romantic; the force of which I shall endeavor to blunt by repeating the words of an eloquent moralist: "I know not whether the allusions of a truly humane heart, whose zeal renders everything easy, be not preferable to that rough and repulsing reason, which always finds in indifference for the public good, the first obstacle to whatever would promote it."

I know that libertines will also exclaim that woman would be unsexed by acquiring strength of body and mind, and that beauty, soft bewitching beauty, would no longer adorn the daughters of men. I am of a very different opinion, for I think that, on the contrary, we should then see dignified beauty, and true grace; to produce which, many powerful physical and moral causes would concur. Not relaxed beauty, it is true, or the graces of helplessness; but such as appears to make us respect the human body as a majestic pile fit to receive a noble inhabitant, in the relics of antiquity.

I do not forget the popular opinion that the Grecian statues were not modeled after nature. I mean, not according to the proportions of a particular man; but that beautiful limbs and features were selected from various bodies to form an harmonious whole. This might, in some degree, be true. The fine ideal picture of an exalted imagination might be superior to the materials which the statuary found in nature, and thus it might with propriety be termed rather the model of mankind than of a man. It was not, however, the mechanical selection of limbs and features; but the ebullition of an heated fancy that burst forth, and the fine senses and enlarged understanding of the artist selected the solid matter, which he drew into this glowing focus.

I observed that it was not mechanical, because a whole was produced—a model of that grand simplicity, of those concurring energies, which arrest our attention and command our reverence. For only insipid lifeless beauty is produced by a servile copy of even beautiful nature. Yet, independent of these observations, I believe that the human form must have been far more beautiful than it is at present, because extreme indolence, barbarous ligatures, and many causes, which forcibly act on it, in our luxurious state of society, did not retard its expansion, or render it deformed. Exercise and cleanliness appear to be not only the surest means of preserving health, but of promoting beauty, the physical causes only considered; yet, this is not sufficient, moral ones must concur, or beauty will be merely of that rustic kind which blooms on the innocent, wholesome, countenances of some country people, whose minds have not been exercised. To render the person perfect, physical and moral beauty ought to be attained at the same time, each lending and receiving force by the combination. Judgment must reside on the brow, affection and fancy beam in the eye, and humanity curve the cheek, or vain is the sparkling of the finest eye or the elegantly turned finish of the fairest features: whilst in every motion that displays the active limbs and well-knit joints, grace and modesty should appear. But this fair assemblage is not to be brought together by chance; it is the reward of exertions calculated to support each other; for judgment can only be acquired by reflection, affection by the discharge of duties, and humanity by the exercise of compassion to every living creature.

Humanity to animals should be particularly inculcated as a part of national education, for it is not at present one of our national virtues. Tenderness for their humble dumb domestics, amongst the lower class, is oftener to be found in a savage than a civilized state. For civilization prevents that intercourse which creates affection in the rude hut, or mud hovel, and leads uncultivated minds who are only depraved by the refinements which prevail in the society, where they are trodden under foot by the rich, to domineer over them to revenge the insults that they are obliged to bear from their superiors.

This habitual cruelty is first caught at school, where it is one of the rare sports of the boys to torment the miserable brutes that fall in their way. The transition, as they grow up, from barbarity to brutes to domestic tyranny over wives, children, and servants is very easy. Justice, or even benevolence, will not be a powerful spring of action unless it extend to the whole creation; nay, I believe that it may be delivered as an axiom, that those who can see pain, unmoved, will soon learn to inflict it.

The vulgar are swayed by present feelings, and the habits which they have accidentally acquired; but on partial feelings much dependence cannot be placed, though they be just; for, when they are not invigorated by reflection, custom weakens them, till they are scarcely perceptible. The sympathies of our nature are strengthened by pondering cogitations, and deadened by thoughtless use. Macbeth's heart smote him more for one murder, the first, than for a hundred subsequent ones, which were necessary to back it. But, when I used the epithet vulgar, I did not mean to confine my remark to the poor, for partial humanity, founded on present sensations, or whim, is quite as conspicuous, if not more so, amongst the rich.

The lady who sheds tears for the bird starved in a snare, and execrates the devils in the shape of men who goad to madness the poor ox, or whip the patient ass, tottering under a burden above its strength, will, nevertheless, keep her coachman and horses whole hours waiting for her, when the sharp frost bites, or the rain beats against the well-closed windows which do not admit a breath of air to tell her how roughly the wind blows without. . . .

. . . .

In France or Italy, have the women confined themselves to domestic life? though they have not hitherto had a political existence, yet, have they not illicitly had great sway, corrupting themselves and the men with whose passions they played? In short, in whatever light I view the subject, reason and experience convince me that the only method of leading women to fulfill their peculiar duties is to free them from all restraint by allowing them to participate in the inherent rights of mankind.

Make them free, and they will quickly become wise and virtuous, as men become more so; for the improvement must be mutual, or the injustice which one-half of the human race are obliged to submit to, retorting on their oppressors, the virtue of men will be worm-eaten by the insect whom he keeps under his feet.

Let men take their choice, man and woman were made for each other, though not to become one being; and if they will not improve women, they will deprave them!

I speak of the improvement and emancipation of the whole sex, for I know that the behavior of a few women, who, by accident, or following a strong bent of nature, have acquired a portion of knowledge superior to that of the rest of their sex, has often been overbearing; but there have been instances of women who, attaining knowledge, have not discarded modesty, nor have they always pedantically appeared to despise the ignorance which they labored to disperse in their own minds. The exclamations then which any advice respecting female learning commonly produces, especially from pretty women, often arise from envy. When they chance to see that even the luster of their eyes, and the flippant sportiveness of refined coquetry will not always secure them attention, during a whole evening, should a woman of a more cultivated understanding endeavor to give a rational turn to the conversation, the common source of consolation is that such women seldom get husbands. What arts have I not seen silly women use to interrupt by *flirtation,* a very significant word to describe such a maneuver, a rational conversation which made the men forget that they were pretty women.

But, allowing what is very natural to man, that the possession of rare abilities is really calculated to excite overweening pride, disgusting in both men and women—in what a state of inferiority must the female faculties have rusted when such a small portion of knowledge as those women attained, who have sneeringly been termed learned women, could be singular? Sufficiently so to puff up the possessor, and excite envy in her contemporaries, and some of the other sex. Nay, has not a little rationality exposed many women to the severest censure? I advert to well-known facts, for I have frequently heard women ridiculed, and every little weakness exposed, only because they adopted the advice of some medical men, and deviated from the beaten track in their mode of treating their infants.* I have actually heard this barbarous aversion to innovation carried still further, and a sensible woman stigmatized as an unnatural mother, who has thus been wisely solicitous to preserve the health of her children, when in the midst of her care she has lost one by some of the casualties of infancy, which no prudence can ward off. Her acquaintance have observed, that this was the consequence of newfangled notions—the newfangled notions of ease and cleanliness. And those who pretending to experience, though they have long adhered to prejudices that have, according to the opinion of the most sagacious physicians, thinned the human race, almost rejoiced at the disaster that gave a kind of sanction to prescription.

*She is referring to breast-feeding them instead of hiring wet-nurses.

Indeed. if it were only on this account, the national education of women is of the utmost consequence, for what a
number of human sacrifices are made to that moloch prejudice! And in how many ways are children destroyed by the
lasciviousness of man? The want of natural affection, in
many women, who are drawn from their duty by the admiration of men, and the ignorance of others, render the infancy of man a much more perilous state than that of brutes;
yet men are unwilling to place women in situations proper
to enable them to acquire sufficient understanding to know
how even to nurse their babes.

So forcibly does this truth strike me that I would rest the
whole tendency of my reasoning upon it, for whatever tends
to incapacitate the maternal character takes woman out of
her sphere.

But it is vain to expect the present race of weak mothers
either to take that reasonable care of a child's body which is
necessary to lay the foundation of a good constitution, supposing that it do not suffer for the sins of its fathers; or, to
manage its temper so judiciously that the child will not
have, as it grows up, to throw off all that its mother, its first
instructor, directly or indirectly taught; and unless the mind
have uncommon vigor, womanish follies will stick to the
character throughout life. The weakness of the mother will
be visited on the children! And whilst women are educated
to rely on their husbands for judgment, this must ever be
the consequence, for there is no improving an understanding by halves, nor can any being act wisely from imitation,
because in every circumstance of life there is a kind of
individuality which requires an exertion of judgment to
modify general rules. The being who can think justly in one
track will soon extend its intellectual empire; and she who
has sufficient judgment to manage her children will not
submit, right or wrong, to her husband, or patiently to the
social laws which make a nonentity of a wife.

In public schools women, to guard against the errors of
ignorance, should be taught the elements of anatomy and
medicine, not only to enable them to take proper care of
their own health, but to make them rational nurses of their
infants, parents, and husbands; for the bills of mortality*
are swelled by the blunders of self-willed old women, who

*Bulletins published weekly by the parishes of London listing
deaths and their likely causes.

give nostrums of their own without knowing anything of the human frame. It is likewise proper only in a domestic view to make women acquainted with the anatomy of the mind, by allowing the sexes to associate together in every pursuit; and by leading them to observe the progress of the human understanding in the improvement of the sciences and arts; never forgetting the science of morality, or the study of the political history of mankind.

A man has been termed a microcosm; and every family might also be called a state. States, it is true, have mostly been governed by arts that disgrace the character of man; and the want of a just constitution, and equal laws, have so perplexed the notions of the worldly wise that they more than question the reasonableness of contending for the rights of humanity. Thus morality, polluted in the national reservoir, sends off streams of vice to corrupt the constituent parts of the body politic; but should more noble, or rather, more just, principles regulate the laws, which ought to be the government of society, and not those who execute them, duty might become the rule of private conduct.

Besides, by the exercise of their bodies and minds women would acquire that mental activity so necessary in the maternal character, united with the fortitude that distinguishes steadiness of conduct from the obstinate perverseness of weakness. For it is dangerous to advise the indolent to be steady, because they instantly become rigorous, and to save themselves trouble, punish with severity faults that the patient fortitude of reason might have prevented.

But fortitude presupposes strength of mind; and is strength of mind to be acquired by indolent acquiescence, by asking advice instead of exerting the judgment, by obeying through fear, instead of practicing the forbearance, which we all stand in need of ourselves? The conclusion which I wish to draw is obvious: make women rational creatures, and free citizens, and they will quickly become good wives, and mothers; that is, if men do not neglect the duties of husbands and fathers.

Discussing the advantages which a public and private education combined, as I have sketched, might rationally be expected to produce, I have dwelt most on such as are particularly relative to the female world, because I think the female world oppressed; yet the gangrene, which the vices engendered by oppression have produced, is not confined to the morbid part, but pervades society at large: so that when I wish to see my sex become more like moral agents, my heart bounds with the anticipation of the general diffusion of that sublime contentment which only morality can diffuse.

SOME INSTANCES OF THE FOLLY WHICH THE IGNORANCE OF WOMEN GENERATES: WITH CONCLUDING REFLECTIONS ON THE MORAL IMPROVEMENT THAT A REVOLUTION IN FEMALE MANNERS MIGHT NATURALLY BE EXPECTED TO PRODUCE

. . . .

SECTION VI
. . . .

Moralists have unanimously agreed, that unless virtue be nursed by liberty, it will never attain due strength—and what they say of man I extend to mankind, insisting that in all cases morals must be fixed on immutable principles, and that the being cannot be termed rational or virtuous who obeys any authority but that of reason.

To render women truly useful members of society, I argue that they should be led, by having their understandings cultivated on a large scale, to acquire a rational affection for their country, founded on knowledge, because it is obvious that we are little interested about what we do not understand. And to render this general knowledge of due importance, I have endeavored to show that private duties are never properly fulfilled unless the understanding enlarges the heart; and that public virtue is only an aggregate of private. But the distinctions established in society undermine both, by beating out the solid gold of virtue, till it becomes only the tinsel covering of vice; for whilst wealth renders a man more respectable than virtue, wealth will be sought before virtue; and, whilst women's persons are caressed, when a childish simper shows an absence of mind—

the mind will lie fallow. Yet, true voluptuousness must proceed from the mind—for what can equal the sensations produced by mutual affection, supported by mutual respect? What are the cold or feverish caresses of appetite, but sin embracing death, compared with the modest overflowings of a pure heart and exalted imagination? Yes, let me tell the libertine of fancy when he despises understanding in woman— that the mind, which he disregards, gives life to the enthusiastic affection from which rapture, short-lived as it is, alone can flow! And that, without virtue, a sexual attachment must expire, like a tallow candle in the socket, creating intolerable disgust. To prove this, I need only observe that men who have wasted great part of their lives with women, and with whom they have sought for pleasure with eager thirst, entertain the meanest opinion of the sex. Virtue, true refiner of joy—if foolish men were to fright thee from earth, in order to give loose to all their appetites without a check—some sensual wight of taste would scale the heavens to invite thee back, to give a zest to pleasure!

That women at present are by ignorance rendered foolish or vicious, is, I think, not to be disputed; and, that the most salutary effects tending to improve mankind might be expected from a REVOLUTION in female manners appears, at least, with a face of probability, to rise out of the observation. For as marriage has been termed the parent of those endearing charities which draw man from the brutal herd, the corrupting intercourse that wealth, idleness, and folly produce between the sexes is more universally injurious to morality than all the other vices of mankind collectively considered. To adulterous lust the most sacred duties are sacrificed, because before marriage, men, by a promiscuous intimacy with women, learned to consider love as a selfish gratification—learned to separate it not only from esteem, but from the affection merely built on habit, which mixes a little humanity with it. Justice and friendship are also set at defiance, and that purity of taste is vitiated which would naturally lead a man to relish an artless display of affection rather than affected airs. But that noble simplicity of affection, which dares to appear unadorned, has few attractions for the libertine, though it be the charm, which by cementing the matrimonial tie, secures to the pledges of a warmer passion the necessary parental attention; for children will never be properly educated till friendship subsists between parents. Virtue flies from a house divided against itself—and a whole legion of devils take up their residence there.

The affection of husbands and wives cannot be pure when they have so few sentiments in common, and when so little confidence is established at home, as must be the case when their pursuits are so different. That intimacy from which tenderness should flow will not, cannot, subsist between the vicious.

Contending, therefore, that the sexual distinction which men have so warmly insisted upon is arbitrary, I have dwelt on an observation that several sensible men with whom I have conversed on the subject allowed to be well founded; and it is simply this, that the little chastity to be found amongst men, and consequent disregard of modesty, tend to degrade both sexes; and further, that the modesty of women, characterized as such, will often be only the artful veil of wantonness instead of being the natural reflection of purity, till modesty be universally respected.

From the tyranny of man, I firmly believe, the greater number of female follies proceed; and the cunning, which I allow makes at present a part of their character, I likewise have repeatedly endeavored to prove is produced by oppression.

. . . .

Asserting the rights which women in common with men ought to contend for, I have not attempted to extenuate their faults; but to prove them to be the natural consequence of their education and station in society. If so, it is reasonable to suppose that they will change their character, and correct their vices and follies, when they are allowed to be free in a physical, moral, and civil sense.*

Let woman share the rights and she will emulate the virtues of man; for she must grow more perfect when emancipated, or justify the authority that chains such a weak being to her duty. If the latter, it will be expedient to

*"I had further enlarged on the advantages which might reasonably be expected to result from an improvement in female manners, towards the general reformation of society; but it appeared to me that such reflections would more properly close the last volume." (Wollstonecraft's note). Although Wollstonecraft originally intended to write a second volume on the rights of woman, she seems never to have begun it.

open a fresh trade with Russia for whips; a present which a father should always make to his son-in-law on his wedding day, that a husband may keep his whole family in order by the same means; and without any violation of justice reign, wielding this scepter, sole master of his house, because he is the only being in it who has reason: the divine, indefeasible earthly sovereignty breathed into man by the Master of the universe. Allowing this position, women have not any inherent rights to claim; and, by the same rule, their duties vanish, for rights and duties are inseparable.

Be just then, O ye men of understanding! and mark not more severely what women do amiss, than the vicious tricks of the horse or the ass for whom ye provide provender—and allow her the privileges of ignorance, to whom ye deny the rights of reason, or ye will be worse than Egyptian taskmasters, expecting virtue where nature has not given understanding!

An Historical and Moral View of the Origin and Progress of the French Revolution

WOLLSTONECRAFT'S 522-page history of the French Revolution, ambitiously titled and advertised as "Volume the First," was completed in 1794, though the project was never carried further. Since most of the volume reviews what had taken place prior to her arrival in Paris in December 1792 (she was criticized for relying heavily on the reports in *The New Annual Register,* the periodical for which Godwin had worked), and since it lacks the eyewitness view of events (and of women's participation in them) that the author of *A Vindication of the Rights of Woman* seemed so fortunately situated to provide, it fails to justify its length.

Her individual voice does assert itself, however, in general reflections on the trends in society that had led to the revolution, and a concern with the devastation revolution leaves in its wake. In the book's most frequently quoted passage, she thrills to the silence of Versailles, another ruin of the sort that appeals to the Gothic element in her sensibility, but she turns from imagination of the past to a prophecy of the future, when farms and "hospitable mansions" will replace such monuments to the privileges of the few. Progress to a rational reformer, after all, means not only sequence but improvement. While she censures the excesses of the mob, she points out the more vicious excesses that provoked them. Although her fiction is filled with irreparable loss and problems without solutions, in her works on society and human rights she has a grand vision of promise, as "liberty with maternal wing" soars above "to shelter all mankind." She asserts in observing the French Revolution: "We must get entirely clear of all the notions drawn from the wild traditions of original sin: the eating of the apple, the theft of Prometheus, the opening of Pandora's box."

In her preface, Wollstonecraft hails the French Revolution as an expression of the "enlightened sentiments of masculine and improved philosophy." Liberty may be a matron, but her adjective reiterates her criticism of the pettiness she found in the typical "feminine" situation, a criticism which she pursues in two striking ways in this history. Sketching the enslavement of the masses that eventually must lead humanity to rebellion, she offers several illustrations from the common experience of women. Even the cultural flowering of antiquity, she reminds us, left women "in a state of bondage"; and among the injustices that still plague the world she cites one that she had closely observed as she grew to womanhood: enforced obedience to undeserving parents and to tyrannical husbands. Thus deprived of the right to self-determination, women become indolent and mindless.

In analyzing the fickle and dangerous Parisian mobs, she explains that "the French may be considered as a nation of women." The source of their mindlessness curiously resembles the mindlessness of their queen and eventual victim, Marie Antoinette, whose shallow but enchanting character Wollstonecraft typically believes resulted from the queen's faulty upbringing. Ever the educator, Wollstonecraft asserts that "education, and the atmosphere of manners in which a character is formed, change the natural laws of humanity." As Marie Antoinette was depraved by early influences, the untaught masses of human beings must similarly be expected to act unreasonably. Yet even among the French, Wollstonecraft recalls, testifying here to her own enjoyment of French hospitality, progress in human culture may be charted. Instances of domestic equality and sensible child care encourage the reformer to hope for more widespread improvement, and in the spirit of hope her history concludes: "People thinking for themselves have more energy in their voice than any government." Wollstonecraft writes best when she too thinks for herself and when, as is so frequently the case, her thoughts call for a humane and independent moral view that transcends the restrictions imposed by the ages according to class and sex.

AN
HISTORICAL AND MORAL VIEW
Of THE
ORIGIN AND PROGRESS
Of THE
FRENCH REVOLUTION
AND THE
EFFECT IT HAS PRODUCED
IN
EUROPE.

PREFACE

The revolution in France exhibits a scene, in the political world, not less novel and interesting than the contrast is striking between the narrow opinions of superstition, and the enlightened sentiments of masculine and improved philosophy.

. . . .

By ... attending to circumstances, we shall be able to discern clearly that the revolution was neither produced by the abilities or intrigues of a few individuals; nor was the effect of sudden and short-lived enthusiasm, but the natural consequence of intellectual improvement, gradually proceeding to perfection in the advancement of communities, from a state of barbarism to that of polished society, till now arrived at the point when sincerity of principles seems to be hastening the overthrow of the tremendous empire of superstition and hypocrisy, erected upon the ruins of Gothic brutality and ignorance.

FROM BOOK I:
PROGRESS OF SOCIETY

. . . .

America fortunately found herself in a situation very different from all the rest of the world; for she had it in her power to lay the first stones of her government, when reason was venturing to canvass prejudice. Availing herself of the degree of civilization of the world, she has not retained those customs which were only the expedients of barbarism; or thought that constitutions formed by chance, and continually patched up, were superior to the plans of reason, at liberty to profit by experience.

When society was first regulated, the laws could not be adjusted so as to take in the future conduct of its members, because the faculties of man are unfolded and perfected by the improvements made by society . . .

. . . .

We must get entirely clear of all the notions drawn from the wild traditions of original sin: the eating of the apple, the theft of Prometheus, the opening of Pandora's box, and the other fables, too tedious to enumerate, on which priests have erected their tremendous structures of imposition to persuade us that we are naturally inclined to evil: we shall then leave room for the expansion of the human heart, and, I trust, find that men will insensibly render each other happier as they grow wiser. It is indeed the necessity of stifling many of its most spontaneous desires to obtain the factitious virtues of society that makes man vicious, by depriving him of that dignity of character which rests only on truth. For it is not paradoxical to assert that the social virtues are nipped in the bud by the very laws of society. One principle of action is sufficient—respect thyself—whether it be termed fear of God—religion; love of justice—morality; or self-love—the desire of happiness. Yet, how can a man respect himself, and if not, how believe in the existence of virtue, when he is practising the daily shifts which do not come under the cognizance of the law, in order to obtain a respectable situation in life? It seems, in fact, to be the business of a civilized man to harden his heart, that on it he may sharpen the wit, which, assuming the appellation of sagacity, or cunning, in different characters, is only a proof that the head is clear, because the heart is cold.

Besides, one great cause of misery in the present imperfect state of society is that the imagination, continually tantalized, becomes the inflated wen of the mind, draining off the nourishment from the vital parts. Nor would it, I think, be stretching the inference too far to insist that men become vicious in the same proportion as they are obliged, by the defects of society, to submit to a kind of self-denial, which ignorance, not morals, prescribes.

But these evils are passing away; a new spirit has gone forth, to organize the body politic; and where is the criterion to be found to estimate the means by which the influence of this spirit can be confined, now enthroned in the hearts of half the inhabitants of the globe? Reason has, at last, shown her captivating face, beaming with benevolence; and it will be impossible for the dark hand of despotism again to obscure its radiance, or the lurking dagger of subordinate tyrants to reach her bosom. The image of God implanted in our nature is now more rapidly expanding; and, as it opens, liberty with maternal wing seems to be soaring to regions far above vulgar annoyance, promising to shelter all mankind.

. . . .

The French Revolution is a strong proof how far things will govern men, when simple principles begin to act with one powerful spring against the complicated wheels of ignorance; numerous in proportion to their weakness, and constantly wanting repair, because expedients of the moment are ever the spawn of cowardly folly, or the narrow calculations of selfishness. To elucidate this truth, it is not necessary to rake among the ashes of barbarous ambition, to show the ignorance and consequent folly of the monarchs, who ruled with a rod of iron, when the hordes of European savages began to form their governments, though the review of this portion of history would clearly prove that narrowness of mind naturally produces ferociousness of temper.

. . . .

Men exclaim, only noticing the evil, against the luxury introduced with the arts and sciences; when it is obviously the cultivation of these alone, emphatically termed the arts of peace, that can turn the sword into a ploughshare. War is the adventure naturally pursued by the idle, and it requires something of this species to excite the strong emotions necessary to rouse inactive minds. Ignorant people, when they appear to reflect, exercise their imagination more than their understanding; indulging reveries instead of pursuing a train of thinking; and thus grow romantic, like the crusaders, or like women, who are commonly idle and restless.

. . . .

But . . . if the degeneracy of the higher orders of society be such that no remedy less fraught with horror can effect a radical cure; and if enjoying the fruits of usurpation, they domineer over the weak, and check by all the means in their power every humane effort to draw man out of the state of degradation into which the inequality of fortune has sunk him; the people are justified in having recourse to coercion, to repel coercion. And, further, if it can be ascertained that the silent sufferings of the citizens of the world under the iron feet of oppression are greater, though less obvious, than the calamities produced by such violent convulsions as have happened in France, which, like hurricanes whirling over the face of nature, strip off all its blooming graces, it may be politically just to pursue such measures as were taken by that regenerating country, and at once root out those deleterious plants which poison the better half of human happiness. For civilization hitherto, by producing the inequality of conditions which makes wealth more desirable than either talents or virtue, has so weakened all the organs of the body politic, and rendered man such a beast of prey, that the strong have always devoured the weak till the very signification of justice has been lost sight of, and charity, the most specious system of slavery, substituted in its place. The rich have for ages tyrannized over the poor, teaching them how to act when possessed of power, and now must feel the consequence. People are rendered ferocious by misery; and misanthropy is ever the offspring of discontent. Let not then the happiness of one-half of mankind be built on the misery of the other, and humanity will take place of charity, and all the ostentatious virtues of an universal aristocracy. How, in fact, can we expect to see men live together like brothers, when we only see master and servant in society? For till men learn mutually to assist without governing each other, little can be done by political associations towards perfecting the condition of mankind.

Europe will probably be, for some years to come, in a state of anarchy; till a change of sentiments, gradually undermining the strongholds of custom, alters the manners without rousing the little passions of men, a pack of yelping curs pampered by vanity and pride. It is in reality these minor passions which during the summer of idleness mantle on the heart and taint the atmosphere, because the understanding is still.

Several acts of ferocious folly have justly brought much obloquy on the grand revolution which has taken place in France; yet, I feel confident of being able to prove that the people are essentially good, and that knowledge is rapidly advancing to that degree of perfectibility when the proud distinctions of sophisticating fools will be eclipsed by the mild rays of philosophy, and man be considered as man—acting with the dignity of an intelligent being.

. . . .

FROM BOOK II:
CHARACTER OF THE QUEEN OF FRANCE

. . . .

It is certain that education and the atmosphere of manners in which a character is formed change the natural laws of humanity; otherwise it would be unaccountable how the human heart can be so dead to the tender emotions of benevolence which most forcibly teach us that real or lasting felicity flows only from a love of virtue and the practice of sincerity.

The unfortunate queen of France, beside the advantages of birth and station, possessed a very fine person; and her lovely face, sparkling with vivacity, hid the want of intelligence. Her complexion was dazzlingly clear; and, when she was pleased, her manners were bewitching; for she happily mingled the most insinuating voluptuous softness and affability with an air of grandeur, bordering on pride, that rendered the contrast more striking. Independence also, of whatever kind, always gives a degree of dignity to the mien; so that monarchs and nobles, with most ignoble souls, from believing themselves superior to others, have actually acquired a look of superiority.

But her opening faculties were poisoned in the bud; for before she came to Paris, she had already been prepared, by a corrupt, supple abbé, for the part she was to play; and, young as she was, became so firmly attached to the aggrandizement of her house that, though plunged deep in pleasure, she never omitted sending immense sums to her brother, on every occasion. The person of the king, in itself very disgusting, was rendered more so by gluttony, and a total disregard of delicacy, and even decency in his apartments; and, when jealous of the queen, for whom he had a kind of devouring passion, he treated her with great brutality, till she acquired sufficient finesse to subjugate him. Is it then surprising that a very desirable woman, with a sanguine constitution, should shrink abhorrent from his embraces; or that an empty mind should be employed only to vary the pleasures, which emasculated her circean court? . . .

Lost then in the most luxurious pleasures, or managing court intrigues, the queen became a profound dissembler; and her heart hardened by sensual enjoyments to such a degree that when her family and favorites stood on the brink of ruin, her little portion of mind was employed only to preserve herself from danger. As a proof of the justness of this assertion, it is only necessary to observe that, in the general wreck, not a scrap of her writing has been found to criminate her; neither has she suffered a word to escape her to exasperate the people, even when burning with rage and contempt. . . . Still, she was a woman of uncommon address; and though her conversation was insipid, her compliments were so artfully adapted to flatter the person she wished to please or dupe, and so eloquent is the beauty of a queen in the eyes even of superior men, that she seldom failed to carry her point when she endeavored to gain an ascendancy over the mind of an individual. Over that of the king she acquired unbounded sway, when, managing the disgust she had for his person, she made him pay a kingly price for her favors. A court is the best school in the world for actors; it was very natural then for her to become a complete actress, and an adept in all the arts of coquetry that debauch the mind, whilst they render the person alluring.

. . . .

How silent is now Versailles!—The solitary foot that mounts the sumptuous staircase rests on each landing place, whilst the eye traverses the void, almost expecting to see the strong images of fancy burst into life. The train of the Louises, like the posterity of the Banquoes, pass in solemn sadness, pointing at the nothingness of grandeur, fading away on the cold canvas which covers the nakedness of the spacious walls— whilst the gloominess of the atmosphere gives a deeper shade to the gigantic figures that seem to be sinking into the embraces of death.

Warily entering the endless apartments, half shut up, the fleeting shadow of the pensive wanderer, reflected in long glasses that vainly gleam in every direction, slacken the nerves, without appalling the heart, though lascivious pictures, in which grace varnishes voluptuousness, no longer seductive, strike continually home to the bosom the melancholy moral that anticipates the frozen lesson of experience. The very air is chill, seeming to clog the breath; and the wasting dampness of destruction appears to be stealing into the vast pile on every side.

The oppressed heart seeks for relief in the garden; but even there the same images glide along the wide neglected walks—all is fearfully still; and, if a little rill creeping through the gathering moss down the cascade over which it used to rush bring to mind the description of the grand waterworks, it is only to excite a languid smile at the futile attempt to equal nature.

Lo! this was the palace of the great king!—the abode of magnificence! Who has broken the charm? Why does it now inspire only pity?—Why, because nature, smiling around, presents to the imagination materials to build farms, and hospitable mansions, where, without raising idle admiration, that gladness will reign which opens the heart to benevolence, and that industry which renders innocent pleasure sweet.

Weeping—scarcely conscious that I weep, O France! over the vestiges of thy former oppression, which, separating man from man with a fence of iron, sophisticated all, and made many completely wretched; I tremble, lest I should meet some unfortunate being, fleeing from the despotism of licentious freedom, hearing the snap of the *guillotine* at his heels, merely because he was once noble, or has afforded an asylum to those whose only crime is their name—and, if my pen almost bound with eagerness to record the day that

leveled the Bastille with the dust, making the towers of
despair tremble to their base, the recollection that still the
abbey is appropriated to hold the victims of revenge and
suspicion palsies the hand that would fain do justice to the
assault, which tumbled into heaps of ruins walls that seemed
to mock the resistless force of time. Down fell the temple of
despotism; but despotism has not been buried in its ruins!
Unhappy country!—when will thy children cease to tear thy
bosom? When will a change of opinion, producing a change
of morals, render thee truly free? When will truth give life
to real magnanimity, and justice place equality on a stable
seat? When will thy sons trust, because they deserve to be
trusted; and private virtue become the guarantee of patriotism? Ah!—when will thy government become the most perfect, because thy citizens are the most virtuous!

. . . .

STATE OF CIVILIZATION AMONGST THE ANCIENTS

. . . though bad morals, and worse laws, have helped to deprave the passions of men to such a degree as to make the
benefits which society have derived from the talents or exertions of individuals to arise from selfish considerations, still
it has been in a state of gradual improvement, and has
arrived at such a pitch of comparative perfection that the
most arbitrary governments in Europe, Russia excepted,
begin to treat their subjects as human beings, feeling like
men, and with some powers of thinking.

The most high degree of civilization amongst the ancients,
on the contrary, seems to have consisted in the perfection
the arts, including language, attained, whilst the people,
only domesticated brutes, were governed and amused by
religious shows that stand on record as the most egregious
insult ever offered to the human understanding. Women were
in a state of bondage, though the men, who gave way to the
most unbridled excesses, even to the outraging of nature,
expected that they should be chaste, and took the only
method to render them so in such a depraved state of soci-

ety by ruling them with a rod of iron, making them, excepting the courtesans, merely household breeding animals.

The state of slavery, likewise, of a large proportion of
men, tended probably, more than any other circumstance, to
degrade the whole circle of society. . . .

. . . .

The laws made by ambition rather than reason treated
with contempt the sacred equality of man, anxious only to
aggrandize, first the state and afterwards individuals: consequently, the civilization never extended beyond polishing
the manners, often at the expence of the heart, or morals. . . .
Sentiments were often noble, sympathies just—yet the life
of most men of the first class was made up of a series of
unjust acts, because the regulations thought expedient to
cement society did violence to natural justice. . . . where
. . . will be found the man who will simply say that a
king can do no wrong; and that, committing the vilest crimes
to sully his mind, his person still remains sacred? Who will
dare to assert that the priest who takes advantage of the
dying fears of a vicious man, to cheat his heirs, is not more
despicable than a highwayman? or that obedience to parents
should go one jot beyond the deference due to reason, enforced by affection? And who will coolly maintain that it is
just to deprive a woman, not to insist on her being treated
as an outcast of society, of all the rights of a citizen,
because her revolting heart turns from the man whom, a
husband only in name, and by the tyrannical power he has
over her person and property, she can neither love nor
respect, to find comfort in a more congenial or humane
bosom? These are a few of the leading prejudices, in the
present constitution of society, that blast the blossoms of
hope, and render life wretched and useless . . .

. . . .

It is by . . . teaching men from their youth to think that
they will be enabled to recover their liberty; and useful
learning is already so far advanced that nothing can stop
its progress. . . .

. . . .

FROM BOOK III:
CHARACTER OF THE PARISIANS

. . . .

... sudden transitions from one extreme to another, without leaving any settled conviction behind to confirm or eradicate the corroding distrust, could not be seen in such a strong light anywhere as at Paris, because there a variety of causes have so effeminated reason that the French may be considered as a nation of women; and made feeble, probably, by the same combination of circumstances as has rendered these insignificant. More ingenious than profound in their researches; more tender than impassioned in their affections; prompt to act, yet soon weary; they seem to work only to escape from work, and to reflect merely how they shall avoid reflection. Indolently restless, they make the elegant furniture of their rooms, like their houses, voluptuously handy. Everything, in short, shows the dexterity of the people, and their attention to present enjoyment.

And so passive appears to be their imagination, it requires to be roused by novelty; and then, more lively than strong, the evanescent emotions scarcely leave any traces behind them. From being devoted to pleasure in their youth, old age is commonly passed in such merely animal gratifications that a respectable looking aged man or woman is very rarely to be seen. Independent, likewise, of the vanity which makes them wish to appear polite, at the very moment they are ridiculing a person, their great susceptibility of disposition leads them to take an interest in all the sensations of others, which are forgotten almost as soon as felt. And these transient gusts of feeling prevent their forming those firm resolves of reason that, bracing the nerves, when the heart is moved, make sympathy yield to principles, and the mind triumph over the senses.

. . . .

... The mob, it is true, in the heat of rage, inhumanly butchered ... the vile instruments of despotism. ... The behavior ... of the hardened children of oppression in all countries is the same, whether in the amphitheater at Rome, or around the lantern post in Paris.

. . . .

Strange, that a people who often leave the theater before the catastrophe should have bred up such monsters! Still, we ought to recollect that the sex called the tender commit the most flagrant acts of barbarity when irritated—so weak is the tenderness produced merely by sympathy, or polished manners, compared with the humanity of a cultivated understanding. Alas! It is morals, not feelings, which distinguish men from the beasts of prey! These were transactions, over which, for the honor of human nature, it were to be wished oblivion could draw the windingsheet that has often enwrapped a heart whose benevolence has been felt, but not known. But if it be impossible to erase from the memory these foul deeds, which, like the stains of deepest dye revived by remorse in the conscience, can never be rubbed out—why dwell circumstantially on the excesses that revolt humanity, and dim the luster of the picture, on which the eye has gazed with rapture, often obliged to look up to heaven to forget the misery endured on earth? Since, however, we cannot "out the damned spot," it becomes necessary to observe that, whilst despotism and superstition exist, the convulsions which the regeneration of man occasions will always bring forward the vices they have engendered to devour their parents.

. . . .

Fortunately, in spite of the various impediments that have thwarted the advancement of knowledge, the blessings of society have been sufficiently experienced to convince us that the only solid good to be expected from a government must result from the security of our persons and property. And domestic felicity has given a mild luster to human happiness superior to the false glory of sanguinary devastation, or magnificent robberies. Our fields and vineyards have thus gradually become the principal objects of our care—and it is from this general sentiment governing the opinion of the civilized part of the world that we are enabled to contemplate, with some degree of certainty, the approaching age of peace.

All that could be done by a body of manners, without a soul of morals, to improve mankind, had been tried in

France—the result was polished slavery, and such an inordinate love of pleasure as led the majority to search only for enjoyment, till the tone of nature was destroyed. Yet some few really learned the true art of living, giving that degree of elegance to domestic intercourse which, prohibiting gross familiarity, alone can render permanent the family affections, whence all the social virtues spring.

It is a mistake to suppose that there was no such thing as domestic happiness in France, or even in Paris. For many French families, on the contrary, exhibited an affectionate urbanity of behavior to each other seldom to be met with where a certain easy gaiety does not soften the difference of age and condition. The husband and wife, if not lovers, were the civilest friends and the tenderest parents in the world—the only parents, perhaps, who really treated their children like friends, and the most affable masters and mistresses. Mothers were also to be found who, after suckling their children, paid a degree of attention to their education, not thought compatible with the levity of character attributed to them, whilst they acquired a portion of taste and knowledge rarely to be found in the women of other countries. Their hospitable boards were constantly open to relations and acquaintance, who, without the formality of an invitation, enjoyed there cheerfulness free from restraint, whilst more select circles closed the evening by discussing literary subjects. In the summer, when they retired to their mansion houses, they spread gladness around, and partook of the amusements of the peasantry, whom they visited with paternal solicitude. These were, it is true, the rational few, not numerous in any country—and where is led a more useful or rational life?

In the provinces, likewise, more simplicity of manners prevailing, their morals were more pure: though family pride, as in England, made the most noble house the royal family of each village, who visited the grand court only to import its follies. Besides, in France, the women have not those factitious, supercilious manners, common to the English; and acting more freely, they have more decision of character, and even more generosity. Rousseau has taught them also a scrupulous attention to personal cleanliness, not generally to be seen elsewhere: their coquetry is not only more agreeable, but more natural: and not left a prey to unsatisfied sensations, they were less romantic indeed than the English; yet many of them possessed delicacy of sentiment.

It is, perhaps, in a state of comparative idleness—pursuing employments not absolutely necessary to support life—that the finest polish is given to the mind and those personal graces which are instantly felt but cannot be described: and it is natural to hope that the labor of acquiring the substantial virtues, necessary to maintain freedom, will not render the French less pleasing when they become more respectable.

FROM BOOK IV:
PROGRESS OF REFORM

People thinking for themselves have more energy in their voice than any government which it is possible for human wisdom to invent; and every government not aware of this sacred truth will, at some period, be suddenly overturned. Whilst men in a savage state preserve their independence, they adopt no regular system of policy, nor ever attempt to digest their rude code of laws into a constitution, to ensure political liberty. Consequently we find in every country, after its civilization has arrived at a certain height, that the people, the moment they are displeased with their rulers, begin to clamor against them; and, finally rejecting all authority but their own will in breaking the shackles of folly or tyranny, they glut their resentment by the mischievous destruction of the works of ages, only considering them as the moments of their servitude.

From the social disposition of man, in proportion as he becomes civilized, he will mingle more and more with society. The first interest he takes in the business of his fellow men is that of his neighbor; next he contemplates the comfort, misery, and happiness of the nation to which he belongs, investigates the degree of wisdom and justice in the political system, under which he lives, and, striding into the regions of science, his researches embrace all human kind. Thus he is enabled to estimate the portion of evil or good which the government of his country produces, compared with that of others; and the comparison, granting him superior powers of mind, leads him to conceive a model of a more perfect form.

. . . .

ON THE CHARACTER OF THE FRENCH

The occupations and habits of life have a wonderful influence on the forming mind; so great that the superinductions of art stop the growth of the spontaneous shoots of nature, till it is difficult to distinguish natural from factitious morals and feelings; and as the energy of thinking will always proceed, in a great measure either from our education or manner of living, the frivolity of the French character may be accounted for without taking refuge in the old hiding place of ignorance—occult causes.

When it is the object of education to prepare the pupil to please everybody, and of course to deceive, accomplishments are the one thing needful; and the desire to be admired ever being uppermost, the passions are subjugated, or all drawn into the whirlpool of egotism. This gives to each person, however different the temper, a tincture of vanity, and that weak vacillation of opinion which is incompatible with what we term character.

Thus a Frenchman, like most women, may be said to have no character distinguishable from that of the nation, unless little shades, and casual lights, be allowed to constitute an essential characteristic. What then could have been expected, when their ambition was mostly confined to dancing gracefully, entering a room with easy assurance, and smiling on and complimenting the very persons whom they meant to ridicule at the next fashionable assembly? The learning to fence with skill, it is true, was useful to a people whose false notions of honor required that at least a drop of blood should atone for the shadow of an affront. The knack also of uttering sprightly repartees became a necessary art, to supply the place of that real interest only to be nourished in the affectionate intercourse of domestic intimacy, where confidence enlarges the heart it opens. Besides, the desire of eating of every dish at table, no matter if there were fifty, and the custom of separating immediately after the repast, destroy the social affections, reminding a stranger of the vulgar saying—"Every man for himself, and God for us all." After these cursory observations, it is not going too far to advance that the French were in some respects the most unqualified of any people in Europe to undertake the important work in which they are embarked.

. . . .

EXCUSE FOR THE FEROCITY OF THE PARISIANS

The deprivation of natural, equal, civil, and political rights reduced the most cunning of the lower orders to practice fraud, and the rest to habits of stealing, audacious robberies, and murders. And why? because the rich and poor were separated into bands of tyrants and slaves, and the retaliation of slaves is always terrible. In short, every sacred feeling, moral and divine, has been obliterated, and the dignity of man sullied, by a system of policy and jurisprudence as repugnant to reason as at variance with humanity.

The only excuse that can be made for the ferocity of the Parisians is then simply to observe that they had not any confidence in the laws, which they had always found to be merely cobwebs to catch small flies. Accustomed to be punished themselves for every trifle, and often for only being in the way of the rich, or their parasites, when, in fact, had the Parisians seen the execution of a noble, or priest, though convicted of crimes beyond the daring of vulgar minds? When justice, or the law, is so partial, the day of retribution will come with the red sky of vengeance, to confound the innocent with the guilty. The mob were barbarous beyond the tiger's cruelty: for how could they trust a court that had so often deceived them, or expect to see its agents punished, when the same measures were pursuing?

Let us cast our eyes over the history of man, and we shall scarcely find a page that is not tarnished by some foul deed or bloody transaction. Let us examine the catalogue of the vices of men in a savage state, and contrast them with those of men civilized; we shall find that a barbarian, considered as a moral being, is an angel, compared with the refined villain of artificial life. Let us investigate the causes which have produced this degeneracy, and we shall discover that they are those unjust plans of government which have been formed by peculiar circumstances in every part of the globe. Then let us coolly and impartially contemplate the improvements which are gaining ground in the formation of principles of policy; and I flatter myself it will be allowed by every humane and considerate being that a political system more simple than has hitherto existed would effectually check those aspiring follies, which, by imitation, leading to vice, have banished from governments the very shadow of justice and magnanimity.

Thus had France grown up and sickened on the corruption of a state diseased. But as in medicine there is a species of complaint in the bowels which works its own cure and, leaving the body healthy, gives an invigorated tone to the system, so there is in politics: and whilst the agitation of its regeneration continues, the excrementitious humors exuding from the contaminated body will excite a general dislike and contempt for the nation; and it is only the philosophical eye, which looks into the nature and weighs the consequences of human actions, that will be able to discern the cause, which has produced so many dreadful effects.

Letters Written during a Short Residence in Sweden, Norway, and Denmark

IN THESE LETTERS, written between May and October 1795 and published in January 1796, Wollstonecraft's many selves coalesce. Acknowledging her book as an unusual amalgam of public and private concerns, she refuses to apologize for her frequent use of the first person and bids her readers decide for themselves if they wish to know her. This refreshing openness helps us see in retrospect the unwittingly autobiographical cast of her earlier work. She omits the practical details of the business transactions of the trip she undertook for her faithless lover, Gilbert Imlay, perhaps judging them unsuitable for publication. By alternating descriptions of her often arduous travels through the countryside with her impressions of the women of Scandinavia, she makes of her own activity a standard by which she judges what she observes. As always she deplores laziness of body and of mind. Her own energy impressed everyone who met her, but the personal reflections in the letters reveal that familiar Wollstonecraft paradox: while briskly discharging her duties, she broods on the pains of being a woman and the chaos of her own life.

Although she thought it best to leave her year-old Fanny with a nurse, her daughter is never far from her thoughts as she moves around Scandinavia. She fears that in bringing her up to be an independent and thoughtful woman, she will only prepare her child to suffer as her mother suffers: "I dread to unfold her mind, lest it should render her unfit for the world she is to inhabit—Hapless woman! What a fate is thine!" Nevertheless, Wollstonecraft pursues her own independence, identifying strongly with the ill-fated sister of George III, Caroline Matilda, who was married in 1766 to the Danish King Christian VII, when she was only fifteen. The marriage was an unhappy one, and Matilda entered into an affair with the court doctor, by whom she bore a daughter after she had mothered Christian's son. She escaped from Denmark but died in 1775; Wollstonecraft clearly felt that Caroline had been victimized more for her reforming zeal than for her conduct: "Disgusted with many customs which pass for virtues ... she probably ran into an error common to innovators, in wishing to do immediately what can only be done by time."

With Imlay as the principal recipient of her correspondence, Wollstonecraft often comments bitterly on men's treatment of women: Danish men, for instance, are described as domestic tyrants. Indeed all men prefer to exercise power in their sexual relations. Smarting at Imlay's abandonment, she records the liberal Scandinavian custom of maintaining illegitimate children, but as always she sets no store on custom for its own sake, musing that a person of sense and means might improve matters greatly by setting an enlightened example for the impressionable and lackadaisical, repeating her own views on sensible clothing, nursing, and feeding.

To be sure, Wollstonecraft's tenuous act of balancing conflicting emotions could not be sustained indefinitely. When this competent businesswoman, loving mother, enterprising tourist, and insecure mistress returned home to discover that Imlay had taken a new mistress, she threw herself from a bridge into the Thames. But these letters, bridges of another sort, formed a span to her new life as well. If Imlay was indifferent to her outbursts of passion and grief, another reader was not. Three weeks after meeting her, William Godwin had got a copy of what he admiringly referred to as "Wollstonecraft's Travels." No Swiftian satire, this confessional volume moved him to a tender tribute in the *Memoirs* of his dead wife: "If ever there was a book calculated to make a man in love with its author, this appears to me to be the book."

LETTERS
WRITTEN
DURING A SHORT RESIDENCE
IN
SWEDEN, NORWAY, AND DENMARK.

ADVERTISEMENT

The writing travels, or memoirs, has ever been a pleasant employment, for vanity or sensibility always renders it interesting. In writing these desultory letters, I found I could not avoid being continually the first person—"the little hero of each tale." I tried to correct this fault, if it be one, for they were designed for publication; but in proportion as I arranged my thoughts, my letter, I found, became stiff and affected: I therefore determined to let my remarks and reflections flow unrestrained, as I perceived that I could not give a just description of what I saw, but by relating the effect different objects had produced on my mind and feelings, whilst the impression was still fresh.

A person has a right, I have sometimes thought, when amused by a witty or interesting egotist, to talk of himself when he can win on our attention by acquiring our affection. Whether I deserve to rank amongst this privileged number, my readers alone can judge—and I give them leave to shut the book if they do not wish to become better acquainted with me.

My plan was simply to endeavor to give a just view of the present state of the countries I have passed through, as far as I could obtain information during so short a residence, avoiding those details which, without being very useful to travelers who follow the same route, appear very insipid to those who only accompany you in their chair.

FROM LETTER IV: [ON SWEDEN]

The severity of the long Swedish winter tends to render the people sluggish; for, though this season has its peculiar pleasures, too much time is employed to guard against its inclemency. Still, as warm clothing is absolutely necessary, the women spin, and the men weave, and by these exertions get a fence to keep out the cold. I have rarely passed a knot of cottages without seeing cloth laid out to bleach; and when I entered, always found the women spinning or knitting.

A mistaken tenderness, however, for their children, makes them, even in summer, load them with flannels; and, having a sort of natural antipathy to cold water, the squalid appearance of the poor babes, not to speak of the noxious smell which flannel and rugs retain, seems a reply to a question I had often asked—Why I did not see more children in the villages I passed through? Indeed the children appear to be nipped in the bud, having neither the graces nor charms of their age. And this, I am persuaded, is much more owing to the ignorance of the mothers than to the rudeness of the climate. Rendered feeble by the continual perspiration they are kept in, whilst every pore is absorbing unwholesome moisture, they give them, even at the breast, brandy, salt fish, and every other crude substance, which air and exercise enables the parent to digest.

The women of fortune here, as well as everywhere else, have nurses to suckle their children; and the total want of chastity in the lower class of women frequently renders them very unfit for the trust.

The Swedish ladies exercise neither [mind and body] sufficiently; of course, grow very fat at an early age; and when they have not this downy appearance, a comfortable idea, you will say, in a cold climate, they are not remarkable for fine forms. They have, however, mostly fine complexions; but indolence makes the lily soon displace the rose. The quantity of coffee, spices, and other things of that kind, with want of care, almost universally spoil their teeth, which contrast but ill with their ruby lips.

The manners of Stockholm are refined, I hear, by the introduction of gallantry; but in the country, romping and coarse freedoms, with coarser allusions, keep the spirits awake. In the article of cleanliness, the women, of all descriptions, seem very deficient; and their dress shows that vanity is more inherent in women than taste.

FROM LETTER VI: [ON NORWAY]

As the Norwegians do not frequently see travelers, they are very curious to know their business, and who they are—so curious that I was half tempted to adopt Dr. Franklin's plan, when traveling in America, where they are equally prying, which was to write on a paper, for public inspection, my name, from whence I came, where I was going, and what was my business. But if I were importuned by their curiosity, their friendly gestures gratified me. A woman, coming alone, interested them. And I know not whether my weariness gave me a look of peculiar delicacy, but they approached to assist me, and inquire after my wants, as if they were afraid to hurt, and wished to protect me. The sympathy I inspired, thus dropping down from the clouds in a strange land, affected me more than it would have done, had not my spirits been harassed by various causes—by much thinking—musing almost to madness—and even by a sort of weak melancholy that hung about my heart at parting with my daughter for the first time.

You know that as a female I am particularly attached to her—I feel more than a mother's fondness and anxiety, when I reflect on the dependent and oppressed state of her sex. I dread lest she should be forced to sacrifice her heart to her principles, or principles to her heart. With trembling hand I shall cultivate sensibility, and cherish delicacy of sentiment, lest, whilst I lend fresh blushes to the rose, I sharpen the thorns that will wound the breast I would fain guard. I dread to unfold her mind, lest it should render her unfit for the world she is to inhabit. Hapless woman! what a fate is thine!

But whither am I wandering? I only meant to tell you that the impression the kindness of the simple people made visible on my countenance increased my sensibility to a painful degree. I wished to have had a room to myself; for their attention, and rather distressing observation, embarrassed me extremely. Yet, as they would bring me eggs and make my coffee, I found I could not leave them without hurting their feelings of hospitality.

It is customary here for the host and hostess to welcome their guests as master and mistress of the house.

My clothes, in their turn, attracted the attention of the females; and I could not help thinking of the foolish vanity which makes many women so proud of the observation of strangers as to take wonder very gratuitously for admiration. This error they are very apt to fall into; when arrived in a foreign country, the populace stared at them as they pass: yet the make of a cap, or the singularity of a gown, is often the cause of the flattering attention, which afterwards supports a fantastic superstructure of self-conceit.

FROM LETTER VIII: [ON NORWAY]

... Though I could not speak Danish, I knew that I could see a great deal: yes; I am persuaded that I have formed a very just opinion of the character of the Norwegians, without being able to hold converse with them.

I had expected to meet some company; yet was a little disconcerted at being ushered into an apartment full of well-dressed people; and, glancing my eyes round, they rested on several very pretty faces. Rosy cheeks, sparkling eyes, and light brown or golden locks; for I never saw so much hair with a yellow cast; and, with their fine complexions, it looked very becoming.

These women seem a mixture of indolence and vivacity; they scarcely ever walk out, and were astonished that I should, for pleasure; yet they are immoderately fond of dancing. Unaffected in their manners, if they have no pretensions to elegance, simplicity often produces a gracefulness of deportment, when they are animated by a particular desire to please—which was the case at present. The solitariness of my situation, which they thought terrible, interested them

very much in my favor. They gathered round me—sung to
me—and one of the prettiest, to whom I gave my hand, with
some degree of cordiality, to meet the glance of her eyes,
kissed me very affectionately.

At dinner, which was conducted with great hospitality,
though we remained at table too long, they sung several
songs, and, amongst the rest, translations of some patriotic
French ones. As the evening advanced, they became playful,
and we kept up a sort of conversation of gestures. As their
minds were totally uncultivated, I did not lose much, perhaps gained, by not being able to understand them; for
fancy probably filled up, more to their advantage, the void
in the picture. Be that as it may, they excited my sympathy;
and I was very much flattered when I was told, the next
day, that they said it was a pleasure to look at me, I appeared so good-natured.

The young women here, as well as in Sweden, have commonly bad teeth, which I attribute to the same causes. They
are fond of finery, but do not pay the necessary attention to
their persons to render beauty less transient than a flower;
and that interesting expression which sentiment and accomplishments give seldom supplies its place.

The servants have likewise an inferior sort of food here;
but their masters are not allowed to strike them with impunity. I might have added mistresses; for it was a complaint
of this kind, brought before the mayor, which led me to a
knowledge of the fact.

The wages are low, which is particularly unjust, because
the price of clothes is much higher than provisions. A young
woman who is wet-nurse to the mistress of the inn where I
lodge receives only twelve dollars a year, and pays ten for
the nursing of her own child; the father had run away to get
clear of the expense. There was something in this most
painful state of widowhood which excited my compassion,
and led me to reflections on the instability of the most
flattering plans of happiness that were painful in the extreme, till I was ready to ask whether this world was not
created to exhibit every possible combination of wretchedness.
I asked these questions of a heart writhing with anguish,
whilst I listened to a melancholy ditty sung by this poor
girl. It was too early for thee to be abandoned, thought I,
and I hastened out of the house to take my solitary eve-

ning's walk—and here I am again, to talk of anything but the pangs arising from the discovery of estranged affection, and the lonely sadness of a deserted heart.

The father and mother, if the father can be ascertained, are obliged to maintain an illegitimate child at their joint expense; but, should the father disappear, go up the country or to sea, the mother must maintain it herself. However, accidents of this kind do not prevent their marrying; and then it is not unusual to take the child or children home; and they are brought up very amicably with the marriage progeny.

I took some pains to learn what books were written originally in their language; but for any certain information respecting the state of Danish literature, I must wait till I arrive at Copenhagen.

The sound of the language is soft, a great proportion of the words ending in vowels; and there is a simplicity in the turn of some of the phrases which have been translated to me that pleased and interested me. In the country, the farmers use the *thou* and *thee;* and they do not acquire the polite plurals of the towns by meeting at market. The not having markets established in the large towns appears to me a great inconvenience. When the farmers have anything to sell, they bring it to the neighboring town, and take it from house to house. I am surprised that the inhabitants do not feel how very incommodious this usage is to both parties, and redress it. They indeed perceive it; for when I have introduced the subject, they acknowledged that they were often in want of necessaries, there being no butchers, and they were often obliged to buy what they did not want; yet it was the *custom;* and the changing of customs of a long standing requires more energy than they yet possess. I received a similar reply when I attempted to persuade the women that they injured their children by keeping them too warm. The only way of parrying off my reasoning was that they must do as other people did. In short, reason on any subject of change, and they stop you by saying that "the town would talk." A person of sense, with a large fortune to insure respect, might be very useful here, by inducing them to treat their children and manage their sick properly and eat food dressed in a simpler manner: the example, for instance, of a count's lady.

FROM LETTER XVIII: [ON DENMARK]

The men of business are domestic tyrants, coldly immersed in their own affairs and so ignorant of the state of other countries, that they dogmatically assert that Denmark is the happiest country in the world; the prince royal the best of all possible princes; and count Bernstorff the wisest of ministers.

As for the women, they are simply notable housewives without accomplishments or any of the charms that adorn more advanced social life. This total ignorance may enable them to save something in their kitchens; but it is far from rendering them better parents. On the contrary, the children are spoiled, as they usually are, when left to the care of weak, indulgent mothers, who having no principle of action to regulate their feelings become the slaves of infants, enfeebling both body and mind by false tenderness.

I am perhaps a little prejudiced, as I write from the impression of the moment; for I have been tormented today by the presence of unruly children, and made angry by some invectives thrown out against the maternal character of the unfortunate Matilda. She was censured, with the most cruel insinuation, for her management of her son; though, from what I could gather, she gave proofs of good sense, as well as tenderness in her attention to him. She used to bathe him herself every morning; insisted on his being loosely clad; and would not permit his attendants to injure his digestion by humoring his appetite. She was equally careful to prevent his acquiring haughty airs and playing the tyrant in leading strings. The queen dowager would not permit her to suckle him; but the next child being a daughter, and not the heir apparent of the crown, less opposition was made to her discharging the duty of a mother.

Poor Matilda! thou hast haunted me ever since my arrival; and the view I have had of the manners of the country, exciting my sympathy, has increased my respect for thy memory!

I am now fully convinced that she was the victim of the party she displaced, who would have overlooked, or encouraged, her attachment, had her lover not, aiming at being useful, attempted to overturn some established abuses before the people, ripe for the change, had sufficient spirit to support him when struggling in their behalf. Such indeed was the asperity sharpened against her that I have heard her, even after so many years have elapsed, charged with licentiousness, not only for endeavoring to render the public amusements more elegant, but for her very charities, because she erected, amongst other institutions, a hospital to receive foundlings. Disgusted with many customs which pass for virtues, though they are nothing more than observances of forms, often at the expense of truth, she probably ran into an error common to innovators, in wishing to do immediately what can only be done by time.

FROM LETTER XIX: [ON DENMARK]

Wealth does not appear to be sought for amongst the Danes to obtain the elegant luxuries of life; for a want of taste is very conspicuous at Copenhagen, so much so, that I am not surprised to hear that poor Matilda offended the rigid Lutherans by aiming to refine their pleasures. The elegance which she wished to introduce was termed lasciviousness: yet I do not find that the absence of gallantry renders the wives more chaste, or the husbands more constant. Love here seems to corrupt the morals, without polishing the manners, by banishing confidence and truth, the charm as well as cement of domestic life. A gentleman, who has resided in this city some time assures me that he could not find language to give me an idea of the gross debaucheries into which the lower order of people fall; and the promiscuous amours of the men of the middling class with their female servants debases both beyond measure, weakening every species of family affection.

I have every where been struck by one characteristic difference in the conduct of the two sexes; women, in general, are seduced by their superiors, and men jilted by their inferiors; rank and manners awe the one, and cunning and wantonness subjugate the other, ambition creeping into the woman's passion, and tyranny giving force to the man's; for most men treat their mistresses as kings do their favorites: *ergo* is not man then the tyrant of the creation?

Still harping on the same subject, you will exclaim—How can I avoid it, when most of the struggles of an eventful life have been occasioned by the oppressed state of my sex: we reason deeply, when we forcibly feel[?]

But to return to the straight road of observation. The sensuality so prevalent appears to me to arise rather from indolence of mind and dull senses than from an exuberance of life, which often fructifies the whole character when the vivacity of youthful spirits begins to subside into strength of mind.

I have before mentioned that the men are domestic tyrants, considering them as fathers, brothers, or husbands; but there is a kind of interregnum between the reign of the father and husband, which is the only period of freedom and pleasure that the women enjoy. Young people who are attached to each other, with the consent of their friends, exchange rings, and are permitted to enjoy a degree of liberty together which I have never noticed in any other country. The days of courtship are therefore prolonged, till it be perfectly convenient to marry: the intimacy often becomes very tender: and if the lover obtain the privilege of a husband, it can only be termed half by stealth, because the family is wilfully blind. It happens very rarely that these honorary engagements are dissolved or disregarded, a stigma being attached to a breach of faith, which is thought more disgraceful, if not so criminal, as the violation of the marriage vow.

Do not forget that, in my general observations, I do not pretend to sketch a national character; but merely to note the present state of morals and manners, as I trace the progress of the world's improvement. Because, during my residence in different countries, my principal object has been to take such a dispassionate view of men as will lead me to form a just idea of the nature of man. . . .

THE MENTOR LIVING HISTORY LIBRARY
John Anthony Scott, General Editor

MENTOR Books of Special Interest

MENTOR Books of Plays

Buy them at your local

bookstore or use coupon

on next page for ordering.

SIGNET CLASSIC for Your Library

(0451)

- [ ] **EMMA by Jane Austen.** Afterword by Graham Hough. (515242—$1.95)
- [ ] **MANSFIELD PARK by Jane Austen.** Afterword by Marvin Mudrick. (517520—$3.50)
- [ ] **NORTHANGER ABBEY by Jane Austen.** Afterword by Elizabeth Hardwick. (517482—$2.50)
- [ ] **PERSUASION by Jane Austen.** Afterword by Marvin Mudrick. (517156—$2.95)
- [ ] **PRIDE AND PREJUDICE by Jane Austen.** Afterword by Joann Morse. (516621—$1.50)
- [ ] **SENSE AND SENSIBILITY by Jane Austen.** Afterword by Caroline G. Mercer. (515536—$2.50)
- [ ] **JANE EYRE by Charlotte Brontë.** Afterword by Arthur Ziegler. (515560—$1.75)
- [ ] **WUTHERING HEIGHTS by Emil Brontë.** Foreword by Goeffrey Moore. (516508—$1.75)
- [ ] **FRANKENSTEIN or THE MODERN PROMETHEUS by Mary Shelley.** Afterword by Harold Bloom. (511328—$1.50)
- [ ] **THE AWAKENING and SELECTED SHORT STORIES by Kate Chopin.** Edited by Barbara Solomon. (517490—$2.95)
- [ ] **ADAM BEDE by George Eliot.** Foreword by F. R. Leavis. (515781—$2.95)
- [ ] **DANIEL DERONDA by George Eliot.** Introduction by Irving Howe. (512049—$3.50)
- [ ] **MIDDLEMARCH by George Eliot.** Afterword by Frank Kermode. (517504—$4.95)
- [ ] **THE MILL ON THE FLOSS by George Eliot.** Afterword by Morton Berman. (515439—$3.50)
- [ ] **SILAS MARNER by George Eliot.** Afterword by Walter Allen. (516788—$1.75)

Buy them at your local bookstore or use this convenient coupon for ordering.

THE NEW AMERICAN LIBRARY, INC.,
P.O. Box 999, Bergenfield, New Jersey 07621

Please send me the books I have checked above. I am enclosing $_____ (please add $1.00 to this order to cover postage and handling). Send check or money order—no cash or C.O.D.'s. Prices and numbers are subject to change without notice.

Name_____

Address_____

City _____ State _____ Zip Code _____

Allow 4-6 weeks for delivery.
This offer is subject to withdrawal without notice.